Privileged Lives

A Social History of
Middle-class Ireland
1882–1989

Tony Farmar

A. & A. Farmar

British Library Cataloguing in Publication Data
A CIP catalogue record for this book is available
from the British Library

ISBN: 978-1-906353-26-1

Index by Helen Litton
Cover design by Kevin Gurry
Cover image 'St Stephen's Green' c 1936 by Harry Kernoff
Courtesy of Catriona Kernoff
Illustrations on pages 33, 57 courtesy National Library of Ireland

Contents

Introduction

History has traditionally been concerned with causes, consequences and reasons-why. *Privileged Lives* is not. This is because there is a specific difficulty with social history that does not afflict narratives of diplomatic, military or political history.[1] In the absence of war, plague or famine, social change works insidiously and mostly unbeknown to those it is affecting. We can date exactly the appearance in 1965 of the mini-skirt on the fashion cat-walks—but what effect (and when) did it have on sexual attitudes in north Dublin? More, history is not an inevitable progression towards the light.

It is clear, for instance, that the social and intellectual world of Dublin was freer and livelier in 1907 (including a thriving vegetarian restaurant) than in 1932. Sir Walter Scott illustrated this point with a story about his great-aunt, a Mrs Keith. One day she asked him to procure for her the stories of the novelist Aphra Behn, which she remembered being much admired in her youth. But when she started the stories she found them shocking and impossible to read. 'Is it not,' she commented, 'a very odd thing that I, an old woman of eighty and upwards, sitting alone should feel myself ashamed to read a book which sixty years ago I have heard read aloud for the amusement of large circles, consisting of the finest and most creditable society in London?' Somehow, between the lively Mrs Keith's twentieth and eightieth birthdays (i.e. between 1750 and 1810), a wholesale change in social manners had occurred, the extent of which was surprising even to her who had lived through it. (This change,

---

1 The straightforwardness of these disciplines can be deceptive. Sir Harold Nicholson, with the authority of a participant in the Peace Congress of 1919, wrote: 'Nobody who has witnessed history in the making, and observed how infrequent and adventitious is the part played in great affairs by planned intention, can believe that it is ever quite so deliberate as it seems in retrospect. The apparent relation between cause and effect is rarely what at the time and in the circumstances actually determines the course of affairs. . . . Nobody who has seen statesmen dealing with each other can forget the immense part played in human affairs by such unavowable causes as lassitude, affability, personal affection or dislike, misunderstanding, deafness or incomplete command of a foreign language, vanity, social engagements, interruptions and momentary states of health.'—*Congress of Vienna* (London 1946) chap 1.

incidentally, predates Queen Victoria by more than a generation.)[2]

The solution to the narrative problem adopted here is to show how things seemed *at the time* in one period and the next, and by implication the changes. The years chosen for special scrutiny, starting in 1882, the high point of the land agitation, are roughly 25 years apart, the conventional period of a generation.

Privileged Lives starts with the assumption that the two core elements in a person's self-evaluation are gender and class. The period between 1882 and 1989 produced remarkable changes in the way gender and sex roles were perceived, and these are covered in some detail. Class is more controversial. In Ireland as in the United States it has been common to deny the existence of a class system. Sociologists have even declared that, though a useful term, 'there was strictly no Irish middle class as such'.[3] Nonetheless, the idea was well understood and freely used throughout the period. In 1932 a government enquiry specifically endorsed the idea that there was 'a middle class style of living, with its attendant emphasis on suburban residence, maidservant, education, holidays, etc.'[4] According to its search engine, in 1989 *The Irish Times* used the term over 300 times in the year, averaging once an issue.

In that year the political commentator James Downey wrote that the Irish middle class 'became in the course of the nineteenth century not only the dominant class in most of the country but the most important class on the island as a whole.' Since 1932, he believed, the representatives of the urban middle class had held a small share of political office, but 'a disproportionate share of political power, being especially influential in business, the professions, academic life and the church'.[5] In 1998 two ESRI scholars noted how 'the middle classes of the Republic have suceeded admirably' in setting their superior resources to maintaining their privileged position in the strategically critical educational system.[6]

---

2 H. Grierson (ed) *Letters of Sir Walter Scott 1826–1828* (London 1936) p 96 circa 6 September 1826. Aphra Behn, famous as the first Englishwoman to earn her living by her pen, would not now be at all startling, though in her most famous story, *Orinooko*, she does certainly dwell vividly on the naked beauties of her leading male and female characters.

3 For instance, M. Peillon *Contemporary Irish Society* (Dublin 1982) p 28

4 *Committee on the Cost of Living Figure*, P. no 992 (Dublin 1932)

5 J. Downey *All things new* (Dublin 1989) pp 9, 17

6 C. Whelan and D. Hannan 'Trends in educational inequality in the Republic of Ireland' *ESRI Working paper no 100* (Dublin 1998) p 17

The importance of class lies in the ability of members to hand on to their children a privileged start in life, through education, through membership of the right clubs, through investment in professional training, through the hundred ways not available to non-members. With this comes respect, prestige and access to a host of valued social goods including better housing, diet, clothing and, as a consequence, health and longevity. At the same time, there have been certain expectations imposed on members: where and how they lived, whom they might marry, where they might work, not to mention family manners, entertaining, consumption patterns and dress codes. The disproportionate stress felt by those unable to maintain such 'standards' underlines how central class is to identity.

As well as the evolving themes of gender and class there has been a century-long debate about Ireland's development. One side (typically adopted by the urban middle class) said that without economic independence cultural freedom was not sustainable—as the Yiddish expression has it, 'a language is a dialect with an army'; others, notably including de Valera, believed that the most thriving economy in the world would be worthless if the Irish people were unable to express their souls in the language and in the culture uniquely forged to do so. In practical terms, were the children to learn Latin and Irish or German and mechanical drawing?

The debate starts in the 1880s when a combination of global economic shifts and local politics hustled the Ascendancy off the land, leaving social and economic space for the middle class to expand into. For a brief while it seemed as if the modernisers were winning, but the political dominance of Sinn Féin ideas, combined with the enormous and crucially conservative influence of the Catholic Church, led to a decisive shift. Only in the 1960s was it acceptable to query the intellectual consensus that had been created.

By 1989, the grand narratives of Land, Religion and Nationalism had more or less lost credibility. Agriculture had ceased to be the majority employer; Mass attendance was slipping; and people no longer spoke of the fourth green field. With the enormous help of television, urban middle-class life-styles, aspirations and attitudes had become the norm—at least for two-thirds of the population. This was not, of course, 'The end of history' as Francis Fukuyama's 1989 article famously proclaimed, but it was the beginning of a new era.

—1882—

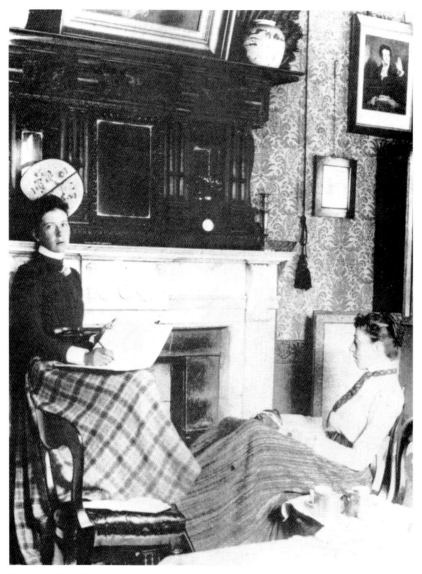

Tales of the old Ascendancy: Violet Martin and Edith Somerville in the drawing-room of Drishane, Castletownshend. Thick, warm, skirts, blouses, hair up in the style of the day.

Chapter 1 The day of the landlords is over

The passing of the Land Act 1881 marked the beginning of the long revolution which transferred the land from the Ascendancy to the small farmers of Ireland. The descendants of the planters who had so violently imposed their will on the country in the seventeenth century—'no petty people' as Yeats would vainly proclaim—were, over time and with comparatively little violence, hustled off the stage. Space was left for the Catholic urban middle class to expand socially and economically, as their counterparts had done and were doing in other countries.

In global terms this class revolution was only the Irish aspect of a larger continental movement. Just as the motor car and the bicycle were about to edge the horse towards the margin of history, the caste with which the horse was identified was losing the mandate of heaven all over Europe, from Lampedusa's Sicily to Chekov's Russia. By the end of the process that caste had become, like royalty before it, largely decorative.

Behind this revolution was a tectonic shift in the global market for food. In the late 1870s, agricultural goods from the new world began to upset the balance of the old-world markets. As the historian David Cannadine put it:

> [the] world-wide collapse in agricultural prices meant that estate rentals fell dramatically, and [that] land values plummeted correspondingly. As a result the whole territorial basis of patrician existence was undermined . . . at the same time prodigious unprecedented plutocratic fortunes were now being made around the world in business, in industry and in finance. . . . [The] sudden and dramatic collapse of the agricultural economy [occurred] partly because of the massive influx of cheap foreign goods from North and South America and the Antipodes, and partly because of the final and emphatic burgeoning of the fully fledged, large and highly concentrated industrial economy. Across the Continent, agricultural prices and rentals collapsed.[1]

As the territorial basis of aristocratic dominance was undermined, eminently practical people such as Oscar Wilde's Lady Bracknell noticed that 'land has ceased to be either a profit or a pleasure. It gives one position and prevents one from keeping it up.' Without rents the landowners could no longer afford to devote themselves to public life. Their authority and status drained away accordingly. In France, the nobility had made up half of the National Assembly in 1871; by 1889 they contributed no more than one-fifth. In Germany, Austria-Hungary, Russia and Britain middle-class political movements successfully attacked the old hegemony.

Irish landowners, a mere 744 of whom owned nearly half the country,[2] were not immune from the shocks felt by their cousins and old school-fellows on 'the mainland'. They too felt heaven's mandate slipping away. In a series of anonymous articles in the *Freeman's Journal*, Sir George Fottrell, Secretary of the Land Commission, declared that it was time for the Irish landlords to go. 'The Land Act has brushed away the legal cobwebs which settlements and entails had woven round his title'; the owner of such an encumbered, unpaying estate is now 'no longer an object of admiration, but of pity'. Why should they not take the easy way? 'By selling [the Ascendancy landlord] will free himself from all the expenses of agents and bailiffs and other management; all allowances and drawbacks and subscriptions and claims of one kind or another which as landlord he has to accede to or which he in his heart feels he ought to accede to.'

Landlords were invited to envisage the comfort of cash to invest in 'stocks or shares of whatever form of security might be most remunerative'. This inflammatory series of articles, published as a pamphlet by the *Freeman's Journal* in 1882, cost Sir George his job.[3]

The landlord controversialist William Bence Jones (who died in London in 1882, having been harassed from his house in Clonakilty by the Land League) had attempted to refocus his class by declaring: 'Landowning is a business as much as cotton-spinning. And farming too is only another business . . . if this fact were fully recognised, there would be an end to all feudal and semi-feudal views on the relation of landlord and tenant. They are simply two men dealing with one another in a matter of business.'[4]

But there was too much freight for that kite to fly.

Not everyone thought the decline of the Ascendancy was a tragedy. The distinguished scientist Sir Robert Kane, who had just been made Chancellor of the newly founded Royal University, was strikingly forthright, even bitter, about the landed class in his evidence to the Select Committee on Industries (Ireland) in 1884: 'I think the greatest evil under which we have laboured both financially and socially in Ireland for a long time has been people who were really worth nothing, or next to nothing, or less than nothing, preserving a position and station and appearance and influence both in public and private life which they were not in the slightest degree entitled to.'[5]

The secret ballot, introduced in 1872, had freed tenants to vote as they chose, away from the sharply scrutinising eyes of landlords and agents with whom they might in a week or two have to renegotiate their rents.[6] The result shocked Irish landlords into realising that perhaps their tenants did not, as they had fondly imagined, love them dearly. When the tenants of James Martin of Ross, one of the great landlords of Galway, voted against his wishes in 1872, he was so astonished and hurt by this 'betrayal' that he neglected his health and died a month or two later. 'It was not,' as his daughter Violet—the 'Ross' of Somerville & Ross—later wrote, 'the political defeat, severe as that was, it was the personal wound, and it was incurable.' The family's view was that the voters were simply graduating from landlord to clerical control—'like sheep who passed in a frightened huddle from one fold to another', as Violet Martin was to put it many years later.[7] The contempt is palpable.

There was a war on, about which the twenty-three-year-old Edith Somerville had no illusions, as she made clear in her diary: 'Uncle Josc's tenants have paid up £300 and refuse to give more. The amount due is £1,600. Pleasing prospect for Uncle Joscelyn until eviction forces the brutes to pay.'[8] Helpless in the face of the tide of history, some of the Anglo-Irish grew sour. In Somerville & Ross's *An Irish Cousin* (1889) a landlord expostulates: 'Do you mean to tell me that one of my tenants, a creature whose forefathers have lived for centuries in ignorance and degradation, is my equal? . . . it is absurd to suppose that the natural arrangement of things can be tampered with.'[9]

Although some few landlords did organise assistance to their boycotted fellows, contemporaries were surprised by the general failure of the class to combine and defend itself. George Moore (himself of landlord stock) ascribed this to simple cowardice: 'For fear of drawing attention to themselves individually, they shrank from meeting in council, and declined to adopt any common course of defence'.[10] This was a hard saying about a caste that valued physical courage above all virtues.

The Ascendancy wilted under the twin attack of international economic forces and tenant muscle. Men slipped out at night to stick posters on walls and trees calling for the boycott of richer neighbours.[11] A symbolic grave was dug outside Bence Jones' front door. George Moore described how

> the air was filled with threats, murder, and rumours of many murders. Land League meetings were held in every town, in every village rustic orators fearlessly proclaimed the extermination of the owners of the soil. Each post brought letters marked with coffins and crossbones, or almost equally

melancholy epistles from agents, declaring that the law was in abeyance, that whole armies of people assembled to prevent the bailiffs from serving their notices of eviction. Some of them had been thrown into lakes, others had been dragged out of their beds and shot in the legs, for daring to disregard the occult law that from Seventy-nine to Eighty-two governed the island. It was a time of darkness and constant alarms. It was by night that prosperous tenants and leaseholders paid their rents; the reductions the League demanded often amounted to the entire balance coming to the mortgaged landowners; and they saw themselves deprived of their only means of existence. For how many generations had they lived on the taxed soil? For how long, when other industries had failed, had they laughed and said 'The fools! There is nothing like the land; all else fails, but it cannot be taken away.' And now they saw that which they had taken to be eternal vanishing from them even as a vapour. An entire race, a whole caste, saw themselves driven out of their soft, warm couches of idleness, and forced into the struggle for life.[12]

In a scathing article in the *Contemporary Review*, Professor Mahaffy of Trinity College, who could never have been accused of nationalistic tendencies, castigated the failure 'to enter into a defence association with a strong feeling of public spirit'. What was the cause? Mahaffy believed that the best children of the class 'scatter throughout the world, and those who remain at home are the idle and good for nothing who think they can live by amateur farming and mismanaging an agency business till they succeed to their property, when they do little but hunt and pass the time in idleness at home.'

Indignantly he condemned the intellectual laziness of the Ascendancy: 'The splendid libraries so common before famine times are scattered and it is now an exception to find a good library in a country house. They tell you it is not needed. Have they not their daily papers, and can they not get books down from a library in Dublin?'[13]

In a later novel, Edith Somerville described the childishness of many of the contemporary Anglo-Irish, as exemplified by Major Dick Talbot-Lowry: 'Though a pessimist in politics [he] was an optimist in most other matters, and found it impossible to conceive of a state of affairs when he would be unable to do—approximately—whatever he had a mind for. At the age of fifty-eight, fortitude and endurance are something of a difficulty for a gentleman unused to the exercise of either of these fine qualities.'[14] Early in 1882 the Church of Ireland decreed a Day of Humiliation and Prayer—since 'all the future of a land justly dear to us may be at stake', as the Archbishop's call had it. Congregations were recorded as fuller than usual for a weekday, including many businessmen. The nationalist *Nation* quoted with grim satisfaction from two sermons given on the day.[15] First, the sermon of the Venerable Archdeacon of Kildare: 'Let us confess today that in the former days of our ascendancy we have [word missing] ourselves too proudly, and too harshly leaned on the strong arm of physical force . . . again there has been throughout our land a recklessness and love of pleasure of which we have been for some time reaping the bitter fruit.'

In Sandymount in Dublin, the Rev. Houston declared: 'The landed gentry were too often absentee or idle, evil livers, extravagant, and constantly getting into debt, while our leaders had the reputation of being an overreaching class, hard-fisted and hard-hearted.' These were not the words of a self-confident class.

This is not the place to discuss the detail and progress of the Land War, the Land League and its doings and the political stars such as Parnell, O'Kelly and Biggar (though the latter's breach of promise case in late 1882 will be noted). But there is no doubt that at the time most recognised either with satisfaction or horrified disbelief the momentousness of the political decisions being made. Many years later Violet Martin summed up the result: 'It left the Irish tenant practically the owner of his land, with a rent fixed by Government, and the feudal link with the landlord was broken forever.'[16] Her childhood neighbour, the Countess of Fingall, wrote of feeling at the time that 'the day of the landlords is over. Even the greatest recluse among them, locked up within his strong wall or behind his thick woods must be aware of the battering on the gates.'[17]

Getting

The historic change in the social and economic structure took time to work its way through. In 1882, landlords remained at the top of society. According to *Thom's Directory* of that year 120 of these had estates valued at £10,000 or more, including Arthur Barry (£32,000), the Duke of Abercorn (£35,000), the Duke of Leinster (£48,000), Sir Richard Wallace (£74,000), and, top of the pile, the Marquess of Downshire (£91,000). In the conditions of the Land War, of course, these valuations were distinctly theoretical. Several hundred landowners had estates supposedly worth £5,000 or more.

In practice, these apparently lavish sums were never unencumbered. As Table 1 shows, a network of psychological and practical obligations consequent on his position severely circumscribed a landlord's freedom of manoeuvre.

Table 1 How to spend an estate income of £5,000 a year

Pensions etc., say £1,300
  Mother, upkeep of the lodge across the park plus £700 a year
  An unmarried aunt, £180
  Unmarried sisters, 2 x £150 each
  Bridie, the old nurse, and other pensioners, say £150

Staff costs, say £1,400
  The agent, including his house, £600
  Steward/bailiff (manager of the home farm), £200
  Labourers, stablemen etc. perhaps 20 x £25 each
  Indoor staff, perhaps 8 at an average of £10–15 each plus board

General costs
  Mortgages, depending on what happened in the low rent years, say
    £650
  Local charities, perhaps a school, and especially the Church of
    Ireland after disestablishment in 1869
  Annual visit to Dublin for the Season (6 weeks in February and
    March, including renting a house)
  'Pin-money' for wife
  Stables, and hunters, £30 each
  Subscription to local hunt, £25

Household and family costs
  Education, boarding school in England if possible for the boys,
    governess for the girls
  Jointure (dowry) for the daughters
  Allowance for son in the army
  Income tax at 4d in the £

Source: Based on Bateman *The Great Landowners of Great Britain and Ireland* London, 1883, pp xxiv–xxv

This network of obligations did not encumber the incomes of the bishops of the Church of Ireland, who despite coming off the state payroll after disestablishment in 1869, had managed to maintain a very good income. There were twelve of them in all, with an average of just under £5,000 a year each. Top of the heap were the Archbishops of Armagh (£9,800) and Dublin (£7,400). The average parish clergyman, on the other hand, earned a mere £260 a year.

Lawyers had for centuries competed with the Church of Ireland hierarchy for the top of the state-paid listings. In 1882 they were still just second, with the Lord Chancellor being paid (as the official accounts record with typical precision) £6,782 12s 2d in the year ending 31 March 1882—somewhat less than the statutory annual salary of £8,000 because he had been appointed during the year. The Lord Chief Justice received £5,074.

These judicial salaries were considerably higher than those of the Chief Secretary, the cabinet minister in charge, with £4,425, or the Under-Secretary (in effect the top civil servant), who got a mere £2,000. This was, however, 40 times the salary of the lowest paid worker in his office. As it happens, this was much the same as the ratio between the ordinary parish parson and the Archbishop of Armagh. (The ratio from highest to lowest in the modern Department of Finance is 10:1.) The salaries paid in 1882/3 to the staff in the Chief Secretary's office present a typical gradation.

Table 2 The hierarchy in the Chief Secretary's office 1882

Title	No.	Av. salary £p.a.
Clerks of the 1st class	3	810
Parliamentary draughtsman	1	600
Clerks of the 2nd class	5	449
Private secretary to Chief Secretary	1	420
Clerks of the 3rd class	5	267
Librarian	1	185
Office keeper	1	150
Clerks of the lower division	5	137
Messenger 1st class	3	112
Messenger 2nd class	7	93
Coal porter and gas attendant	1	52
Cleaners	5	32

Source: 1882/3 Civil Service Estimates

Some other official salaries were: the Inspector General of Police £1800, Secretary of the Land Commission £1000; the resident magistrates £550 (enough for Somerville & Ross's Major Yeates in West Cork to hunt and shoot regularly, and to employ a cook, several housemaids and outside servants such as a gamekeeper). The Director of the National Gallery was paid £500. Gerard Manley Hopkins, newly appointed professor at the Royal University, received £400, as did the Governor of

Mountjoy; a DMP police inspector was on £150, a sergeant £90 and a constable £75. At the bottom of the scale of official salaries was the average of £49 (plus a house) given to national school teachers.[18]

Non-official salaries are harder to rescue from history, but a few high-lights survive. Thus the leading accountant of the day, Robert Gardner of Craig, Gardner (now PriceWaterhouseCooper) averaged £3,000 a year between 1870 and the First World War. Charles Eason, soon to take over from W. H. Smith the business that was to be named after him, received an average of £1,250 for the nine years up to 1882; the most senior of his 150 or so employees got £6 a week.[19] The two partners in the coal importing firm Thomas Heiton got a basic salary of £500 plus interest on capital of £225, and a share in profits which started at £673 in 1880 and progressed rapidly from there.[20] Thomas Edmondson, the manager of the Manor Hill Laundry at Dundrum, had a basic salary of £200 plus a half share of profits, which in 1882 gave him a total of £734.[21]

Spending

What did these earnings mean in practice? Generalisations are dangerous, firstly because widespread information is lacking, and secondly because the typicality of what information we have is impossible to judge. However, as the social historian Mona Hearn reckoned, perhaps too pessimistically, 'a young man marrying on £300 a year and hoping to start a family, would have found it necessary to budget very carefully. Food would have accounted for at least 30 per cent of income; clothing 17 per cent; rent 12½ per cent; fuel 4½ per cent; 8 per cent for servants.'[22]

A detailed cash notebook of the late 1850s, kept by John Findlater of the grocery chain, broadly confirms these figures. His average income was more than twice the £300 a year which Mona Hearn regarded as the very minimum on which a middle-class man could marry. He spent about 16 per cent of that income on rent and insurance and 24 per cent on food and fuel. His meticulous records note that he gave his wife 7 per cent of his income for her personal expenses (some £40 a year—a new silk dress would probably cost £5 5s), and as much as 16 per cent to donations and pious subscriptions.[23]

Obviously, family spending patterns, then as now, varied greatly, but as Eason's company historian Louis Cullen shows, it was clearly possible on an income of £1,250 or more to save considerably for various capital investments. 'Housekeeping expenses' for the Eason family in

Kenilworth Square, Rathgar, 'were only £520 in 1872 and only reached £600 for the first time in 1885'. With eight children, schooling was obviously an item, at £150 a year; Charles Eason's one luxury was the maintenance of a coach (rather grand for Kenilworth Square) which cost him £100 or more. Gifts and charities ran to £150; seaside holidays (in Ireland until the 1880s) were modest.[24]

Marriage entailed finding somewhere to live. Generally this meant renting rather than buying. 'Fools build houses for wise men to live in', as the contemporary saying had it. Behind this was the intuition that if the cost of living was drifting slowly downwards, as it was to do from the Famine to the First World War, there was little sense in buying a house now that would be cheaper next year. The wide availability of rental properties meant that a growing family could adjust its accommodation as necessary; if the chimney smoked or the neighbours were disagreeable, one could simply move on. This resulted in great mobility: John Findlater lived in three houses in the first six years of his marriage. He and his family moved into Upper Leeson Park in 1864 and left in 1868. In those four years 57 out of 119 houses on the road had changed hands.[25]

Building or buying houses was normally done not to provide a home, but to generate an income. In the absence of regular pension arrangements or a substantial stock market, the return on housing property was attractive. A house purchased for £500 in Rathmines, for instance, could attract a rent of £45 (less ground rent). This relationship between purchase price and rental seems to be common, and the return, in this case at around 9 per cent—assuming tenants could be found—was certainly better than the 5 per cent available to shareholders, for instance in the Dublin Artisans Dwelling Company, or the 3 per cent from government bonds. So Paterfamilias would often buy various properties and bequeath them to his daughters as a source of sustained income. In 1884, George Plunkett and Josephine Cranny (the parents of the future 1916 leader Joseph Plunkett) married, and their fathers, who were substantial southside property developers, gave them not only a house in Fitzwilliam Square, but also seven houses in Belgrave Road, Rathmines, and a further seven in Marlborough Road, Donnybrook—a total rental of more than £700 a year.[26]

Dublin was spreading, even sprawling, as speculative builders created new streets of aspirational housing with the characteristic little gardens in front and rere and (until the 1880s) an elaborate entrance. In October 1882, *The Irish Times* reported that some sixty new streets were

being built in the area between the canals, and many more in the townships outside. These were growing rapidly, catering for a wide range of
house-seekers, from the grandees in Clyde or Waterloo Roads to the
diarist Mary Hayden, who on the death of her physician father in 1881
(her mother had died earlier) had to leave Merrion Square and retreat
with her brother and a servant to what she called a 'sardine box' of a
newly-built house on Moyne Road in Ranelagh.[27] In October 1882 a
neighbouring house, number 32, was advertised as 'a comfortable house'
with seven apartments (rooms), bathroom, WCs etc. for £40 a year. The
presence of a fixed bath and indoor WC was worth commenting on.[28]
Ranelagh was nothing like as built up as it has become—in October
1883 Mary Hayden describes how she left Moyne Road and 'ran across
the fields in the moonlight to post a letter.'[29]

In the 1880s, the townships housed just over a quarter of the population of Dublin, but two-thirds of the city's rentier class (described
as 'Gentle' in the 1881 Census). This group would have included Mary
Hayden and her brother John. Half the accountants in Dublin lived in
the townships, and a third of doctors, clerks and commercial travellers.
Barristers were slower to move, but by 1891, 36 per cent them also lived
in the suburbs. In 1881 a quarter of the labourers living in Dublin lived
in the suburbs, but as the century progressed the growing labouring
population became concentrated in the inner city. By 1901, 88 per cent
of the labourers in Dublin lived between the canals. So by the time
of the 'Lockout' of 1913, there had been at least a generation of class
segregation by area.

In 1882, to rent a 'desirable residence' in Waterloo Road cost £80,
which implied earnings of at least £500 a year. This was one of the
'Roads' of the fashionable Pembroke Estate, where many senior state
officials lived. Wellington Road, for instance, housed officials from the
Chief Secretary's office, the Bank of Ireland, the Board of Public Works,
the Court of Chancery, two senior academics from Trinity College and
the American consul. There were 24 top civil servants in the offices of
the Chief Secretary and the Board of Works (1st- and 2nd-class clerks
earning over £400); of these we can identify addresses for nineteen,
and virtually all lived in the southside townships.[30] Wellington Road,
Leinster Road, Leeson Park, Morehampton Road, Rathgar Road,
Lansdowne Road crop up more than once. Only two lived on the north-
side, in Sherrard Street and Henrietta Street respectively. By the end of
the century, most of the houses in Henrietta Street were in tenements
(one had already succumbed by 1882), but at this time it was still full of

barristers and judges.

Rathgar was then more down-market. Brighton Square, for instance, where James Joyce was born in February 1882, had several junior officials, an assistant surveyor from the Board of Works, an official from the Collector-General's office (James Joyce's father), a commercial traveller, an accountant, two Bank of Ireland officials and a commission agent. In October, 24 Brighton Square was offered for £36 a year '2 sitting rooms, 3 bedrooms, kitchen, pantry, w.c. and gas—newly papered and plastered—garden front and rere'. No. 61, renting for £34, was described as a 'neat, dry, comfortable, two storey house. 5 rooms, closet, kitchen, servant's room etc'. If we apply Mona Hearn's rule that rent probably represented 12.5 per cent of income, a rental of £36 implied an income of just under £300.

At least a quarter of the ordinary middle-class income was spent on food. Unfortunately, although there are facts in abundance about how the poor ate, and about prison diets and workhouse regimes, exactly what and how the middle class ate remains shadowy. We can take hints from British publications such as Mrs Beeton, whose book was certainly regularly advertised in Irish publications, but the fact that her suggestions for 'Plain Family Meals' invariably include some form of meat on Fridays suggests caution.

The diet was probably monotonous, with a lot of meat, and not much else. As *The Irish Times* commented: 'The average householder knows but two vegetables—the potato and the cabbage—for ten months of the year, with green peas and beans in the summer.'[31] If we estimate that between 25 and 30 per cent of income was spent on food, our middle-class householders on £300 and £500 a year would spend between £2 10s and £3 a week. Beef was about 11d a pound, and mutton somewhat cheaper. So a 10lb roast rib ('sufficient for 8–10 persons' says Mrs Beeton), would in May 1882 have cost about 9s (just about a week's wages for a rural labourer); 14lbs of potatoes only cost 6d, and cabbages were equally cheap at 1s a dozen.[32]

In 1878 a Dublin woman with the unexpected pseudonym of 'Short' wrote a book called *Dinners at Home*. This is probably the first printed cookbook by an Irishwoman (published, of course, in London). The reviewer for *The Irish Times* evidently knew the author. As he put it, this 'Dublin lady' explains how to produce 'the plain, tidy little dinners that all men like but do not always get'. The book was sufficiently popular to be followed up two years later by *Breakfasts and Luncheons at Home*, and the series remained in print for twenty years.

'Short's' motive in writing the book, as she explains in the preface, was to improve the very dull quality of domestic cookery. 'It must be acknowledged,' she wrote in the preface, 'that at the present day most ladies of moderate incomes do not pay sufficient attention to their cuisine.' The deplorable result was that 'many gentlemen are driven to dine at their Clubs rather than incur the risk of having both their temper and digestion spoiled by the incompetency of their cooks.'[33] The cover shows two images of Paterfamilias: one dining alone in gloomy splendour in his club, the other in jolly conviviality at home with the women of the family. There was no question as to which alternative was preferable.

'Short' did not intend, however, to make her readers slaves to the stove. '*Dinners at Home,*' she wrote, 'is specifically designed to give the Mistress of the House such information as will enable her, without her constant attendance in the kitchen (as is erroneously supposed essential by many), with a cook of moderate pretensions to have a thoroughly satisfactory dinner served at home.' One visit a day to the kitchen should be enough: 'Write your orders for the cook daily, with separate orders for the greengrocer, fishmonger etc. as they call. A visit once a week to the butchers is quite sufficient as a general rule.' A key principle was to get away from the tyranny of roasted meat, 'large joints, which are in reality more extravagant than the smaller and more tempting made-dishes. It is a mistake,' she notes, 'to have these "for company only"; for the cook accustomed to serve nothing but joints gets confused and lamentable results follow.'[34] The cook should be encouraged to produce a 'made-dish' every day until it becomes second nature.

The chapter on vegetables makes it clear that the process is starting from a low base of skill and variety. No mention is made of cabbage, onions or carrots, presumably because the handling of these would be expected to be known, but the cooking of peas ('boil in bubbling salt water for a quarter of an hour and serve with lumps of fresh butter'), French beans, cauliflower, turnips and spinach ('boil, chop fine and serve with melted butter and cream') are carefully explained. The 'made-dishes' are not much more sophisticated, as can be seen from the menus she suggests.[35]

For a table of four to six persons, she proposes the following:[36]

Wednesday
    Tapioca soup
    Whitings with plain butter sauce
    Boiled steaks of mutton
    Cold beef

Salad (winter or summer)
Apple Charlotte
Macaroni and cheese

Sunday

Soup (reheated from the day before)
Saddle of mutton (2nd loin left over from Friday roasted again
with buttered pepper)
Mayonnaise chicken
Apple tart (cold)

She does not specify vegetables. Sunday's menu is designed to reduce the amount of work required in the kitchen. Otherwise, there are for an ordinary family at home four or five courses every night. The prevalence of mutton is marked, and none of the dishes are such as to excite a gourmet. We may take it that daily reality in most houses fell short of this not very high standard both in terms of variety and culinary skill.

Mary Hayden's diaries contain very little about food—except to criticise—but since she was only twenty in 1882, this is not surprising. On 13 March, for instance, 'we dined on a fowl as old as Methusalem and as sinewy as a racehorse', and on 1 August 'nasty boiled mutton, when I buy meat it's never nice'. (The city's medical officer Charles Cameron and his team condemned some 250,000 lbs of diseased meat every year.) She often scolds herself for over-indulgence in cake-shops in town, but says very little about day-to-day diets. On the other hand, she frequently records drinking champagne—thus: 'Spent the evening studying in my room, it being Lent I could not have anything to eat, but I got some champagne'[37]—it is difficult to imagine the daughters of senior physicians in the Dublin of the 1930s, 1960s or even the 1980s so casually helping themselves to champagne, even as a study aid. She sometimes takes ale or coffee: 'I provided myself with a tin of preserved coffee and some hot water and by their aid worked away until 5 o'clock in the morning'. After two hours sleep rolled in a cloak (fully dressed) she got up but, perhaps not surprisingly, 'felt so giddy and queer that I could hardly stand at first, but a dose of strong tea made me nearly all right'.[38] She does not say whether the tea was India or China; the fashion was moving from the latter to the former.

In later chapters of this section we shall see more of Mary Hayden, especially to explore the early views on the 'Woman Question' of one who became a well-known Irish feminist.

Chapter 2 The wonderful nineteenth century

The Land War was, not surprisingly, an overwhelming topic of conversation even among urban professionals with no direct interest. Mary Hayden notes that during a visit, 'the gentlemen got onto the Land Question at once and it is needless to remark stayed there ... [the subject] must lose the charm of novelty when one has heard it discussed as I have on an average four days in the week (for say 2 hours daily) for the last year and a half.' With characteristic sharpness, she adds: 'also I have noticed that when those who discussed it began with different views on the subject, they invariably ended with these views unchanged'.[1]

There were plenty of other possible topics. Charles Darwin died in April, a revered intellect. His theory of natural selection, first published more than twenty years before, had won the day in the field of natural history. The problem was what did the theory imply in other arenas, such as theology, politics and economics? This was the hey-day of the 'social Darwinism' promoted by the contemporary philosopher, Herbert Spencer, and eagerly touted by hard-nosed 'practical men', especially in post-Civil War America. The slogan 'survival of the fittest' was elevated to a moral imperative implying, among other things, that any state assistance flew in the face of nature. The Belfast hymn writer, Mrs Alexander, whose husband was Bishop of Derry (and later became Archbishop of Armagh), declared:

The rich man in his castle
The poor man at his gate
God made them high or lowly
And ordered their estate.

There was something impious about questioning why the absentee Duke of Devonshire should have (in theory at least) nearly £20,000 a year from his lands in Cork, while a labourer on his estate would be doing well to take home 10s a week. Up-to-date thinkers subscribed to Spencer's idea that there was a naturally evolved state of society, and that to force changes by legislation was somehow perverse. This strong idea of the 'natural order of society' was crushingly evoked in other arenas, such as the economy and relations between the sexes.

Where exactly God fitted into all this was doubtful. The fashionable

Society folk 'telephoning New Year's greetings' as the caption puts it. The first patents for telephones were issued less than six years before, in 1876. The unfamiliarity of the apparatus can be seen by the fact that the artist shows all his subjects listening, and none speaking. (Illustrated London News *7 January 1882*)

spiritualism—the Society for Psychical Research, with Professor William Barret of Trinity as a co-founder, began its earnest work in March—was one response to Darwin's bombshell. Another was the route of the atheist Charles Bradlaugh, who refused to take the oath under God on election to Parliament, and had to be re-elected four times between 1880 and 1886 before the House of Commons reluctantly allowed him to affirm.

Other current interests included the possibility of a tunnel under the Channel—'madness' said the military, envisaging hordes of heavily armed Frenchmen (for Germans were not yet perceived as likely aggressors) clambering up the white cliffs of Dover; or the fading prospects for the newly-built Dublin South City Market in George's Street, intended as the covered market commercial hub of the city. Most people thought of vegetarianism as 'an outrage on common sense' as Dr Edward Mapother, Medical Officer of Health, once called it: nonetheless a vigorous minority advocated its claims. Such advocates very likely also had strong views on the evils of vivisection and inoculation.[2]

In a Catholic group, there might be discussion of the supposed apparition of the Virgin in Athlone in August, after a mission for females. This was only a year after the apparitions at Knock, where, according to a full and detailed list published in the *Nation* in May 1880, over 150 cures had already been recorded. In Athlone, the local priests quickly stopped a similar cult developing by briskly throwing a cloth over the statue involved and making the people disperse.

More sombrely, conversation might turn to the Jules Ferry laws being enacted in France, imposing mandatory secondary education up to the age of fifteen and simultaneously removing Catholic religious from all schools, nuns from hospitals and chaplains from the army. The gradual easing of Bismarck's *Kulturkampf* attack on the Church (which had included the expulsion of Jesuits, state control of schools and seminaries, and compulsory civil registration of marriage) was by contrast a relief. Nonetheless, the campaigns against the Church in these two major European states contributed to an increasing feeling of isolation and defensiveness in the Vatican, compounding the distancing initiated by Pius IX's anti-Modernist encyclicals. This year also saw the first anti-Jewish pogroms in the Russian Empire as Jews were scapegoated for the assassination of the Tsar the previous year.

Today a men-only group might discuss sport, but in 1882 there was little more in the newspapers than reports on racing and occasional notices of rowing, cricket, football, cycling and billiards. Team games, and organised space- and rule-bound spectator sports as we know them, were in their infancy. The older and less constrained sports such as hunting, horse-racing, coursing and shooting were still dominant. At home, archery, cricket, tennis and croquet were played. Ireland's first golf club, the Royal Belfast, was founded in November 1881 with a six-hole course. Neither the *Freeman's Journal* nor *The Irish Times* devoted more than two or at most three columns (out of 64) to sporting matters. The GAA had yet to be founded, though Michael Cusack was working behind the scenes. In the first international soccer matches in February 1882, the Irish team was beaten 13–0 by England and then 7–1 by Wales a week later, with Ireland's first international goal being scored by fifteen-year-old Samuel Johnston.

In the drawing-room, apart from 'the wretched details of weddings and balls',[3] the ladies' conversation might turn to the report by the Postmaster-General that although the British had sent 1.6 million Valentines, in Dublin the practice had been 'almost entirely discontinued'. Or perhaps it would turn to fashion. The general look was of a very slender waist with a long tightly-laced corset, making a smooth frontal shape. The skirts were usually drawn back over a bustle at the back. But the variations were infinite. Here the fashion correspondent describes a 'particularly tasteful and elegant' toilette: 'Black is always fashionable, for many do not really look well in colours. A visiting dress of black satin and *broché* is very handsome, the skirt divided into draped, festooned panels having almost the effect of pleated crenellations over a rich Cordoba lace flounce, sustained by three satin balayeuses.'

Thus the Countess de B - - - in *The Irish Times*. Such reports purported to come from fashion's very front line, fashionable gatherings in Paris. Declaring that 'X are worn', or such-and-such a colour 'is much seen', in practice she presumably recounted what couture houses such as Worth or Poiret had announced.

Not discussed, except in the most general way, was the voluminous underclothing—five or six petticoats were normal, not to mention stays. Some idea of their extent can be gleaned from the Rational Dress Society's recommendation that female underclothes should weigh no more than 7lbs (an ordinary modern tweed jacket weighs about 2lbs). Since, however, 'laughter and cheers' greeted a speaker at one of their meetings who asked 'could any woman look without a shudder at the garments she wore three or four years ago?', the Society clearly had an uphill struggle on its hands against the allurements of fashion.

'The wonderful 19th century'

The Victorians of the 1880s saw themselves as living in 'the wonderful 19th century ... what changes in life ideas, knowledge, it has seen—the century of Science'.[4] In a reaction from the *a priori* rationalising of the utilitarians (Godwin, Bentham and Mill), the mid- to late-Victorians liked to accumulate facts. This mania was constantly under attack: from quarters such as Dickens' satirical portraits in *Hard Times*, from religious writers such as those in the *Irish Ecclesiastical Record* (complaining, for instance, about 'the hard cold materialism of our day, which treats as shadowy and unreal whatever does not submit itself to the arbitrary tests of science and sense', and 'the boast that our age puts its trust in facts only') and from aesthetes such as Oscar Wilde, who wrote in his 1889 essay 'The decay of lying', 'if something cannot be done to check, or at least to modify our monstrous worship of facts, Art will become sterile and beauty will pass away from the land'.

Nonetheless, the iconic books of the era, *The Origin of Species* and *Das Capital*, both bristle with facts. Marx's writings had in 1882 as yet scarcely penetrated Ireland, the library of Trinity College, for instance, not holding copies of any of his books until much later. References to Darwin, on the other hand, who died in April, frequently occur in *The Irish Times*, mostly quoting 'on the authority of Mr Darwin', or 'his great theory'.

In time, various methods of summarising and assessing these unwieldy mountains of facts would develop into statistics. This was not an exclusively English phenomenon: in France, Quetelet introduced his notion of the 'average man' as the touchstone of social policy, and in Italy, Lombroso laboriously measured the craniums of criminals.

At a simple day-to-day level, practical science and engineering seemed to improve everything. In the home, the noisy and noisome water-closet was being transformed into the relatively silent and much more efficient flush toilet. Ironically, the high-pressure Vartry water supply exposed many a middle-class Dubliner to enteric fever. The old drains, designed for water runaway, could not cope with the new sewage and drinking and washing water became contaminated. Frederick Pim of the Sanitary Association noted: 'Every autumn we have an outbreak of typhoid among our well-to-do classes, by which prominent citizens are struck down, some never to rise again ... the proportion of deaths from this disease is nearly twice as great amongst the well-to-do middle classes as among the artisans and labouring classes'.[5] (In 1878, the wife of one of the richest men in the city, the accountant Robert Gardner, had died of such an outbreak of typhoid in their Clyde Road house.) Although the tenements were still a running sore, by the end of the nineteenth century the scourges of previous generations—plague, smallpox, cholera and typhus—were largely eradicated.

The dreaded laundry-work was increasingly mechanised and indus-trialised. The telephone was creeping in, at least to public offices. In their advertisements, Wallace Brothers coal merchants made much of the fact that orders taken in the branch in Rathmines could be telephoned straight to the quays. Comedians joked about the perils of mistaken identity; businessmen were warned in a court case about relying on tele-phoned orders. Writers in the *Irish Ecclesiastical Record* worried about whether it would be legitimate to give absolution over the phone—it was decided not. So far only a few public arenas had electric light, but its potential was obvious.

In February, the *Irish Ecclesiastical Record,* which regularly covered science issues at this time, published the full text of a lecture by Father Gerald Murphy on electricity and lighting, explaining the new marvel to the parish priests of Ireland. Another issue contained an admir-ing review of the International Exhibition of Electricity in Paris. Mr Edison, said *The Irish Times,* 'has succeeded in creating a lamp which burns no air, gives off no heated products of combustion, is unaffected by draughts, can set nothing on fire, can neither smoke nor blaze up and is extinguished only by contact with air'.[6] By the end of the year Edison had established the first public generator, in Manhattan, and 193 buildings were being lit. The rival system, gas lighting, had had a head start, and was even now sadly revealing (and adding to) weaknesses in domestic cleaning. To meet the need, specialised cleaning products and brushes came into the market. Another source of domestic dirt, coal, had for domestic consumption and railways doubled in usage in twenty years (the gas company alone took 11 per cent of tons used).

The bicycle was just now being transformed by the development of the chain system of propulsion from the elegant but perilous 'ordinary' (penny-farthing), used exclusively by men as a sporting vehicle, to the new and practical 'safety bicycle'. Advertised in Ireland from late 1881, it took a little time for the new device to catch on. An early adopter was the politician Tim Healy, who 'startled Dubliners by joining the noble army of cyclists. He rides a safety bicycle'.[7] The horseless carriage was in the wings. Ireland's first motor casualty had occurred ten years before on the Earl of Rosse's estate, and in Germany, Daimler and Benz were busy developing a petrol-driven engine. As if in preparation for this enormous new market, in Philadelphia Rockefeller and his associates created the ingenious Standard Oil Trust in January 1882, thereby consolidating their control over 90 per cent of US oil capacity.

In medical circles, the great topic, as fundamental to medicine as the Land Acts were to Irish politics, was the newly confirmed germ theory of disease. The importance of this intellectual moment can hardly be overemphasised. Throughout the 1870s, report after report had shown that surgery under the antiseptic conditions proposed by Lister dramatically increased the survival rate of patients. But there was some vagueness as to what exactly *were* the germs, organisms, seeds or viruses, as they were variously called, that caused fatal putrefaction. In March 1882, Dr Robert Koch of Berlin announced his discovery of the bacillus responsible for tuberculosis. At last there was a meticulously researched, coherent and realistic theory to account for the fevers which carried off so many people (and continued to do so until the development of penicillin sixty years later). These infectious diseases—typhus, typhoid, diphtheria, smallpox, cholera, measles, and, worst of all, tuberculosis—were in 1882 responsible for just over 1 in 10 of all deaths in Ireland.

Apart from quibbles from the anti-vivisectionists, the profession's response was excited and positive. Dr F. J. Quinlan, addressing the winter meeting in St Vincent's Hospital, declared: 'The whole subject is profoundly interesting and important . . . [and] opens up a vista of preventive medicine of the most useful kind'. Dr Kendal Franks told the winter meeting of the Adelaide Hospital that germ theory 'promised to revolutionise both branches of [the medical] profession'. He went on, presciently, to describe the potential: 'we are but children playing on the shore of an unknown and boundless ocean.'[8]

Finding the cause was unfortunately not the same as finding the cure. Tuberculosis, politely called consumption, had begun its steady rise in the 1860s and was to continue until reaching a peak in 1900–05. As an increasing proportion of the population lived in towns, this disease had an opportunity to infect more and more. Before Koch's ideas became generally understood (much later), a certain vagueness about the cause of disease allowed free play to quacks and their remedies.

Regular advertisers of such nostrums included Hamilton Long with their *Celebrated Chest and Lung Protector*, available from their shop in Sackville Street, and 'recommended for delicate chests, consumption, asthma, rheumatism etc.'. Dr de Jongh's *Light Brown Cod Liver Oil* (price 4s 9d per pint, or four times the cost of a bottle of Findlater's 1874 claret) unusually made no claims to cure anything but consumption. Dr Barry's delicious *Revelenta Arabic Food*, on the other hand, cured 'asthma, consumption, palpitations, giddiness, low spirits etc.' and *Pepper's Quinine and Iron Tonic* went even further, with a formidable list of targets, from flatulence and 'wasting of the system', to consumption, heartburn, loss of zest for exercise, tendency to fall suddenly and scrofula. Over the next thirty years, as the medical profession became increasingly sceptical about its ability to do anything but diagnose, reassure and console, quack medicines became more and more outrageous. By the turn of the century three-quarters of the advertising in publications such as the *Weekly Freeman* were for patent medicines.

How to get on in society

As the middle classes consolidated their position and became more prosperous, they began to expand into unfamiliar territories of entertaining and sociability. The freedoms and easy ways of a close community of neighbours and relations were not sufficient in that strange new land. Over time, various ways had evolved of handling the complicated mix of nearness and distance enjoyed by social acquaintances. These ways had the added glamour of aristocracy, a glamour that was to retain its strength for generations after the class had imploded economically.

So there was a market for books about 'How to get on in society'. These replaced the books of courtesy aimed at instilling *l'art de vivre* in young men that (in English) culminated in Lord Chesterfield's chilling *Letters to his Son*, published in 1774. The new breed of etiquette books was aimed at middle-class readers who wanted specific details of how to comport themselves in social gatherings. In the late nineteenth century titles such as *Habits of Good Society* (1859), *Laws and Byelaws of Good Society* (1867), *Manners and Tone of Good Society* (1879), *Etiquette of Good Society* (1880), *Etiquette of Modern Society* (1881), and *Manners and Rules of Good Society* (1888) sold, so the publishers claimed, in the tens of thousands. Serving a similar purpose were titles such as Eastlake's *Hints on Household Taste* (1868), Kerr's *The Gentleman's House* (1871), and *Society Small Talk, or What to say and how to say it* (1880).

These books were typically addressed to women rather than men, since it was on the women that the burden of calling and entertaining typically fell. The manuals laid down strict rules about the elaborate rituals of visiting cards and morning calls, how to give luncheons and teas and dinners, and the etiquette surrounding a death in the family. Some, as for instance *The Habits of Good Society*, go into intimate details such as the recommended personal washing regime—'the shower-bath should only be used with the sanction of a physician'—and hair care—'a lady's hair should in ordinary life be dressed twice a day even if she does not vary the mode'. The books are comfortingly prescriptive. 'Pork', says the author of *Etiquette of Good Society*, 'was a very favourite dish. Now we dream as little of placing it on our tables (except they be very homely ones) as do the Jews.' Another declares: 'The *only* dances danced by society are quadrilles, lancers, valses and the lately revived polka . . . such dances as the Mazurka are unknown in good society'. Perhaps it was not necessary to believe that these rules were always and everywhere followed: it was enough that no mistake would ever be made by following them.

The books mentioned were all published in London, so there would be some doubt as to their applicability in Ireland had not a writer in the *Irish Ecclesiastical Record* endorsed the 1879 *Manners and Tone of Good Society* as 'the latest and most reliable work on etiquette'.[9] (According to Michael Holroyd, this was the very book consulted in the British Museum by the young Bernard Shaw in preparation for his entry into London society a few years later.[10]) The full title of this 200-page volume is *Manners and Tone of Good Society or, Solecisms to be Avoided, by a Member of the Aristocracy*. The nub is in the subtitle. In the introductory remarks the author explains that 'the most comprehensive instructions are given . . . that it may be clearly understood what is done and what is not done in good society'. This will enable the reader 'to feel at ease in whatever sphere he may happen to move and cause him to be considered well bred by all with whom he may come in contact.' It was obviously unlikely that anyone reading such a book would actually *be* well-bred.

As with modern cookbooks, there is an amalgam of practical information, fantasy and aspiration. *Manners and Tone*, for instance, carefully prescribes how one should pronounce such names as Cockburn and Colquhoun and Cholmondeley should one ever meet such grandees, the correct way to address a duchess, or how a lady should react if a prince of the royal family chose to dance with her. (Once the equerry has made the introduction, 'The Prince would bow and offer his arm; the lady would courtsey and take it. She would not address him until addressed by him, it not being considered etiquette to do so.')

The books respond to a real anxiety that in this sphere of armed neutrality that is called society there is a correct way of doing things, and that if one fails to follow the latest style one risks being recognised as not quite 'one of us'. In *The Real Charlotte*, the Dublin girl Francie, her card case in hand, heart beating fast 'with shyness and conscious inferiority', mingles with Co. Galway society, and then sadly notices that 'she alone, among a number of afternoon callers at Castle Ffolliott, had kept her gloves on during tea.'[11] Lest any of his readers were tempted not to take the prescriptions seriously, the 'Member of the Aristocracy' chillingly recalled 'how an illustrious politician alluded in the House of Commons to the famous Pytchley Hounds [normally pronounced 'poitchly'] as the Pitchley Hounds, and how this was received with much laughter and how the joke is still remembered against him'.[12]

A visiting card such as Francie had was the first essential. With this, one could quietly extend and consolidate one's social circle. Cards were quite simple thin pieces of pasteboard, the size of a modern credit card, with the lady's name and address typically in small copperplate type; she would, of course, put her husband's Christian and surnames, not her own. 'Young ladies' did not have cards of their own; their names were added on to their mothers' cards. Once her mother died, Mary Hayden had her own card—on 3 April 1883 she records 'left a card on the Kellys'. Cowen's of Sackville Street and Rathmines would print fifty for 3s 6d—and fifty more from the same plate for 1s—a total sum that would otherwise buy you a 5lb joint of beef or a pound of green tea.

Cards were left at the homes of friends and acquaintances; they were always dropped in personally and given to the servant opening the door—it was a gesture just short of a 'call' (and only appropriate in the 'servant-keeping class' as it was called). Cards were left in after dinner parties and other entertainments, and were in general the light oil of all social activity.

The etiquette of 'morning calls' (which took place between three and six in the afternoon) demonstrates the delicacy involved in treading this ground strewn with so many mutual unacceptabilities—such as differences of rank, religion, politics, social circle, occupation. There was a sense also that the introducer was in a manner vouching for the social acceptability of the introduced. As a consequence, introducing people, we are told, must never be done *indiscriminately*. 'So for instance a lady would not introduce two of her acquaintances residing in the same town, although moving in different circles, unless they had each expressed such a desire.'

Dinner

Public dinners were a major feature of social life. Victorians loved to gather in large parties to celebrate anything at all. These dinners were typically long, elaborate and wordy affairs—and for men only. The dinner to celebrate the foundation of the Institute of Chartered Accountants in 1888, for instance, had numerous guests, and no fewer than fourteen speeches. In June 1882, the Irish Medical Association invited 150 guests to its annual dinner. The menu was as follows:

First service

Soups: turtle, consommé with asparagus; turtle punch, East Indian sherry

Fish: turbot and lobster sauce, salmon sauce, Tartar, Marcobrum, hock

Entrées: lamb cutlets and cucumber, sweetbreads with fresh peas, Bollinger champagne 1875

Rélèves: roast Spring chicken, tongue, cold lamb and salad, roast sirloin of beef

Second service

Goslings, asparagus, pâté de foie gras, entremets and dessert.

After all this, the tablecloth was removed and the Queen was toasted. Then followed at least eight speeches.[13]

Scarcely less elaborate were the formal dinner parties held at home. The author of *Manners and Tone* strongly recommended the giving of good dinners as 'there is no better or surer passport to good society'.[14]

At such a dinner the guests arrived at about eight and they expected to begin dinner at quarter past. Each male guest would 'take down' the woman allocated to him by the host. The allocation followed complicated rules of precedence, a table of which, formally authorised by Dublin Castle, was helpfully printed in *Thom's Directory* every year. This listing enabled you to confirm that, for instance, the younger sons of an earl went down to their dinner before the Lord Chief Justice, the Master of the Rolls and the General Commanding the Forces in Ireland, but after the Chief Secretary. For the women in particular this was a moment of some tension, as Mary Hayden implied: 'I got a man to entertain who was awfully hard to get on with; he talked under his breath in a dead level kind of tone. Conversation with him felt like dragging a weight up a hill, or perhaps rolling a stone would be a better simile, for when one started a subject he got on at it a little bit and then came back on you again for a fresh push'.[15] In England, débutantes faced with this problem were taught to work their way letter by letter through the alphabet in search of suitable conversational topics. The wide diversity of experience, knowledge and life, particularly between the sexes, often made dinner conversation a general ordeal. 'Ladies at dinner parties,' thought Mary Hayden, then seventeen years old, 'are an awful nuisance.' She added, endearingly: 'NB when I say I do not like ladies at dinner-parties I mean Papa's dinner-parties, when I have my own friends it is different, of course.'[16] 'Wits' specialising in light patter not too burdened with facts, such as Professor Mahaffy or Father Healy from Bray, were accordingly much prized.

Led by the host, the whole party processed to the dining room, where the gentleman seated his lady on his right-hand side. She would immediately remove her gloves, unfold her napkin and place the enclosed bread on her *left* side. She now prepared to make her choice of soup— 'White or consommé, madame?' Twenty years before, all the dishes, including poultry and roasts to be carved by the host, would have been placed on the table and the guests would have helped each other, with the gentlemen taking particular care of the ladies on their right. 'Society' had however recently adopted *diner à la Russe*, in which the dishes were handed round by the servants to each guest in turn. This innovation was a great blessing to maladroit hosts who no longer had the embarrassment of carving in front of the guests.

The meal would wind its elaborate way, with each course presenting additional pitfalls for the unwary. For instance, 'made' dishes, such as rissoles and patties, should be eaten with a fork only, the 'Member of the Aristocracy' declaring that it would be a vulgarism to use a knife. A knife and fork were used for eating salad or asparagus (it would be extremely vulgar to pick these, or the legs of poultry, up in your fingers). As to puddings, the general rule was again to use a fork only, if possible—this applied to pastries, jellies, iced puddings etc.

At the end of the meal the servants would help the guests to fruit (they should not be tempted to help themselves from the display on the table). Cherries were tricky—bending your head to drop the stone from your mouth 'is regarded as inelegant and is seldom done'; better to gently ejaculate it into a half-closed hand held over the mouth and drop it thence on to the plate. Pears or apples should be peeled and quartered, and pineapples eaten with knife and fork.

After dessert the ladies would withdraw, and the gentlemen take coffee, wine and cigarettes. 'It is not now the fashion,' says our author, 'for gentlemen to sit over their wine beyond fifteen or twenty minutes'. As

Mary Hayden related, the ladies would retreat 'in solemn state to the drawing-room' where 'time passes slowly until the gentlemen appear'. When they did, they were 'in high good humour, of course, they having lots of good stories over their wine downstairs.' Tea would be served and, after about half an hour, the time being now ten-thirty, the guests would start to leave, the whole process having taken no more than two and a half hours. Guest were urged not to tip the servants as they left: 'it would be considered extremely vulgar and ill-judged were anyone to do so.'

The last ceremony

The last ceremony of a lifetime of forms and ceremonies involved death and its concomitants. Perhaps the greater sense of vulnerability heightened awareness, but death certainly had a different place in public discourse than now. The vulnerability was real, and affected all ages: on 28 February 1882, for instance, *The Irish Times'* deaths columns reported ten deaths. There were two widows and one 'beloved wife'; otherwise the ages went from 68 to 59, 33, 28, 17, 15 years and a mere 22 days.

The patterns of the deathbed scene, with the soon-to-be widow or widower and the children gathered solemnly round a decorous bed, are familiar to us from literature. Mary Hayden's account of the death of her father has more of the messiness of real life.

> Papa's face was getting whiter and whiter; his breathing more and more difficult. [Dr] O'Carroll presently called to the sister to make a mustard plaster. My impression is that she refused, at all events he told me to send down to the kitchen for it. I returned to the room and climbed on to the bed to kiss Papa. He was lying on his side, gasping and did not seem to notice me, Suddenly his breath appeared to stop, I ran out of the room thinking he was dead, but when outside I heard the gasping still going on and I returned. A few minutes passed. Suddenly Papa sprang up in the bed. His eyes rolled fearfully and he threw himself down on the other side. O'Carroll caught him as he fell. Looked at him and laid him down. Then, turning to John, he said 'Your poor father is dead'. I could not believe it and catching at his arm asked 'Are you sure?' 'Yes, quite sure, come away. There is no use in staying here' he answered; and after I had given a single glance at the bed I followed him out of the room.[17]

Dr Lombe Atthill declares in his 1911 memoirs that in fact doctors were seldom present at the point of death: 'When the event is at hand he can do no good and his presence is seldom desired'.[18] Dr O'Carroll's devoted attentions to his patient may perhaps be explained by the fact that not many months afterwards he proposed to Mary. She refused him.

The next day, family friends and relatives came, with flowers. Dr Hayden was laid out in the brown habit of the Third Order of St Francis. Crâpe was put on the door and the blinds were pulled down. The following day 'a good many people' came to pay their respects. Dr Hayden was lifted from the bed and put into his coffin, and the lid fastened down. A priest relative said Mass in the bedroom where the coffin stood on trestles. The funeral was on Thursday (he had died on Sunday); as was customary the body was taken straight from the house. Such a funeral normally got under way at nine or ten in the morning. Although it was increasingly acceptable for close female relatives to go to the funeral, Mary did not, so it was an all-male funeral. As befitted a senior physician 'the funeral was very large, nearly 100 carriages.'[19] Most of these would have had occupants, but it was also the custom for closed, empty carriages to be sent to follow the cortège by acquaintances wishing to show respect. The number of carriages was a source of comment: when the well-connected chairman of the Munster Bank, William Digges La Touche, went to his rest in September 1882 people noted that he was followed by over 200 carriages.

Large public demonstrations of sympathy and regret were common. Thus, when the Countess of Moy died in June, the little town of Moy was closed—'every shop was shut, and all business suspended, though a market day'. Mr Webb, a miller from Mallow, was followed to his grave by a procession two and a half miles long, including many of his work people. When the old Fenian, Charles Kickham, died in August, his funeral procession was attended by delegates from London, Belfast and Liverpool. As the open hearse bearing white plumes and drawn by four black horses wound its way from Blackrock to Glasnevin, 'the walls and footways along the Rock road were thronged' and then there were the 'dense masses in waiting at the city side of Balls Bridge'.[20]

Under pressure from various funeral reform associations (and perhaps Dickens' satire) over-the-top displays of black crâpe scarves and headbands, mutes, riderless horses, plumes etc. that had characterised a grand funeral of the 1850s were no longer fashionable. Nonetheless, considerable if restrained shows of emotion were appreciated and carefully reported. In March, *The Irish Times* told its readers that a Mrs Lilly's reaction 'elicited the sympathies of all who saw her. When the grave was being closed in over the remains of her husband the poor woman utterly broke down.'[21] At the funeral of Thomas Burke, one of the Phoenix Park victims, 'the two brothers of the murdered gentleman appeared to have completely broken down under their sad bereavement'. Their mother's steps 'were slow and tottering'. The funeral of the other victim, Lord Frederick Cavendish, gave *The Irish Times*' colour-writer a chance to let himself go. He knows that 'a most melancholy interest' will be felt in the details. Here is 'the aged Duke [father] bent with the burden of his 74 years but still more by the crushing weight of his terrible sorrow. There are the ladies of the house, whose grief is something too sacred to touch upon. Exquisite flowers lie near the coffin, placed there by loving and gentle and reverent hands . . . who shall dare to tell the poignant anguish of those affectionate hearts?'[22]

No doubt there were occasions when women were less affected. However, both sad and merry widows were expected to follow the dress-code of mourning. Widows stayed in mourning for two years, two-thirds of that time being full mourning (i.e. deepest black with no hint of colour). They were not expected to pay or receive calls, or to entertain or be entertained for a least a year. (Different rules applied to men, who were permitted to return to society much more quickly.) Custom laid down various lesser periods of mourning: three weeks only for a second cousin, six for a first cousin, nine months for a grandparent and twelve for a child or parent.[23] No wonder the provision of mourning clothes was an important part of the drapery business.

Chapter 3 The condition of Ireland

In the years following the 'mighty collapse' of the Famine, Irish society had recovered well. To contemporaries the recovery was even a kind of economic miracle. As the Registrar General, Thomas Grimshawe, put it, referring to the twenty-five years after the Famine: 'It may be that Ireland has advanced more rapidly, and recovered from a condition of almost wreck more completely than any other country would have done or ever has done.'[1]

Grimshawe reported that most of the economic indexes had risen very substantially since 1851. Crucially, rents and farm receipts were up. The rapidly growing English manufacturing towns exhibited a constantly increasing demand for Irish meat and butter. As a response, Irish farming had cut the area under crops and expanded the pasture. There were 37 per cent more cattle in the country than there had been in 1851, but cereals were down from 3 million acres in 1851 to 1.8 million. There were now 2 million acres under hay and clover.

The population was gradually urbanising. There were in 1881 19 towns with more than 10,000 people, holding 16 per cent of the population, compared to 10 per cent in such towns in 1851. The biggest of these was Dublin, which (if you included the suburbs) had grown by 22 per cent since 1851. Belfast had doubled in size in the same time. Emigration had removed the very poorest people, so the proportion of families living in first- or second-class houses had gone from just over a quarter of all families to just under a half. The number of pupils attending primary school had gone up by 40 per cent; the number attending universities and colleges had doubled.

Other indicators were positive also. Bank deposits had gone from £8 million in 1851 to £30 million in 1881; money in the humbler savings banks had risen from £1.3 million in 1851 to £3.7 million in 1881. In 1851, there were only 580 miles of railway track; by 1881 this had grown to 2,400 miles.[2] Usage of these tracks had gone up fivefold. Shipping activity in and out of the country had more than doubled, and linen and beer production were both substantially up. Fishing employment, on the other hand, had halved, which was a puzzle. Even emigration had shrunk, to the extent that the Registrar General estimated that there had been in 1876 a small increase in population for the first time in thirty years.

The Irish industrial question

After a generation of progress, the economy turned rapidly worse after 1876. A succession of bad harvests (including in 1879, supposed to be the worst since 1816) revealed the vulnerability of the marginal populations. Added to this, as we have seen, was the dramatic restructuring of the market for agricultural goods caused by competition from America. The quantity of wheat imported from the US into the UK in 1878–82 was three times what it had been only ten years before. 'We have been disposed to complain very bitterly,' wrote *The Irish Times* in February 1882, 'of American food competition, and to dread still worse competition from that source.' And now frozen meat began to come into the London and Liverpool markets from across the world: Argentina sent its first consignment in 1875, Australia in 1880, New Zealand in 1882. In 1882, Australia sent only 1,400 tons—by 1900 it was 50,000 tons. In 1885 a witness told a parliamentary committee that 'to live and thrive is now an impossibility with the farmer . . . liners from America are bringing over corn and even flour freight free.'[3]

Looking across the water, men of a speculative turn noticed that equally bad conditions for English agriculturalists did not produce the same devastating effects. The power of British industry was more than able to compensate in bad agricultural times. In the old days farmers had said to themselves 'down corn, up horn', meaning that if the arable was having a bad year, the pasture would supplement it. In the new international market this comfortable model would no longer work. This gave an urgency to the question: how could Irish industry be developed sufficiently to balance the natural instability of agriculture in Ireland?

In the summer of 1885, a serious attempt was made to address this question by the House of Commons Select Committee on Industries (Ireland). Chaired by Sir Eardley Wilmot, a lawyer with a long-standing interest in Irish affairs, the committee called in expert witnesses, who were asked a grand total of 13,500 questions. Taken together the answers vividly reveal how the segment of Ireland that was neither landlord nor farmer saw the problems the country faced. As the historian E. R. R. Green noted, the committee's report 'marks the beginning of industrial revival if only by drawing attention to a truly alarming state of affairs.'[4] But it did more than that, for it also was the beginning of a century-

Two early motors on the quay at Waterford, attracting considerable attention. The first motor car in Waterford was registered to Herbert Goff, the son of a local business-man. The first commercial garage in Ireland was established in Waterford in 1900. (National Library of Ireland)

long argument about how the fundamental welfare of the Irish people was to be achieved. On one side was the view that without economic strength nothing could be done. On the other was a conviction that there were more important things than mere economic success. Were the children in schools to learn German and mechanical drawing or Latin and Irish?

No conclusions were reached in the report, 'not having been able to take sufficient Evidence to enable them to agree upon specific recommendations', as the committee told the House. However, every single one of the questions, with the answers, was carefully printed as backing for future deliberations. They were, after all, Facts, or something like them.

The report is in itself a monument to the Victorian work ethic. The committee sat for 34 days over May, June and July 1884. The report (intended as merely interim) is over 1,100 pages in length; it includes 700 pages of evidence, 50 appendixes filling over 200 pages, and a further 205 pages devoted to an index (including a 4-page index to the index). Despite the Chairman's urging, the select committee was not reappointed, the government preferring to address specific issues by royal commissions.

The basic reason why the committee failed to produce any answers was because the question was too complex and intractable. The more the members learned, the more difficult the problem seemed. At bottom the question was not: why is there no industry in Ireland?—but the more complicated: how can we account for the decay of Irish industry and how can we reverse that decay? Stories such as this about Bandon sixty years before were uppermost in the committee's mind:

> The town of Bandon in the county Cork had a population of 14,100 in 1824, the majority of whom were artisans employed in the manufacture of linens, woollens, corduroys etc. which were produced by hand looms; females being employed in weaving and spinning. There were two extensive cotton mills, driven by water power, in full work for upwards of half a century until 1826, when the protective duty was removed and the country became flooded with English manufactures.[5]

The population of Bandon in 1883 was 5,800.

As a preliminary, the Chairman sent a questionnaire to a number of industry leaders asking 'whether the trade is carried on as extensively as formerly?' Virtually all, from agricultural implement makers, bootmakers and basket makers to salt refiners, silversmiths and spade manufacturers replied with the same message, as, for instance, did Thomas

Hoey, pin-maker: 'The trade is not carried on as extensively as in former times. The commercial depression, the impoverished condition of the country and English competition are the causes of this decline.'⁶ It was estimated that 5–6 million pins and nails were used every day in Ireland, 'barely a tithe of which' were made in the country. The tendency to buy from English manufacturers for various reasons, ranging from ease of supply and cheapness to snobbery, was noted also by gun-makers, iron founders and even the spade manufacturers. The decline of landlord purchasing power naturally affected specialised industries such as coach and cabinet builders.

In the course of days and days of questions, the witnesses reverted constantly to particular aspects of the problem, ranging from competition from British manufacturers to the refusal, following current economic theory, to provide state assistance to one economic group rather than another. Much time was also spent on resource questions, such as the lack of coal, and whether and how far water power could substitute. Particular attention was paid to railway freight charges, which seemed especially prejudicial. As several witnesses showed, it was often cheaper to convey goods from London or Liverpool to Galway than from Dublin to Galway, and shorter distances inside Ireland were even more penalised. Viewed from London, this was no more than the practice of giving discounted rates to large customers; viewed from Ireland it looked like another way in which established large-scale English businesses could strangle new Irish businesses.

It was clear that Ireland's major problem was Britain—or more specifically the staggering industrial machine that had been developed in England. British trade in iron, coal, cotton and ships had until very recently been larger than that that of the USA, France and Germany combined. Since the development of the railways throughout the country, British goods were able to penetrate deep into the Irish countryside. In country towns and villages, tea and shop-bought clothes had replaced oatmeal and home-made clothes in everyone's budget.

Several witnesses mentioned how things had gone downhill in the last decades. For instance, the wool merchant, William Keating, remembered Birr as it had been, with perhaps a touch of nostalgic exaggeration:

They had extensive factories of tobacco, soap and candles; they also had a large production of combs, brushes and hats; they had two extensive distilleries and two breweries; they had extensive production of woollen stuff goods, both for public sale and for home consumption by farmers in the neighbourhood. Of all these industries there remains but one distillery working about half the extent it did previously and one weaver; that is all the small manufacturing in the district. Then in the neighbouring town of Roscrea in Tipperary there were a 1,000 men employed as weavers and wool-combers; those 1,000 are now represented by 2.[7]

Sir Robert Kane, the author of *The Industrial Resources of Ireland* (1845), was a key witness, among other things reporting that years ago there had been 28 mills on the Dodder—'it was one succession of mills from the source to the mouth almost . . . most of those mills are idle now'. From Waterford, Alderman Cornelius Redmond told the same story: the Portlaw linen factory, down from 3,000 employees to 500; the famous Waterford glass factory brought to its knees by a strike; shipbuilding and iron-founding had also disappeared. As it happened, the collapse of the mighty Malcolmson empire, which at one time sent ships across the world, from China to the United States, and made Waterford a more important shipbuilding centre than Belfast, owed more to the second generation's incompetence and extravagance than British competition. Only bacon curing survived.

Sir Robert Kane was asked about trade unions. The problem, as he conceived it, was that the men were all members of English unions, which of course had their own interests to protect. (Membership enabled the men to get work in England or even on the continent if they wished.) He recounted an instance where a British union (no doubt in pursuit of some 'no new technology without negotiation' policy) told its members to prevent a Dublin foundry from upgrading its machinery.[8] In another case, William Sullivan shockingly described how rival English manufacturers actually financed a long strike in a glass factory in Cork: 'an attorney in Cork paid the wages provided by glass-makers of St Helen's and Birmingham for two years.'

The committee spent a considerable time exploring the butter market. Years before, the Cork butter market had been one of the largest in the world; but over the previous twenty years a disastrous decline in exports had been experienced. One London merchant gave evidence that in 1851 butter from Ireland had represented one-third of all his imports; thirty years later, Irish imports represented less than 1 per cent. The key problem was that Irish butter was made by farmers' wives all over the south in the same rough and ready manner as it had been for generations. Unfortunately, the Danes and the French and the Swedes had improved their methods, and the market had responded.[9]

The witnesses presented the committee with an almost intractable complex of problems. Irish butter was an important source of income for small farmers, especially in the south. But it came from low-yielding cows fed on mossy, poor grass (the best seed was dear, and not available from the local shopkeepers who gave long credit). As a result of this, and cattle-raising customs, the average Irish cow gave only 430 gallons of milk a year, while Yorkshire cows gave 640. Irish butter-makers had no technical education and were therefore ignorant of non-traditional methods. The butter they produced was salty, which improved its keeping qualities but did nothing for its flavour. Because of the traditional butter-making technique it was also watery and poorly packed. The new, expensive, cream separator used abroad eliminated water almost completely.

However, merchants colluded by buying the poorest quality for ready money. Relying on their experience of exporting butter in the previous century, the trustees of the Cork butter market continued to insist that all butter be packed in oak (which had to be imported, as opposed to locally available beech); barrels were insisted on, rather than the more suitable tubs which could not be rolled to the damage of their contents. The Danes had designed special ventilated trains to carry their butter, while Irish butter was frequently loaded straight into carriages that had previously held paraffin oil or coal.[10] Freight rates were high, partly because of the low volumes.

Faced with this web of problems in one industry alone, some of which, such as the improvement of the quality of cattle and dairying, touched on deep issues, it is perhaps not surprising that the committee failed to make any recommendations.

Several witnesses noted the poor support that the banking sector provided. As one pointed out: 'The present banks lend only in very limited circumstances and to a very small extent'.[11] On average, Irish households had savings of £34 each in the banking system (this represents more than the annual wages of a labourer). Part of the reason for at least some of such savings not being invested even in the land was the need for the farmer to supply a portion to enable his daughters to marry. Most witnesses believed that this money was sent by the banks to London to be invested from there in English firms.

The banks certainly did not invest this money in Irish industry. In the first instance, neither they nor their British counterparts saw industrial investment as their business; the key to successful banking was to borrow long and lend short. Thus they were happy to, for instance, help out respectable farmers for a few months before harvest, but if the loan ran for more than three months the farmer had to renew, pushing his effective interest rate up to 10 per cent (i.e. nearly double the usual rate). Without security of tenure Irish farmers had very little substance to back loans.

This had not mattered in the good days before 1876, when banks had been relatively free with loans. But snap! 'the farmers were shut out from banking accommodation as soon as the agrarian crisis came on.'[12] So, unable to 'borrow money at a moderate rate of interest to purchase seeds or cows at the beginning of the season, they take credit from shopkeepers and borrow money from the class of men known as gombeen men, who will give them extended credit but charge them grossly exorbitant rates of interest.'[13]

Witnesses also criticised the tendency of banks in the south of the country: 'The smaller the sum, the more exacting they are . . . and they have been anything but careful in the larger transactions'. Peter McDonald, who had travelled throughout Ireland for twelve years as partner of the distillers and wine merchants Cantwell & McDonald identified 'a want of caution in these large advances.'[14]

McDonald clearly knew something, for at the end of the very day on which he was speaking, the Munster Bank based in Cork suspended payment, causing immense distress. Poor management and fraud were clearly indicated. It emerged, for instance, that two of the directors had very large unsecured loans (nothing like as much as rumour had it, they declared indignantly) and enormous loans of £25,000 had been made to a building contractor, an undischarged bankrupt, called Commendatore Delaney. It later emerged that virtually unsecured loans of £13,000 had been made to a Mr O'Brien, and another of £24,700 to a Mr Nicholas Murphy. The chairman of the bank, William Shaw MP, had outstanding loans of £90,000. A few days later the astonished public was told that Robert Farquharson, one of the joint-managers of the Dublin branch, had defrauded the bank of some £70,000 and was on the run, probably beyond the law's reach on the Continent. The money had gone on stock exchange speculation.

The following year the bank was wound up, but not before real hardship was caused to shareholders. As was customary, the shares had been only partly paid up. The liquidators discovered that after all the defalcations a call was necessary. Suddenly, instead of receiving a dividend, conceivably a major source of income, the 3,500 shareholders,

1,300 of whom were widows and spinsters, had to pay £2 a share. As the *New York Times* reported: 'A number of Irish ladies who had all their means invested in the bank will be reduced to poverty'. (The fate of Miss Matty in Elizabeth Gaskell's popular 1853 novel *Cranford*, who loses £150 of her income of £163 by the failure of a bank, would have been well remembered.) In due course the assets were reconstituted into the newly-founded Munster and Leinster Bank, which itself in 1966 became part of Allied Irish Banks.

The habit of the day was to believe strongly in 'essential' or racial characteristics, and several witnesses were asked anxiously whether there was anything fundamental in the Irish people that would prevent them from engaging in industry. Those asked absolutely denied it. The Irish were quite strong enough, as Sir Robert Kane confirmed from various international statistics comparing Irish, English, Scottish and Belgian workers.[15] They were also hard-working, as was evident from the success they had made as emigrants in Lancashire and in the United States. William Keating continued: 'They have not the same plod, but they are more reliable in many ways than the English and Scotch mechanics.' Robert Kane believed that 'in quickness of appreciation and intelligence' Irish workers surpassed English and Scottish workers, though he conceded that in 'severe reasoning and judgement', such as was required by management, 'their superiority is not so manifest'.

The difficulty, as more than one witness declared, was in habit of mind. Keating saw it like this:

> A man accumulates in Ireland a few thousands, and if he keeps them he does not invest them; in England or Scotland his sons would consider that a good foundation for developing the industry or business. In Ireland the sons want to be professional men; they want to go into the army, or they take up the profession of a walking gentleman and do nothing; the father dies and the business ceases. That is a very common thing in Ireland, because in the higher classes there is what I may be permitted to call a vulgar contempt for work; and with those who aspire to mingle with them the same contempt for work obtains. The first thing the Irishman of the upper middle class does is to get out of any connection with business the moment he can.[16]

These were the attitudes that the young William Butler Yeats (and not him alone) was being brought up with in the 1880s, perhaps as recompense for the bourgeois reality of cramped houses in Harold's Cross and Sandymount. A descendant of wool merchants, he later sneered at 'the merchant and the clerk [who] breathed on the world with timid breath' and told his friends moodily that if he had his rights he would himself be Duke of Ormonde, and live 'among men who ride upon horses'.[17] The strongest creative voice of his generation tragically turned to the dark side of the European inheritance: magic, irrationality (what he called in his idiosyncratic spelling 'the greater renaesance—the revolt of the soul against the intellect') and a social and economic system represented by pitiless agricultural grind for the many, supporting leisure for the very few.

William Sullivan put another gloss on the analysis:

> It must not be forgotten that the small farmers of the present are the descendants of the gentry of the past . . . the successive famines and pestilences of the past have naturally swept away the lower classes, and the present farmers represent to a considerable extent, more than perhaps you could imagine, the descendents of the gentry who were dispossessed and who still, I regret to say, in one sense, retain many of the traditions and instincts of their class.

Prominent among which was a dislike of the 'labour of the hands' involved in craft work.[18]

Although the witnesses were perfectly clear that there was no intrinsic bar to the Irish reviving their industrial past, there were other obstacles. One of these, identified by Sir Robert Kane, was an intense lack of self-confidence. 'It was the famine of 1846,' he believed, 'which shattered the confidence of the people in themselves, and broke down any spirit of confidence and energy they had, and they had a great deal of it before then . . . at that time there was very much more tendency to industrial enterprise than there has been since.' (Seventy years later Seán Lemass was to highlight this lack of confidence, of what Keynes called 'animal spirits', as the key problem in developing Irish industrialisation.[19]) Do you think, Sir Robert was asked by one of the committee, 'that we have recovered from that famine forty years ago? I think not; of course there has been a very large amount of recovery, but I think we have not by any means completely recovered.'[20]

Witness after witness reverted to the education system. They noted that the syllabus of the national schools, and the same applied to private schools, was so literary as to lead the children to think of clerking or teaching as their natural destinations rather than manual work. 'The system of teaching is altogether a mistake . . . the girls want to be mistresses and governesses and boys to be clerks. If they had practical education and a little education in the use of tools and models the result would be different'. Ireland was behind in this matter, so Professor Sullivan said, because of 'the entire social transformation that was effected at the time of the famine . . . besides the previous history of the country in which every little industry has gradually and gradually died out.'[21]

Payment by results, by which a sucessful teacher could double his or her basic income, favoured rote-learning and thorough knowledge of set texts. But it did not allow much space for variation. Since the teachers themselves were generally those who had done well in the system and were specifically rewarded for following it slavishly, there was little likelihood of deviation. (This was not unique to Ireland, as the characters of Bradley Headstone and Charley Hexam in Dickens' last completed novel *Our Mutual Friend* make clear.)

In considering what might be done to revive Irish industry, witnesses frequently mentioned some form of protectionism. This proposal, however, met both ideological and political barriers. In his seminal work, *Principles of Political Economy*,[22] which had taught a generation how to think about economics, John Stuart Mill clearly set his face against any attempt to bolster or protect a country's native industry. 'This was certainly', he wrote, one of 'those cases in which government interference works ill because grounded on false views.' The theory of international trade showed that protectionism merely 'renders the labour and capital of the country less efficient'. The result can only be waste and national loss.[23] For Mill, and for many of his readers, this was one of the laws of economics, to break which would be as counterfactual and indeed irresponsible as expecting the waters of a canal to flow uphill. As one witness stated: 'In my opinion in this 19th century it would not be possible to return to protectionism pure and simple.'[24] Sir Robert Kane stressed the need to keep within 'the ordinary functions of government', when rejecting the idea of government loans to industry.[25] (For the very latest economic thinkers of the time, such as W. S. Jevons, Mill's categorical 'laws' which had purported to be as solid as physical or astronomical laws were nothing of the sort. But perhaps it was unlikely that such views would be represented on a parliamentary select committee.)

As well as being 'right', these *laissez-faire* policies were politically popular. When William Lane suggested state assistance for the butter industry he was told, 'You are probably aware that State interference with industry is very much objected to . . . this is a principle and a popular principle'.[26] The speaker went on to stress 'the immense difficulty there would be in asking the Legislature of the United Kingdom to take a special trade under its protection and foster it either by education or subsidies for centres of education'.

On the whole, the witnesses agreed with Sir Robert Kane that 'as long as Ireland is an integral part, legislatively and politically considered, of the United Kingdom' differential duties were impossible. Another concurred: 'I cannot conceive the possibility of [England] permitting any protective duties on its manufactures going into Ireland'. But, asked one questioner, would it not be to Ireland's advantage? Sir Robert had no doubt: 'looking at it from a purely Irish standpoint, it would be a very popular sort of Utopia'.[27]

The Select Committee on Industries (Ireland) could not agree on any conclusions, though the evidence strongly favoured at least the development of technical education in the national school system and also rebalancing of railway freight charges so that they did not penalise Irish manufacturers. Nonetheless, the distinguished witnesses did together provide a wish list for the economic development of the country—elements in the list were to recur in Sinn Féin's policies and in other policy formulations up to the present day.

Chapter 4 The Angel in the House

Social change effects its magic in gradual steps rather than jumps. Although the prescient saw that the landlord system was finished in the 1880s, it took another generation before the Wyndham Act of 1905 completed the task, and much longer before the glamour of the old Ascendancy faded. The economic analysis of the witnesses to the select committee was not put firmly into the political arena until Sinn Féin's manifesto twenty years later. The 'woman question', as the style of the day described it, was another slow burner.

Given the religiously and socially conservative tendencies of the time, it is perhaps not surprising that debate about the status of women did not loom large in Ireland. Even in England many, perhaps most, men and women would have agreed with Queen Victoria's private opinion of votes for women that 'this mad wicked folly of Women's Rights with all its attendant horrors, on which her poor feeble sex is bent, forgetting every sense of womanly feeling and propriety' ought to be stopped in its tracks.[1] The issue was regularly debated in the House of Commons in the 1870s, but in the 1880s the appetite seemed to have waned, for it only came up once.

More soberly, the *Handbook to Political Questions* rehearsed some of the arguments against giving women the vote:[2]

That women are already represented in that they exercise influence on the male votes;
That the majority of women do not want and would rather be without the suffrage;
That women can never be physically the equals of men; and cannot therefore claim the suffrage on equal terms;
That if women were enfranchised the disposal of their votes would cause family jealousies, ill-feeling and greater political strife;
That men's respect and reverence for women would be fatally undermined, while the finer edge of women's nature would be blunted;
That the concession of the suffrage would inevitably be followed by the demand that women should be qualified to sit in the House of Commons, on the Bench etc.;
That to grant the suffrage to women on the grounds that as they are bound to obey the laws they ought to have a hand in making them would

logically oblige us to concede the suffrage to every man, woman and child in the kingdom;

That the electorate is large enough now, and any increase to it would be a misfortune.

These opinions were not gathered from old fogeys sitting in the windows of Piccadilly clubs, but can be found in the pages of the liberal monthly review *Nineteenth Century* (whose contributors included William Gladstone, Thomas Huxley and Oscar Wilde), frequently in articles written by women. The distinguished editor of the *Economist*, Walter Bagehot, gave his opinion that to seek equality was 'a struggle against Nature; a war undertaken to reverse the very conditions under which not men alone but all mammalian species have reached their present development'.[3]

In 1877, towards the end of his life, the nationalist MP Isaac Butt intervened in the debate about the Women's Disabilities Removal Bill. He was against it, being a firm proponent of the 'women's place is in the home' theory. 'By the arrangement of God,' he thundered, 'man was intended for the busy walks of life, woman for the sanctuary of home and for those offices far higher than man could perform in the busy scenes of life, and which make home and life holy. That is her place.' To change that would 'sever relations which have existed since the Creation . . . let [a woman] make political speeches, and never again could you restore her purity of thought, her innocence of heart, her affection for home, husband and children. All these would be ruthlessly destroyed.' And, he declared, 99 out of 100 women in Ireland thought the same.[4] Published a few years later was Olive Schreiner's best-selling novel *The Story of an African Farm* (1883), which was one of the very first to explore the issues of 'the New Woman'. In that novel, the protagonist Lyndall, though pregnant, refuses to marry. She acerbically notes how the rhetoric declaims 'it is delightful to be a woman', and then concludes, 'but every man thanks the Lord devoutly that he isn't one.'[5] In 1884, Mary Hayden, then twenty-two, echoed these words with a cry of dismay and self-doubt in her diary:

If I were a man I should never omit thanking God for my sex every morning and night. A weak body, weak intellect for a woman what trials you are . . . a second place always, or a first yielded with polite contempt, hemmed in with restrictions because 'weakness must be protected' going the same weary round of dull toil or vapid amusement from youth to age, slaves or toys unable to join in the eager interesting work of business life. Too delicate forsooth for anything but 'the peaceful life of home', bearing children who

The lavish wedding of George Noble, Count Plunkett and Josephine Mary Cranny, the offspring of two south Dublin building families. One of their children, Joseph Mary Plunkett, was a poet and the key strategist for the 1916 Rising. At the centre of the photograph, the demure new 'angel of the house'. (Honor O Brolchain)

will soon learn to despise them, leading that dreary weary life till they die and are forgotten. With intellects that cannot originate, that perhaps may grasp and comprehend some of that wisdom which has come down from the past but cannot add to the store, ever following, unable to lead. 'When shall women be found equal to men?' when indeed, hereafter perhaps, not certainly here.'[6]

Middle-class women, those Butt had in mind, were, in the terms of Coventry Patmore's sequence of popular poems, 'the Angel in the House' (1854–63); delicate creatures whose sphere of responsibility was the preservation and nurturing of the family home. Given the available technology, this was not a light or insignificant assignment. When the Hayden family cook left, to her disgust Mary (then aged seventeen) was told that she herself 'must assist in that odious, undefined, stupid yet complicated business of "minding the house". I shall certainly make a mess of it. If I had certain defined duties to perform, I should perhaps succeed well enough, but the watching and noting what requires to be settled needs a good memory and a natural fondness for order—neither of which I possess'.[7]

The primary fuel in Dublin homes, for instance, was coal. This had to be delivered by one of the hundreds of vans criss-crossing the city all day carrying coal, bread, fish, vegetables and so on. Coal is heavy as well as being smelly and dirty. But without it there would be no cooking and no hot water. A typical Dublin household used one ton a month during the winter and less in the summer, at a cost of anything from 15s to 24s a ton. Having been deposited in the cellar, it then had to be collected in coal scuttles for the stoves and fires where it was wanted. Cooking (including tending the ever-hungry stove) and cleaning were equally physical work with very little mechanical aid. The worst chore of all was laundry, and maids seeking work often specified that they would not do it. Luckily, commercial laundries were becoming more common— replacing the weekly washer-woman.

Unfortunately, the educational system provided very little help. As Michael Davitt told a parliamentary committee on technical education in 1884: 'There is a complete absence of any interest in commonsense domestic training in the education of girls'.[8] As one result, he claimed that 'the Irish people have about the worst system of cooking in the world.' The fault lay with the prevailing taste for being 'accomplished'. To this end, parents and teachers had developed a style of education 'which echoed in the frivolity of its approach to the serious facts and duties of life what is believed to be the education of the wealthy and fashionable'. He deplored this model of 'accomplished uselessness' and 'learned indolence' as adopted by nuns and other educators of girls. To reinforce the seriousness of his message he claimed (without much evidence) that the ignorance of hygiene and other subjects 'which could scarcely be mentioned', added as much as 5 per cent to the mortality of Dubliners. Davitt would not have been happy to read the controversy in the letters column of the *Freeman's Journal* in September 1883, where the main concern of the writers was that the girls in convent schools should learn deportment and society manners.

The thousands of new houses being built in the Dublin suburbs represented a new idea of life: that the workplace and the home were separate arenas with little in common and little overlap. In the ideology of the day, the husband was seen as grappling at work with the neo-Darwinian horrors of the struggle for existence. After work he would come back home to sweetness and light, to moral and physical delicacy and refreshment. The home stood for honesty, warm feeling, love and truthfulness—virtues not to be found in the average office or workplace. The gentle satire of the lawyer's clerk Wemmick, in Dickens' *Great Expectations* (1860), perfectly exemplifies the division between home and work: while he walked back to work 'by degrees Wemmick got dryer and harder and his mouth tightened'.[9] Those professions which did not require office backup were slow to adopt the new idea—indeed, Irish barristers were until very recently actively discouraged from establishing offices. Doctors typically used part of their house as a surgery. Middle-class men in newer professions, such as solicitors, accountants, engineers, had offices with (male) clerks; female office workers came in a decade or so later. This is an urban, middle-class pattern, not, for instance, represented in the Anglo-Irish world, where the same demesne contained the stables and the home farm and the magistrate's room, where Lady Fingall remembered her father receiving rents, settling leases and dispensing justice; or for that matter in the farmer's world, where work and home were one—only the farm labourer 'commuted' to work.

To support this new life-style, large shops (later called department stores) such as Arnotts and Pims stocked a widening range of goods from ribbons and pins to chairs and carpets. They encouraged Materfamilias to decorate her home to look as unlike an office or factory as possible—coaxed by words we scarcely use now, such as 'dainty', 'tasteful' and 'refined'. (She was not, however, encouraged to consider the lives of the dressmakers, or the shop-girls who could be seen any

Saturday in the drapers' shops on their feet still at ten at night, having started at nine in the morning. This for ten shillings a week.[10])

The theory of the law on the position of women was clear: as Blackstone explained, in English law 'the very being or legal existence of the woman is suspended during marriage, or at least is incorporated and consolidated into that of the husband.'[11] A plethora of consequences followed this idea. For instance, as Blackstone explained, a husband could not legally grant or covenant anything to his wife; he was responsible for her debts (incurred before and after marriage); neither could testify against the other in court; and if someone injured her she must sue in his name. But in 1882 the passing of the Married Women's Property Act made a major breach in this theory. By allowing married women to retain rights over their property and their earnings, it quite clearly recognised their 'legal existence'.

In practice, middle-class women of all ages were still severely limited in all sorts of ways: in what they could wear (the divided skirt proposed by the Rational Dress Society, thought *The Irish Times*, was a step towards the genuinely shocking idea that men and women would dress similarly), how they could ride (anything other than the elegant if precarious side-saddle was out of the question), what they could read, what they were taught, where and when and with whom they could go out. Mary Hayden records her dismay at being spotted outside without gloves, or travelling on the top deck of a tram, and at forgetting to return a visit. The occasion when, greatly daring, she dined alone in a London restaurant is carefully recorded. When she goes to a party in the evening she has to be escorted home (by a man such as her brother, or by their maid); if no one is available she cannot go. As she progresses in her studies, her best friend's husband (a timber merchant of Thomas Street) rails against 'women going out of their sphere'.[12]

For a young woman of the middle class, the constraints were all the more irritating because of the freedoms enjoyed by contemporary young men. Mary Hayden frequently mentions the contrast. In June 1878, aged sixteen, she notes 'how I wish I could have a game of cricket as I see some fellows doing in the square . . . John [her brother] is far too grand to play it with me even in the garden'. (Croquet and tennis she would be allowed, but they are 'stupid'—football is not mentioned.) In July, by the sea, 'spent hours learning to throw a stone and didn't succeed.' The comparison with the freedoms of boys' lives was constantly galling: '[A former playmate] is now I suppose a man, while I and in fact all girls go on *semper eadem* with few pleasures and no liberty and in fact behave better than the boys who have so much enjoyment.'[13]

On her eighteenth birthday she looks forward with no enthusiasm to 'balls and parties and all that', and mourns 'the general liberty of action which ladies have not'. A year later she sees some (male) students rowing on the river, and poignantly reflects: 'How I envied them. I wish that the doctrine of transmigration of souls was true and then I might be a man sometime, might sometimes walk and ride about day and night by myself: if only it could be.'[14]

Not that she had any aspirations to equality as such. In August 1880 (aged eighteen), she read a science fiction story by Bulwer Lytton called *The Coming Race* (1871) in which 'the female is the dominant sex, a notion absurd in itself and impossible, for though some women rise far above men in intellect and occasionally in strength, yet nothing short of a radical change in them physically and morally could make ordinary women the equals of ordinary men.'[15]

On the other hand, she was not a bit starry-eyed about men. Her regular rows with her brother John, and his disobliging refusals, for instance to escort her to the theatre or the debates at the L&H, the University College Dublin debating society, certainly cured any tendency to 'talk painful sentimental rubbish about men' as her friends were wont to do. In April 1882, she and her friend Josephine chatted after breakfast: 'For a good while our discourse turned on the male portion of mankind ... the faults she ascribed to men were—slowness in comprehension, immorality, drunkenness and selfishness. The faults were certainly undeniable and worse in themselves than those of women.'[16]

Nonetheless, as she recorded a month later, 'I dread having men [to tea] for I am haunted with a perpetual fear that they are bored, and in fact their superiority has a chilling effect on my spirits.'[17] Marriage did not seem a particularly tempting prospect. Seeing Josephine pampered and engaged, she was inclined to repine 'at my harder and rougher lot, then suddenly I think "but she is going to get married" and I feel more than content with my destiny'.[18]

The idea of women's votes was floated in Dublin in 1882, but not to any great acclaim. A meeting held in Russell's Temperance Hotel in St Stephen's Green on 14 April to hear an address by Caroline Biggs, a leading light of the English National Society for Women's Suffrage, was very sparsely attended. Perhaps this was simply because the weather was bad, or perhaps because, as the Rev. Carmichael, in the chair, commented:

'One of the reasons why the cause of women's suffrage had not made more progress was owing to the small amount of attention given to the subject by women themselves.'

Before Caroline Biggs delivered her 'able and argumentative address', the meeting was addressed by the chairman and two other men, one of whom pointed out that women in Ireland were even worse off in point of representation than those in England. There, at least women had local government votes and were entitled to become Poor Law guardians. In Ireland, the only recent reform, he said, was that women were now entitled to be arrested under the Coercion Act! After Miss Biggs' speech, the motion calling for the extension of the parliamentary franchise to women was passed unanimously.[19] Mary Hayden does not mention this meeting in her diaries; she spent that afternoon 'making visits', got caught in a heavy shower and returned home early.

George Moore's 1886 realist novel *Drama in Muslin* describes the lives of a number of young women leaving their grand convent school in England and entering the Irish marriage market. As Moore puts it, 'while the island rocked with the roar of five million peasants claiming the right to own the land they tilled', these young women concentrated on their own tough contest, fuelled by a great imbalance of the sexes. In this world, as one of their mothers says, 'a woman is absolutely nothing without a husband; if she does not wish to pass for a failure she must get a husband, and upon this all her ideas must be set.' Without a husband, how was a woman to aspire to those 'other and higher things', or to participate in the 'glory and honour of the homes of England, aye and of Ireland', that Isaac Butt so enthused over?

The anxious mother made it clear to her daughters that the method was straightforward:

> Make yourselves agreeable, try to learn how to amuse men. Flatter them, that is the great secret; nineteen out of twenty will believe you, and the one that doesn't can't but think it delightful. Don't waste time thinking of your books, your painting, your accomplishments; if you were Jane Austens, George Eliots and Rosa Bonheurs it would be of no use if you weren't married. A husband is better than talent, better even than a fortune—without a husband a woman is nothing; with a husband she may rise to any height. Marriage gives a girl liberty, gives her admiration, gives her success; a woman's whole position depends on it.[20]

Depressingly, one of the daughters, Alice, realised that 'she was no more than a plain girl, whom no man would care to marry, and who would have to live without any aim or object in life, an ever-increasing burden to her people, an object of derision to her acquaintances.'[21]

Faced with this possible fate, as Moore writes waspishly, the girls quickly learned to use what allure they had.

> To snigger, to cajole, to chatter to any man who would condescend to listen to them, and to gladly marry any man who would undertake to keep them. For this and only this did the flower-adorned bosoms swell sweetly beneath the laced corsets; for this were the red laughs that cajoled behind shadowy curtains; for this were the pretty feet advanced, with the flesh seen through the open work of the stockings; for this and only this was the pleasing azure of the adoring eyes.[22]

Today, the fashions of the 1880s with their bustles and layers seem impossibly demure; for contemporaries, as Moore describes, they were implicitly alive with sexuality. Here, for instance, he describes the beauty, Olive, entering a ball room: 'She was in white silk, tightly drawn back so that every line of her supple thighs, and every plumpness of the superb haunches was seen; and the double garland of geraniums that encircled the tulle veiling seemed like flowers of blood scattered on virgin snow.'[23] Alas, for all her beauty, Olive does not marry Lord Kilcarney, who was instead infatuated by Violet's infinite fragility—'irresistibly suggestive of an Indian carved ivory were the wee foot, the thin arm, the slender cheek'.

Lower down the social scale there was less pretence. In his book on the winter of 1880/1 and the experiences of Captain Boycott, the English journalist Bernard Becker recounts the story of a Kerryman offered by the match-maker a choice of two brides: one with one cow and the other with two. He liked the girl with one cow far better than her rival, so he consulted a local patriarch: "'Take the girl with two cows," said he, "there isn't the difference of a cow between any two women in the world.'"[24]

Marrying for love

In the middle-class world one was supposed to marry for love. Indeed, to give too much weight to prudential considerations was regarded as cold. So, perhaps confused by mixed messages, things could go too far in the course of the wooing. The young woman might be seduced and become pregnant, the dreaded fate worse than death. Unless a quick marriage could be arranged, or the girl be spirited away to have her baby abroad, this was a social disaster whose consequences would affect her sisters' life chances as well. Without any form of social welfare, if the family abandoned her, it was easy for the unmarried mother to crash through the various social levels and end up very impoverished indeed.

The law, in its old-fashioned way, did not concern itself with such matters, but was very clear as to one aspect of the event. The father or guardian or master with whom the woman was living was entitled to sue the seducer for 'loss of service'—though not if she was living away from home. The action rested not on the damage of the seduction itself, but on the interruption of the daughter's or servant's practical service which he had a legal right to expect. As a contemporary expert pointed out, 'instead of the servant getting protection as a daughter, the daughter only gets protection as a servant.' One consequence of what, even then, was regarded as an antiquated law was that the father was not obliged to spend any compensation he might get on either the child or the seduced woman herself.[25]

Another hazard on the way to the coveted state of matrimony was being strung along by a reluctant suitor, or even jilted. The law provided a remedy for those wronged in this way. In theory, both men and women could sue for breach of promise, but breach of promise cases were nearly always brought by women suing men. Indeed, the law had some distaste for men sueing, recognising the imbalance between the sexes: as Judge O'Brien put it, the fact that 'women had so much less freedom of action' meant that if a long understanding was arbitarily broken off 'she would find herself unable to form a new engagement'.[26] What made these cases so titillating (and deplorable) to contemporaries was the way the law tore down the customary veil of privacy in such matters. Just as the home and the workplace were increasingly separate, so the Victorians sought to place undignified money and elevated love on quite different planes. The breach of promise cases explicitly combined and equated the two, to great comic effect. Reports of the cases are peppered with 'laughter in court'.

Judge O'Brien's comments were made in the unusual case of Kingsley *v* Peile in which the plaintiff, 'a gentlemanly medical student of about 35', sought damages for £1,000 from Miss Peile. As well as being, as the court reporter noted, a lady of attractive appearance and manners, she had £2,900 of shares in the Royal Bank, £1,700 in Grand Canal and £320 in Great Northern Railway stocks and others, giving her an income of something like £150 a year. He had a small property, some in Parsonstown, which produced £120 a year. The case came to court in January 1883 and revealed the very difficult path a woman had to tread.

She and the plaintiff had first known each other years before when he and her brother had been fellow medical students in Dublin. He went to England and they had corresponded, no doubt with more persistence and enthusiasm on her part than his. In 1878 a wedding had been arranged and settlements drawn up (this was before the Married Women's Property Act). At the last minute, he demanded £100 cash immediately, supposedly to enable him to complete his long-deferred medical degree. She refused, they had a flaming row, and the engagement was eventually broken off. As she admitted in court, one of the reasons was the revelation that, far from having £170 of his own as she supposed, £50 of that came from a job as a doctor's assistant which he had since given up, and £30 was payable to his mother. 'It dawned on me,' as she said, 'he wanted my money in place of myself.'

The judge summed up very much against the plaintiff, accepting the defence characterisation of him as 'a thoughtless designing fellow'; the jury found that there had indeed been a promise of marriage, but assessed damages at one farthing.

A more traditional scenario was presented when Miss Fanny Hyland sued the Parnellite nationalist politician, Joseph Biggar. (The political connection no doubt gave an agreeable picquancy to the case for the readers of the unionist *Irish Times*.) After the Land League was suppressed in October 1881, the headquarters was moved to Paris. There, Biggar and others spent the winter. To pass the time, he enjoyed visiting the home of Miss Hyland and her mother, offspring and relict of the late Mayor of Kilkenny. Miss Hyland was thirty-five at the time, he sixty-three. Amorous nothings, explored in some detail by the court, were exchanged.

By her report, Miss Hyland certainly understood that the bachelor politician was serious in his attentions, as indeed the casual remarks, gifts of lockets, and presents such as gloves seemed to signify. He even kissed her, a significant freedom the lady showed no sign of resenting. Indeed, 'she liked being kissed,' claimed the defendant. The sensitivity of the events described in court gave rise to a kind of nervous skittish hilarity, as the contrast between the traditional sentimental details of courtship and the raw facts of life were paraded in court, as in this exchange:

[Prosecuting barrister] Had he the appearance of a man who had lost his heart?
[Miss Hyland] He had—(laughter)
Had you lost yours at this time?
No

Were you in a fair way to losing it?
Yes—(laughter)
When did you actually lose it?
On the 19th—(laughter).

However, when things appeared to get serious, Biggar had withdrawn, citing mysterious and unspecified 'obstacles'. The court elucidated that two of these obstacles were his illegitimate children, by different mothers, whom he was educating. Prompted by Patrick Egan, a fellow Parnellite with whom Biggar had fallen out, Miss Hyland sued for breach of promise. The jury believed her story rather than his, and awarded her £400 damages. This would be enough to pay all her expenses for two years or so. It was a mere pin-prick to the old rogue, however; when he died a few years later he left a £37,000 fortune (having told the court he was worth £20,000).

However much deplored by high-minded lawyers and parliamentarians, who mooted the possibility of abolishing the action in six different debates between 1879 and 1890, breach of promise cases made great reading in the newspapers, opening a window on other people's lives, a window we can still look through. It was argued, indeed, that the scandalous and sensational reports were an additional reason for abolishing the action.

Even more sensational than breach of promise was the action for damages arising from seduction of a wife, or 'crim. con.', as *The Irish Times* continued to call it. Technically, the action for criminal conversation had been abolished with the ecclesiastical courts in 1857. The new divorce law, however, allowed a plaintiff to sue the spouse's lover for damages as a preliminary to full divorce. The sensational Irish case of the day was Joynt *v* Jackson, in which the editor of the *Ballina Herald* sued the manager of the Ballina branch of the Bank of Ireland for seducing his wife.

Charlotte Joynt had married at twenty and had nine children, of whom five survived. She had started as a model wife, a genuine Angel in the House, but something had gone wrong. Perhaps, hinted the lawyers, her husband's fidelity was not all it should have been. She began to drink wine and whiskey, even, so it was claimed, in public houses. She met James Jackson, the bank manager, a man who, counsel claimed, 'had a reputation for that kind of work in Ballina', and a year later was seduced by him.

Things went from bad to worse. Eventually, by 1879, she found herself in a local mental asylum, and from there wrote a letter to her husband admitting her infidelities with Jackson. In an effort to minimise the damages, Jackson claimed that he was not the first with whom she had had an affair. The question for the jury, as one of the barristers put it, was whether 'the vortex of licentiousness into which Mrs Joynt had plunged' was the consequence of his seduction or not. The evidence, though plentiful, was circumstantial. The husband won £1,000 damages (he had initially sought £5,000, so presumably the jury believed some at least of the tales of her previous misdeeds). He then successfully sued her for divorce.

The last we hear of this unfortunate woman is that she had disappeared into America, no doubt helped by her family, but of course without her children.[27]

In the practical details of life, at every stage women were at some sort of disadvantage, and their options were few. Occasionally, as in the case of twenty-five-year-old Maryanne or Marian Stanley, it all became too much, and suicide resulted. Marian lived with her mother and siblings in a house on Ranelagh Road. It was not a happy home. As Marian's brother reluctantly told the coroner's court, at one time his parents had such violent rows that they had come to the attention of the police court. They had violently assaulted each other, and since then they had lived apart.

Marian herself began to be out at all hours, eventually ending up with a child at the age of twenty. Her mother helped her look after the baby, and it seemed that she was going back to a respectable life. Then she met Frederick Wade, the young son of a publican, and began staying out with him 'in a house in Great Brunswick Street' until two in the morning. Her family knew something of this, and, while not approving, took the view that she and her sister were grown women who, as the brother said, 'knew perfectly well what they were doing'. Since the family knew what was happening, the coroner noted that there was no question of 'seduction' in the formal legal sense.

The next step was for herself and Wade to move in to lodgings—a front parlour doubling as bedroom and sitting-room—in the opportunistically named Land League Terrace, North Circular Road. Mrs O'Flaherty, the landlady, stated that they arrived without luggage, and claimed to have been married by registry office that morning. Wade stayed that night. Marian remained in the lodgings for two months, with Wade coming once a week or so. The infrequency of his visits made her unhappy. The landlady and she became quite friendly, but her own family, who were still looking after her little son, seem to have made no effort to discover where she was.

But then disaster struck. Frederick Wade's mother, on whom he completely depended, found out about the liaison. Urged on by her clergyman (a priest from Gardiner Street), the mother put her foot down, cut off money supplies and insisted Wade drop Marian for good. Wade, who comes out of the affair as more pathetic than sinister, during a long conversation on Friday 18 January explained the situation to Marian. Marian (who was not Catholic) made an attempt to contact the Gardiner Street priest but with no luck. The next morning (Sunday) a letter arrived from Wade definitively breaking off the connection and enclosing a postal order for £3. When Mrs O'Flaherty returned from Mass she found Marian lying across the bed. She had swallowed carbolic acid, and was dead before she could be got to the Mater Hospital.

The coroner took the kindly view that she was in an unfortunate family situation and was perhaps trying to establish herself in a respectable way at last. But clearly the forces of society, represented by her man, the respectable widow and the priest of Gardiner Street, were too much for her.[28]

One might have supposed all this was far from the life of the scholarly Miss Hayden, but Dublin was a small place still. A year afterwards she records being on the tram when 'at Ranelagh, young Stanley, the son of the poor girl who committed suicide last year, got in. He is a lovely little boy with great dark eyes and dark hair. We all stared at him till he became quite shy.'[29]

—1907—

A group of priests in Waterford in the early twentieth century. The 'sagart aroon' of the Famine days has been replaced by the powerful leader of the parish, who found it easier to be right than to be kind. (National Library of Ireland)

Chapter 5 The whole face of the country is changing

The world of 1907 was changing, in unpredictable, unsettling, ways. A contemporary writer commented that 'the experience of stress, cross-currents, and changing conditions in the religious, theological, intellectual, social and other domains was so considerable . . . the whole drama fascinates the imagination and challenges examination'.[1] Most generations feel this, but in 1907 there really was something in the air. The inventions that had been surfacing twenty-five years before—the motor-car, electricity, food importation, weaponry—were having a cumulative impact. Not only were new questions being asked, but radically new answers were being taken seriously. Theories that would have been regarded as beneath consideration a generation earlier—or indeed later—were argued and discussed in full seriousness. Fresh ideas were in the air about sex relations, local and international politics ('Bolshevik' was one of the new words of the year), and religion—under pressure from the occultism of Yeats and AE and the Modernism of the Irish Jesuit, Father George Tyrrell. Some other new words of the year, as identified by the *Oxford English Dictionary,* give a flavour of the time: activism, bemusement, challengingly, changeover, pacificism, intelligentsia, New Thought, structuralism and tough-minded. Less seriously, the *OED* also identified first uses in this year for Meccano, Snakes and Ladders and Teddies.

Men and women

Among the ideas swirling around the ether were fundamental ones about the relations between men and women. Ideas of woman's self-possession (in several ways) were explored in plays by Ibsen and George Bernard Shaw, and pursued in novels by the so-called 'New Woman' writers. The most famous of these novels, *The Woman Who Did,* features a woman who lives with a man without marriage and suffers social estrangement as a result. A bundle of elements, including a hunger to see and experience the world without chaperones, the pursuit of economic self-sufficiency and the rejection of inevitable marriage were loosely attached to this headline. (As a small indicator of the limitations the New Woman was contesting, we have seen in the 1880s how Mary Hayden recorded the first day she ate alone in a restaurant as one to be remarked. Mary Hayden was to become a leading figure in the Irish suffrage movement, chairing various organisations including the Irish Women's Franchise League and the Catholic Women's Suffrage Society.)

The opposition to the New Woman was no longer couched in the measured tones of the 1880s, and frequently reflected a low opinion of actual women. In March 1907, *The Weekly Irish Times* quoted the popular novelist Marie Corelli, author of *The Sorrows of Satan* and other best-sellers, as deploring the idea of women's suffrage: 'shall we sacrifice our Womanhood to politics? Shall we make a holocaust of maidens, wives and mothers on the brazen altars of Party?' To do so, she declared, 'would be nothing less than a national disaster.' The argument was, of course, conducted purely in a middle-class context. No one expected the women working long hours in shops, or in Jacob's biscuit factory or the Dublin Laundry, earning perhaps 10s for a 60-hour week, to have the 'natural heritage of her sex, which is the mystic power to persuade, enthral and subjugate man', in Marie Corelli's words. Doubting that the great majority of women were intellectually fitted for the franchise, she dismissed the counter-argument about 'the illiterate yokel with the vote' by saying that, unlike a woman voter, at least he is not likely to be carried away by a candidate's 'admiration for her beautiful eyes.'[2]

In the same month, a spiteful article called 'A lecture to young ladies' by 'Felix' deplores their 'want of sympathy with the strenuousness of men's lives'. They 'chatter about their new hats, their dances and tea parties and a score of other frivolities while their actual welfare is being fought for by the male members of their families'. Not, admittedly, that they should be encouraged to invade what is essentially men's domain; 'Felix' favoured rather an intelligent interest and womanly sympathy.[3]

More often the comment was no more than mildly patronising: thus a review of a novel by Dorothea Gerard about four young women characterised them as 'bitten with the modern spirit of dissatisfaction and the craze for constant change and excitement'. We are reassured, however, that 'the author is no believer in the new woman or in women's rights or women's movements, except of course the old old women's movement towards love and marriage.'[4]

Behind this concern lay a fear that, displaying such independence of the family, the New Woman would probably also not want babies. The dreadful example of France, whose population had stagnated at around 40 million, while Germany surged ahead from 45 million in 1881 to some 60 million in 1907, was vivid with strategic implications. Britain had gone from 30 million to 37 million in the same period, and, worryingly, Ireland had slipped from 5.1 million to 4.4. In 1903 President Roosevelt had alerted his country to the fearful risk of 'race suicide' as he called it. By this he meant that native white Americans were having fewer children than immigrants.

The theme was taken up in London by Sidney Webb in a series of article in the London *Times* of October 1907 when he raised the alarm that what he called 'the servant-keeping class' was being outbred. Statistics quoted showed that the birth rates of 'those sections of the population which give evidence of thrift and foresight' had collapsed by 50 per cent. Clearly, the decline in birthrate was due to deliberate 'regulation of the married state . . . in other words the situation is deliberate race suicide.' Unfortunately, less advanced nations and less prudent people continued 'to produce a torrent of children', which gave Mr Webb (who had no children of his own) worries for the future of the human race. The term 'race suicide' had a long life. Twenty years later James FitzGerald-Kenney, the Minister for Justice, declared in the Dáil that 'great nations do commit race suicide', specifying France; and correctly added that the Catholic notion that birth control was wrong was 'accepted by the overwhelming majority of people of all classes and shades of religion.'[5]

British suffragettes had been agitating for many years for the vote and for greater participation in public affairs by women. In isolated areas this call had also been heard in Ireland; but for most people (male and female) the position of women was clearly in the home. Most men took the view that woman's suffrage was probably against the natural law. And if it was not, there were more pressing things to be worrying about, such as one's career, one's family and even the National Question. (Although claims have been made that the 1916 Rising had feminist credentials, the absence of a woman signatory of the Proclamation suggests differently.) In June, the *Freeman's Journal* gave its plain man's view: 'The "smart" woman and sometimes the advanced woman sneer at the old-fashioned notion that a woman's life should be lived for her husband and her children. The man who is worth his salt realises that his first duty is by the toil of his brains or his hands to make and keep a home for his wife and family. The woman can have no higher duty than to make that home happy'.

But there was the worrying business of the low marriage rate. At 4.8 per 1,000, this was 40 per cent below that of England and Wales and 35 per cent below that of Scotland. Some blamed feminism, others blamed men. The *Freeman* took a middle line: 'It is said that men have grown selfish. They shirk the trials, the expenses, the dangers of matrimony. They prefer the selfish ease of bachelor life. But men are not wholly to blame. If men are no longer attracted it is because women are no longer attractive. It is the domestic virtues that make a home desirable. For womanly women there will always be marrying men.'[6]

The Church took the view that marriages were made in heaven, and that any attempt to interfere with the process on earth was to be deplored. Canon Sheehan's lovable old priest, Father Dan, expressed this in an extraordinary passage from the novel *My New Curate*, first published in 1899.

> The Christian ideal of marriage was nowhere so happily realised as in Ireland, where, at least until recent times, there was no lurid and volcanic company-keeping before marriage, and no bitter ashes of disappointment after; but the good mother quietly said to her child: 'Mary, go to confession tomorrow, and get out your Sunday dress. You are to be married on Thursday evening.' And Mary said 'Very well, mother', not even asserting a faint right to know the name of her future spouse. But then, by virtue of the great sacramental union, she stepped from the position of a child and a dependant into the regal position of queen and mistress of her own hearth.[7]

It is difficult to know what to make of this wildly unlikely scene.

Similar ideas were discussed in detail in the popular treatise *The Mirror of True Womanhood*, by Rev. Bernard O'Reilly, subtitled 'A Book of Instruction for Women in the World'. For Father O'Reilly and his readers, 'no woman animated by the spirit of her baptism ... ever fancied that she had or could have any other sphere of duty than that home which is her domain, her garden, her paradise, her world.' Women were warned against vanity, and the appetite for display and enjoyment. The wife was urged never to seek to please 'any eye but that of her husband, or to value any praise on dress, personal appearance, accomplishment of any kind, but what falls from his dear lips; or to wish for any amusement that is not shared by him; or to wish to have any theatre for the display of any gift, natural or otherwise, save in the bosom of one's family.'[8]. (The fantastical tone adopted by Father O'Reilly may stem from the fact that his mother died when he was young; Canon Sheehan's mother died when he was only eleven.)

Even in the universities, the middle-class students took little interest in their sisters' position. In the L&H, the UCD debating society, there was a long-running battle to prevent women students attending the debates unaccompanied. The President of UCD, Father Delany SJ, was as unenthusiastic about the idea as were most of the students. As he pointed out, it would involve the ladies in great dangers being out late at night, and having to cross the city on their return home. (This advice was not always needed, if the vigour of Miss Nelly MacCarthy was at all typical. While on holiday in Paris, she lost her way. She was quickly latched on to by a passing woman who took her down various side streets to her own room, and immediately demanded money. This was refused, so she attacked and attempted to strangle Miss MacCarthy, who at once took a revolver out of her handbag and shot her assailant in the leg. The sound of the shot aroused the police who immediately appeared on the scene. Miss MacCarthy was released and the attacker was later put on trial.[9]) Father Delany also worried about the male students, whose morality might be jeopardised by conversations with the ladies, not to mention the possibility of the undesirable or unhappy marriages that might be brought about. The society agreed, until December 1910, when a vote to allow their entry was passed by 19 votes to 17, with Arthur Cox and future Taoiseach John A. Costello voting against.[10]

Economically, women were finding that it was increasingly possible to swap the traditional immersion in the family work unit for separate functioning. As a contributor to *Open Doors for Irishwomen* maintained: 'The girl of the 20th century has a wide range of professions from which to choose nowadays—very different to that of her mother for whom the one opportunity of earning a livelihood was the everlasting governess.' She somewhat undermined the point, however, by continuing 'and it is well and better work should be the result since each worker can now suit her own taste be it music or literature, flowers or children.'[11] If sufficiently resolute, she could even become a physician, via the Irish Royal College; but she could not expect much welcome from her male colleagues. As one wrote in the Carmichael Prize Essay of 1905: 'The whole position of the female sex in the social economy of the world—passive as opposed to the active male, makes it extremely undesirable that a woman should engage in ordinary general practice, or include men among her patients.' An exception might be made in gynaecology, especially for the poor.

Open Doors for Irishwomen was produced by a new organisation called the Irish Central Bureau for the Employment of Women, an initiative of the Countess of Dudley, wife of the Lord Lieutenant. As the fore-word explained, the book was for 'women of good birth and education who for lack of means are forced to take up remunerative work. And in Ireland this class is by no means a small one.' Stimulated by the times, these young middle-class women were open to activities and roles that would not have been available to their mothers.

The book begins with jobs in the civil service, as women clerks with annual salaries starting at £55 and mounting to £90 after ten years for seven hours work a day, five and a half days a week (candidates 'must be at least 5 feet tall'). Other possibilities listed, not always in glowing colours, are dairying, dispensary work, homework (embroidery, needlework, lace damask), journalism ('limited field offered'), librarianship (demand small and pay not large, 'the hours in public libraries are long'), matron-housekeeper in a residential business house such as Clerys (£30–£35 plus full board), medicine ('the number of hospital appointments open to women are few and not very highly paid').

Then there was the eternal nursing: children's ('the Lady Nurse does for a child what its mother would do for it were she not prevented by ill-ness or social duties'), hospital, massage, mental or midwifery. The sister in a major hospital could earn up to £50 a year plus full board; a success-ful midwife with a private practice up to £60 for a succession of live-in assignments. A lady cook could earn between £30 and £60 plus full board, but she would require very good skills and her in-between social position meant that 'great tact is required in dealing with servants'.

For girls coming from the country there was the problem of where to live. Dublin was scarcely ready to accommodate single young women of this sort. As a result, jobs with residential prospects were at a premium. Being a secretary of a charity or similar organisation was a possibility for an active businesslike person, but unfortunately 'there are but few resident secretaryships in Ireland.'

Class

By 1907 the class shifts resulting from the Land War were twenty years or more in evolution. But it was only very slowly that the native middle class extended their range. If, rather crudely, we might take the Catholics as a proxy for the native Irish, and the Protestants as repre-senting the incoming British, we can measure progress through succes-sive Censuses. In 1901, Protestants still held a disproportionate grip on the top professional and business jobs. In Dublin City and County, for instance, Catholics represented only 43 per cent of barristers, not very much more than the 37 per cent recorded in 1881; 41 per cent of doctors (34 per cent in 1881), 37 per cent of civil engineers (35 per cent in 1881) and 33 per cent of bankers (26 per cent in 1881). Lower down the scale, two-thirds of commercial clerks and 97 per cent of general labourers were Catholic.

The militant Irish-Ireland journalist, D. P. Moran, claimed that class distinctions were 'ridiculously minute and acute in Ireland',[12] perhaps because, in addition to the growing social gradations of wealth and position, there were the extra dimensions of religion and race. Only at the very top of society did the two religious and racial goups mingle easily. Thus, the shrewd observer of Irish life, Arthur E. Clery of UCD, educated at Catholic University School and Clongowes, related his experience from 'something like the middle of the Irish upper-middle class'—a placing, incidentally, that neatly confirms D. P. Moran's comment about the minute distinctions. 'I have only once in my life dined in a Protestant home,' he writes.

> I have never drunk afternoon tea in the drawing-room of a member of [the Church of Ireland]. Though I am entering on middle life [he was 33], and my dancing days are nearly over, I have never been at a dance in a Protestant home. I don't include in this the ménages resulting from mixed marriages; they are neutral ground. Years ago, by accident, I once found myself at a charity ball organised by Protestants of the middle upper-middle class for some non-sectarian purpose. I found that the only girl I knew in the room was the only Catholic. With trifling and accidental variations this is, I believe, the general experience of Catholics of my own class and the classes below it.[13]

On the other hand, Clery bluntly confirms the theory that class was a greatly more significant differentiator than religion. As he saw it, 'the hatred existing between religions in Ireland is much less than the hatred existing between the different classes of the same religion. Women of different religions do not refuse to speak to each other. Catholic and Protestant do not edge away from each other on a tram, as the middle-class man edges away from an artizan.'

Although later it was to be absurdly claimed in nationalist circles that there was no such thing as class in Ireland, it remained an important token of personal identity. D. P. Moran continued his article quoted above by deploring the failure of the Gaelic League 'in attracting the active co-operation of the professional and middle classes; it has thousands of sympathisers among these classes, but too few attend the branches.'[14] Moran's point was taken extremely seriously by Gaelic

League organisers, and for some years afterwards they insisted on officers of the League wearing evening dress at the more important functions.[15]

Though now largely landless, the Anglo Irish held the social high ground, and their complacent attitudes to work and wealth prevailed. As the egregious Page Dickinson (an architect by profession) commented: 'There was little commercial element in the best of social life. No pushful newspaper man had captured the public taste; few profiteering industrial magnates had attained social success through the power of their purses. Dublin was more free from the meaner elements in its social life than was London of that time.'[16]

In *Dublin Made Me,* C. S. Andrews described the class line-up from his viewpoint:

> At the top of the Catholic heap—in terms of wordly goods and social status—were the medical specialists, fashionable dentists, barristers, solicitors. wholesale tea and wine merchants, owners of large drapery stores and a very few owners or directors of large business firms. These were the Catholic upper-middle class; they were the Castle Catholics . . . Below the Castle Catholics were the Catholic middle-middle class. They were the general practitioners, less successful solicitors, grocers, publicans, butchers, tobacconists who did not live over the shop (when they moved from over their shops they ascended in the social scale), as well as corn merchants, civil servants, journalists, coal merchants and bank managers. In politics these people were nationalist, and from them came the municipal politicians. Lower down the scale were the shopkeepers and publicans who lived over the shop, as well as clerks, shop assistants, lower grade civil servants, and skilled tradesmen . . . at the bottom of the heap were the have-nots of the city, consisting of labourers, dockers, coal heavers, messenger boys and domestic servants.[17]

Outside the home, in business and professional life, as Arthur Clery noted, 'men of all religions mingle freely. They become firm friends and appreciate each other's good qualities. They lunch together; they drink together; and in one sense they forget the religious question. Yet . . . a single shot, a blast on the bugle, a tap on the drum and they rush to take their places in the opposing firing lines.'[18] In Clery's view the underlying motive for such social exclusiveness was the fear of mixed marriages. 'One of the points about which all religions in Ireland are in complete agreement is a rooted objection to mixed marriage.' Consequently, 'a Protestant girl who dances with a Catholic knows that she is wasting her time; and why should her mother have fresh tea made and distribute her cakes to a man who is plainly unmarriageable?' This explained why there was so little clamour in Ireland about the *Ne Temere* decree (promulgated in 1907) in which the Catholic Church effectively insisted that any children born to a Catholic mother or father be brought up

Catholic. Taking religion seriously, both sides so completely deplored the idea of mixed marriage that it hardly seemed an issue, and was not to be one until the 1940s.

The virtues the increasing middle class cherished were notably different to those of the aristocratic Anglo-Irish. For instance, where the upper class fêted honour, flair and physical courage, the new class valued respectability, persistence and hard work. Although the old virtues never lost their glamour, gradually the new became what were rewarded. Even in sports, a contrast can be seen between the dashing individuality of upper-class sports such as hunting and shooting and the team efforts of the increasingly popular cricket and soccer. The insistence on respectability led to the general reluctance to marry without a good income, and the high value given to being correctly dressed. Commonsense, domesticity and religious observance (if not necessarily belief) were important too. Presumably because of how they got their livings, the middle class brought a new professionalism and moral rigour to the attitude to money and debt—they did not think it honourable to keep tailors and other tradesmen waiting years for their money, and the financial irresponsibility that characterised previous generations (as exemplified in *Castle Rackrent*) was disapproved of.

The family was significant, but in the sense of valuing concrete persons—sons and daughters especially—not the abstract Family of the Anglo-Irish who so greatly cherished their ancestral trees. Education was clearly perceived as the route to success, though commercial men doubted the value of universities for those destined for business; with education came a respect for the new and the modern. It was doctors, for instance, who were typically the first in a neighbourhood to own a motor-car. Upper-middle-class homes were also typically the first to have WCs, heating systems and electricity. In Ireland, as in England, the aristocracy froze in great houses noisy with unreliable plumbing.

Religion

The certainties of twenty-five years ago, when religious belief of some sort was simply taken for granted, had slipped away. Even the traditional rationalism of the Enlightenment was under attack. At a meeting of the L&H, Jack B. Yeats declared that not only was there never a more religious man than Walt Whitman, but he was a primitive man posing as a modern, and asked 'was that not the note most intensely modern—to be a primitive man?'[19] Spiritualism, theosophy, the occult and even

[67]

atheism were now part of the general conversation. Even inside the Catholic Church there were substantial divisions, from full-blooded acceptance of Roman discipline, through the 'liberal Catholics' who looked to Cardinal Newman for inspiration, to Modernism, in which modern-minded thinkers proposed ways in which the Church might or ought to accommodate itself to new thinking. (The idea that the Pope ought to 'come to terms with progress, liberalism and modern civiliza- tion' had been roundly condemned by Pius IX in 1861.) One strand of Modernism was to stress the profound unknowability of God, which by implication threw doubt on the use of reason in theology. This in turn undermined the whole rational theological element of Catholicism which had been so elaborately affirmed since the Council of Trent. This was anathema.

To prevent these ideas spreading, Pope Pius X initiated a marked tightening of clerical discipline, to a sinister point. Bishops were to report to Rome every three years on doctrines current among their clergy; they were to strictly censor the opinions of all professors and directors in seminaries; and they were to establish a secret vigilante group in each diocese to monitor opinion.[20] None of this could avert the tremendous attacks on the Church's establishment by Catholic bar- rister Michael McCarthy, notably in the sustained polemic, *Priests and People in Ireland* (1902), for which sales of 60,000 copies were claimed, in which he described the Church as an incubus on the people.

As it happened, one of the best-known Modernists was Father George Tyrrell SJ, who was born in a Protestant family in Dublin's Dorset Street. He was condemned as a heretic in October 1907 fun- damentally for undermining the long tradition of rationalism in the Church. In practice, few Irish priests and fewer laypeople were tempted by Modernism or indeed liberal Catholicism. Most stayed with the tra- ditional (since the Famine, at least) Rome-oriented '*Catholicisme du type irlandais*', a unique combination of Roman Thomist theology, European piety and English puritanism.

As a sign of the times, the *Irish Ecclesiastical Record,* which in the 1880s had regularly carried articles on scientific matters, now rarely did. One of the very few purely scientific articles published in 1907, on non- Euclidean geometry, is principally concerned to prove that it had been invented by an eighteenth-century Jesuit. Much space was taken up in the 1907 issues with attacks on 'modern rationalism' and with sneering at 'the revolt of the semi-learned of modern times' against the Bible. This, the writer continued, 'like many another crawling and creepy thing, has its origins in the Reformation.' International Catholic solidarity was a key value. Thus, in January 1907, the *Record* denigrated Roger Casement's exposure of the atrocities perpetuated by Belgium in the Congo. 'Things were never one-eighth as bad as the United Kingdom newspapers said,' it commented. 'The well-organised campaign' was stimulated by the 'commercial greed of England and the dissatisfaction of English Protestant missionaries.' (This view of Casement and the agitation against Congo atrocities was to be repeated in *Irish War News*, issued from the GPO during the 1916 Rising.)

The anti-intellectual note, very different from years before when the name Darwin was mentioned with respect, was not reserved for the 'semi-learned'. Another writer attacks modern anthropology, recommending that archaeologists should abandon their 'pieces of sharpened stone and bits of broken bones' and attend to 'the best authenticated record of man's primitive state' i.e. the Bible. A third deplores the interest of current Catholic periodicals in doctrinal matters. In a contemptuous dismissal, he declares 'a priest of 10, 15 or 20 years' ministry may find it hard to recall any cases in which his penitents were really hindered by difficulties in dogma . . . the advancing of such reasons being usually either a preliminary or a pretence. On close inspection the root of bitterness was found not to have its bed in the First Commandment but further on, more than half way down the field of the Decalogue.'[21]

A network of publications had emerged to re-imagine Irish history and life through this lens. Among these were the *Irish Ecclesiastical Record* (1864), *Irish Monthly* (1873), *Irish Messenger* (1887), *Irish Catholic* (1888) *Irish Rosary* (1897), the *Father Mathew Record* (1908), *The Cross* (1910), *Catholic Bulletin* (1911) and *Studies* (1912).[22] Typical of the way writers in these publications propagandised the relationship between priest and people was the oft-told story of how well Irish priests had behaved in the Penal times. As Sissy O'Brien remembered in *The Farm by Lough Gur*, in those days when her grandmother was a small girl, the priests were close to the people, sharing their lives and hardships, and 'our holy religion was persecuted and forbidden. The priests were hunted. They took their lives in their hands every time they said Mass in a barn or a lonely house or in caves or the mountains—for half a dozen people at a time.'[23] It is possible that the remarks may have been true of the 1690s, but certainly not the 1790s when Sissy's grandmother was most probably born. Behind the propaganda can be detected a sense that the 'sagart aroon' of olden times had been submerged in the newly disciplined parish priest, whose formation made it easier for him to be right than to be kind.

Politics

Common sense said that the world was naturally ordered into carefully graded and evaluated hierarchies. In the human world men controlled women (were they not physically stronger and with larger brains?), white men ruled non-whites, and strong countries dominated weak ones. For more than twenty years it had seemed the manifest destiny of the English-speaking 'Anglo-Saxon races' (by which was meant Britain and the United States) to dominate the world. As one enthusiast wrote in 1882, 'the work which the English race began when it colonised North America is destined to go on until every land on the earth's surface that is not already the seat of an old civilisation shall become English in its language, in its political habits and traditions and to a predominant extent in the blood of its people.'[24] The laureate of this mission, Rudyard Kipling, became in 1907 the first English Nobel prizewinner for literature. *The Irish Times* noted that this achievement by a man whose main lessons were of 'national pride, manliness and fidelity to great traditions . . . may not gratify narrow-minded advocates of the peace movement'.[25]

The firm belief in the hierarchy of races added a special frisson to the shock when in 1905 a non-white race, the Japanese, defeated the Russians in battle. Nonetheless, the whole doctrine made any proposal for radical change, such as Home Rule for Ireland, effectively a challenge to this natural order. Since 23 per cent of the world's population was under British control, did not this prove that the British were natural rulers? And anyway, what kind of track record did the Irish have? They were certainly a spiritual, creative people, but surely lacking the gravitas of natural rulers such as the Romans and the English? George Bernard Shaw had fun with this myth in his *John Bull's Other Island*, written in 1904 and published in book form in 1907 and performed on the Dublin stage to great applause. Everyone enjoyed the paradox of the romantic and impulsive Englishman contrasted with the cool, calculating Irishman.

Despite this, by 1907 the British had lost the battle for the hearts and minds of the Irish. Many people felt it was simply a question of when and how much Home Rule would be won. On St Patrick's Day the *Freeman's Journal* picked up the mood: 'Now,' wrote the leader writer, 'from the ends of the earth comes a chorus of confidence, a voice that brings not merely cheerfulness but strength . . . this celebration of the National Festival has been marked by a brightness and hope too often lacking in the past.'

With the recent change of government from Tories to Liberals, the dashing Lord Dudley had been replaced by Lord Aberdeen as Lord Lieutenant, the titular head of government. The Aberdeens, known to Dublin wits as Jumping Jack and Blowsy Bella, were, as one of their officials put it, 'an earnest, kindly, well-intentioned couple'[26]. Nobody could deny that Lady Aberdeen in particular did a tremendous amount of good work; they used their influence among the poor, for the battle against the 'white plague', tuberculosis, which was then killing 12,000 people a year, to aid local industry and so on. Unfortunately, they lacked the vice-regal style.

The Dudleys, on the other hand, had this quality in abundance. One morning, for instance, Lord Dudley noticed he needed a haircut, so he sent to London for Truefitt, his hairdresser, whose man arrived by the night mail. Unfortunately, Lord Dudley had an important yacht race at Kingstown the next day, and couldn't spare the time for a haircut, so the barber had to wait. Next day, Lord Dudley motored to Meath, and on his return was summoned immediately to London. On arriving in London he noticed to his surprise that his hair still wanted cutting, so he summoned Truefitt himself by telephone, and the job was done. The following day he returned to Dublin, and he was reminded that Truefitt's man still waited to cut his hair. 'Too late, too late,' said Dudley, 'send him back to London. Why can't these people come when they are wanted!'[27]

The Aberdeens' lack of style was translated into their entertaining, which was deliberately democratic. This did not please everyone. As Page Dickinson complained in his autobiography: 'Social amenities were thrown to the winds, and the rag-tag and bobtail of Dublin went to Court . . . many people of breeding gave up all idea of going to the Castle . . . Man after man of my own generation who formerly would, as a matter of course, have gone to the Court functions, avoided them, and laughed when the Castle was mentioned. Without being a snob, it was no pleasure and rather embarrassing to meet the lady at dinner who had measured you for your shirts the week before.'[28]

Nonetheless, people still went to the Castle. The *Freeman*'s report of a levee in February 1907 veered between the sarcastic and the sycophantic.

The usual small crowd of leisured folk assembled along Cork Hill and round the tow path of the Upper Castle Yard and took the customary interest in and made the customary remarks, occasionally more candid than complimentary, about the occupants of 'growlers' and 'outsiders' and carriages. Court suit is a trying costume to those who have said eternal farewell to youth, and it seldom looks imposing or appropriate reposing in a 'cab' or flaunted on an 'outsider' . . . the troops made a brave show, particularly the officers of the 11th Hussars in their picturesque cherry trousers and with their jaunty aigrettes. The visitors, the officers of the garrison being especially to the fore, began to make their appearance before midday. The Viceroy having taken up a position in front of the throne . . . the visitors filed in from the Picture Gallery, making their obeisance in passing.

Below the Lord Lieutenant were the real political and administrative powers, headed by the Chief Secretary, Augustine Birrell, who had a seat in the cabinet, and senior civil servant, Sir Antony MacDonnell, the son of a Catholic landowner, who had made his name as an administrator in India—this and his temper gave him the nickname of 'the Bengal tiger'. Below them were an extraordinary accumulation of boards and offices that had grown up over the years—sixty-seven in all, all ultimately answering to London, dealing with national and intermediate education, local government, public works, congested districts, prisons, trade, lunatic asylums—enough boards to make Ireland's coffin, as the nationalists frequently said. In 1907, the Irish Council Bill was introduced into Westminster to devolve the running of a few of these boards to Ireland; it was a sad compromise, limited to local government, education, the congested districts and a few other responsibilities. It excluded any say in the police, the judiciary, the Land Commission, even the Post Office. No wonder that the nationalists rejected it as contemptible, while for unionists it went a sight too far down the Home Rule trail.[29]

Many of the Castle officials were English, and acutely conscious that with the collapse of landlordism, their position was increasingly anomalous. As Birrell himself said in a speech in the House of Commons in March,

> I do not think that any Chief Secretary with the slightest tincture of popular feeling in his bones could enter the gloomy portals of Dublin Castle without a sinking of the heart . . . No pulse of real life runs through the place. The main river of Irish life as it rushes past its walls passes by almost unheeded. There it stands 'remote, unfriended, melancholy' regarding this great stream of National life and feelings with a curious expression of cynicism and amusement, coupled also I admit, with a passionate tutorial desire to teach the wild Irish people how to behave themselves (laughter). Just and exactly so might a Roman Provincial Anno Domini 120 living in his delightful villa in York, Colchester or Bath have regarded the vagaries of the inhabitants of these islands.[30]

This waning of confidence meant that the Anglo-Irish gentry increasingly took their tone from the military. The system of massing troops in large barracks adopted after the Crimean War, and the disproportionate tendency of the Anglo-Irish to go into the army or navy had spread a loyalist and military influence throughout the class. Country society in Ireland was no more able than Jane Austen's Hampshire to resist the exciting influence of so many smart young men readily on tap for dances, theatricals, picnics or tennis. As one memoirist put it, 'It was only a convinced anti-Britisher who could hold off his daughters from associating with these fascinating creatures, so . . . well turned out and so ready to enjoy themselves.'³¹ Even in Dublin, the military were conspicuous in social events.

Political allegiance ran from the hard-line unionists to the inheritors of the physical force Fenian tradition. In between were constructive unionists, Home Rulers, Sinn Féiners and the theoretically non-political GAA and the Gaelic League. The United Irish League (the re-united Parnellite and anti-Parnellite wings of the old Irish Parliamentary Party) still dominated the hustings. But its characteristically overblown style carried its own retribution. As the historian Alvin Jackson wrote: 'The Irish Parliamentary Party had created an elaborate mechanism for its own destruction. It helped to maintain a contempt for British rule and therefore a contempt for its own association with that rule. In addition, its ferocious rhetoric allowed little tolerance for the necessary compromises of political life . . . the Irish Parliamentary Party had thus taken a steam-hammer to the superficially impressive shell of British administration in Ireland; but it was Sinn Féin who picked up the kernel.'³²

In the meantime, so complete was their political hold that some (particularly southern unionists) complained of their oppressive dominance of local affairs. However, John Redmond, the leader of the party, was not especially secure in his tenure; his followers' allegiance was known to be volatile, and to require considerable reinforcing by local priests, by nationalist journalism as exemplified by the *Freeman's Journal*, and by judicious patronage.

A piercing scrutiny affected every member of parliament. The *Freeman* regularly published lists of attendance records at Westminster, and questions to the Chief Secretary in parliament had the particularity, aimed at local consumption, familiar to us from the reports of the Dáil. In March, for instance, the Chief Secretary was asked about a pier in Gooseroun in Kerry, about a teacher's salary in Ballybunion, and a robbery from a postman in Co. Cork; in April, Mr Jeremiah McVeagh asked the Chief Secretary if his attention had been drawn to the condition of the schoolhouse in Barnmeen, Co. Down (it had); in August, Birrell was asked if he was aware that the schoolhouse at Ahascragh, near Ballinasloe which was used as a (Protestant) parochial hall had been vandalised. He was, and he said he could not understand it as the rector was, as far as he knew, one of the most popular men in the community.

The predominantly middle-class nationalists had reasons for believing that their country was on an upward spiral: an American journalist quoted the veteran campaigner John Dillon as saying that 'Ireland has made more progress in the last ten years than during the previous two hundred years . . . the whole face of the country is changing, and the spirit of the people with it.'[33]

Chapter 6 A poor man's paradise

By 1907, Ireland's urban middle classes were comfortably benefiting from the economic boom of Edwardian England. They had accommodated themselves to the shift in Dublin's economy from manufacture and industry to the less labour-intensive import/export business, so much deplored by the witnesses to the 1884 Select Committee. Cattle (on the hoof) and near-agricultural goods such as stout and biscuits went to England, and back came clothes, shoes, sugar and tea, as well as machinery, paper and such-like manufactured goods. To run this enormous warehouse business required lawyers, accountants and clerks, supported by thousands of unskilled labourers precariously employed. Skilled and semi-skilled workers, the backbone of working-class movements in other countries, were few.

The division of Dublin into the haves in the suburbs (the still independent townships outside the canals) and the have-nots in the city was well advanced. In the suburbs, nearly 1 in 5 of the population were independent or professional, while only 1 in 20 of the city's population fell into that class. As many as 43 per cent of the suburban population pursued clerical, managerial or professional lives: less than a quarter of the city's population fell into those categories. No wonder then that the new food and grocery chains, Findlaters, Leverett & Frye and Bewleys all set up branches in these lucrative middle-class areas. At the other end of the scale, 88 per cent of the conurbation's unskilled workers lived between the canals.[1]

The range of incomes in all areas was still very wide. The senior civil servant, the Under-Secretary, Sir Anthony MacDonnell, was paid £2,000; the Inspector-General of Police got £1,800, the Crown Solicitor £2,200, the Recorder of Dublin £2,400. (These salaries were more or less the same as they had been in 1882, reflecting the fact that the cost of living had gently declined since then.) As before, judges earned more than this: the Lord Chancellor had £6,000 (recently reduced from £8,000) and other judges £3,500. This represented a 120:1 ratio between the Chancellor's salary and that of the ordinary labourer.

Lesser functionaries earned considerably less: the Treasury Remembrancer received £1,200, as did the Registrar-General, and the Keeper of the King's Arms, Sir Arthur Vicars, who was to lose his job

The comfort and elegance of a successful Catholic Edwardian physician and his family are clearly seen in this photograph of 1910. Sir Andrew Horne was a leading obstetrician and the first Master of the National Maternity Hospital, Holles Street. In 1931 his otherwise well-qualified son Andrew (on the left) was prevented from succeeding him by Archbishop Walsh, the ex-officio Chairman of the hospital, solely on the grounds that he had studied at Trinity, as recommended by his Belvedere masters.

during the year over the theft of the Irish Crown jewels, had £500. The 127 officials in the Board of Works earned an average of £285 a year; a national schoolteacher as little as £100.[2]

Table 3 Scales of earnings in 1907

Over £5,000	Lord Chancellor (£6,000),
£3,000–£5,000	Master of the Rotunda
£1,000–£3,000	Provost of Trinity, Under-Secretary, senior partner Craig Gardner
£750–£1,000	Junior Fellow TCD
£500–£700	W. B Yeats' annual literary earnings (1912–1917)
£300–£500	Fellow of UCD, top manager in Eason's
£200–£300	Board of Works official; proposed salary for nationalist Member of Parliament
£100–£200	National schoolteacher, dispensary doctor
£50–£100	Skilled worker
Less than £50	Rural labourer

University teachers were reasonably rewarded: the Provost of Trinity was paid £1,751 in 1905, and the senior Fellows had between £1,300 and £1,600 each. The famous Mahaffy earned £1,495 2s in that year from the college. Junior Fellows averaged £800, while the assistant to the registrar and the accountant had £450 each.[3] The (Jesuit) Fellows of University College Dublin still earned £400 a year.

In the professions the range was equally wide; the mastership of the Rotunda was said to be worth 'some thousands a year',[4] and certainly Surgeon McArdle of St Vincent's had no trouble building himself a substantial house and elaborate garden in the Wicklow mountains, where he lived for two months of the year, taking few or no cases.[5] Dispensary doctors, the GPs of the day, lived on a different scale, as George Birmingham's Dr Lucius O'Grady discovered.

He enjoyed, as a dispensary doctor, £120 a year. He received from Lord Manton an additional £30 for looking after the health of the gardeners, grooms, indoor servants and others employed about Clonmore Castle. He would have been paid extra guineas for attending Lord Manton himself if the old gentleman had ever been ill. He could count with tolerable certainty on two pounds a year for ushering into the world young O'Loughlins. Nobody else in the district ever paid him anything.[6]

The few top barristers could earn as much as £5,000, though the average of those in practice was nearer £800–£1,000;[7] the senior partner of Craig Gardner, the leading accountancy firm, had £2,700; the five executive directors of Boland's averaged £1,400. An alimony claim in a divorce case in June 1907 revealed that a well-off Derry merchant, with three boot and shoe shops, had £700 a year. In another alimony claim (4 December), a jeweller in Nassau Street was judged to have an income of £300 a year. (There was some argument about this: his wife said he had at least £600, while he claimed he had only £100 a year. Her counsel was felt to have made a point when he queried the possibility of dining regularly at Jammet's, Dublin's top restaurant then in St Andrew's Street, on £100 a year.)

Down the social and economic scale, though still in the 'middle classes', the wages in the retail department of Eason's, for a few years before 1907, show the range possible. The head of this relatively unprofitable department, an old and respected employee, had £4 10s a week, but only one other employee in the department had as much as £2 a week; there were three at £1 18s and nine below that, with figures ranging from £1 10s to trainees at 7s.[8] In the larger stores, it was common for staff to be provided with accommodation: contemporary Censuses record that over one hundred employees of Clery's slept on the premises at this time. A small ad in the *Freeman* in January announced: 'Young Lady engaged in City wants situation immediately as Assistant to general Drapery, can also help as Milliner, able to serve through; good reference: salary £12 (indoor) six years experience'.

The top employees in Eason's earned £9 a week at this time. In Eason's, therefore, a young starter on a few shillings a week could look forward to a steady and secure job, with his income steadily progressing to £100 a year, then £200 and perhaps even to the giddy heights of £400 or £500 if he was really successful. On this there was no problem in keeping a modest yacht in Dublin Bay—indeed one of Eason's executives was a founder member of the Dublin Bay Sailing Club. Not only were there enormous differences between the earnings of one group and another, but even in a man's own lifetime he could, without excessive optimism, expect to run from comparative poverty to riches as he grew older.

However, to enjoy the delights of Dublin a middle-class bachelor did not need to be particularly well-off. In his memoirs describing life in pre-war Ireland, Page Dickinson noted that 'people could do themselves well in Dublin at that time, and hunt or yacht or go in for any similar sport on incomes that would scarcely have covered living expenses in London. A poor man's paradise, surely.'⁹ This last sentence could have been more sensitively expressed, given the well-known privations of the real poor.

Dickinson and his friends frequently enjoyed what he describes as 'a simple and very cheap dinner' at a little pub in Leinster Alley before going to further entertainments at the newly founded United Arts Club. A typical menu ran as follows:

A steak or chop	6d
Potatoes and bread	no charge
A glass of draught stout	1d
Cheese, bread and butter	2d
Glass of port	2d

Total, elevenpence, plus a twopenny tip for the waiter.¹⁰

Then as now the successful business venture was a possible route to rapid riches. Ernest Bewley was one example. In 1890, Bewley's was a modest coffee- and tea-selling business: his cousins' other businesses, in shipbuilding, in import/export and in wines and groceries, were much better known. In 1894, the first Bewley's café was opened, to be followed in 1896 by another in Westmoreland Street. By the 1900s, Ernest Bewley was rich enough to set up house in the substantial 'Danum', in Zion Road, Rathgar, which he built for himself on the grounds of the old Rathgar sawmills (one of the Dodder businesses that had not survived). He also bought new premises in Fleet Street, intending to diversify into bicycle repair, an idea which came to nothing. By 1907, he had developed the Fleet Street property into a series of offices above an extended café, had started his famous Jersey herd, and had just been elected an alderman of the city of Dublin.¹¹

Another, more traditional, route to riches was demonstrated with the death in December of 'Banker' Patterson, an illiterate miser. The *Freeman's Journal* reported that he began business as a loan shark after finding a sum of money on his way to Belfast. He loaned single shillings at a penny a week interest. To save money, he sat in the dark, wore no trousers in the house in summer, and possessed only a cup, a plate and a knife. He left all his money, £80,000, to charity.

The problem, then as now, was how to get started. The first significant factor was religion. Many firms and other organisations deliberately or effectively discriminated against Catholics. Nationalists frequently complained that the best civil service and other government appointments went to Protestants. In the Local Government Board, for instance, there were 34 Protestants and only 13 Catholics; in the Board of Works the 79 Protestants earned an average of £326, while the 48 Catholics averaged only £197.

Table 4 Proportion of Catholics in selected jobs in Dublin

	Total	RC	RC %
Barrister, solicitor	917	392	43
Physician, surgeon	564	227	40
Author, editor, journalist	261	167	64
Civil engineer	369	136	37
Insurance [clerk/broker]	858	440	51
Railway official	2139	1594	75
Accountant	533	169	32
Commercial clerk	7506	5881	78
Banker	715	236	33
Publisher, bookseller, librarian	235	149	63
General labourer	24084	23334	97

Source: Census 1911, Table XX combined Dublin City & County

This was partly because, as one acerbic writer pointed out in a letter to the *Freeman's Journal*: Ireland was 'but a small part of the British Empire, and its population a not very essential part of the aggregate population of the United Kingdom. We are still under the government of the United Kingdom—not that of the Kingdom of Ireland, just yet— and that is a government of an overwhelmingly Protestant community, by an overwhelmingly Protestant parliament, and, most naturally, in the interests of that Protestant majority.'[12]

The writer maintained that since Catholics had been, with a few exceptions, generally disloyal in Ireland, this was good reason for not appointing them to positions of power. On the other hand, even this loyal unionist could not help but feel that home rule was imminent.

For many of the brighter Irish recruits the wider possibilities of empire must have been tempting. Could they, too, not become, like Sir Robert Hart, head of the entire Chinese customs service, or, like Sir Anthony MacDonnell, ex-administrator of millions of Indians? A typical pathway would have been that of Joseph Brennan, later the first Governor of the Central Bank. After a couple of terms in UCD he went to Cambridge, graduating from there into the first division of the civil service, attached to the Board of Customs and Excise. A year or two later he was transferred to Dublin Castle.[13] Certainly, most of those who entered the medical profession, Protestant or Catholic, expected to emigrate. The 1901 Census recorded that there were 2,200 practising doctors in Ireland and as many as 1,331 medical students (46 of whom were female); the most promising of these looked forward to a job in Britain or the empire.[14]

Because businesses lacked elaborate staff organisation, recruitment was a very personal matter. Modern executive functions such as finance, marketing, quality assurance and personnel were completely unknown; in general the employment of such experts, even in accounting, was a late development—it was not until 1945 that there were as many chartered accountants working in industry as in professional practice. The Bank of Ireland did not employ a professional accountant until the 1950s.

As a result, except in the railways or banks, and enormous firms such as Guinness, opportunities were few. *Thom's Directory* listed only 38 public companies registered in Dublin, excluding banks and insurance companies, and while there were companies such as Guinness and Gallaher registered elsewhere, the corporate sector was not large. As a result, personal introductions were vital, and recruits tended to follow the religious adherence of the owner and his friends. This remained the case until the 1960s.

The narrow range of possibilities meant that sons tended to do the kind of work that their fathers had done. Some of this immobility was caused by the fees, premiums and capital investments that employers demanded of their recruits. Professional firms such as solicitors and accountants might ask for £150 or more as premium, and then pay little or no wages during the period of training. Similar arrangements applied to trainee barristers, with the added penalty of hazardous earning patterns in the early years. Banks and large firms such as Guinness frequently demanded a surety payment of £100 (a crippling two years' wages for a labourer) as well as a personal introduction and the passing of a stiff examination. Competition for eligible jobs was severe. In November, Kingstown announced that it had had 69 applicants for the post of librarian of the municipal library. It was eventually offered to a woman librarian at 30s a week with residence, coal and light.

Once the money was earned, the question of what it was to be spent on could be addressed. As we have seen in 1882, middle-class family respectability was difficult to maintain on much below £250 a year. Wealth was conventionally defined as an annual income of £700 or more. Todd Andrews' parents, with only two children, and living in the parental home, found life a hard struggle on £150 a year.[15] Single men could just about manage on that. 'Many men, curates for instance, live on less', as Dr O'Grady knew; what's more, they 'face the world in tolerably clean collars and succeed in looking as if they generally had enough to eat.'[16]

Slow promotion, and the high ratio of senior earnings to junior, meant that young middle-class men, whatever their prospects, could hardly earn enough to keep a wife and family until their thirties or even later. Of course, people would marry before then. The problem then was that, as the author of the 1903 book *Marriage on £200 a Year*, put it: 'Because a woman has decided to marry on a small income, she is no whit changed as far as her tastes and likings are concerned; it will be her aim and ambition to live as far as possible in the old manner, to drop none of the refinements to which she has become accustomed, and to bring up her children as she herself has been brought up.'

With no welfare benefits (the old age pension, the very first state benefit, was introduced in 1909) it was easy for the financially struggling to drop disastrously in social status. The maintenance of respectability, at all levels, was therefore extremely important. Appearance was much cherished. Mrs Andrews, for instance, who ran a dairy and provision shop in Terenure, 'never went out in the street with ungloved hands (she would regard it as not respectable to be seen without gloves)'.[17]

The first item to acquire was some form of accommodation. It was still the case that only the very rich bought their houses: nearly everyone else rented. The question was: where? A clue to the most desirable areas for middle-class Catholics can be gleaned from the results of the annual collection of Peter's Pence, to support the Vatican. The *Freeman* devoted two whole pages in early August 1907 to an elaborate record of the donation of every parish in the diocese. By this listing we can detect the richer Catholic parishes. Top of the list was Haddington Road in the Pembroke area, which donated £59. (Haddington Road church was to become the only Catholic church in Ireland to erect a memorial to its parishioners who fell in the Great War.[18]) Next came the fashionable church of St Andrew's, Westland Row, which catered for the doctors and professional families of Merrion and Fitzwilliam Squares; they gave £54.

The Pro-Cathedral, with its large but not wealthy catchment area, gave £50. Kingstown gave £38 and Monkstown only £16, reflecting the fact that, uniquely in Dublin, it still had a minority Catholic population. By contrast, the predominantly working-class area of Ringsend gave £6.

The church in the centre of the grander and older (and more Protestant) Rathgar, the Three Patrons (known as 'the servants' church'), gave only £30, while Cullenswood and Milltown (Beechwood Avenue) gave £42.

This area of Ranelagh (built on the old nursery grounds that had once provided ready-made trees for their avenues to the purchasers of decayed estates after the Famine) was at this time expanding rapidly with smaller houses to appeal to the newly-wed and less well-off middle classes. It had just been defined as a separate parish. Work was about to begin on the substantial new church at the top of Upper Beechwood Avenue, and perhaps in response, the renters of houses in the street went from being three-quarters Protestant in 1901 to three-quarters Catholic in 1911. The predominance of renting allowed these rapid changes to occur: *Thom's* shows that even in the grand Clyde Road, Ballsbridge, 43 per cent of houses changed hands in the five years between 1891 and 1896, and again between 1896 and 1906. A similar pattern can be traced in, for instance, Temple Road, Rathmines. These houses were sold as investments for the typical price of £450, and could attract rents of perhaps £40 a year (net of ground rent). In one advertisement, Macarthur's, the prominent auctioneer, offered 78–80 Lower Beechwood Avenue as an investment: 'two good modern houses, ornamental design, 5 bedrooms, bath (hot and cold) separate wc,' to be let at £42 each p.a. At the same time, two three-room cottages off the North Circular Road in Drumcondra were available for £5 or £6 per year, and in the 'nice quiet neighbourhood' of Sandymount houses were rentable for £24 a year. (This is a substantial increase on what an equivalent house in Rathgar would have fetched twenty-five years before.) Although returns of 8 per cent or more such as these were not unknown on the stock exchange, they were in the riskier stocks; returns from ultra-safe government bonds were much lower.

It was common for family men to buy houses (in lieu of life insurance) for their wives and daughters, so there was a web of female property ownership across Dublin. The best-known of these owners is Brendan Behan's Granny English with her tenement houses in Russell Street and Fitzgibbon Street. At one extreme was Countess Plunkett, mother-to-be of the 1916 signatory Joseph Mary Plunkett and daughter of Dublin southside property developers, who managed a large portfolio of houses in Donnybrook and Rathmines. Lower down the social scale were the clients of the Workingmen's Building Society. In 1909, this small operation had 46 applicants for loans (one of whom was Patrick Pearse looking to shore up the finances of St Enda's in Ranelagh—he was not successful); of these, 16 were women. Among the women applicants were a Mrs Marcella Mooney of 6 Eblana Terrace, Grand Canal Street, borrowing £650 on the security of Nos 6, 8, 10 and 12 Eblana Terrace, a Mrs Geoghegan (whose husband, says *Thom's*, was a stevedore) proposing 71 and 73 Bath Avenue as security, and a Mrs Hand, who offered the tenements of 11–17 Coleraine Street.[19]

The next item to buy was food. For the working-class family, this might account for as much as two-thirds of the average income.[20] For the average middle-class family, food represented considerably less of the budget. In the *Economic Cookery Book*,[21] first published in Dublin in 1905, Mary Redington suggests that the following expenditures would be typical at certain levels of income.

Table 5 *Expenditure by annual income range*

Income per year	£150–£220	£250–£300
Expenditure	%	%
Food	50.0	45.0
Clothing	18.0	17.0
Lodging	12.0	12.0
Fuel	5.0	4.5
Education	5.5	8.0
Tax, rates	3.0	4.0
Health	2.0	4.0
Recreation	3.5	5.0

The figures for the larger income match in expenditure patterns those given in more detail by Dorothy Peel, in her 1902 book *How to Keep House*, for a family living on £250; in her listing, 12 per cent was allocated to rent (much the same as we have seen suggested for 1882), 41 per cent to food and 20 per cent to clothing. Mrs Peel provides a guideline to the quantities of certain staples that might be required for a normal family, which she calculates would cost between 8s 6d (for 'plain but sufficient living') and 10s (for 'nice living') per head per week.[22]

Meat—¾ lb (uncooked) per head per day
Table butter—½ lb per head per week
Bacon—1 lb per head per week for breakfast rashers
Sugar—1 lb per head per week
Tea—¾ lb per head per week
Milk—1/3 pint per adult per day
Jam—1 lb per head per week.

Eggs, bread, fruit etc. were extra according to the household's taste. She does not mention vegetables. By our standards there is a formidable amount of meat (over 5lbs a week each) and jam and sugar.

There had been a significant change in the retailing of food over the previous thirty or forty years. Instead of skilled grocers selecting and purchasing loose goods such as tea, sugar, and flour, manufacturers were beginning to provide tins, pre-packed and branded goods. As Willie Findlater, who as head of the chain of shops was the leading grocery retailer in the country, presciently told a staff conference in 1902: 'One of the great alterations that have taken place in our trade is the number of proprietary articles that have been introduced of late years . . . if this is encouraged much further it will mean the passing of the grocer, and he will be replaced by a mere hander-out of packet goods, or we will have nothing but girls behind our counters'.[23]

The old skills of the grocery trade, however, were still in use: blending tea to suit exactly the local water; chipping salt and sugar from large blocks into saleable quantities; ripening cheese, selecting and buying butter by the barrel and patting it into blocks; smoking hams; selecting and washing fruit according to season (oranges only between November and April and so on); attending to special customers—a chair for Madam, and a biscuit for her dog—down to folding twists of brown paper into cups to carry loose goods such as flour, rice, semolina. No wonder there was a seven-year apprenticeship to the trade.

By 1907, products unknown before were rapidly gaining popularity: branded packaged tea, such as Mazawattee (the up-market favourite), and Liptons; biscuits, from Jacobs and from English firms such as Peak Frean and McVitie; jams, from Williams & Woods in Great Britain Street; pickles and sauces, Lever's heavily advertised Sunlight Soap, margarine, Fry's cocoa, Bovril, Cherry Blossom boot polish, ginger ale from Cantrell & Cochrane. The new packaged products always made a great play of their purity and wholesomeness, for adulteration had long been revealed as the besetting temptation of the old-style grocery trade. Findlater's *Grocery List* shows how far this branding process had gone by 1904. Over fifty different types of biscuit (but as yet no breakfast cereals); and a fine range of tinned goods, from lobster parts, calves' tongues and grated Parmesan to soups and Swiss condensed milk. Compared to a modern supermarket, the range is weak on imports from France or Italy and any food from east of Suez (except curry, for the old India hands) but strong on tinned fish and fruit, pickles and bottled sauces.[24]

Milk was a special case. It was supplied to the customer by one of the two hundred or more private dairies scattered throughout the city, often with their own cattle sheds and herds. Delivery vans criss-crossed the entire city. In the winter, there were as many as 6,000 cows housed in byres and yards in the middle of the city, some of which as Dr Flinn, medical inspector of the Local Government Board, reported, were in an intolerable condition. 'Some time since I visited a number of dairy-yards at milking time. The cow byres were then in a very filthy state, full of recent manure . . . the hands of those milking were not in a cleanly condition . . . In a few places pigs were kept on the dairy premises, a condition fraught with danger where there is a supply of milk being daily distributed to the public . . . In many cases the surface is very irregular and soft, and consequently in damp or wet weather pools of stagnant water are in evidence.'[25]

The country dairies, said the *Freeman's* leader writer, were even worse than those in Dublin. No wonder then that the milk supply was a prime target of the anti-tuberculosis campaign.

The supply of meat was not much more enticing. Three-quarters of Dublin's meat was slaughtered in private abattoirs of which there were still more than fifty around the city. Dubliners were well used to strag-gling herds of cattle wending their way through to the slaughterhouses in Moore Street, Townsend Street, Westland Row, Thomas, Francis and Dorset Streets and elsewhere. Because of the condition of some of these yards, they were a serious health hazard. Ramshackle huts and shanties, permanently stained with offal, blood and entrails, vividly suggested the less than humane methods of slaughter frequently used.[26]

For those who didn't have accounts with chains such as Findlaters and Leverett & Frye, there were individual grocers, who often still brought traditional skills to bear (and generated traditional rich odours as well), such as Murphy's in Mary's Abbey, at the end of Capel Street, a large draughty shop where Austin Clarke's mother bought 'the best Danish bacon, butter, eggs in winter, and in summer the best Irish bacon, butter, eggs'. Behind the shop was a smoke house, with glowing ashwood where, almost hidden in the gloom above, hung the Limerick hams. Or Barry's sweetshop, where Mr Barry boiled all the sweets himself, rarely emerging from the hidden sugariness, the thickenings, skimmings and ladlings.[27] Mrs Andrews' provision shop in Terenure had 'two counters facing one another, from one of which was dispensed eggs, butter, bread, cheese, tea and sugar, and from the other sweets. Behind the shop was a parlour which we used as a living and dining room.'[28]

Efficient rail and sea transport ensured that Dubliners had available as many products as their contemporaries in Canterbury or York, if not

London. Elizabeth Bowen and her governess used to shop in Upper Baggot Street, where 'two rows of well-to-do shops faced each other over the wide street . . . [there was] a chemist, with the usual giant bottles of violet and green, a branch of Findlater's, a baker's, a post-office (encaved at the back of a fancy stationers) and a draper's . . . everything was, in its way, classy: where white cotton coats were worn these were chalky clean, and sweet dry sawdust covered victuallers' floors.'[29] The Junior Army and Navy in D'Olier Street was another favourite haunt, as was the high-class grocers, Andrews, in Dame Street, with the elaborate ball arrangement for sending cash and change between the cashier and the counter.

Added to these interests were the smells. The basic smells were of dust and hay and straw and horse droppings, and the Liffey; there were also, depending on the wind, the malt and barley from Guinness, the rich baking of biscuits from Jacobs in Bishop Street, the suds from Barringtons of Great Britain (now Parnell) Street, where, as Austin Clarke wrote, 'it was always washing day, always Monday'. Individual shops had their own smells: the sugary tang from the sweetmaker, the cool milky dairy shop, the spicy and curranty grocer, the keen reek of drugs and the dusty dry smell of the loofah from the chemist ('smell almost cure you, like a dentist's doorbell', thought Leopold Bloom) or the hucksters' shops which sold bread and paraffin oil and kindling sticks and hot boiled peas, or the less pleasant smells from the shop at the corner of Marlborough Street where tripe and crubeens and black puddings were prepared.[30]

Since the 1850s Christmas had become an increasingly important time for shopkeepers. On Christmas Eve 1907, the *Freeman's* reporter noticed that

> Dame Street [predominantly offices] was dull and dirty. Most of the shops were closed and the only gleam of brightness came from the passing brilliantly illuminated tramcars. But when one turned into George's Street there was a complete change of scene. All the shops were doing a furious business, crowds filled the side walks; happy children grabbing their mothers' skirts halted in front of the windows, where confectionery or toys were displayed, . . . in Thomas Street and James Street there are still stalls on which were displayed turkeys and geese that are to be got cheap . . . the shops suggest a conspiracy on the part of poets, pastry cooks and butchers to overfeed us . . . every window front appealed irresistibly to the passer-by, from the time-honoured sawdust doll and dancing nigger, the model motors, the silks and satins, the turkeys and the geese, down to the fragrant mixtures of Apothecaries Hall. O'Connell Street and the other business streets in the

area presented constant streams of people crossing by Nelson's pillar between Henry Street and Earl Street . . . shops which catered for the Christmas card traffic continued thronged throughout the greater part of the day. The provision shops, too, of O'Connell Street, Henry Street, Mary Street, Capel Street remained open after most of the other establishments had put up their shutters, and they continued to be well patronised even up to midnight, many of the poorer classes with slender purses waiting till an advanced hour in the hope of getting the bargains.

For men, a suit was *de rigueur*: with a waistcoat, completed with boots and a watch chain, and a long-tailed shirt (with detachable collar), a tie, and long underwear. The prices varied widely, depending on cloth and cut. In April, the Henry Street Warehouse, a department store, had flannel suits at 10s 6d, 15s and 21s; striped tweed suits at 15s and 21s; and Irish tweed suits at 22s 6d, 27s 6d, and 35s. For more sporting occasions, jacket and trousers might be adopted; Irish-Irelanders, following Douglas Hyde's lead, frequently sported kneebreeches.

For women, clothing started with long knickers, still usually made by themselves or by devoted elderly relatives;[31] a chemise and a corset, which ran from the breasts to the thighs, contorting the body into the conventional S-shape, with a narrow waist and protruding chest and bottom. (Only advanced feminists and socialists ventured forth without stays or in any kind of 'rational dress'.) Over this, went another petticoat or two and a dress, or a skirt and blouse. For day wear, the collar was closed; in the evenings, arms and some of the chest might be revealed.

The long-term trend of twentieth-century fashion, attributed particularly to the influence of Chanel, has been increasingly to adapt sporting clothes to more formal occasions. William Bulfin noted an early version in Cork, at a regatta. One tall girl, he noticed, sported 'a motor cap, cycling skirt, golf blouse, and walking shoes' while her companion wore 'a yachting cap, tennis shoes, and a man's light waterproof coat . . . [over] a dainty muslin costume.'[32]

Personal tailoring was so prevalent that for some it was a luxury to buy shop goods; Austin Clarke remembered Mrs Carney, 'our family tailoress', who used to make his boyhood suits, and how he envied his school contemporaries their 'splendid shop suits', and how he lived in constant apprehension 'lest the boys from the high-class suburbs would detect a woman's hand in the cut of my breeches.'[33] Another innovation was dry cleaning, announced as 'the new French process, *nettoyage à sec*' by Prescott's laundry.

A family that had comfortably covered the basics could start to look round. Education was generally the next priority. As income went up, so did expenditure on education, which meant success in examination results. For the Intermediate examinations of 1907, the top boys' schools were five Christian Brothers' schools, then Clongowes, Blackrock College, Inst. of Belfast, Rockwell College, O'Connell School; for girls the Loreto convents took the place of the Christian Brothers schools, with five out of the top twelve placings; then St Louis (three convents), Victoria High School, Londonderry, Victoria College, Belfast, the Dominican Convent, Eccles Street. The exam orientation of the Intermediate system was deplored by educationists: the Chief Secretary (in words echoed later by Pearse) described it as a system of 'cram, cram, cram ... which murders the growing intelligence of the people, ... turning the little boys and girls of Ireland into money-making machines.' The *Freeman* would have none of this: 'The only reason he and his advisors are against the system,' it wrote, 'is that Irish-Ireland is using it for self-advancement.'[34]

One item of expenditure the middle-class household could not economise on was help. There were 28,000 servants in the city area, or just over one servant for every four members of the middle classes. At the simplest level, the household would run to only one servant, usually living in. With complete board and lodging, this was not expensive: in March a lady in Kingstown, with three in the family, offered a wage of £8 (per year), and that was typical. In November, Mary Foley sued her employer for loss of wages under the newly passed Workmens' Compensation Act. She had badly burned her hand with a defective gas iron, and was off work for a month. Her wages were 3s a week (£7 16s a year) and her board 7s (she obviously lived out), so she was claiming 10s a week. She was awarded £4, i.e. eight weeks' wages.

As well as board and lodging, there was the possibility of the servants' living standard being boosted by perks, though these depended on the mistress. Garments that the household no longer wanted were frequently given. With luck there might also be a chance of a few backhanders. The rag-and-bone man would pay for items such as bones, dripping, empty bottles and jars, and tradesmen frequently gave the cook Christmas presents, and occasionally a commission on purchases. (The recently passed Prevention of Corruption Act made both of these perks illegal, to the dismay of many a pantry.) More legitimately, visitors would give tips: for those staying a few nights, tips of as much as a week's wages were normal.

While the servant saved her tips, there was much hard work to be done. In *Marriage on £200 a Year*, Mary Halliday gives a suggested daily routine in a small household with only one servant. It was a long, relent-less and generally lonely day, with the periodic arrival of delivery men the only light relief.

6.30 Open house: see to kitchen

6.50 Sweep and dust dining-room; lay breakfast table

7.20 Brush boots

7.30 Brush stairs

7.40 Clean front door and hall

8.00 Make breakfast

8.15 Serve breakfast

8.45 Take pail upstairs, empty slops (from the utensils in the bed-rooms); strip and make beds, tidy bedrooms

9.30 Wash breakfast things

10.00 Allocated work for that day—e.g. washing, clean kitchen, iron-ing etc.

12.00 Prepare vegetables for dinner—in this small household, the mistress will actually cook the meal

12.30 Change into more formal wear

1.00 Serve dinner

1.45 Wash dinner things

2.30 Afternoon walk (with children)

4.45 Prepare and serve nursery tea

6.30 Bath children

7.00 Wash tea things

7.30—9.00 own time, except on Monday and Thursday

9.15 Serve supper

9.45 Bedtime.[35]

The larger and richer the household, the more elaborate the division of function. There was a fine gradation of skills. Cooks, for instance, were either plain cooks, who worked on their own, and also did house-work; cooks-general, who usually had an assistant; or professed cooks who had at least a scullery-maid and a parlour-maid under them, and possibly a 'tweeny'. This last was the lowest form of servant life—she was frequently worked into the ground by her fellow-servants.

In a well-off town household, the servants might consist of a pro-fessed cook, a parlour-maid, a housemaid and a tweeny. More specialist help such as a lady's maid, and a nurse or governess, could be added to the household as required. So far, all the servants are female: grander arrangements started with a boy (for messages, boots, etc.) and pro-gressed through a single-handed manservant, a footman, a valet and a butler. The bachelor household of Sir Arthur Vicars and his friend, Francis Shackleton, the Dublin Herald, with a joint income of some £750 a year, consisted of a cook, a manservant, a boy and a coachman.

Transport was normally the next consideration. The bicycle was extremely popular, and at £5 for a reasonable model just about afford-able on £250 a year. It was only for the reasonably athletic, though, for the roads were generally rough, and spills were frequent. For richer excursionists, the choice was between a horse carriage or a motor car. In the long run, a motor car worked out cheaper. A four-seater at a price of £300, with 53,000 miles' capability at 4,000 miles a year, would cost £167 a year to run, while a brougham and two horse, with harness, etc., also at £300, would cost £244 a year and be capable of only some 3,000 miles a year. The car was also more rugged: 'In the majority of places the carriage horses are not taken out at night. The motor can be used at all hours and in all weathers. It makes distant places accessible that with a horse are impossible.'[36] But the motor car was not only a status symbol. It was also an instrument of government. Sir Henry Robinson, head of the Local Government Board, pointed out that with a motor car a Chief Secretary wishing to find out at first hand about conditions in Dingle or Ballycroy could arrive and visit more places in 24 hours than he could have seen in five days with horse-drawn transport.[37] He was no longer dependant on the self-interested reports of local magistrates and police for information. There is, however, no evidence that the quality of administration was improved as a result.

A somewhat overcooked artist's impression of the entrance and main building of the 1907 Exhibition in Herbert Park *(Illustrated London News)*

Chapter 7 The last great Irish Exhibition

Both before and during its six-month run, the great Irish international exhibition of 1907, in what is now Herbert Park, was a constant source of gossip, of news, of drama and of simple jollity. Over two and three-quarter million visitors streamed through its turnstiles between May and November; halls and entertainments were spread over 52 acres. They came to see the stands of over a thousand exhibitors of commercial and industrial products, to listen to a long series of concerts by military and civilian bands, to see the native Somalians in their village (complete with spears and shields), to admire the paintings in the Palace of Fine Arts, to watch the performers, or to try out the water-chute that whooshed with much splashing and shrieking through the lake. (Much too dangerous, said Mrs Andrews to the seven-year-old Todd, who longed to try it).[1]

These exhibitions had four functions: they stimulated trade, by allowing manufacturers to display their wares in a world where retail outlets were few and advertising was inadequate (trade fairs still perform this function); they educated the public, in taste and in the organisation of ideas; they attracted foreign tourists; they encouraged artists and others to deploy their talents in the creation of beautiful and practical objects. That at least was the original motivation; by 1900, when the most luxurious of the great nineteenth-century exhibitions, the Paris Exposition of 1900, took place, the element of tourist show was predominant. The promoters of the Irish International Exhibition of 1907 were working a seam that was past its best, and it is no surprise that the entreprise made a financial loss.

The project started with the International Exhibition held in Cork in 1902–3. It attracted many visitors, and William Dennehy, the editor of William Martin Murphy's newspaper, the *Irish Daily Independent*, wrote a series of articles praising the venture and proposing that something similar should be done in Dublin. He also suggested that there be set up a National Institute of Commerce and Industries. This idea, which was apparently a cross between the Irish Management Institute, Córas Tráchtála and the Irish Goods Council, never got off the ground. The exhibition idea did, however, and by 1904 a committee had been set up and a guarantee fund was being gathered from interested parties. It was originally planned to hold the exhibition in 1906.[2]

The question of the site had first to be settled. At first the Phoenix Park was proposed, and was an obvious starting point, but it was strongly felt that the southside would be more financially attactive. Accordingly, the 40-acre site of rough wooded ground between Donnybrook and Ballsbridge was investigated. This land had already been promised by Lord Pembroke to Pembroke District Council for a park, and they were quite happy, in exchange for a fee, to waive their claim for a year or two.

The site was well supplied with handsome trees, but was frequently flooded by the Dodder in winter, so considerable work had to be put into draining and landscaping it before the exhibition buildings could be erected. During the course of clearance the workmen came across a mysterious and macabre find: a body, buried without a coffin, in the seated position, about two feet from the surface. No police action was taken. Once cleared, the park was filled with great halls and a lake, like a city created by a mad dictator, with all public and and no private buildings.

By May, all was ready, and the exhibitors were largely in place. There were over 1,000 of these, of which 538 were Irish, 278 French, 187 English; other exhibitors came from Hungary, Italy, Holland, Germany, Japan, Armenia and the Argentine. Unlike previous exhibitions, in which exhibits were carefully categorised, it had been decided not to allocate space according to a definite scheme. As they walked along the corridors visitors were exposed to a bizarre succession of products, natural and manufactured, serious and trivial. The *Freeman's Journal* described the effect:

> The stalls are arranged in the buildings without any reference to their contents . . . commencing at the Central Hall the visitor meets the following stands, taking them in order: printing, furniture, evening gowns, post cards, woollens. In the North Wing off this hall, walking along one avenue, are jewellery, carpets, pianos, furniture (again), upholstery, church decoration, sewing machines. In the South Wing, taking them in order, comes: matches, photographs, glass bottles, laboratory stores, ropes, electricity, account books. In the Hall of Industries one avenue gives this assortment, taking the stalls in order: bacon, zinc and alkalis, salt, spinning bobbins, oats, sugar, steel pens, fishing rods, sacking, hides, soap; in another are woollens, chemical fertilisers, laundry requisites, barometers, medicines. In another avenue comes chemical manures, ropes and cords, band instruments, sheep dips, marbles, inks, boot paste. Another avenue is made up in the order of jewellery, saddlery, horse hairs and bristles, hunting requisites, woolwork, agricultural fertilisers.[3]

The systematic order characteristic of previous world's fairs, notably the Great Exhibition, had been abandoned. On the other hand, as the official record noted, monotony was avoided.

The *Freeman*, along with most of nationalist Ireland, was by this time an increasingly hostile witness, a stance taken from the beginning by the Gaelic League. In January 1907, the League issued a statement urging all Gaelic Leaguers to have nothing to do with the project and to give it no support. There was even talk of boycotting exhibitors. The League feared that local manufacturers would be swamped by foreign companies, which would use their presence in Ireland to explore and further penetrate the Irish market. In June, several Irish societies in London, including the GAA, the Gaelic League, Cumann na nGaedheal, and the Dungannon Club, issued a joint manifesto denouncing the Exhibition, and the Irish Party maintained a constant posture of opposition to it. In the event, only 308 out of 2,371 Irish firms listed in the *Irish Manufacturer's Directory* were represented.

The organisers certainly had a knack of alienating opinion. No doubt the choice of a British building contractor was influenced by the £26,000 Humphreys put into the guarantee fund, but the handling of the catering tender was bungled. Jammet's (who then ran a hotel as well as a restaurant) and other locals applied, but J. Lyons of London eventually got the job, but only after dark accusations that they had been given an inside track in the bidding. Quite soon after the opening, when it was discovered that the appallingly bad weather, and perhaps nationalist doubts, had reduced the expected stream of visitors, 200 Irish workers were sacked from the catering staff. Lyons had brought over 400 English people of their own, who were kept on. Though it was understandable from Lyons' point of view, and the blow was softened by a handout of £7 each to the disappointed workers, this was a stick readily to hand with which to beat the organisers.

The choice of some of the paintings in the displays of Fine Arts could also have been more tactful. Not only were there vivid representations of the martyrdom of sixteenth-century French Protestants at the hands of Catholic priests, but also there were, as one complainant put it, 'a couple of glaringly naked pictures; . . . to the naturally refined tastes of the ignorant world, which have not been vulgarised by education, such things are repulsive and disgusting.' The organisers persisted to the end with a myopically Protestant view of the world, though the hyper-sensitivity of the nationalists was such that it was hard to avoid offence. Among the hymns chosen for the closing ceremony was a Protestant favourite, 'The Old 100th', which had been sung at ceremonies for Dargan's exhibition of 1853. Father Ambrose Coleman OP, editor of *The Irish Rosary*, worked himself into a fine rage, describing the tune as that to which Cromwell and his men masssacred thousands of poor Irish Catholics. 'It is, therefore,' he went on, 'the most barefaced impudence and hypocrisy on the part of the Ascendancy clique at the Exhibition to invite Catholics to voluntarily join in prayers, whose ancestors suffered heavy fines and rigorous imprisonment for refusing to have anything to do with them.'

The official opening of the exhibition was on Saturday 4 May. Great crowds attended the route to watch the Lord Lieutenant, Lord Aberdeen, and his Countess process to the Donnybrook entrance and thence to the official opening ceremony. It was a bright day, but very windy, and abnormally cold. In fact, the weather throughout the six months of the exhibition's life was to be markedly bad. As a result, regular attendances were well down on expectations. On the first day, about 25,650 turned up and found the famous water chute still being tested, the Canadian pavilion still undergoing finishing touches, and in various ways preparations still going on.

For those who braved the weather, there was always plenty to see, quite apart from the formal displays of products. On a typical day, the grounds would open at ten o'clock, and the various entertainments, such as the water chute, the helter skelter, the Indian theatre, the switchback railway, and the displays of the rivers of Ireland, ants and bees, the Somali village, the crystal maze and the shooting range would open at 10.30. From 12.30 to 10.30 at night, military and civilians bands, organ recitals and other musical entertainments filled the air. In the afternoon and evening, there was often a 'cinematograph performance', and, later at night, fireworks.

As well as these regular entertainments, there was a constant stream of special attractions such as Japanese jugglers, tight-rope walkers, novelty bands and trick cycling displays to keep up the public interest. The Somali village was by far the most successful side-show, grossing nearly £10,000 in 6d entrance charges. In this exhibit, various native Somalis went about their daily lives in as near a replica of home as the damps of Dublin would allow. Early on, a correspondent of the *Freeman* described the scene: 'The Somali Village was more active than on the opening day, but the coloured gentleman who walks along outside, uttering hideous noises, making faces, and brandishing his spear might usefully be allowed to moderate his zeal somewhat. Ladies and children are apt to be startled suddenly coming upon him thus enraged.'

Later on, another correspondent described the villagers as uttering grunts and whoops of joy at the visit of King Edward, which was explained as the nearest they could get to cheers. (There was a strong element of the zoo about the village.)

The visit of King Edward VII and his Queen, Alexandra, took place on one of the few fine days in this dismal summer. The royal couple, accompanied by Princess Victoria, stayed on the royal yacht in Kingstown harbour. On the morning of 10 July, they landed and took carriages to the exhibition grounds, pausing only to receive a loyal address from the burghers of Kingstown. This was the first of thirteen sycophantic addresses from various organisations that the King had the pleasure of receiving that day. On the way to the exhibition, the royal couple (who were still King and Queen of Ireland) were greeted by the Irish people with what the *Freeman's Journal* described as a 'respectful and hostlike attitude to their foreign visitors'; it was reported that large and enthusiastic crowds were marked only in such areas as Ailesbury Road, Donnybrook and near Trinity College.

On arrival, the royal couple went blandly and amicably around the exhibits, expressing general though vague enthusiasm. A small incident marred the occasion for Lord Aberdeen, who as Lord Lieutenant was the host. Somebody had decided that William Martin Murphy, as the leading organiser of the exhibition, should receive a knighthood. Unfortunately, no one had mentioned this to Lord Aberdeen, so there was no ceremonial sword. Furthermore, no one had mentioned it to Murphy either, and on the spot he declined the honour. There followed a pause, which, as Lord Aberdeen describes the scene in his auto-biography, was 'exceedingly awkward . . . during the subsequent brief interval before the luncheon some observations of a very emphatic sort were addressed to myself.'[4] Coming on top of the recent theft from the heart of the Castle of the Irish Crown jewels, this incident exposed the Castle establishment as strikingly incompetent.

The exhibition presented an opportunity for violent moblike larking that simply does not occur today. On the very last night, in November, a large body of Trinity students assembled at eight o'clock by the band-stand. They had an apparently unlimited number of fire crackers and other fireworks, which they let off with great abandon. Led by a young man in a Turkish fez, and another who waved the Union Jack, a group rushed over to the Somali village, where they caught one of the men, hoisted him high, and vociferously demanded that the unfortunate

Somalian make them a speech on the fashionable subject of technical education. (This is no doubt the source of the Dublin folklore that
relates how certain Trinity students actually kidnapped a Somali baby
for a few days during the exhibition.)

After they had rampaged about for a while, throwing fireworks, the
police charged them, and they scattered. About two hundred of them
quickly regrouped and took control of the central bandstand. At this, the
police vigorously intervened. They scaled the platform, and after a fierce
tussle the intruders were hurled off. The students then began to tear bits
off the pillars and throw them at the police; the students were again
routed, so they surged off to the outside bandstand, where they seized a
bandsman, put him on a chair and hurled him over the stand. They then
began to smash the chairs and throw squibs at the crowd. Eventually,
they were ejected bodily out of the grounds just before midnight.[5]

It was not for nothing that the nationalist MP, Tom Kettle, (a UCD
man) joked that the reason Dublin needed such a large police force
relative to other cities was nothing to do with the lawlessness of the
Irish, but was to keep the loyalist Trinity students in order. For, despite
the country's continuing reputation for drunkenness, in fact there
had been a remarkable transformation in the previous thirty years. In
Dublin, arrests for drunkeness had considerably reduced (from 5,200
per 100,000 population in 1870 to less than 1,000 per 100,000);[6] and
other crime was down similarly.

For serious drinkers, the beginning of 1907 brought a change to the law.
A new licensing act enforced weekend closing at 10 p.m., and extended
the 'bona fide' distance from three to five miles. (Bona fide travellers were
by law entitled to a drink at any time; thus to get a drink out of hours
you had to prove that you had travelled at least the decreed distance.)
The new law enabled small traders, such as drapers and grocers in the
city, which normally stayed open until 11.30 or later at night to catch
the post-pub business, to close earlier on Saturdays. Reporters noted
that streets normally crowded at that hour were deserted. Temperance
restaurants and shellfish establishments also did better business as a
result of the early closing.

By the last weeks of the exhibition's course, it was clear that the
takings were simply not enough to cover the costs. In the event, the
accounts showed that the total expenditure had been £340,000, and the
receipts, including the organisers' shares from all the concessions, was
£240,000—a loss of £100,000. Part of the failure was blamed on the
weather, which had been exceptionally wet and cold all summer. Not

only the exhibition was hit. The Dublin Horse Show was also rained out, as a *Freeman's Journal* reporter graphically described. 'Rain, rain, rainclouds like dirty blankets, not a vestige of life in the air, underfloor inches of slush, beauty checked, restrained, marred, almost destroyed; not a horse in good humour, horsemen scowling and growling, not a bit of colour or picturesqueness about; nothing but a wearisome, monotonous, merciless downpour.'[7]

J. P. Nannetti, the nationalist Lord Mayor, took the opportunity to renew the attack on the exhibition as a whole. The traders of Dublin, he declared, generally believed they had lost by the exhibition. 'Hotels, restaurants and theatres had all lost money through the Exhibition being here,' he claimed, somewhat wildly. 'Instead of spending money in the city, visitors went to the Exhibition and traders in the city never saw them.' A director of two city centre hotels, the Metropole in O'Connell Street and the Grosvenor in Westland Row, disagreed; in the event his receipts were more than doubled. Many restaurant keepers undoubtedly had had a bad start to the year, but as the Hotel and Tourist Association confirmed at a meeting a few days later, the exhibition generally had been a boon. One Association member spoke of trebling his business, and sending away thirty or forty people every night. After all, he said, a million people had visited the city. In the official record of the exhibition, published two years later, William Martin Murphy noted that the chairmen of public companies were all having to apologise for the relatively dull performance of their companies in 1908 compared to 1907.[8]

The land was cleared and (not without some argument between the organisers and the Council about depredations) returned to the people as Herbert Park, complete now with its own lake, the sole memento. This was the most tangible result of the Irish International Exhibition of 1907. For various reasons, its aims in stimulating Irish industrial enterprise were particularly ineffective. For Irish life as a whole, however, the most powerful single result of the exhibition was the stimulation and direction it gave to the anti-tuberculosis campaign, which, like the home industries section, was chaired by Lady Aberdeen.

The general improvement in health, echoing that in most other European countries, has been variously ascribed to improved nutrition, sanitation, housing and water quality and personal hygiene practices. In urban centres such as Dublin, water-borne sewage rendered the night-soil men redundant from the 1880s. In the 1911 preface to *The Doctor's Dilemma*, George Bernard Shaw confirms a change: 'Ireland is certainly a transfigured country since my youth,' he writes, 'as far as clean faces and pinafores can transform it.' Nonetheless, new habits took time to evolve; maintaining personal hygiene was nothing like as easy as it is today. In *Ulysses*, the characters shave, urinate, fornicate, eat in bed, and perfume themselves, but they rarely wash: Stephen Dedalus apparently hadn't had a bath for nine months. Bloom himself is the exception: he buys with pleasure a bar of Barrington's lemon soap (price 4d) and enjoys a bath in the Turkish baths in Leinster Street. Jewish women, who for ritual reasons had a bath once a month, had a reputation for exceptional cleanliness. Some medical men even warned against washing excessively with soap, lest the skin's natural oils be depleted. On the other hand, in 1907, Surgeon Tobin (whose nickname was 'Daddy') urged the medical students at St Vincent's to adopt two rules 'firstly cleanliness of body . . . secondly self-restraint in regulating his appetites.'

Even at the time, medical men did not claim that the quality of medical care had much to do with the large improvement in healthiness. Indeed, many were quite pessimistic about the power of medical intervention to achieve much. Oliver St John Gogarty facetiously described the medical ideal of his mentors in Vienna as 'a good diagnosis confirmed by an autopsy'.[9] Though the sheer presence of ordinary dispensary doctors (not just attending the sick, but vaccinating and registering births, marriages and deaths) must have had some effect in promoting norms of cleanliness.

The Irish people were undoubtedly healthier at the beginning of the century than their parents and grandparents had been. Life expectancy at birth had gone from under forty before the Famine to fifty in the 1870s and was to rise to nearly sixty by the 1920s. Having survived infancy, more young men (and to a lesser extent young women) survived middle age. In an analysis of his Co. Wicklow dispensary practice, Dr Langford Symes of Kiltegan noted that out of his 4,200 population 244 attended his dispensary and he visited 110 at home. Digestive problems (often caused by an excess of salty bacon), fevers and respiratory afflictions made up half of the cases.[10] Decade after decade, the Census records a steady improvement in the health of the nation since the Famine. On Census night in 1851, there were 104,000 people recorded as bedridden (i.e. 15 people per 1,000 living); ten years later this had fallen to 12 per 1,000. At the turn of the century the number of sick had dropped further to 8 per 1,000 living, ten years later the number had dropped again to 7 per 1,000.[11] A little prematurely, Dr John Moore, in his inaugural address to the students of the Meath Hospital in 1895 lamented 'the triumph of Hygiene means the pasing away of Medicine . . . already there are signs which seem to indicate that at least in certain directions the doctor's occupation will be gone.'[12]

Tuberculosis was at that time by far the most fatal malady that afflicted Ireland. In 1907, deaths from all forms of tuberculosis numbered 11,679; this represented 15 per cent of all deaths in that year. It was a fearful, mysterious disease, which struck particularly at the young, the female and the urban dweller. Rates seemed, if anything, to be getting worse, fluctuating between 2.7 and 2.9 per 1,000; thirty years before, the rates had been 2.3 and 2.5 per 10,000. The Women's National Health Association, led by Lady Aberdeen, began an unprecedented public education exercise, which, as a side effect, brought about a general change in people's ideas of disease. Travelling caravans were established by the Association to bring the message of fresh air to the country; model dairies, selling pasteurised milk, were set up; lectures, leaflets, booklets, and other instruction methods were exploited.

First of all, people had to be convicced of the relatively new germ theory. Tuberculosis, they were told, was not hereditary, as everyone had believed, but was actually caused by unbelievably tiny 'plants'. Lady Aberdeen's lecturers struggled with homely metaphors to express the scale: four hundred million of these bacilli could comfortably sit on a penny stamp, said one. Another noted that the 'monster steamship the *Lusitania*' was 'just as many times larger than this matchstick as this match exceeds in size a tubercle bacillus'. What was more, they multiplied alarmingly: 'An enterprising bacillus who may wake up in the morning to find no child about him to fetch his slippers, at sundown may have a tidy little family of twelve or fifteen millions of young germs to minister to his evening comfort.'[13]

Not everyone was immediately convinced. Lady Aberdeen recorded a conversation between two country-women after a lecture about TB and germs. 'One said all that talk about germs was just a lot of nonsense, but she was overwhelmingly discredited when another . . . declared there was a power of truth in it, so there was, for when she washed out a room after a girl had died in a decline there was germs in it as big as a young babby's finger!'[14] All this bustle and talk of dirt and sickness irritated nationalists and imperial officials alike, and they snidely referred to Lady Aberdeen as 'the vice-regal microbe'.[15]

The campaign focused especially on the widespread habit of spitting. According to the lectures reprinted in *Ireland's Crusade against Tuberculosis*, people spat on the floors of churches, offices, shops and pubs, in trams and, of course, on the pavement. Lecturers gave frighteningly vivid description of how a consumptive was 'capable of coughing up millions of tubercle bacilli even during a single hour . . . as long as the phlegm remains moist the tubercle bacilli are as securely locked up in the sticky mass of phlegm as flies in amber; but let the phlegm once get thoroughly dried, then there is no longer anything to hold the bacilli and the first current of air which comes along floats them up and blows them about to the common danger.'[16]

To ram home their points, well-meaning medical commentators deliberately stimulated fear. Tuberculosis was infective, they insisted, not hereditary, and infectivity could lurk in pocket-handerchiefs, in second-hand clothes and furniture, in an innocent kiss, in wallpaper, in the pages of a library book, even in the dust on a shop floor. (As a result of this campaign, middle-class people shunned the public libraries for a generation.) Furthermore, as the great physician, William Osler, put it, consumption was 'a house disease'—infection occurred where microbes could accumulate, so domestic customs and practices had to be changed radically. Under penalty of allowing their families to become sick, women were urged to force open windows; to burn bedding that had been in the family for generations; to provide nutritious food; to avoid dubious milk; and, above all, to keep all living rooms scrupulously clean. By the 1920s, these messages amounted to a sacred duty laid on the woman of the house. As the Catholic Truth Society's *Woman in the Home* pamphlet put it, 'once disease germs find access to dust it acts as a veritable hot-house or breeding-ground for them and for this reason it is absolutely necessary that dust should be removed from our homes daily'. [17]

In her autobiography, Lady Aberdeen details the continuing success of the campaign: by '1913 the rate had fallen to 2.15 per 1,000, meaning 9,387 deaths; and thus in 1913 there were 44 fewer deaths every week from tuberculosis than in 1907 . . . in 1924 the rate of deaths from all forms of tuberculosis had fallen to 1.45 per 1,000, meaning 4,582 deaths.'[18] By 1932, the rate had dropped to 1.32 per 1,000.

Chapter 8 The seething pot

In her novel *Mount Music*, published in 1919 but based on earlier work, Edith Somerville characterises the fall of the Anglo-Irish economic power and the corresponding Catholic middle-class rise. 'When one ancient and respectable family-coach runs down hill', she wrote, 'another vehicle, probably of more modern equipment, will go up.'[1] The novelist saw clearly how this was happening, though her sympathies were with the losing side. As she says of the rather stupid Major Talbot-Lowry, the Anglo-Irish representative character, 'it may be easy to deride him, but it is hard not to pity him.'

In the 1880s the clamour had been for progress, especially economic; but now the fastidious began to perceive this as coarse and unworthy. Advanced Irish nationalists, in particular, inherited from the Fenians a desire to demonstrate a purely spiritual patriotism, uncontaminated, as they would see it, by any material aspirations. There was an unconscious echo of the struggle in Russia between the Slavophiles and the Westernisers, between Moscow and St Petersburg, between the ancient traditions and moral purity of Old Russia and a Europe-led, Enlightenment-accepting vision of a new future. Just as the Slavophiles perceived the country and its villages as more purely Russian, as places without pretension but with a deep native spirituality, the Irish-Irelanders saw the life on the land as representing something truly and authentically Irish in a way that urban life could never be.[2] This contest was the background to Irish political life for generations. In the short term the country lobby carried all before it, and the voice of the urban middle class was weak.

The Irish-Irelanders wanted to be released, as George Birmingham wrote in his second political novel, 'from the shameless trickery of English statesmen, the insatiable greed of the merchants, the degraded sensuality of the workers'.[4] These nationalists burned with contempt for 'England', and believed, according to Eimar O'Duffy, that 'Ireland, set free, would have her mission. As once she had been the refuge of learning and religion in a Europe overrun by barbarism, so she might yet be the stronghold of the spirit in a world overwhelmed by materialism.'[5]

Not all the ideas were on the left wing: the more conservative toyed with militarism and anti-semitism, and a kind of intense nostalgia for the imagined rural order of the past.

Ireland was in fact relatively prosperous, with a per capita income perhaps as high as the top ten of the world, just below France.[6] Some Irish observers thought that the current prosperity was due to the British connection and argued for the necessity of sustaining it. Others took a less positive view, declaring that the Irish had been over centuries 'bled white' by the English, that it was even now 'bleeding to death'. A French writer melodramatically declared that the Irish were a 'weakened and exhausted race', battered by centuries of famine, emigration, alcoholism and colonial exploitation. Those remaining, he thought, seemed scarcely to have the will to thrive. The birth and marriage rates were the lowest in Europe; 9 per cent of the population lived off the Poor Rates; emigration seemed an unstaunchable haemorrhage; the number of lunatics per head had quadrupled since 1851; the 'white plague' (consumption) was killing 12,000 of the youngest and most hopeful of the country's citizens a year; 30,000 licensed public houses (one for every 146 people) exacted their toll.[7] 'The country is doomed,' said the gloomy clothing manufacturer in George Birmingham's 1906 novel *Hyacinth*, 'the best of them are flying to America and those that remain are dying away, drifting into lunatic asylums, hospitals and workhouses.'[8]

The economic penetration of English goods brought with it an increasing prominence of English media and habits. Ireland was, it seemed, steadily becoming an English shire, a province of England, as had Wales and Cornwall. The so-called 'slow process of denationalisation' was obvious as English goods and cheerfully vulgar mass-market English publications flooded into the new markets. In 1912, the Dubliner William Dawson noted the 'steady encroachment of London daily papers. It is fast becoming as common a sight to see the man in the tram with a London morning paper as with a Dublin one.'[9]

Manufacturers in England wooed the Irish market with bogus 'Irish' names—'The Colleen Bawn', 'Erin's Own', 'The Kathleeen Mavoureen'. British flour brands were called 'Slainthe', 'Faugh-a-Ballagh', 'Emerald' and 'St Patrick'; still others put harps, shamrocks and similar symbols on their bags. In 1907, to combat this passing-off, the Irish Industrial Development Association began issuing a 'made in Ireland' trade mark.[10]

Yet at the same time, in the country a transition was occurring from the traditional practical home-made clothes—'the younger women

THE RIVAL HURDY=GURDYS.

MISS ERIN. "Go away, please, gentlemen; this noise is awful. If you expect me to pay you for discord, you're quite mistaken. When you've practised a little harmony you can call round again."

Not everyone felt equally strongly about the political situation. This cartoon, from an Irish comic journal the Leprachaun (a predecessor to Dublin Opinion) portrays a certain weariness on the part of the ordinary middle-class voter. Neither Sinn Féin ('for ourselves and no one else') nor Redmond's Parliamentary Party (with its monkey, the Freeman's Journal) are flattered.

think they look prettier in gowns made artfully by the local dressmaker' in light imported cloth.[11] The number of commercial travellers spreading these goods through the country had quadrupled in twenty-five years. The enveloping shawl worn over the head was to remain, nonetheless, the characteristic garment of the Irish country-woman for another generation at least.

Many who were later to become ardent Republicans, for example C. S. 'Todd' Andrews, imbibed their first ideas of the world from English comics such as *Chips, Comic Cuts, The Magnet, The Gem* (Billy Bunter's home territory) and the *Union Jack*. Andrews' life-long nickname was actually derived from a character in *The Magnet*. Adult publications such as *Titbits, Photo Bits, Pearson's Weekly, Lloyd's Weekly News* (all of which were read by Leopold Bloom and his milieu) were deplored by the churchmen and the puritanical Gaelic Leaguers alike.

Although scholars have described the excitement of the literary revival, it affected only a few. The vast majority of the Irish people were literate, and readership of newspapers (notably the weeklies such as the *Weekly Freeman*) was widespread, but they were not book readers. As W. B. Yeats observed: 'The people of Ireland respect letters and read nothing. They hold the words "poet" and "thinker" honourable, yet buy no books. They are proud of being a more imaginative people than the English, and yet compel their own imaginative writers to seek an audience across the sea.'[12]

William Dawson, a member of the group of UCD intellectuals that included Tom Kettle and Arthur Clery, declared that 'nobody in Dublin buys books—if we except text-books and sevenpenny novels—but even the "intellectuals" will scarcely borrow from a library a book by a Dublin man published in Dublin.'[13] (He believed that 'a Parliament in Dublin would remedy at least this state of affairs'.) The matter was the subject of jokes—as, for instance, Dr O'Grady, who bought a few books every year 'quite privately, for no one in the west would admit that he threw away his money wantonly'.[14]

Although the Public Libraries (Ireland) Act 1851 had enabled local authorities to establish libraries, by 1880 only Sligo and Dundalk had taken advantage of its terms. Four public libraries were established in Dublin between 1884 and 1905, but the stock was small and the borrowers few; when the system was temporarily closed for lack of funds in 1908 there were a mere 6,000 books on loan, for a population of 375,000 people. The Carnegie gifts ensured the erection of handsome buildings, but not the supply of books, so that when the new library in Great Brunswick Street was completed in 1909 it remained empty for two and a half years 'like a canal without water'. Eventually newspapers and magazines appeared, but no books for a further two years.

Out to the theatre

The general Dublin theatre audience certainly lacked 'national-mindedness'. The 565 seats in the Abbey were very often not filled; the inveterate playgoer Joseph Holloway records an occasion when only fifty people attended. In the same week that the Abbey showed *The Playboy of the Western World*, less serious citizens enjoyed *Casey's Circus* at the Empire ('Screamingly funny acts! Roars of laughter! with the Latest English and American sensation! Man versus Motor—a wonderful cycling and motor racing exhibition'); or the last week of *Sinbad*, the pantomime, at the Gaiety, and *Mother Goose* at the Theatre Royal; at the Tivoli, Chas. Fisher and Co. played their musical farce, *The Music Master*. The Theatre Royal and the Gaiety had initially requested that the Abbey's licence be restricted to plays written by Irish writers on Irish subjects, presumably not deeming them any threat. This restriction was later waived.[15]

Finally, there were Living Pictures at the Rotunda. These were short one-reel films in a wildly mixed programme. A typical selection would include: *The Short-sighted Sportsman's Mortification, Canadian Salmon Fisheries, A Model Husband, New Tour in Switzerland, The Sultan of Morocco and his Army, Flowers for Mother's Birthday, Professional Skiing from Norway* and so on. Later in the year the Empire (always the raciest of the theatres) had 'artistic' poses 'representative of undraped statuary' by La Milo, and in May an exhibition by Miss Juno May, the female wrestler. Wrestling was extremely popular with both sexes: in July, the *Freeman* noted the presence of a 'galaxy of ladies' at a contest between the great Russian, George Hackenschmidt, and the Belgian Constant le Marin in the Theatre Royal. Later that month the 'knights of the grip and tumble arena' were part of a variety programme that began with the 'accomplished comédienne' Kitty Wagner, and included Collins and Rice, who called themselves the Breezy Comedy Duo.

As soon as things were managed by Irishmen for Irishmen, thought the nationalists, matters would rapidly right themselves, and all this vulgarity would wither away. However, the experience of nineteenth-century nationalists in Poland, Hungary and Italy was that abstract ideas of political and economic freedom were insufficient to inspire fighters. The movement needed the heat fuelled by a legendary past, a flag, a national anthem, a traditional enemy, a language and a literature, and—crucially—a burning frustration that these rights were being denied by the occupying power. The Irish-Ireland movement was subliminally aware of the essentially synthetic nature of the task: 'We are nation-makers', wrote a correspondent to the Sinn Féin paper *United Irishman*,[16] echoing the famous statement 'we have made Italy, now we must make Italians' after the unification of Italy.

The process often required a ruthless smoothing of the complexities of the actual event. In 1831, for instance, thirteen policemen were stoned and bludgeoned to death by an infuriated crowd of several hundred farmers in the townland of Carrickshock, Hugginstown, Co. Kilkenny (a notable incident in the so-called 'Tithe War'). Nearly eighty years later, in 1907, to promote his election chances, a local man, Nicholas Murphy, boasted of the epochal 'Battle of Carrickshock'. A brutal outburst was thus transformed, and the three farmers also killed in the melée had become martyrs. Murphy extolled the blessed spot where 'tyranny and ascendancy received their first blow'—subsequent blows being understood to have been delivered during the Land War. In a speech the following year the new editor of the *Munster Express* declared (to cheers) that the crushing victory over Crown forces in Carrickshock had 'turned the tide, and marked not alone an epoch in the history of our country, but that of the civilised world'. The monument that was eventually erected twenty years later simply does not mention the dead constables (who were mostly local men, and Catholics). By 1931, just before the Eucharistic Congress, the event was being glossed as ' a fight for religion, first and before all. This was the motive, the religious motive that inspired the people of South Kilkenny to make this stand.'[17]

In 1907 the nationalist movement erected statues to the Manchester Martyrs (in Tipperary), to the Irish 'wild geese' who fought at Fontenoy (in Belgium) and to Parnell (in O'Connell Street). At the very beginning of the year a massive 'indignation meeting' gathered in Dublin to prevent the despoilation of Conquer Hill, which was described as 'the venerated and historic mound under which have lain for 900 years the relics of the Irish heroes who fell in the Battle of Clontarf'.[18] The mythic rhetoric was an essential part of these meetings. At the unveiling of the monument to the Manchester Martyrs, for instance, one of the speakers claimed that 'the longest war in history was only a fraction of that between Ireland and her enemies . . . the Manchester Martyrs died defending the flag that had floated for 1,000 years in the face of the enemy.' As he cycled through Ireland (in a tour described in a book published in 1907), the journalist William Bulfin reflected on ancient glories, waxing lyrical over Tara ('old when Christ was born, for it had held the throne of Ireland from days far back beyond the morning of our history ... one of the world's chief capitals, and a great centre of political, legislative and literary activity'),[19] and seeing in every mountain and field some echo of the greatness of the Gael. In Belfast, however, this (Protestant) centre of Irish industrial effort, Bulfin's uncritical enthusiasm for things Irish failed. He disliked the place intensely. It was not, he thought, an Irish city. It seemed foreign; the street life lacked Irish geniality, it was cold, austere, rigid, grim—in the very primness and newness and spaciousness of the city there was something basically un-Irish. Elsewhere, the reader was urged to feel in himself 'the unconquerable spirit of the lion whelps of Gaeldom'.

In his Belvedere classroom, one of the lion whelps, the fourteen-year-old Arthur Cox, later to become the country's leading business solicitor, imbibed the rhetoric readily. Writing in a prize essay he declared that 'even those pages of [Ireland's] history which are stained with blood and tears are witnesses to her undying conquests.'[20] This style was such a contrast to the factually precise speech of England that it was a constant small irritant between colonist and colonised. George Birmingham described how 'occasionally an English Government official pounces on a fervid orator or scribe and insists that his words bear their obvious meaning. No one is more surprised than the victim ... for he knows he did not mean what he said and that no one except a Government official would suppose he did.'[21] The habit of wide statement was not limited to any particular field. Quite soon after the opening of the new National Library building in 1890 a reader complained about the draughts in the Reading Room, declaring indignantly that this was 'a real national grievance, which concerns all classes of the community'.[22]

Although it would not have been admitted in 1907, globally it was English speech that was (and is) abnormal. The English had taken seriously the strictures of Locke as to the difficulty of making a true statement. Combined with the Royal Society's promotion of plain, simple, unadorned language, this left English speech especially rich in diminishers, approximaters, qualifiers and compromising adverbs (such as rather, nearly, just about, there or there abouts, comparatively, relatively, hardly, almost, scarcely etc.).[23] The English did not talk of 'the mother of all battles', insist 'mi casa es su casa', or declare that 'the dogs in the street' know such-and-such. A modern English observer reports that in Italian 'the blunt expedient of communication guaranteed through brutish straight-talking is secondary to the beauty of the sound . . . that's why it's often impossible to render in English a passage of Italian'.[24]

With imperial insouciance, the typically monoglot English simply assumed that their way of speaking was normal and any deviation humorous. The educationist P. W. Joyce recalled how 'a very distinguished Dublin scholar and writer . . . mentioned to me once that when he went on a visit to some friends in England . . . they often laughed at his roundabout expressions'.[25]

Language was a key battlefield for nationalists. In an essay first published in 1772 the German philosopher, Johann Herder, had rejected Enlightenment advocacy of a universal language as mistaken, claiming that language reflected mental make-up and that consequently people of one language were significantly different to those of another. Each language encapsulated its speakers' experiences of blood, soil, environment, experience and destiny.[26] Clearly, therefore, for the true Irish person, the Irish language should not be difficult to learn. As Eimar O'Duffy wrote: 'If there was anything in heredity its germs must be in his brain. They would grow once more, given the chance, like some temporarily suppressed bodily faculty.'[27] To lack the native language, as de Valera declared much later, was 'to abandon part of ourselves, to lose our key to our past, to cut away the roots from the tree.'[28] Without this key, a vital part of the Irish spirit must remain in the dark, and the race cruelly and arbitarily suppressed.

For some the language's origins in a 'purer' time reinforced a denial of economic reality: 'In these days of coarse materialism, Gaelic is for the Gaels an intellectual stimulant and a moral anti-septic,' wrote one commentator.[29] Others, following Davis, saw the language as a surer barrier and a more important frontier for a nation than a mountain or a river. Douglas Hyde said at a Gaelic League meeting in May 1907, that the League was engaged in 'the last struggle of the Irish race to preserve not its language, but its identity as a nation'. In stuffy rooms in Dublin enthusiasts argued as to whether Connacht, Munster or Ulster Irish represented the best basis for a standardised modern Irish language. So, in practice, as in other European countries, a small urban élite chose the language by which they intended to unify the state. Thus had the French imposed Parisian French on the speakers of hundreds of dialects (as late as 1880 only one-fifth of the population were reported as fluent and comfortable in French); in Italy only 2.5 per cent understood Tuscan Italian in 1860, and as recently as 1970 30 per cent used dialect only.³⁰ Despite wistful glances towards the revival successes of other European languages, such as Czech, Flemish and Polish, few saw Irish totally replacing English. English was a vulgar commercial necessity, said Hyde, but Irish was a national one.

By far the most exciting outing for Irish-Ireland in 1907 was the protest against the staging of Synge's *The Playboy of the Western World* at the Abbey in the early part of the year. As was the way of these things, there was a strong element of contrived farce mingled with genuine emotion.

The Abbey was in the habit of announcing its new offerings in advance, and in late January a small paragraph appeared in the papers, which with hindsight appears as a doomed attempt to ward off trouble by stressing Synge's knowledge of the Irish peasants of the west.

> Mr Synge's new three-act comedy *The Playboy of the Western World* will be played for the first time on any stage tonight at the Abbey Theatre. It is a peasant play pure and simple, and the scene is laid in the vicinity of Belmullet. No one is better qualified than Mr Synge to portray truthfully the Irish peasant living away in western Ireland. He has lived with them for months at a stretch, in the Aran Islands and Mayo. He has noted their speech, their humours, their vices, and virtues. He is one of the best Irish speakers in the country, and is thus bought into the closest contact with the people. *The Playboy* is founded on an incident that actually occurred.

Synge had, as the Abbey well knew, chosen sensitive ground. The moral quality of Irish peasant life, especially native Irish-speakers, was an important part of the nationalist myth. It was thought that they represented authentic Irishness in a way that city-soiled intellectuals could not hope to. The parts of the country where Irish was spoken were, it was thought, 'morally, on a higher level than those of other parts of the country'. In the same way had the mid-nineteenth century Slavophile insisted on the moral superiority of the Russian peasant. Hyde himself maintained that native Irish speakers were cleaner, more virtuous, better mannered than others, and churchmen declared that their faith was stronger and their religious feeling more profound.³¹ To address this environment in anything other than the most positive way was to attack the core of the nationalist myth.

The *Playboy's* first night was Saturday 24 January 1907. On the following Monday, the *Freeman* contained a review and an indignant letter about the play, though there was no mention of riots or large scale disturbances. The reviewer affected a solemn, self-righteous tone immediately, saying that 'a strong protest must be entered against this unmitigated, protracted libel upon Irish peasant men and worse still on Irish peasant girlhood'. However, according to the reviewer's report, the audience was quiet though restless until the third act, when Peg ties Christy and prods him with burning turf. At this point 'angry groans, growls, hisses and noise broke out, while the pinioning of Mahon went on. It was not possible—thank goodness—to follow the dialogue for a while. The groans, hisses and counter-cheers of the audience drowned the words.' In his final summing up, the *Freeman's* reviewer came out strongly against the play.

> The mere outline of the plot does not convey the offensiveness of the piece. No adequate idea can be given of the barbarous jargon, the elaborate and incessant cursings of these repulsive creatures. Everything is b----y this or b----y that, and into this picturesque dialogue names that should only be used with respect and reverence are frequently introduced. Enough! the hideous caricature would be slanderous of a Kaffir kraal.

Just below this attack the paper printed a letter from 'A Western Girl' which introduced the 'shift' issue into the debate. The writer knew the West as well as Mr Synge did, she claimed, and 'in no part of the South or West would a parricide be welcomed'; what's more, she added 'not only would such a man be shunned, but his brothers, sisters and blood relations would be more or less boycotted for generations' thus somewhat weakening her case for the innate Christian sensitivity of the region. Her main concern was reserved, however, for 'a word, indicating an essential item of female attire, which the lady [i.e. Miss Sara Allgood, who played the Widow Quinn] would probably never utter in ordinary circumstances, even to herself'. This was not, we can be sure, intended to be interpreted as a 'fact'; it was more a vividly expressed response to the discomforting eroticism of the piece.

These attacks alerted some attention, for the audience on the Monday night was considerably more volatile, and well prepared to be shocked. It was described as 'a very thin house', which received the curtain-opener, *The Riders to the Sea*, most favourably. The *Freeman's* reporter described what ensued:

> For a few minutes after *The Playboy* had started the rather smart dialogue was applauded [clapping during a scene being evidently customary]. As soon as Mahon was taken to the arms of the peasants, and it became clear that Margaret was to be left alone with him, the uproar reached massive proportions. Stamping, booing,

vociferations, in Gaelic, and striking of seats with sticks were universal in the gallery and in the pit . . . Amidst this babel of sounds the refrain of *God save Ireland* was predominant . . . cries of 'Sinn Féin for ever' were also heard. Someone shouted 'such a thing could not occur in Ireland'. Another rather irrelevantly shouted 'What about Mullinahone and witchburning?'[32] This query was responded to with very emphatic execrations.

Eventually the police were called and the noise calmed down a bit. At the end of the act the police left (perhaps thinking the play was over), and the nationalists began singing again songs such as 'The West's Awake', 'A Nation Once Again' and other patriotic compositions.

By the Tuesday night farce began to follow tragedy. Everyone knew that a thoroughly enjoyable confrontation was in the air. Thirteen-year-old Walter Starkie went that night, and 'found a great crowd assembled in the streets adjoining the theatre. Inside the atmosphere was electric . . . as if everyone was expecting a political revolution to break out.'[33] Starkie noted that in addition to the usual middle-class theatre-goers, there were numbers of workers, and various Dublin intellectuals, who had come to see and be seen. In short, everyone wanted to be in on the fun. At 7.30 the police arrived at the Abbey, as well as a mysterious group of young men, not apparently Trinity students. One of them stripped off his overcoat and offered to fight anyone in the audience who disagreed with him—an offer received with great hilarity. He then announced (to no one's surprise) that he was 'a little bit drunk' before moving to the piano and playing a waltz, very badly. The stewards eventually hustled him away from the piano. At 8.15, W. B. Yeats entered and the curtain went up. *Riders to the Sea*, the curtain-opener, was again received with general applause. Then Yeats stood up and suggested that there should be a public debate on the issues raised by *The Playboy*. At this stage a number of Trinity students appeared in the stalls, with the avowed intention of suppressing interruptions. ('The students of Trinity being then, as ever, the "death or glory" boys of Irish loyalty,' as George Birmingham put it.[34])

A few minutes into the play, uproar began, a good deal of it contributed by the drunken gentleman who once again offered to fight all and sundry—he was eventually persuaded to leave. The noise continued throughout the play; as the *Freeman* reported 'not half a dozen consecutive sentences had been heard by the audience . . . groans and hisses greeted the sentence "you are a man who killed your father: then a thousand welcomes to you". This revolting sentence led to further disorder . . . [as did reference to] an article of female attire.'

Yeats and his supporters ran up and down the aisles, acting as spotters for the police, pointing out people who were making noise, with a view to having them ejected. They succeeded in getting a number of the most vociferous thrown out in this way. Among those arrested was Padraic Colum's father, later indicted in the magistrate's court. Yeats gave evidence in court against him, claiming there was an organised attempt to prevent the play being heard, which was, in effect, true. A 40s fine was imposed (perhaps half a week's salary for a clerk).

By Wednesday, the lines of confrontation were clearly drawn, and everyone came expecting a row, especially the police, who this time lined the side of the pit. The *Freeman's* reporter was there again, and described the scene. 'As usual the first ten minutes passed off quietly, in fact there was a fair share of applause ... however when the self-described parricide was greeted with open arms by the peasants things changed. Shouts of "get out" were hurled from all directions, whilst cat-calls, strident bugle notes, and fierce denunciations added to the terrific din. But, on the other hand, there were shouts of "order" and "fair play".'

In the third act, with old Mahon chasing after Christy, one of the cast, Philly Cullen, says: 'I'm thinking we'll have right sport before night will fall'; at this point the combatants in the pit momentarily forgot the deep seriousness of the issues. 'This was so very apropos to the exciting situation,' wrote the *Freeman*, 'that all parties in the theatre joined in an outburst of hearty laughter.' However, things quickly reverted, and the police were kept busy ejecting interrupters. At the end of the play the audience hung on, and a number of gentlemen stood on the seats and began to make speeches to knots of their supporters.

D. P. Moran's journal *The Leader*, the locus of much Irish-Ireland thinking, was predictably against the play:

> Had the production been submitted to the less artistic appreciation of the commercial audience it would have been hooted off the stage in half an hour ... throughout the play there runs an undercurrent of animalism and irreligion really as rare in the much-decried Theatre of Commerce as it is undesirable in the National Theatre of Ireland. One looks in vain for a glimmer of Christianity in the acts or utterances of the characters. Superadded must be the frequent repetition of words for the use of which any corner-boy would be arrested, and touches of coarse buffoonery which would not be tolerated in a pantomime.[35]

For the moment the excitement about *The Playboy*, which was to recur when the play was taken abroad, ended with a great debate on the subject at the Abbey on 5 February. W. B. Yeats opened the batting, and there were contributions from Francis Sheehy Skeffington (who said he was both for and against the play), Cruise O'Brien, leader writer of the *Freeman*, Jack Yeats, Joyce's friend C. P. Curran and others, most of whom took up more or less predictable positions. A theme that the play opens to the modern audience, the striking ability of the emigrant to recreate him or herself, an activity that was forced on tens of thousands every year, was not mentioned in the discussions.

A contribution from Mr D. Sheehan, a medical student, took the debate to an arena that appealed to neither side. He was, reported the *Freeman*, strongly in favour of the play, which he said represented in Christy the widely distributed type of sexual melancholic. This comment was greeted with hisses and disorder. Sheehan went on to say that he had come that night to object to the pulpit Irishman just as they objected to the stage Irishman (renewed noise) . . . they ought, he said, to defend the women of Ireland from unnatural pathological—(the rest of the sentence was lost in the noise). Mr Synge, Sheehan continued, had drawn attention to a particular type of marriage, which while not confined to Ireland (disorder) was very common here (disorder). Here is a fine young woman like Pegeen Mike (hisses) and a tubercule Koch's disease man like Shaun Keogh (some laughter, groans, hisses and noise).

At this stage in the speech, reported the *Freeman*, many ladies 'whose countenances plainly indicated intense feelings of astonishment and pain', rose and left the place. Many men also retired. The rest of Mr Sheehan's speech was drowned in noise. The new tradition was in thorough agreement with the old as to the necessity for reticence on sexual matters. Sheehan's note of blunt speaking was hardly to be heard in public debate again for sixty years. After some more speeches the meeting broke up with cheers and hisses and the singing of 'A Nation Once Again'.[36]

These activities were exciting, but still of minority interest. Even students and young intellectuals did not automatically become Irish-Irelanders. De Valera, for instance, was twenty-four in 1907 and spent his time teaching in Carysfort and playing rugby. He did not join the Gaelic League until 1908, nor did he, so it is said, consider seriously the idea of an Irish Republic until 1911.[37] For Joe Brennan, later to become Secretary of the Department of Finance, the *Playboy* row was less interesting than the Rector of UCD's attempt to censor a student paper. In the L&H, students with political views, many of whom would become the country's leaders, largely supported Redmond and the parliamentary party. Irish was never spoken, and more radical views barely heard.[38] At a less intellectual level, twenty years after the foundation of the GAA, only 3 of the 32 playing fields in the Phoenix Park were required for Gaelic games, the rest being used for soccer.[39]

Sinn Féin had only just been founded as a separate movement, and its ideas had still to become the dominant orthodoxy. For most people in 1907, Joseph Chamberlain's famous dictum of 1904, that 'the day of small nations has long passed away. The day of empires has come' contained a brutal truth. In this context connection with the British empire was acceptable as long as increased political, cultural and economic independence was granted. Such independence was even politically thinkable in Westminster, as it simply had not been years before. In its pursuit, the United Irish League was steadily advancing the parliamentary road to Home Rule. Sinn Féin was seen as clearly extremist; the *Leader* (2 March) reported as typical the reluctance of one man to join the Gaelic League, which was in theory non-political, because if he did so he would be expected to adopt Sinn Féin policies. It would take a surprisingly few years before its ideas became the dominant opinion.

—1932—

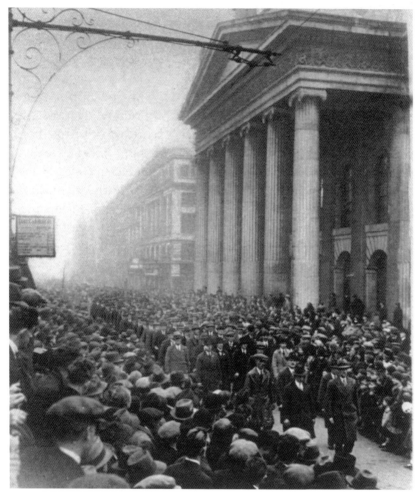

Easter 1932: a crowd lines O'Connell Street to watch five battalions of the IRA march past in celebration of the Rising. Though still proscribed by the Church, the IRA had just been unbanned by the incoming Fianna Fáil government. Many believed that the IRA was importing arms and ammunition on a growing scale. (Illustrated London News)

Chapter 9 Nothing but unrest

By 1932 the empires, powers and principalities that had dominated the nineteenth century scene had largely joined feudalism in the dustbin of history. The 'age of empires' so confidently diagnosed by Chamberlain in 1904 had suffered a quick collapse. The key exception of course was Ireland's immediate neighbour Britain, whose flag still waved over one-fourth of the earth's arable surface and some 485 million people. Although the ineffable self-confidence of the pre-War period was never to be recovered, Britain was still immensely rich; London was by far the most populous city in the world. If you wanted to suggest stability, you said 'as safe as the Bank of England'. It was also culturally dominant; Irish people felt acutely the gravitational pull of their overmighty neighbour.

In the place of the old easy-to-spot empires, sinister destabilising forces, such as communism, the Yellow Peril, international finance and fascism, not to mention more occult powers, preyed on people's minds, as if the horrors unleashed in the First World War could not be quieted. As ever, unworldly people believed that, after all, *somebody* must be to blame—for the Great War, the Russian Revolution and the Depression, as well as such deplorable items as jazz, the skimpiness of women's skirts, the White Slave Trade, pornography and the morality of the cinema. They brooded on Edmund Burke's famous remark, that 'a rat, gnawing at a dyke, can drown a nation'. Among the conspiracy theorists was Nesta Webster whose inflammatory book *Secret Societies* (1924), was politely if sceptically reviewed in *The Irish Times*. The reviewer explained her conspiracy theory that 'a secret society of Jews has worked with every revolutionary force down the centuries . . . seeking to achieve the overthrow of the Christian religion and the Christian order and morality. This secret society is, though she does not use the word, Anti-Christ.'[1]

The world view of certain Catholic writers was not dissimilar and just as cataclysmic. They saw a manifestation of 'the eternal struggle between good and evil'. As Father T. F. Ryan SJ saw it, this 'had entered a new phase, and the future of civilisation depended on whether God or Satan would triumph.'[2] In Ireland for the Eucharistic Congress, Archbishop

McDonald of Edinburgh elaborated: 'Bolshevism has rocked religion to its very base; and that blasphemous anti-God campaign, led by powers of wickedness in high places, is threatening to engulf in the chaos of impiety the civilisation of the entire world.'[3] In a sermon preached in his native Cavan the headmaster of Blackrock College, John Charles McQuaid, confirmed that the perennial battle against Christ's church and his angels was being fought by Satan and his earthly allies, Jews, Freemasons, Protestants and communists.[4] Foremost in the armies of Satan were the Jews ('a Jew as a Jew is utterly opposed to Jesus Christ and all the Church means' said McQuaid); they had infiltrated and corrupted the Freemasons, who in turn controlled the Protestants generally. The effect such apocalyptic visions had on ordinary lives in Ireland is difficult to assess. Perhaps a near analogy is 'the shadow of the bomb' under which the children of the 1950s to 1970s lived; very few brooded much about such matters, but, for all, the fact was always there as a background.

A few optimists saw a chance to create a new world order that would not make the same mistakes. Some agreed with H. G. Wells, who looked forward to a world state, run by an upgraded League of Nations.[5] Others, such as the Catholic publicists G. K. Chesterton and Hilaire Belloc in England, and their many followers in Ireland, yearned for a return to the world before the Reformation. They urged, as Chesterton put it, 'the sanity of field and workshop, of craftsman and peasant, from the inanity of trusts and machinery, of unemployment, over-production and unemployment'.[6] Dr Gilmartin, the Archbishop of Tuam, expressed in a sermon the recurrent wish that 'Ireland would return to the simple life of our fathers with home industries, small farms worked by the family, fireside stories, Irish dances, Irish games and native music, with Irish the language of the home.' Unfortunately, this did not appeal in practice. The Archbishop had been told that a million pounds a year left the country to pay for silk stockings. Surely, he wondered, Irish hosiery could be made capable of supplying all *reasonable* demands?[7]

Right at the end of the 1920s, gross and uncontrolled speculation had thrown the economy of the USA, the richest country in the world, into collapse. (The events are familiar: weak regulation, over-lending by banks, uncontrolled speculation on margin by ordinary people. Among the highlights discovered during the subsequent investigation was the leading US banker who had set up a private company to sell his own bank short.) The repercussions echoed far beyond the private gambling club of Wall Street. By the summer of 1932, industrial production in many leading countries was only half what it had been a few years before, and world trade had slumped by one-third.[8] World unemployment stood at over 20 per cent; coal production dropped 30 per cent between 1929 and 1932.

Big changes in the old ways were looked for: 'half the European countries' thought the nature writer Henry Williamson 'were in process of altering their entire conception of economic and physical life, an evolutionary process that was not understood in complacent, mature England.'[9] It seemed that capitalism (and probably democracy itself), was in trouble. As a correspondent to the *Catholic Bulletin* wrote: '[capitalism's] impotence in the presence of the financial and economic problems of the hour has raised the first serious doubts with respect to its soundness'.[10] From the communist Peadar O'Donnell to the Jesuit Father Edward Cahill, thinking people believed that the basic liberal democratic model was dead or dying, and a replacement was urgently needed. A branch of the British Fascist party was formed in the Free State in 1930, and in 1931 Saor Éire, the socialist republican group, was founded and quickly condemned by Cumann na nGaedheal.[11]

Country after country was abandoning democracy. Not only did this seem increasingly inevitable, but even in many respects a Good Thing. Mussolini, who seized power in 1922, was widely regarded as the saviour of his nation. (For years, Canon Hayes, the founder in 1931 of Muintir na Tíre, kept a photograph of him above his desk.) Russia, Germany, Poland, Bulgaria, Turkey, Hungary, Rumania, Yugoslavia, Spain and Portugal all had or would soon have forms of dictatorial government, and were all surging ahead economically. One country unlikely to fall into dictatorship was the United States, where, *mirabile dictu*, a Catholic (Al Smith) was the Democratic candidate for the presidency—the Irish were urged to pray for his success. In the event he was thoroughly defeated by the Republican Hoover.

'The year 1931 has departed, unwept and unhonoured,' wrote the leader-writer of the *Irish Independent* on 1 January 1932.

> It was a time of almost universal distress and anxiety ... in Germany alone it is said that almost 20,000,000 citizens are living on relief ... But unemployment has not been the only spectre ... budget deficits, increased taxation, and political crises have been the lot of the wealthiest nations. In Great Britain and Austria political landslides have brought new Ministers into power. In Spain the last of the Bourbon dynasties has given way to a Republic. In India the year has ended with rumblings of a storm that may soon become a terrifying hurricane.

On the plus side, the *Irish Independent* reported in November 1931 that 'Herr Hitler's last chance of becoming German Chancellor seems to have gone.' In August 1932, the paper returned to the theme with a note that 'the disintegration of the Hitler party is proceeding apace.'[12] There was, no doubt, a similar element of wishful thinking in the report in December 1932 that 'the question of Stalin's retirement is again being freely discussed in Soviet Russia.' A more realistic analysis of Hitler's prospects was provided to the Department of External Affairs, and summarised in *Studies* in 1933, by Professor Daniel Binchy who had just returned from a stint as the country's representative in Berlin. Binchy had experienced at first hand the hypnotic effects of Hitler's beer-cellar oratory, and left the reader in no doubt about his power over the German people, his enthusiasm for war and his megalomaniac hatred of the Jews.[13] Binchy's successor, Charles Bewley, was considerably more sympathetic to German policy, even to the point of staying in Europe when war broke out.

In October, the newspapers reported the first successful flight from Ireland to Berlin—it took eight hours, as opposed to three days by the overland route. The *Irish Independent* commented that it and its readers were 'accustomed to think of Central Europe as a place almost as far away from us as America; in some respects indeed much further.'[14] The *Independent* was smug about Ireland: 'Ireland has come through the ordeal of the world waves of depression and distress with fewer bruises and a greater residue of vigour than most countries . . . foreign observers speak with envy and admiration of conditions in this country and of its sound Administration.'

The last remark was in the context of an election year, in which Fianna Fáil were going to make another attempt to unseat William Cosgrave's Cumann na nGaedheal party. The *Independent*, along with most of the business establishment and the strong farmers, supported Cosgrave warmly. But unemployment was high, emigration continued (though at a reduced rate, no doubt because of overseas conditions) and both rural and urban poverty were marked. Young women were leaving the countryside, determined not to face the life of drudgery endured by their mothers. Father MacCarthy of Aughadown, west Cork, complained bitterly that he could not get a girl to look after him, 'even at ten shillings a week and her keep'. As a result, he was obliged, so *Irish Times* readers were told, to cook his own dinner, and 'to combine housework with his arduous parochial toils'.[15]

Like its readers, the *Irish Independent* was pious, nationalistic, right-wing in its instincts, conservative in its opinions and its style. With audited sales of 130,000 copies a day, it was the mouthpiece of Catholic middle-class Ireland, the successor to the *Freeman's Journal*, and the voice of the new establishment. It was published for 'the new emerging middle classes, the civil service and the professions, to whom the sectarian state was primarily addressed' as John McGahern put it.[16] *The Irish Times* was still resolutely 'Anglo', and the *Irish Press*, which was launched in 1931, was vehemently and vigorously a Fianna Fáil party paper—in early 1932 its editor, Frank Gallagher, was arraigned by the military tribunal for publishing supposedly seditious attacks on the government. The *Independent*'s values were largely Dublin-based, with a nod in the direction of England. (The social column always led off, if possible, with some tit-bit about the British royal family—on 1 January, for instance, readers were told that the Queen, with a number of friends, had driven to the sea at Hunstanton from Sandringham; the party walked on the front and then on the beach and stayed by the sea for some time. The Irish interest was catered for a few days later by the intelligence that the Marquess of Waterford had given up the mastership of the Waterford hunt, 'a decision', said the *Independent*, 'that would be regretted by every hunting man and woman in the country'.)

The shadow of the gunman still hovered in the Free State, particularly behind Fianna Fáil, but for the moment the dapperly formal Cosgrave was President (the office was renamed Taoiseach in the 1937 Constitution). There was an interesting year ahead, full of exciting happenings. As the *Independent*'s new year's day leader continued: 'We face the year with confidence. It will be a year of memorable events. The general election, the Tailteann Games, our participation in the Olympiad, will contribute to make it a year out of the ordinary. But all these things will be overshadowed by the Eucharistic Congress, coinciding as this great event does with the 19th Centenary of the coming of St Patrick.'

Some of the *Independent*'s smugness reflected the fact that for most of the middle-class urban Irish, it was a comfortable world. For some, of course, the practical and psychological cost of keeping up appearances was high. Maeve Brennan's sharp vignettes of middle-class Dublin life in Ranelagh show how Rose, who 'was different in her ways when they had visitors', never went out of the house 'without her special look of a person who fears that at any moment she may find herself among people who are beneath her and who will try to be too familiar with her'. The keeping of place applied upwards as well as down: Lily, aged nine, boasted about how she was going to be a famous actress in the Abbey theatre. 'Don't go getting any notions,' she was told, a favourite put-down, especially often aimed at girls.[17] Girls were the typical target also of sharp adult put-downs such as 'catch yourself on', 'notice-box' and 'who do you think you are?'

Nonetheless, many of the standard ingredients for personal happiness were broadly in place. For instance, although there was an established financial hierarchy, there were no wide disparities in personal wealth among people of the same background—a mere 1,500 were assessed for super-tax. Servants were cheap and easily available. If they paid income tax at all, people paid on average no more than 6 per cent of their gross income. Middle-class people, at least, did not work particularly hard; from ten to five daily, with perhaps a Saturday morning, was a typical week. Businessmen regularly met at Bewleys twice a day, and drank considerable amounts of alcohol at lunch. Senior civil servants were entitled to six full weeks holiday. People lived longer than their parents, especially once they had survived the dangerous days of childhood, in which 15 per cent of deaths still occurred. There was an exciting sense also that modernity was humming—in music, in labour-saving devices, in transport (in 1932, the locally designed Drumm electric train hit 52 mph in trials on the Dublin–Bray route). Above all, most people had a deep faith, providing a reassuring sense of the ultimate purpose of life. 'God made the broth,' was the saying, 'let him stir it.'[18]

A marked feature of daily life was the culture of secrecy. The Victorian liberal love of Facts had turned sour (a phenomenon certainly not unique to Ireland) and now at every level authoritarian figures treated information as unpredictable and dangerous, and therefore to be guarded. A characteristic incident was when the Department of Justice was spooked into suppressing the report of an official committee examining sexual offences in 1932. 'What was agreed on,' writes Diarmaid Ferriter, 'was the need to keep discussion of these issues behind closed doors.'[19] The media was quite weak and, accepting the culture of privacy, was disinclined to probe aggressively. Every organisation—church, government, business or family—had privacies and secrets, things outsiders were not to know, mainly from a simple authoritarian distrust of what others might do with it. Inside businesses and organisations financial and other details were tightly guarded.

A typical instance was the Church's demand that knowledge of the perfectly legitimate 'safe period' was kept secret, for fear of the 'dire social consequences' that might ensue. This was part of a larger pattern.

The law of the land not only banned the importation of contraceptives, but even forbade anyone from expounding a theoretical stance 'advocating birth control'. Apart from the normal business of formally banning 'indecent' books, and the Index of prohibited books, there was a more surreptitious control of what might be read. In 1938, *The Irish Times'* diarist reported that books on Spain, Mexico, Russia and 'certain philosophical and sociological issues' were being quietly withdrawn from the Dublin public library stock unless they were published by one of two approved firms.[20]

Secrecy is the obverse of privacy. (*I* am private, *you* are secretive.) In the family, husbands did not usually reveal to their wives how much they earned or how much money they had; parents were undemonstrative and private in their affections; and the mysteries of the human body remained so. The boundaries of what was to be kept secret crept constantly wider, just as did those of the realm covered by the sexual taboo. What happened inside the house was preserved private to those outside—this was one of the first lessons a child learned. Family and personal secrets were common. The children would never be told what had happened to Uncle John, for instance, or what sickness their cousin Mary had. Quite apart from personal considerations, the logic of the latter secrecy was that many illnesses, notably tuberculosis, 'madness', epilepsy and possibly cancer were believed to be hereditary. Revelation of such an illness could perhaps ruin a girl's chances of marriage. It was common for the parents to have a private language (typically French) in which they could converse—*pas devant* was the catch phrase, for keeping servants and children in the dark. Children in return devised their own languages (such as pig Latin and eggy-peggy), and in games swore each other into secret gangs.

The superstitious believed that priests had all sorts of secret powers, to curse, and to make occult things happen by the power of their prayer. The confidences of the confessional were, of course, respected, even in practice by British law. Apart from the long tradition of militant secrecy, with the Ribbonmen, the Fenians, the IRB and their descendants, which affected the committed, there was the archetypal secret society, the Freemasons, whose membership had undoubtedly increased in the 1920s. Against them was their Catholic mirror-image, the Knights of Columbanus, equally secretive.

The highest social respect was paid to those who carried secrets. These were typically professional men such as doctors, lawyers and clergy; but also senior civil servants and top journalists who were privy to state secrets of various sorts. Because of their intimacy with all sorts of physical knowledge, doctors in particular had an aura of insight. A favourite moral conundrum was 'Should a doctor tell?' (The name of a 1930s film starring a young Anna Neagle.) This covered questions such as how far should patient confidentiality go (for instance, does a doctor have a duty to tell a bride-to-be that her prospective husband has epilepsy in the family?), and, should a patient with cancer or heart disease be told of their diagnosis?

High on the list of the Irish public's daily concerns was sport, particularly those sports that offered the chance of a bet. The *Irish Independent* reported an extraordinary range of sports every day, and not in perfunctory detail. In the first week of January, for instance, there were full articles describing athletics, badminton, coursing, camogie, rugby, boxing, lacrosse, Association and Gaelic football, table tennis, hockey, golf, handball, cricket and horse racing. Sporting heroes were public personalities, very often to both sexes—in June, Clery's arranged to have one of the boxing champions of the day visit the store, where he was mobbed by autograph hunters.

The big home event of the 1932 sporting calendar was the Tailteann Games. These were an Irish version of the Olympics, and like the Olympics mimicked an ancient practice—the Oenach Tailten, whose history can be traced back to the eighth century. The Games were intended to be, as the *Independent* described it in the language reserved for such things, 'a racial re-union for the scattered children of the Gael'. They had first been revived in 1924, and again in 1928, when the Olympics had been in Europe, thus ensuring a healthy participation by Irish-American athletes. This year, the Olympics were in Los Angeles so none came to Ireland; not only that but boxers from Ulster were forbidden to attend by their provincial association because the tricolour was to fly over the stadium.

In his guide to Ireland, published in 1935, the humorous writer Lynn Doyle confirmed that for (middle-class) Dubliners, the struggle for existence was not as keen as in comparable British towns. In fact Dublin was, in 1932, the most prosperous town in Ireland, north and south. It was, as the expression went, 'easy to live in'. The beauty of the surrounding country flowed up to the suburban streets, and 'the people (were) as carefree as if Ireland had never known a sorrow'.[21] When the ex-Jesuit Edward Boyd Barrett first went to New York in the 1920s he noted how, in marked contrast to Dublin, 'everyone hurried, everyone was tense, no one breathed deeply'. He saw in New York his first traffic jam, and noticed with amazement that there were 'no children, no beggars, no old men or old women, but smartly dressed young folk to right and left, milling, talking, hurrying . . . and too busy (or was it too suspicious?) to help a stranger with directions.'[22]

Back in Dublin, there was the fun of being once more a capital city: the new ambassadors (from the US, France and Germany) were the great catch at parties, and the burgeoning civil service promised jobs at home for the sons and (at least until they got married) the daughters. The best of times, wrote Doyle, was Horse Show Week.

> There is nothing on earth like those Horse Show Week dances, a phantasmagoria of lights, laughter, mischief, and reckless gaiety; a babel of voices (you can dance to them if you like, for you won't be able to hear the band), a pageant of dress from the newest of Paris to the Silurian, and a pageant of people from Connemara to Jerusalem; lean hunting girls who could speak to Galway without using a telephone, and their bronzed men-folk; an Irish peeress or two, with the Irish predominating triumphantly over the peeress; sleek, well-groomed doctors and barristers from Fitzwilliam Street and Merrion Square; long-haired intellectuals who think deep thoughts and don't drink shallowly; a Minister or so, trying to look European . . . [23]

The city was still small—Greater Dublin held only half a million people, fewer than Dr Johnson's London. Many of these still lived in great poverty and squalor in what were believed to be the worst slums in Europe. During 1932, the *Irish Journal of Medical Science* published the results of Nurse M. O'Leary's four years of district visiting to children in the poorer areas. One in eight suffered from malnutrition, over half from dental caries, one in five from eye trouble. The Sick and Indigent Roomkeepers Society alone had helped over 20,000 people in the previous year (some one in twenty of the city's population). Inside the limits of a pre-Keynesian budget prudently balanced—as they boasted in the 1932 election—the government was rather slowly trying to do something about re-housing and clearing the slums. Housing estates at Fairview and Marino had been built, though there was, as Fianna Fáil sharply pointed out during the 1932 election, much yet to be done.

It was a period that made much of authority, respectability and hierarchy. Ordinary people's opinions were not sought often—even the Letters to the Editor columns were sparse. Doctors, lawyers and clergy were accustomed to be listened to submissively, and their decisions were not questioned. (Advertisers regularly used images of doctors and clergy to promote goods—one long-running series featured a doctor in pin-stripes recommending Skippers sardines; another quoted a clergyman as writing: 'I have been keeping my eyes open for years for the ideal toilet paper and I have at last discovered it. It is Bronco.') More than twenty years later, a Supreme Court case perfectly illustrated the point. In 1954, a doctor was sued for medical negligence because he had left part of a needle in his patient's body, but decided not to tell her about it. The case was dismissed, Mr Justice Kingsmill-Moore declaring 'I cannot admit any abstract duty to tell patients what is the matter with them, or in particular to say that a needle has been left in their tissues.'[24]

If the poor stepped out of line, punishment could be severe: truancy from school, petty thievery, vandalism and 'destitution' all resulted in committal to detention in industrial schools which at this time housed over 6,500 boys and girls. Committal was not quite automatic: when three lads were caught having stolen 30s from their schoolmaster and spent it on sweets, cinema seats and gambling machines, the judge asked the schoolmaster whether he thought he could teach these 'little thieves' to be honest—if not, he would send them to industrial school. When the teacher said he thought he could, they were sent home. One would like to know what happened to Bernard Matthews of Dundalk, the so-called boy roof-climber, who used to retreat for hours together to the roof of his grandfather's shop (he carried up a bag with him, and when he needed food he simply smoked out his grandfather by blocking the chimney), or Thomas Donnellan of Corofin, described by his mother as 'a wild boy' who refused to go to school, alleging the teachers were beating him for not learning Irish, an excuse not accepted by the district justice.

There was a different law for the rich: a Co. Clare district justice complained bitterly about drunkenness at the Shannon Lawn Tennis Club dance. 'The trouble,' he said, 'is that there has never been a prosecution against persons for drunkenness on such occasions, although at any of the dances I have attended I have seen drunkenness, even at so-called reputable dances in the county. It might be [that the guards thought] that the people drunk were too respectable to be prosecuted, but they were not, and what's more,' he went on, he didn't care whether it was a he or a she getting drunk.

Health was a constant worry. In the 1930s, it was thought of as a gift from God, easily destroyed. The big killer was heart disease (a death rate of 1.9 per 1,000 in 1929), then tuberculosis (1.3) and cancer (1.06). In 1932, tuberculosis, though still tragic because it so frequently struck the young, seemed to be waning in virulence. As a result of strenuous state efforts over the previous twenty-five years, rates per 1,000 had gone from 2.55 in 1907 to 1.25 in 1932 (in 1948 the rate was 1.04 per 100,000). To many observers, there seemed more cause for concern in the steadily mounting deaths from cancer, especially since, as the newly set up Hospitals Commission noted, 'the fight against cancer in Ireland has hitherto been carried on in a more or less desultory fashion.'[25]

For lesser ailments there were plenty of remedies. Wild claims were made for patent medicines such as Aspro, which was stated to conquer rheumatism, gout, neuralgia, 'flu, sleeplessness and 'pains peculiar to women'. Both sexes suffered, so the advertisements claimed, from ailments such as nerves, lazy glands, brain fag and other disabilities. Luckily, these problems were easily removed by any number of tonics. Zam-buk, 'the grand herbal ointment' was particularly effective, at least according to the often quoted testimony of Mr T. Mullins of Feakle, who had severely cut his right leg with a scythe, and had been in terrible pain. Zam-buk, however, rapidly removed the pain, and 'knitted the severed flesh'.

Not that the doctors' armentarium was particularly extensive or effective. The Mulcahy family (General Richard was then leader of Fine Gael) GP was typical. He was 'a large, solid, portly and bespectacled man whose mature and professional appearance inspired immediate confidence . . . he prescribed brown bread for most complaints and for all trivial ailments.' Apart from this, 'cod liver oil, Parrish's food (containing iron), Friar's balsam, purgatives, cough medicines, poultices and camphorated applications for lumbago and other painful conditions were the chief items of the pharmacopeia.' In those days, before antibiotics and other drugs, 'there was little he could do apart from relieving symptoms and inspiring confidence in recovery.'[26] Nonetheless the hours by the bedside, the whispered confidences about physical ailments combined to supply his gravitas.

A combination of stodgy food and doubtful plumbing made constipation a favourite worry. An ad for Beecham's Powders claimed that as much as 90 per cent of poor health was caused by constipation. There was a lurking consciousness that, as the Eno's ad warned, 'waste matter which is not dismissed properly and to time remains to create poisons.' Plumbing was still an uncertain factor, especially in older houses, and people were very familiar with the image of the ill-plumbed house exposing its inmates to typhoid and other diseases. Smokers with throat problems were urged to change to Craven 'A', 'made specially to prevent sore throats'.[27]

Personal appearance was, as ever, a fruitful area for quackery. Cosmetics had not long been customary for respectable women—when in June *Woman's Mirror* announced that 'every normal girl uses the powder puff, the lipstick and a soupçon of rouge', there was an element of proselytising in the comment. In New York, Boyd Barrett saw that 'women took mirrors and boxes of cosmetics from hand-bags and powdered and painted themselves. I was amazed that they were not ashamed to do so in public; and I missed the old-fashioned reserve.' [28] When Maeve Brennan (aged seventeen) went to America in the early 1930s, she was surprised to discover how much effort her new school-friends put into making up. As her biographer writes: 'Her bluestocking mentors and wholesome friends in Dublin would have been embarrassed to show so much concern about their appearance and would have found wearing make-up "common". American women and girls used make-up enthusiastically. '[29] So for advertisers the question was often not which cosmetic, but whether to use one at all. One frequently reproduced advertisement for a cosmetic showed a cartoon of a daughter addressing a harassed mother— 'Mother,' the daughter was pictured as saying, 'why does Mrs S. look so much younger than you? She's your age, but I think she uses some kind of skinfood.' 'What a difference that powder makes!' shrieked another regular advertiser over pictures of a spotty and lonely 'before' and a ravishing and husband-catching 'after'.

With the aid of the anti-tuberculosis campaign, personal hygiene was gradually improving—spitting in the streets was declining, and those who could washed more, pushing the city's consumption of water up by 30 per cent in twenty-five years. It was therefore a pity, as the critic of the *Irish Builder* pointed out, that for reasons of economy, bathrooms were not included in the design of the houses of a new estate in Carlow.[30] For the Mulcahy family in Rathmines, a weekly bath and hand washing twice a day 'maintained a reasonable level of cleanliness' though 'the ubiquitous presence of a distinctive odour of poor hygiene was one of the more disagreeable aspects of those days.'[31] In the country, the lack of facilities combined with personal modesty meant that hygiene standards were low. In the 1940s, Dr Ethna MacCarthy found that over 70 per cent of women from the western counties wishing to emigrate had body lice. So common was such infestation that victims were desensitised. 'Sure,' she was told, 'no one can help having those things.' The Dublin poor were not much better off. Students in Baggot Street hospital found that 'fleas were a menace, especially to fair-skinned students, and lice infestation so common that the smell of oil of Sassifra permeated the ward as most new patients had to be deloused.'[32]

Food hygiene also left much to be done. The city's milk was still supplied by city dairies such as Rafters of New Street, where over 150 cows were housed in strong-smelling barns in the shadow of St Patrick's Cathedral. Despite its importance, milk was in fact a dangerous substance: an article in the Irish women's magazine *Model Housekeeping* warned mothers of 'the chance of your child getting tubercular meningitis, or tuberculosis in some other form', and described filthy pails, manure and other dirt falling from cows' legs and flanks into the milk. A report published in 1924 found that a quarter of Dublin's cows had had tuberculosis, and the *Irish Medical Journal* reported in 1932 that the worst milk was often that which had been pasteurised, since many dairies pasteurised only bad or aged milk—what, after all, was the point of pasteurising good?

Her natural qualities

Women had achieved the vote, and shorter hair and lighter clothes; even at the height of fashion they were now able to dress themselves without the help of a maid, which had not been easy twenty-five years earlier. (There were still, however, plenty of maids—over 80,000 of them according to the 1926 Census, one-quarter of all working women.) But though women had for the moment gained a little more control of their lives, conservative Church-led views were closing in. Divorce had been made legally impossible in the 1920s, more and more woman habitually lost their jobs on marriage (this rule was introduced in the teaching profession in 1932), and information about contraception was censored. The Crusade against Immodest Fashions, stimulated by the Pope, echoed some of the Fatima prophecies and harried away at the fashionable short skirt. Skirts, it was declared, should cover the knees even when sitting. In January 1930 the Sacred Congregation issued a summary of what they meant by modest dress: 'a dress cannot be called decent which is cut deeper than two fingers breadth under the pit of the throat, which does not cover the arms at least to the elbows, and scarcely reaches a bit beyond the knee. Furthermore, dresses of transparent material are improper. Let parents keep their daughters away from public gymnastic games and contests; but, if their daughters are compelled to attend such exhibitions, let them see to it that they are fully and modestly dressed. Let them never permit their daughters to don immodest garb.'

In a book published in 1932, Edward Cahill, the Jesuit Professor of Social Science at Milltown Park, explained the Church's position. He firstly clearly up a vexed point. Woman are not, as Aristotle taught, a kind of inferior man; both men and women, he wrote, 'have all the essential attributes of human nature'. But they are different, and the woman's natural qualities 'fit her especially for the activities and the life of the home.' Indeed, for her to work outside the home, especially with men, would risk violating the requirements of Christian modesty. For the Church (whose views in this matter were more or less enshrined in the 1937 Constitution), the family was the key unit of society, with the man as leader, natural head, provider and protector, and the woman 'by her life within the home' giving the state a support without which the common good could not be achieved.[33] In the 1930 encyclical *Castii Connubii*, Pope Pius XI wrote: 'If the woman descends from her truly regal throne to which she has been placed within the walls of the home . . . she will become as among the pagans, the mere instrument of man.'

Only a few years after the state had given women the vote, Father Cahill proposed that it be taken away and given to the family rather than the individual. The vote was to be expressed, of course, by the male head of the family, and having a value based on the size of the family itself (the more children the greater the value—as contrasted to the crude English practice, at least in local elections, of the more property the more value). In this suggestion, he showed himself more a theoretical than a practical sociologist: according to the 1926 Census, less than half of the adult population (aged twenty or over) were married, so the great majority of both men and women lived in extended family groups. This point also escaped Seán MacEntee, who as Minister for Finance a few years later, lyrically described the 'sound organisation of immemorial memory, deeply rooted in the traditions of our race, based on the patriarchal principle that honour, respect and obedience were due to the heads of the household . . . Today [he complained] the man and his wife carrying the whole burden of their families has no more voice in the direction of our public affairs than the flapper or whipper snapper of 21.'[34]

Class and religion

In the country things were relatively simple: Dervla Murphy's parents went from Dublin to Waterford to run the county library in 1930, and found that 'on one side of the deep rural divide were the gentry and aristocracy, mainly Anglo-Irish and Protestant, and on the other were the farmers and tradesmen, mainly native Irish and Catholic. No true middle class had yet evolved . . . and professional men were usually either the sons of impoverished gentry or of prosperous farmers.'[35] Some of the gentry still lived in an isolated Somerville & Ross world, complete with servants and hunting: in January, for instance, the *Independent* reported the result of a stag hunt in Portrane, Co. Dublin. After a long run, the stag headed straight for Portrane House; it leapt through an open kitchen window, hotly pursued by the hounds, to the consternation of the maids. 'The stag was safely taken, but not until considerable damage had been done to the delph.'[36]

In Dublin, where Dervla Murphy's parents had been born and brought up, structures were considerably more complicated. Sets interlocked and intermingled, particularly in public (giving the illusion of classlessness), but were quite exclusive in their family affairs. Still with considerable prestige were the survivors of the Anglo-Irish Ascendancy, becoming fewer and more isolated year by year. The 'lean hunting girls' admired by Lynn Doyle found it increasingly difficult to find suitable husbands. The Protestant business class still dominated the financial institutions, many of the largest businesses, and the clubs. Catholic professionals formed a distinct and well-off set, the sleek doctors and barristers that Doyle spoke of. Other groups included middling owners of businesses, senior officials, bank employees, and finally ordinary clerks, middling civil servants, employees of businesses. Jewish businessmen, most of whose parents had come to Ireland fleeing the Russian pogroms, were not welcome. Thus immediately after the Second World War the Lancashire businessman Jefferson Smurfit was black-balled from one of the golf clubs on the grounds, as he wrote in his autobiography, 'that anyone with an unfamiliar name, a big nose and a successful business must be a Jew'.[37]

By 1932 about 7 per cent of the Free State's population was Protestant, and half of the Protestants lived in Leinster. Every business, club or organisation was clearly defined in people's minds as either Catholic or Protestant (a feature of Irish life that persisted until the 1960s). Dervla Murphy recalled shopping at Miller's of Dungarvan, an old fashioned Select Family Grocer, and being surprised to notice that a neighbour never entered the shop. 'Mrs Mansfield,' she was told, 'doesn't believe in supporting Protestant shops.'[38] (This phenomenon was not exclusively Irish. 'Generally speaking,' wrote William Hale of his English midland town in the 1850s 'there were two shops of each trade: one which was patronised by the Church and Tories, and another by the Dissenters and Whigs.'[39]) In Belfast long after, as Patricia Craig remembered, scrupulous Catholics refused to buy a 'Protestant loaf', i.e. one manufactured by the Ormeau Bakery rather than Hughes'.[40] Protestants were expected to support Protestant firms, which in turn recruited their staff from Protestant schools. As we have seen, the social division between the two religious groups could be deep. Even in the Dublin cattle market, as one veteran recalled, 'a number of stands were owned by Protestants, who sold practically all Protestant cattle. The Catholics sold practically all Catholic cattle.'[41] The day a Catholic consciously met his or her first Protestant was a memorable one. Olivia Robertson, whose father had come from England to be City Architect, records a scene a few years after 1932 in the playgroup she ran.

> One day a crowd of children appeared before me, dragging with them a rather mentally deficient girl. The children's spokesman, a fair little girl called May, spoke up. She was furious with their prisoner.
>
> 'Miss Robertson, Delia's after saying somethin' awful about you!'
>
> 'Oh dear.' I looked round the circle of angry faces. 'What did she say?'
>
> 'She says you told her you were a Protestant!'
>
> There was a horrified pause. Then May, her face pink and anguished, spoke for them:
>
> 'Oh Miss Robertson, say you're not a Protestant, say you're not a Protestant!'
>
> If only the children had been hostile it would have been easier. But they were incredulous, shocked. To complicate matters, my Anglican training had taught me that I was an Anglo-Catholic. Still, I knew what they meant. I had to rescue Delia.
>
> 'Yes,' I said. 'I am a Protestant. Lots of people are Protestants,' I said. 'The King is a Protestant.'
>
> This was not enough. I thought again.
>
> 'The film stars are Protestants.'
>
> It was all right.[42]

The most common Church of Ireland attitude to the new state was to abstain. (The response of the dominant Catholics to this was compounded of relief and resentment.) Many Protestants, as Brian Inglis testified, 'as soon as they found that the new Irish Government could be trusted not to expropriate their land, debase the currency, or make general legislative mayhem, settled down to ignore its existence. And in everyday matters, the fact that an Irish Free State did exist was hardly noticeable.'[43] The politics of the Free State, recalled Alex Findlater of the grocery family, was simply not mentioned at Protestant tables. For some, such as the formidable Archbishop Gregg, the severance from Great Britain was a disaster: for him the British were the trustees of Christianity in a pagan world, and, as his daughter remembered, 'in 1922 he felt that he had been banished from the Garden of Eden'.[44]

The remoteness from the new world was persisted in, even made a virtue of: for them Dún Laoghaire (always referred to as Kingstown) was simply the place one went to the mainland from. In the end, some accommodation had to be made to demography. Brian Inglis describes the nice calculations by which the Protestant committee of the Bull Island golf club committed slow social suicide. Other things being equal, families in trade, Roman Catholics and Jews were excluded.

> On R.C.'s, as we called them, the rule was flexible. It had to be because there were many people of what we called 'good' families in Ireland who 'dug with the wrong foot' (the Jamesons, for instance, and Sir Arthur Chance's family). There were also a few members of good Protestant families who had made mixed marriages. Parental opposition was often fierce before the match, but it rarely survived the birth of children ... but a Catholic without social status stood little chance of becoming a member. A man who was 'in trade' stood even less. [45]

As Arthur Clery had observed, social class was a much more important determinant than religion.

On the Catholic side, many held that there was, in fact, no Irish class system. This was one of the canons of the Republican movement before the Treaty, and was, in the teeth of the evidence, happily rehearsed to English visitors until the 1970s. 'We assumed,' wrote C. S. Andrews, 'that except for the usual tendency of tuppence-halfpenny to look down on tuppence the Irish nation in the mass was a classless society. There was no social immobility based on birth or inherited wealth.'[46] This was as self-deluding as the Republican assumption that one million Protestants would somehow acquiese in a united Ireland. At the time there were half a million pupils in primary schools and fewer than 30,000 in recognised secondary schools (i.e. not including technical or industrial schools). The small number of secondary pupils were certainly not chosen on merit. Anyone crossing the Liffey from Grafton Street to beyond O'Connell Bridge could at once see in the crowd the physical and economic effects of the class system.

Andrews himself was typical of the men whose birth guaranteed an inherited position of power in the new state. His parents ran two small but reasonably prosperous businesses—an auctioneers and a provisions shop. He himself went to university (one of only seven hundred from the entire country in that year); among his fellow students were the later chief executives of Aer Lingus and the Industrial Credit Corporation. At university he was indeed looked down on by the sons and daughters (especially the daughters) of the professional classes, which perhaps enabled him to describe himself as classless. However, when he married he was presented with a £600 house by his father. His brother joined the civil service, and he himself contemplated becoming a professional accountant. The apprenticeship fee of £200 (at this time the average civil service salary was £179 a year) was a disincentive, so he joined the newly formed Tourist Board as an administrator.

The solicitor, Arthur Cox, whose father had been a distinguished physician and knighted, was another inheritor. He had been at UCD with Kevin O'Higgins and many others in the independence movement and quickly became an adviser to the leaders, travelling, it was said, over to London several times during the Treaty negotiations.[47] As the old unionist and Anglican business world faded, he and the accountant Vincent Crowley worked together establishing and advising new Irish businesses from the 1920s onwards. After the passing of the Control of Manufactures Acts in 1932, this 'lion whelp of Gaeldom' specialised in assisting British firms to circumvent its regulations. With the aid of the Knights of Columbanus, established specifically to counter the imagined influence of the Freemasons at this level, gradually the influence of Catholic professionals ousted the Protestant firms such as accountants Craig Gardner. Despite being by far the largest firm, Craig Gardner was undoubtedly Protestant, and they got no government business for twenty years after the foundation of the new state.[48]

The urban Republicans who had fought against the Treaty had inherited the austerity of Fenianism. They were, as Andrews describes with some irony, 'puritanical in outlook and behaviour. We didn't drink. We respected women, . . . and knew nothing about them. We disapproved of any form of ostentation. We disapproved of the wearing of formal clothes—tuxedos, evening or morning dress and, above, all silk hats. We disapproved of horse racing and everything and everyone associated with it. We disapproved of every form of gambling. We disapproved of golf and tennis and the plus fours and white flannels that went with them . . . We ate our meals with the same detachment with which we dressed or shaved . . . we disapproved of elaborate wedding ceremonies, we disapproved of women "making up" or wearing jewellery.'

This austere creed and the socialist ideas which accompanied it did not last in the gregarious Dublin of the 1930s. 'Within ten years', Andrews goes on, 'we had all played golf and tennis. We had worn black ties and even white ones. We had joined Bridge clubs. We had sampled alcohol and eaten out in restaurants. Some of us had developed views on wine and how to cook steak. We had even modified our views on cosmetics and women's dress. We had visited France.'[49]

It wasn't just the gregariousness that changed views. Two new and powerful media had begun to exert their influence—radio and cinema. Irish radio, Station 2RN as it was known, was state-run as a subset of the Post Office, and so was not likely to prove very revolutionary. It broadcast mostly music, solo singers and instrumentalists, some opera, and talks, for which experts were paid a guinea for a quarter of an hour. Occasionally they attempted an outside broadcast, as at Christmas 1932, when, as one publication reported, '2RN proved its value to Christianity and the country as a national radio station controlled by Irishmen replete with Catholic spirit when they broadcast from Kilkenny Cathedral a magnificent rendering of Mozart's Mass in D.'[50] Politicians were lukewarm about radio. As Senator Connolly, the Fianna Fáil Minister for Posts and Telegraphs declared, he had his doubts 'as to the desirability of having a mechanism in the home as against a certain culture'. Only some 5 per cent of households had radio licences in 1932, most of these being in Leinster (though nobody supposed that the fact that you did not have a licence meant that you did not have a set). With the opening of the new high-power transmitter in Athlone in 1933, the number of licences tripled, to 100,000.

The cinema was another thing altogether. The glamorous images of Hollywood, incorporated in films that promised to 'tear the heart-strings of all filmgoers who see this gripping drama of love and sacrifice' contrasted vividly with the mundanity of daily life. Disturbingly, these films began to suggest a set of values that were far removed from those of authority—the professionals, the teachers, the parish priests and the politicians. Attitudes to sex, to marriage, to material possessions, were all challenged, much as the *Late Late Show* was to challenge them again in the 1960s and 1970s. No wonder, as the *Irish Independent* sympathetically noted, 'a great many well-meaning folk might be found, especially in the ranks of the older generation, who would be prepared to see the opportunities for cinema entertainment abolished or at least very much curtailed, on the grounds that this modern form of popular entertainment is one of the most fruitful sources of vulgarity and to a lesser extent crime in the world of today.'[51] (The word 'vulgarity' was a typical marker of class disdain.) These well-meaning folk included Mary Hayden, by now Professor of Modern History at UCD, who proposed that children be excluded from cinemas.

The new media did not, however, stimulate a wide variety of discourse. Hollywood was not led by intellectuals. Compared to the hectic openness of the days before the First World War, the 1930s were steadily closing down on more than women's freedoms. Certain subjects were simply not engaged with. More or less anything to do with sex, for instance, or the effects of the class system, or whether a united Ireland was in fact desirable, or whether the Catholic Church's contribution to Irish society was other than wholly positive were some of the topics that were simply not discussed in public. They were 'what cannot be thought about', about which we can only brood in private and in a secret place, as Brendan Kennelly put it.[52]

Chapter 10 Necessary for class reasons

The Census of 1926 identified a population of just under three million in the Free State. The great majority lived in the country, in villages and in country towns; a small minority—one in six—lived in large cities, basically Dublin and Cork. The lives, assumptions and habits of those living in cities were very different from those living in the country. Before the advent of television and with only limited access to radio, which was still largely an east coast luxury, the forces making for homogeneity were weak.

In no area was the difference between city and country life more vivid than in the basic economic matter of getting a job. Country people emigrated to Britain or America, or they worked on the farm, or possibly in their parents' shop or business. The question of choosing, or looking for a job, hardly arose. The choice was either to do what work was provided or to leave. An American sociologist who spent several months in the depths of Co. Clare in 1932 believed that this remoteness from the operation of the market economy went deeper. Many people engaged in agriculture in Ireland, he noted, worked not for wages and salaries but by virtue of their family relationship. The 'boys' working on the family farm had literally no money; if they wanted a drink on market day or to go to a hurling match, they had to get the cash from their father. If they went on a message they frequently left the paying to 'the da', who would come later. Even money earned away from the farm, on the roads etc., was frequently paid not to them but to the father.[1] (The political implications of this detachment of large numbers of voters from daily economics must have been profound.) In the city, things were different. The price of the extra freedom was uncertainty, especially in an economic crisis such as that which struck the world after 1929.

Work of some sort had to be sought and found. For the middle class there were several options. The civil service was attractive because secure, prestigious and pensionable; unfortunately, entrance was extremely competitive, with fifteen applications for every Leaving Certificate level post, and twenty-two for those at graduate level.[2] The professions were possible only to those who could afford both the very high premiums, the long unpaid training period and, in most cases, the necessity to be

*Anglo-Irish at the RDS Horse Show. They were always better at style, physical
courage and loyalty than more utilitarian virtues. To smoke in public, as the young
woman on the right is doing, was considered rather fast.*

introduced by a partner in the practice. Medicine was a possibility, if the long training period could be afforded, but since three-quarters of doctors ended up overseas, without contacts or luck that was a one-way ticket. Next came the banks, the railway companies and very large firms, of which Guinness was the best organised.

In terms of numbers, the big employers were the civil service, with 20,000 employed, the railways, with 12,000, and the breweries with 4,200. The other big employer in the state was the Sweep, with 4,000 employees, mostly female clerks. After that, various possibilities might appeal: the army, national school-teaching, engineering, nursing, or if family contacts allowed, a job in Eason's, Jacobs, Bewley's or similar businesses. The larger firms were nearly as secure as the civil service. Entrance to them was usually dependent on an introduction and the provision of some kind of security (a Guinness clerk had to provide £200 in this way, equivalent to the first year's earnings). Very few applicants could offer paper qualifications: in 1930 a mere 999 boys and girls sat the Leaving, and 2,659 the Intermediate. Nearly 20 per cent of national school pupils, on average, were absent every day.[3] Consequently, many large firms set and marked their own entrance examinations. Other paper qualifications such as degrees were little regarded by either business people or professionals. Indeed, as the business spokesman, William Hewat, said in the Dáil, 'the man who went through college has always been dissatisfied to enter an occupation which his university training made him think was beneath his dignity'. Even then, the opinion was becoming old-fashioned. The commerce faculty in UCD was the third largest in the campus, after medicine and arts.[4] As it happened, Hewat's practice was not so forthright as his theory: his son Jimmy, who later became chairman of the family firm Heitons, went to Trinity, as did his daughter, Elspeth, who became a doctor.[5]

Although there were pockets of resistance to recruitment of middle-class Catholics (Guinness being the best-known example), the situation had become more equitable since 1907. Now, 85 per cent of civil servants were Catholic, 83 per cent of employers, managers and foremen in industry, 80 per cent of railway officials, 70 per cent of lawyers, 64 per cent of civil engineers, 55 per cent of chartered accountants and 47 per cent of bank officials.[6] Some of the lag would simply be eradicated with the passing of time, but the law and the banking sector were still markedly Protestant. The accountancy figure reflects the fact that the small profession (industry was a long way from employing professional accountants) was dominated by two Protestant firms, Stokes Brothers & Pim and Craig Gardner, which between them audited two-thirds of the Irish stock exchange companies. Craig Gardner would not appoint its first Catholic partner until 1944.[7]

C. S. Andrews pessimistically described the job-hunting prospects for a new graduate from UCD in the late 1920s.

> University degrees, except in the case of the professions, had little value in the job market. Due to the activities of the ESB, electrical engineers were assured of employment and the local authority service provided openings for civil engineers, though often in roles well below what their training and capacity warranted. Apart from institutions such as the State Laboratory there were few opportunities for chemists or physicists and most science graduates were forced to turn to teaching. For arts and commerce graduates, teaching in secondary and technical schools was virtually the only source of employment apart from clerical or administrative posts in the public service.[8]

The alternative was emigration, the route taken, as we have seen, by most medical graduates.

For Andrews, there was the added disadvantage of having been on the losing side of the Civil War, he being one of several thousand released from gaol after the ceasefire. Most businessmen were unsympathetic, and even if they hadn't been, few firms liked the regular raids of their premises and investigations conducted in connection with these marked men, which were apt to happen every time the illegal IRA exploded a bomb.[9] Even the civil service was not immune: a tribunal set up by the new Fianna Fáil government at the end of the year was asked to investigate 700 claims of victimisation since 1922.[10] No wonder very large numbers of Republicans emigrated in the 1920s.

Personal contacts and influence were considered the key to employment. All entrants to banks, businesses and to professional practices had to be introduced by a director or partner. As Andrews wrote, 'The accepted wisdom of job-hunting in Ireland in those days was that it depended heavily on "influence",' so when he applied for a job with the Irish Tourist Board he 'followed the conventional route.'[11] He called, before 9.30, on his friend Seamus Moore, who was secretary of the Motor Traders Association and a TD. Moore was unaccustomed to callers so early in the day, and was only reluctantly persuaded after many protests about the inconvenience of the hour to put in a good word. By 5.30 that evening, Moore had called on Andrews with the good news that his potential employer (an ex-IRA man from Ballyporeen) would see him the following day. After some reminiscing about the Civil War days, Andrews was offered the job at £4 a week. As late as 1958, Aer Lingus infuriated Fianna Fáil backbenchers by writing to them that canvassing on behalf of job seekers would disqualify—'the majority of the party strongly resented the letter' wrote a contemporary.[12]

Whatever the job, £4 a week was a relatively good starting salary (twice the average wage of a labourer). The new state had not changed the fact that society was carefully divided into layers, both in the country and in the city. In financial terms, the gulf between the rich and poor was still wide, though the erosions of inflation and social change meant that the gap was not as wide as it had been twenty-five years previously. In 1930, the top civil servants earned £1,500, whereas a casual labourer in the city, such as a jobbing gardener, was glad to work for 6s or 7s a day, or £100 a year—a labourer in the country (as ever, the very bottom of the pecking order) might get less than 15s a week. The range of incomes in the city was therefore 15 to 1, compared to the 30 to 1 ratio before the First World War. It might not have seemed so to those living in the crumbling tenements of Henrietta Street, watching the dark-suited barristers passing to and fro to the Kings Inns, but this was a less unequal society than before 1922.[13]

A qualified national school teacher could look for £140 a year (£2 13s a week), rising to £300; a railway clerk started at £80 a year, and on promotion could hope to rise to £350 or more. A tax inspector got £221 to start with, and a dispensary doctor £300. An executive officer in the civil service started at £144 a year, and a bank clerk at £100.[14] At this time the average industrial wage was £129 a year, and a live-in cook cum general servant (referred to in the small ads as a 'general', could be had for less than £30 a year). A farm labourer had no more than £50 a year. Probationer nurses got £10–£12 a year in the first year, after paying substantial fees to the hospital for the privilege.

At the other end of the scale, top civil servants earned £1,500 a year (reduced to £1,000 after the election in which Fianna Fáil came to power for the first time); the six partners of Craig Gardner shared £22,000; the managing director of Clerys got £9,460 (including £6,460 commission on profits). The Revenue Commissioners reported that some 1,500 people paid surtax, which meant that they had a taxable income of at least £2,000 a year; 28 people reported a taxable income of over £20,000.[15] The best-paid people in Ireland were the three promoters of the Hospitals Trust, who received an annual fee of £80,000 for their part in organising the Sweep—the top winners of the Sweepstake itself were considered comfortable for life with their £30,000 prize.

Since 1912, as much as 35 per cent of civil service pay had been based on the cost of living figure. This was fine as long as prices went up, but since 1929 prices generally had fallen, and with them civil service salaries. A government committee was set up in 1932 to investigate the grievances of civil servants, whose incomes both in real terms and in relative terms had worsened considerably in the last few years.[16] (In December, the *Irish Independent* noted that a skilled tradesman's wages had gone up 2.28 times since 1914, whereas a typical civil service income had risen only 1.71 times.) Furthermore, this reduction had been marked in the years since 1929. The Civil Service Federation, on behalf of its members, argued that the cost of living index was based on working-class expenditure patterns, not that of the middle class.

The Federation claimed that there was a significant difference in expenditure and life-style between the middle and the 'wage-earning' class, and that middle-class expenditure had fallen considerably less. To make out this claim they had to detail exactly how widely the kinds of things the middle class bought differed from those of the working class. What resulted was an explicit, unselfconscious (and, in the event, officially endorsed) description of the social benefits of the class system to the middle-class civil servants.

The first point they made was that 'the average civil servant's household budget includes items which do not appear at all or only to a negligible extent in that of a working-class household. Such items are travelling expenses, life insurance, restaurant meals, medical expenses, books, maidservants, etc.' (It is curious to see books, restaurant meals, maidservants etc. turned into a burden and grievance.) Travel expenses arose because civil servants were effectively obliged to live in the suburbs rather than the city centre. Medical expenses were listed because middle-class people could not avail of the free services of the hospitals or the dispensary system.

It was clear also 'that the circumstances of a civil servant's household differ greatly from that of a working-class household. At least one maidservant is normally employed, and the period of dependency of the children is more extended than in a working-class family.' Equally revealing was that for the cost of living index 'prices are collected for the index which do not appear at all in the expenditure of the average civil servant. An example is margarine (third grade)'. Not only that but middle-class civil servants 'are usually obliged to purchase [in different shops] from those of the working class and price movements in such not being subject to the same intensity of competition are different from other markets.'

In summary, the Federation declared that the average civil servant's income was spent on a quite different bundle of goods and services from that on the cost of living index. Nothing like as high a proportion of his income went on food, up to three times as much was spent on rent, less was spent on clothing but much more on sundries. 'That is', declared the Federation, 'the result one would expect, i.e. the increase is devoted to a considerable extent in maintaining a middle-class style of living with its attendant emphasis on suburban residence, maidservant, education, holidays, etc.' This was a frank recognition and characterisation of exactly what the Irish class system meant in 1932. After close examination of various sets of figures, the government committee agreed with the Federation, and recommended that a separate index based on middle-class expenditure be set up.

In August 1932, the number of established and unestablished civil servants was just under 20,000, of whom 1,700 were in the top administrative and executive grades, 1,000 in the professional and scientific and the rest in clerical and 'minor manipulative' (e.g. postmen etc.) A third of civil servants earned less than £100 a year and 60 per cent less than £150. The argument was, therefore, largely concerned with the top 3,000 or so civil servants, whose incomes ran up to £1,500 a year. This was virtually all available for spending. Even after the aggressive Fianna Fáil budget of 1932, which pushed the nominal rate up to 25 per cent, income tax rates were trifling by modern standards. Once earned income relief and allowances were taken into account, a married man with three children paid less than 1 per cent tax on earnings of £500 a year, and at £700 he paid only £44. Four out of five civil servants paid no income tax at all.

Table 1 shows how the money was spent at different levels of middle-class income. As is normal, the first call on every income was for food. At the lower levels of earnings just over 40 per cent of net income was spent on food, as opposed to less than one-third at the higher levels. In actual amounts, the higher civil servants spent £200 a year on food; those earning approximately the average civil service salary spent £70 a year. The richer families, by comparison, spent £112 a year on personal expenses such as charities, holidays, subscriptions, amusements. To an extent, the table shows the effects of increasing promotion over time (and increasing family size). An executive officer starting on £144 a year could reasonably hope to increase his income three or four times over his career.

Table 5 Proportionate distribution of expenditure in civil service households (1932)

Income range	<£300	£301–£400	£401–£500	£501+
Average income of group	£166	£341	£451	£726
Average family size	4.3	4.5	5.3	6.2
Food	41.2%	36.7%	35.1%	29.1%
Housing	16.3%	15.8%	18.1%	15.2%
Clothing	9.1%	8.8%	7.7%	10.5%
Fuel and light	6.6%	5.9%	4.6%	3.9%
Household	5.2%	6.9%	7.8%	7.7%
Education, medical	3.7%	4.5%	5.7%	8.6%
Personal expenses	9.9%	13.0%	11.6%	15.6%
Income tax	–	0.9%	1.7%	4.5%
Sundries	8.0%	7.5%	7.7%	4.3%

But what did this mean in terms of actual food eaten? In 1943 *The Bell*, then edited by Sean O'Faolain, published a graphic series of articles exploring how people spent the money they earned.[17] Despite the leap in the cost of living between 1932 and 1943—the retail prices index jumped some 60 per cent in the first years of the Second World War—to say nothing of the distortions caused by rationing and scarcities, it is unlikely that the styles of cooking and organisation of food would have altered markedly in eleven years. Certainly, such menus as these remained the staples of everyday family cookery until the 1970s, when exotics such as pizza, spaghetti, lasagne and curry began to become generally acceptable.[18]

The series began with the spending of a young solicitor who was earning the equivalent of £500 a year in 1932 values. He lived in Clontarf in a relatively new house (about ten years old); he employed a maid, and a gardener who came once a week. He had three children, a car, some books, a radiogram, and a set of golf clubs. He came home from the office only at the end of the day; he did not drink any wine except sherry, though he always had a spot of Irish in the decanter. He dressed carefully, as befitted his profession, was home loving, liked opera, and occasionally went to the Gaiety, but did not care much for the cinema.

In a typical week his family dinner menus were as follows:

Sunday: A roast, with two vegetables, and a sweet, usually fruit and whipped cream. Coffee was served at every dinner.

Monday: Cold meat with hot vegetables; a sweet, typically rice pudding or a steamed sponge pudding.

Tuesday: Soup from vegetables or stock, brown stew with mixed vegetables and again a simple sweet.

Wednesday: Soup, rabbit in casserole with rashers of bacon, potatoes and one other vegetable; junket and stewed fruit.

Thursday: Steak and kidney pie with two vegetables; jelly and cream.

Friday: Vegetable soup, fish and two vegetables, or Spanish omelette; a milk pudding or cream cheese with biscuits and jam.

Saturday: White stew [lamb and potatoes] or hot pot; fruit, biscuits, cheese and jam.

For breakfast, there was always porridge and bacon and eggs or poached eggs or the like, and the children all had eggs. The solicitor took lunch in town every day. To meet this growing requirement, Bewley's and other eating places expanded their original menus of tea or coffee and cakes during the 1930s, and developed snack-type meals.[19] In September 1932, an enterprising entrepreneur announced a service offering businessmen and bridge parties 'a dainty basket containing tea, coffee, cocoa, milk or Bovril and a choice from forty different types of sandwiches'.[20]

On an income of £250 a year, catering was on a less assured scale. Mr X, a civil servant aged forty-five, had four children and lived in a house that he was in the process of buying. He smoked, took a bottle of stout now and then, had friends in for Bridge or penny poker, and once a week went with his wife to the pictures. Two of his children went to a private school, which was a financial strain. It had already necessitated Mrs X doing without her maid, which meant, among other things, that she had to look after all her clothes herself, a significant task in the early days of labour-saving devices such as electric irons ('A practical present for Christmas,' suggested the ESB in December, at only 14s, compared to a weekly housekeeping budget of, say, £2.). However, they both felt private education was necessary for class reasons. 'Well, it would be pretty awkward for Mrs X having to face the people on the road, and Mr X wouldn't feel too good about it in the office either.'

Similar class pressures were felt in the costs of health care. For those who were admitted into the public wards of the charity hospitals, care was free; all others had to pay, and pay dearly. When the young solicitor's wife was confined with their youngest, the total costs worked out at nearly 10 per cent of his comfortable income for the year. As the novelist Annie M. P. Smithson, who was editor of *Irish Nursing and Hospital World*, noted in the July issue: 'The very rich and the very poor have no cause to complain under the present system. The hardship falls on those who are neither rich nor poor. The middle classes are too proud to go into the public wards of our hospitals, and are not wealthy enough to pay the fees required by first class nursing homes.'[21]

The Xs' menus were simpler than the young solicitor's. On weekday mornings, breakfast consisted of sausages, or porridge, or black and white pudding with fried bread; cocoa for the little ones, coffee for the grown-ups. On Sunday mornings every member of the family got an egg for breakfast. When the girls came home from school for the midday break at half-past twelve there was a light lunch—usually soup with plenty of bread and a drink of milk, and whenever possible fruit, either raw or stewed. The soup was made with stock and plenty of chopped vegetables from the garden. The children's tea was ready at half-past four. This consisted of bread, jam, cheese or potato cakes. Dinner was at half-past six on weekdays and two o'clock on Sundays.

On Sundays, Mrs X served a pot-roast or a joint of corned beef. Cold meat or shepherd's pie on Monday, and hamburgers made of minced steak on Tuesday. Wednesday was meatless, and the family got a vegetable compote, or cauliflower cheese, or an omelette and a pudding of some kind. On Thursday there was Irish stew or braised steak or sausage pie. Friday's dinner menu was the same as Wednesday's. On Saturday, there was nearly always fried liver and onions and, whenever the butcher was obliging, a stuffed baked heart. Supper, later in the evening, consisted of either cocoa or coffee with bread and butter and cheese.

Although they were presumably near enough to be believable by a contemporary audience, these menus are more varied and elaborate than seems likely. In considering the typicality of the *Bell*'s menus, the complete absence of tea is suspicious, even in wartime. Also, neither list of menus mentions the old staples bacon and cabbage or steak and onions, for instance, while both include the relatively exotic omelettes. An article in the generally quite adventurous *Model Housekeeping* by their cookery expert Mrs Hughes Hallet starts diffidently: 'I am sure that most of us think that the French are the only folks who can make omelettes and soufflés, but with a little care and patience you will be able to make them equally well.'[22]

In most middle-class homes simplicity and monotony was the rule. Roast meat was relatively cheap, and could be served cold, minced and other ways during the week; fish of course was customary on Friday. Todd Andrews, visiting the de Valera family at home in Blackrock recorded the household meal, which 'consisted of rashers and eggs, bread, butter and jam'.[23] This was in line with the rather narrow and cramping cult of plainness that was common in Irish-language circles. The future Taoiseach Garret FitzGerald's household diets were not much more sophisticated: 'We were very traditional eaters, porridge and bacon and egg [for breakfast] and the main meal would be meat, potatoes and vegetables. A chicken would have been unusual, bacon was more expensive than beef.'[24] In the Mulcahy household in Rathmines, Risteárd and his siblings enjoyed 'simple but adequate fare, with an emphasis on boiled eggs, potatoes and vegetables, mostly the cheaper cuts of meat (including pig's cheek!), dairy foods, bread and jam, rice pudding, apple pie and tart, tripe and our favourite in later years, and Maggie's speciality, cheese and tomato soufflé'.[25]

At this time there were two traditions of evening eating—the provincial high tea, and dinner later in the evening. Terence de Vere White, who went up to Trinity in 1927, described the resulting social struggle, between 'those who had brought to the city the ways of the country and refused to change them; to dine late, like wearing a top hat, was a symptom of political unsoundness.'[26] Even those who dined relatively early, at seven, say, could do it in style. Here a novelist describes a young solicitor being entertained by a newly-married shipbroker and his wife: 'Middle-class comfort had its good points. The bare mahogany table with its blue table-linen, its blue bowls of flowers, the sense of order and cleanliness, the soft light, the burgundy; it was all very attractive.'[27]

There were less formal entertainments, of course. For those with invitations, there were 'at homes'—Oliver St John Gogarty's in Ely Place, where the famous throat specialist paraded, or Sarah Purser's second Tuesdays in Mespil House. At AE's Sunday evenings, the guests ate slab cherry cake while perched on various uncomfortable chairs and boxes, and listened while AE, a mixture of sage and Buddha, boomed away.[28] 'Wit' in the old style was taken extremely seriously. At one of these parties (which were run on nothing stronger than tea or coffee) Olivia Robertson noticed a hush: 'Lennox Robinson, very long and thin, and Walter Starkie, small and plump, had begun a duel of wit . . . they cut and thrust verbally at one another, they backed, they feinted, thrust, parried, attacked and all the time the audience listened as connoisseurs . . . it was not the meaning that mattered, it was the technique. It was a work of art.'[29] As in Mahaffy's day, style was more important than substance.

In August 1932, a dashing new form of entertaining, including alcohol, appeared. The *Irish Tatler and Sketch* reported the introduction of the cocktail party by the Secretary to the American Legation. 'A most enjoyable affair,' wrote the *Tatler*, 'and a new idea to Dublin. Cocktails with the accompaniment of chips and almonds, tiny onions, olives and sandwiches.'[30] In December, *Model Housekeeping* suggested a simple supper party, which, it said 'is always appreciated, especially on Sunday nights. For supper, two courses are ample, or if a third is desired, soup in the winter is always welcome . . . the menu selected is lentil soup, chicken with tomato sauce, and green salad, trifle.' It is striking to compare this meagre offering with the multi-course family meals proposed by 'Short'.

Contemporary cookbooks, such as the *Tailteann Cookery Book* by K. Warren, which was originally published in 1929 and reprinted in 1935, do not suggest much variety. This book, which is aimed at housewives and cookery students, is frugal and unadventurous. The preface notes (somewhat depressingly) that 'special care has been taken to avoid anything in the nature of lavish expenditure in purchasing the different ingredients'. The *Tailteann Cookery Book* is cookery for living. In this it no doubt reflected the tastes of the Irish middle-class eaters. Herbs are rarely mentioned, garlic never; neither wine nor other alcohol appear, though occasionally a teaspoon of Worcester sauce may be recommended to add flavour; meat is heavily cooked (20 minutes is recommended for a steak, 25 minutes a pound for lamb) and frequently accompanied by stuffing, filling or additional pieces such as hard-boiled eggs or dumplings. These were egg-sized lumps of flour and suet mixed in cold water with a little baking powder and then cooked and served, for instance, with boiled beef. Ms Warren's book contains no mention of rice, except for use in puddings, and scarcely any pasta, except macaroni; cheese is simply cheese, presumably reflecting the poor range available on the Irish market; puddings, on the other hand, were prominent—rice pudding, baked bread pudding, tapioca pudding, bread and butter pudding; college pudding (yet another device for using up stale bread), semolina pudding—all good solid vehicles for calories and carbohydrates.

No doubt Ms Warren knew her market, and her opinion as to the unadventurous nature of Irish tastes is backed by anecdotes. Certainly, the remarkably wide range of goods Findlaters had sold before the war had by 1932 shrunk considerably.[31] The enjoyment of food was not a respectable topic of conversation: a contemporary etiquette book bluntly tells the reader that 'conversations whose only subject is eating or drinking are unworthy of a rational being, much less a Christian.'[32] The kitchen was the woman's territory and area of command, so for a man to know anything more than vague generalities about food (oysters in months with an R, the rareness or otherwise of steak) was uncommon, not to say uncomfortable. A mild connoisseurship of wine was much more acceptable. Thus when the district justice Kenneth Reddin wants to describe positively a middle-class meal in his novel *Somewhere to the Sea* (1936) he describes the burgundy evocatively if oddly ('down-right solemn and gently mulled') but for the food he can muster no more than 'excellent'.[33]

More sophisticated attitudes to cooking were to be found in individual households, and notably in restaurants such as Jammet's, still the best restaurant in town, and hotels such as the Russell and the Shelbourne, where the Swiss chef, Otto Wuest, took his job extremely seriously. In a little pamphlet published in 1930, he explained how he planned a dinner for the hotel guests.[34] The chef had noted a new and less lavish trend: 'of course, some dinners are double the amount of what is here described, whereas others are only half the size, or maybe only one or two courses. The tendency is to eat much less than in times gone by.'

Less was being drunk, too. Between 1926 and 1929 the nation's drink bill was estimated to be about £16 million, or some 10 per cent of the national income. Since then expenditure had shrunk to £12.7 million in 1932, a source of some worry to the Department of Finance, since duties on alcohol represented over a quarter of Exchequer receipts (income tax represented less than 15 per cent).[35]

Housing was the next drain on income. Three-quarters of civil servants still rented accommodation, but purchase was gradually becoming more common. The grand places for the Catholic middle classes to live were still on Dublin's southside—Haddington Road church topped the parish donations to the Pope again in 1932, with a donation of £113, well up on the 1907 equivalent. Rathmines was ceasing to be a Protestant stronghold; its donation was only 15 per cent less than Haddington Road. Rathgar, however, still gave considerably less than Beechwood, maintaining its exclusivity rather more stubbornly. Donnybrook was only a little behind Haddington Road, and Blackrock gave less than half.[36]

Perhaps as a result of the prevalence of renting, house prices in the most attractive parts of Dublin were not high; a three-reception, six-bedroom house in Rathgar could be got for £1,400 (just less than the annual salary of a top civil servant before the election); a four-bedroom house in Drumcondra was offered at £835. A new estate near Milltown golf course offered six-bedroom houses for £2,200, and a newly built semi-detached house in Anglesea Road, with two sitting rooms, five bedrooms, a bathroom (with running hot and cold water) was available for £1,650.[37] However, mortgages were not easy to obtain. Banks would only lend money to businesses (and farms, public houses etc.), and the building societies were undeveloped.

After food and shelter, the family budget had to provide clothing. By 1932, the elaborate female clothes of the Edwardian era had been abandoned, and a simpler line was in vogue. Women's fashions had changed so much under the influence of Paris couturiers such as Chanel that the distinctions that formerly obtained between a dress suitable for dinner and full evening dress, or a dress for the town or one for the country had blurred. Nonetheless, for both sexes it was extremely important to wear the right type of garment for each occasion.

The rules for men were more precise than those for women. A correspondent to *The Irish Times* wanted to know if it were *de rigueur* to wear a top hat to the first day of Punchestown: 'Some men,' he noticed, 'wore top hats, others low ones—only fancy the uncomfortable mixed feelings'. The most formal wear was evening dress (tails and a white tie), always worn with black patent leather shoes; next came a dinner jacket; for day, a morning suit (grey tails), a business suit (in black), a lounge suit, plus fours and a sports jacket for golf, flannels or (better) whites for tennis and so on. Each of the suits might cost anything between 30s and 10 guineas, and the full set was only aspired to at the richest levels. Hats, however, were essential—men rarely ventured into the street without one, as contemporary photographs make clear. Ties, socks, shoes and accessories such as scarves, cufflinks, studs, were changed appropriately with the suit.

In daily life one's dress had to be, said one etiquette book, 'consistent with the age and rank of the wearer'.[38] It demonstrated sex, class and status at a time when each of these things was being challenged in different ways. Even the Vatican felt the importance of clothes; in

1931 it reinforced its disciplinary rules about the necessity for priests to wear clerical garb at all times. By this constant display the awe in which the priesthood was held was to be reinforced. According to the *Irish Ecclesiastical Record*, it was to 'give the wearer the prominence and conspicuousness which naturally appertains to a member of a select and very restricted order.'[39] This idea was widely accepted. The Protestant Archbishop of Dublin, John Gregg, loved tennis parties, but was loath to diminish his office by appearing in the Dublin streets in whites. 'So,' his biographer recalls, 'having dressed himself up in them, he would wear over the white shirt his accustomed episcopal black garb and don the episcopal black top-hat; proceed secretly to his garage whence he would be driven—the top part of him alone being visible—in splendid state to his host's door, to whose astonished gaze he would appear in pie-bald state, black above and white below.'[40] In the Fitzwilliam tennis club, guests who unwittingly wore brown belts with their whites were scolded by senior members, and the club secretary kept a supply of white belts for just such an emergency.

Clothes were everyone's barrier between the private body, with its mysterious life and unsettling orifices, and the outside world. The uneasy prudishness of the time made this barrier extremely important. Unfortunately for the moralists, the female fashions were becoming more revealing, in terms both of the amount of leg, arm, even chest on display, and of the actual female shape, no longer twisted and laden down by the corsets, bustles and petticoats of the Edwardian era. Idealists (usually male) tried to create a national costume, but really fashion came at first or third hand from Paris, a fact deplored by more than one writer: 'The leading fashion houses in Paris and other continental cities are almost all in the hands of Jews and Freemasons of an anti-Christian type', wrote Mary Butler in a Catholic Truth Society pamphlet.[41]

In 1932, the spring colours were 'pale green for evening wear; among the new colours were a dark blue and a dark red; black and a colour were again becoming the uniform of the well-dressed woman, with bows and ties rather than buttons.'[42] Clothes were bought in 'Madame shops' or boutiques, or in department stores. Of those surviving now, Clerys was middle of the road, and appealed especially to the country customers; Switzers 'was the very home of Anglo-Irish clothes, sporting hats in the windows, well-cut tweed suits and hand-worked linen blouses.' Brown Thomas ruled the other side of Grafton Street, where it catered for the new culture.[43] Shopping at these great stores was neither a daily chore nor an expedition, but a new pleasure. As a Brown Thomas advertisement proclaimed: 'Thousands of women are finding one of their chief enjoyments in and about the great Department stores . . . women enjoy their visits to these great emporia in just the same way as they enjoy the theatre or the dance.'[44]

President (as the head of the government was still titled) William Cosgrave was always impeccably dressed, and he always, so his tailor reported, wore Irish-made cloth. Just before the spring election readers of the *Irish Independent* were told that according to the editor of *Tailor and Cutter* magazine, President Cosgrave was 'one of the few statesmen who met with the approval of the Editor.'[45] With his morning suit and silk top hat, then the uniform of international diplomacy, the prestige of the country was safe. Ireland could, at least in sartorial terms, take its place among the nations. The Fianna Fáil party took a different view. Republican simplicity was their objective, in line with their appeal to the rural working class and the small farmers. They wore the formal dress of the bulk of Irish men—a dark Sunday suit. This became a political point—opponents felt that the new government was letting the country down by appearing in such informal wear as a lounge suit, as though a modern head of state appeared at a formal occasion in jeans.

De Valera stuck to this policy of simplicity, to the astonishment of the papal party, during the Eucharistic Congress, but felt less sure when planning his visit to Rome in 1933. There was a frantic exchange of telegrams between Dublin and the Irish ambassador, Charles Bewley. Was it necessary, enquired the cables, for de Valera to wear a top hat on his way to his audience with the Pope? The answer was yes, so de Valera took a hat and, as Bewley put it, wore it 'whenever there were no photographers about'.[46]

Not all de Valera's ministers were so scrupulous about top hats and morning suits. At the Imperial Economic Conference in Canada in 1932 Seán T. O'Kelly, Seán Lemass and Jim Ryan all wore morning suits, in marked contrast to their wear for the Eucharistic Congress. The Dublin film censor and wit James Montgomery cracked—'cloth caps for Christ the King and toppers for King George.' The business of standing or not standing for 'God Save the King' was another symbol which provided a regular source of entertainment at the Horse Show, as loyalists attempted to make die-hards stand and remove their hats. At dances, the Anglo Irish always persuaded the band to play 'God Save the King' instead of 'The Soldier's Song'.[47] During the Ottawa conference observers watched with wry amusement as the ministers stood with the other delegates for 'God Save the King', but refused to drink the loyal toast.[48]

HOLYHEAD CONTRETEMPS.

Smuggling a few Sweep tickets to one's friends in Britain was a common middle-class way of making some pocket money. Only the most rigid moralists disapproved either of the Sweep itself or this illegality. (Dublin Opinion)

Chapter 11 Symbols and manners

In July 1932 a thoughtful correspondent wrote to the *Irish Independent* asking why it was that in such a conspicuously Christian country the Cross did not appear on the national flag. 'If external symbolism counts for anything—as I suppose it does—', 'Consistency' wrote, 'this humiliating anomaly' would be rectified at once.' The appeal fell on deaf ears, but certainly not because of a disbelief in the value of symbols. Quite to the contrary. Symbols, signs and manners were crucially important. From international political matters such as the Oath and the role of the Governor General, to the flying of flags, the naming of streets and of children, styles of personal clothing, manners and times of meals, everything had an allusive significance.

A vote in April to remove the Oath of allegiance to the King from the Constitution was won when the combined Fianna Fáil and Labour parties amassed 77 votes—'one for every execution!' shouted a Fianna Fáil TD in symbolist triumph. There was, however, another well-publicised oath controversy in 1932. In January, a rift was created in the Girl Guide movement over proposals to update their traditional oath of allegiance to the monarch. Strong and complicated passions were roused, and there was great backwoods resistance to any change. In the end the head Guide, Viscountess Powerscourt, suggested a compromise oath of allegiance to the Oireachtas (which included the King as well as the Senate and the Dáil). This, alas, was not acceptable to the diehards, who split away.

Meanwhile, another symbol had been reluctantly changed. The letter boxes had all been painted green, but for many the moulded monograms—VR or ER, albeit now no longer red—continued to give offence. For a long time, the council of the Irish Rugby Football Union refused to fly the Irish flag over Lansdowne Road ground; in February, in the middle of the general election, the Connacht branch protested against this, describing the refusal as an act of disloyalty, and a gesture of contempt to the state— which perhaps it was. After political intervention from Cosgrave himself, Lansdowne Road announced, not very gracefully, that it would, after all, fly the flag.

In July, the Governor General, James MacNeill, to sustain 'the honour and self-respect of Irish public life' published a series of letters that had passed between himself and President de Valera over the previous months. They referred to a campaign of petty harassment that the government had inflicted on him as the symbol of the British connection. The first event occurred in April, when two ministers, Seán T. O'Kelly and Frank Aiken, in accordance with cabinet policy, walked out of a dance given by the French Legation when the Governor General appeared. Dublin buzzed with rumours as to what had happened, and MacNeill wrote to the President asking for an apology. A few days later de Valera replied, refusing an apology and saying that the ministers had been as embarrassed as the Governor General: would he in future please submit a list of his engagements so that this should not recur.

The following month, MacNeill was effectively forbidden to invite distinguished foreign Catholics to stay with him during the Eucharistic Congress, a decision conveyed verbally to him by a civil servant; because he was to be present at a reception for the Cardinal Legate, the Army Band was told not to be there. He was not invited to the great state reception for the Cardinal. Eventually, MacNeill told the government that unless he received an apology he would publish the letters that had passed between them, which, after some attempts to censor them, he eventually did.

The mean-spirited campaign against a symbol continued. Since the Governor General could not be kept away from the Horse Show, the Army Band was forbidden to play there. In the long run it was clear that MacNeill could not win, and in November the King accepted his resignation. He was replaced by Domhnall Ua Buachalla, an Irish speaker and 1916 veteran. (The Cathal Brugha Cumann of the Gaelic League announced that to appoint an Irish speaker as a servant of King George was a symbolic insult to the Irish language.) Symbolising the new regime, Ua Buachalla did not use the Vice-Regal Lodge in the Phoenix Park, but lived in a house in Merrion Square. He carried out virtually none of the traditional duties. In December, he announced that he was not going to send King George the traditional woodcock pie for Christmas, on the grounds that he saw no reason for continuing the custom, especially since he hadn't met the King. When King Edward VIII abdicated in 1936, de Valera seized the opportunity to abolish the office. For a time it seemed as if Ua Buachalla was going to be left with the expensive Merrion Square lease, until de Valera eventually relented and accepted it as a government expense.

Personal manners were another symbol, valued as much for what they revealed as for their content. Recognising their importance for the establishment of a new class in Ireland, the Christian Brothers wrote and published a little book of etiquette for their pupils, called *Christian Politeness*. The book was designed to be used in class, it being recommended that pupils should read a chapter a week, and be examined on their mastery of the subject matter. The boys were urged to put the principles of the book into practice, especially at recreation times, when, as the author put it, 'rudeness is so apt to betray itself'.[2] As with any book of etiquette, the detailed rules give an intolerably mincing, and probably out of date, impression of daily life. The prigs who are held up in *Christian Politeness* as models to follow are not endearing. Furthermore, the act of learning such practices in class implies a self-conscious acceptance of the importance of etiquette rules that we now find awkward. Yet they were taken extremely seriously.

'Nothing', the Christian Brothers pupils were told, 'contributes more to exterior dignity and propriety of manners than exactness in preserving the natural position and motions of the body.' (As class marker, children's posture was a constant parental worry: in March the *Irish Independent* urged mothers to take special steps to teach their daughters to walk gracefully, as it was a key aspect of personal beauty.) The boys were urged not to so stoop when walking as to seem aged or feeble, nor to drag their feet, or twirl on their heels. They were to stand with the toes turned a little outward, with the heels slightly apart; on no account were they to rest their heads against the wallpaper. 'Young people should avoid crossing their legs, or keeping their hands in their pockets, or assuming a lounging attitude.'

On waking in the morning the pupils were told first to offer the day up to God, and then to rise and dress modestly. 'The use of the daily bath has now beome very general, and is highly to be commended.' Teeth are to be brushed every morning, and if possible at night: 'an inexpensive mixture of bark and camphor, or soot and salt, or camphorated chalk may be used with safety and advantage as tooth powder.'

The next section of the book deals with the many traps of the dining table. The prohibitions indicate a fairly rough starting point. The author states that 'it is vulgar to play with the salt cellar and spoon, knives, forks, etc.; to sponge up crumbs with your bread or to look curiously at the plates of others.' Other no-nos include loading the fork with large portions and filling the mouth ('excessively rude'), drinking tea from the saucer, handing your emptied plate to the servants, and holding the knife in the manner of a writing pen. One mustn't 'scrape up the last morsel as if cleaning the plate—indeed it is better to leave a little on your plate' (though not so much as to lead your hostess to think that you didn't like the food).

The mysteries of afternoon visits (evidently still a feature of social life) are dealt with at some length: 'While standing in the hall, it is exceedingly improper to hum a tune, speak loudly, finger the furniture, or gaze through the windows.' What to do with the hat, the umbrella ('invariably left in the hall') and the personal visiting cards are all discussed. The guest enters the drawing-room with the right hand ungloved, ready to greet the hostess, who advances a little way down the room for the purpose. He then sits, and enters into conversation with those nearby (even if he has not been introduced). Obvious conversational pitfalls the Christian Brothers' pupils might have expected, such as joking about religious matters, wounding Christian modesty, discussing the faults of a clergyman, or mocking the physical defects of others, are prohibited. Less obviously, they were warned against the use of irony, puns and the frequent introduction of proverbs. Slang —'objectionable and inelegant phrases such as "beastly dull", "rotten", "you bet", "all jolly rot"'—was deplored.

The Church generally took the view that class distinctions were natural and even beneficial: as Leo XIII had written 'inequality is far from being disadvantageous either to the individual or to the community'.[3] The working out of these subtle rules, the clash of symbols and the distinctions between people that they implied, were important hidden issues in the battle fought at the beginning of the year in the general election.

The Sweep

At the end of the 1920s the Dublin hospital system was in trouble. There were twelve general hospitals, thirteen special hospitals and four nursing homes, serving a population in the Greater Dublin area of 420,000. Most of the hospitals were small, with 150 beds or less. They were also largely in need of repair and of considerable investment in new equipment. Before the First World War, a surgeon had needed little more than a peg on which to hang his blood-soaked operating coat. Many operations had been performed in the patient's home, so a hospital needed no more than one theatre. By 1932, a self-respecting hospital needed six or

eight theatres, as well as X-ray machines, pathology laboratories, phys-
iotherapy apparatus and so on.[4] There were three maternity hospitals,
the Rotunda, the Coombe and Holles Street; they provided 169 maternity beds and 85 gynaecological beds. Fewer than half of the deliveries in
the Greater Dublin area were in hospital compared to over 80 per cent
in comparable American and European cities. The richer patients went
to nursing and maternity homes, the poorer gave birth at home. There
was a steadily growing trend towards hospital births, however, with the
number increasing by one-third between 1925 and 1933.

For years the main source of income for all hospitals had been the
subscriptions of the rich. Unfortunately, a combination of the increasing capital costs of equipment and facilities, and the fact that the most
generous of the rich had either removed themselves to England or lost
much of their money as a result of independence, left most of the city's
hospitals struggling to make ends meet. Even the best-endowed hospital for its size in the city, the all-Protestant Adelaide, in 1933 had an
income of £16,500 and an expenditure of £19,000.

Without the contribution from the Sweep, the three maternity
hospitals would have lost £7,500 in that year, which represented nearly
a third of their income.[5] The state certainly had no money to spare,
so when it appeared that the National Maternity Hospital in Holles
Street might have to close its doors for lack of finance, the government
reluctantly agreed to authorise a lottery to raise funds for the hospitals
generally. Thus was born the Irish Hospital Sweepstake. The idea was
not a new one. Governments had supplemented their finances by lotteries for hundreds of years before the efficiency of the income tax and
the abuses surrounding the lottery persuaded the British government to
abolish them in 1826. Since then they had been illegal, although winked
at on a parish scale. In 1918 an extremely successful lottery had been
organised to compensate the victims of the *Leinster*, the mailboat sunk
by German U-boats. The organiser of this lottery was a forty-year old
bookmaker called Richard Duggan—whose racetrack slogan was 'what
Duggan lays, he pays'.[6]

Ten years later Richard Duggan was one of the three organisers of
the sweepstake. His partners in the scheme were Joe McGrath, the
political contact, who had been in the IRA and also a minister in the
Cosgrave government, but had resigned after the army mutiny in 1925;
and Spencer Freeman, an engineer who had spent the First World War

in the British army organising munitions and supplies. Duggan designed the gamble, McGrath had the key task of generating sales, using his wide connections in government and among the scattered Republicans of the old IRA, and Freeman looked after the organisation and publicity. The ultra-respectable and Protestant firm of accountants Craig Gardner, where both McGrath and his brother had briefly worked, was appointed to perform the treasury and audit functions.

Hospital Trust Ltd set up offices in 13 Earlsfort Terrace, and the staff began to organise the first sweep, which was based on the November Handicap of 1930. Basing the gamble on English races such as the Grand National and the Derby, rather than Irish equivalents, ensured both that there would be large fields, but also that the race itself would be widely known especially in the key market for tickets. The English media gave the Sweep widespread coverage, at least until they were prohibited from doing so. The operation was from the beginning very well thought out in this as in other aspects. Rather than a simple lottery, which only allows one bite of the publicity cherry for each draw, the partners had decided on a sweepstake. This meant that there were two phases of excitement: firstly when the tickets were drawn against the horses, and then when the race itself was run.

From the beginning the venture was a staggering success. The promoters had promised a prize fund of £25,000, based on projected ticket sales of £100,000; they privately hoped for as much as £125,000. The structure of the gamble was different to the current state lottery in that two-thirds of the income was allocated to the prize fund as opposed to just over half in the lottery; beneficiaries consequently got less, and declared expenses (including promoters) were lower than the lottery, typically 10 per cent as opposed to 14 per cent.

The actual sales for the first sweep were a stunning £658,000.[7] The Public Charitable Hospitals Act earmarked 20 per cent of this for the hospitals, and two-thirds for prizes. This one sweep had increased the national expenditure on hospitals by one-quarter overnight. Expenses of running the sweep were declared to be £71,000, and the three promoters received the 7 per cent allowed in the enabling legislation, which came to over £15,000 each—or ten times what de Valera was getting as head of government. This sum swept them comfortably to the top of the highest earners' league. For the next sweep, on the Grand National of 1931, the sales receipts nearly trebled, to £1.7 million, and the hospitals got £439,000. The total expenses were less than 10 per cent, including the reduced promoters' share of 2.4 per cent, which worked out at £42,000.[8]

By the Grand National Sweep of March 1932 more than six million tickets were sold, worth £3.3 million. (Audited accounts were prepared after each sweep by Craig Gardner. Results were frequently reported in the newspapers, and a copy was despatched to each TD.) Each sweep was specifically and separately authorised by the Minister for Justice; theoretically he could stop the whole thing at any time, at the expense of over 900 jobs. Controversially, the enabling Acts allowed income to be declared after certain sales expenses. The nature and destination of these expenses have been the source of much negative comment since the 1970s. Then the journalist Joe MacAnthony suggested that less than 10 per cent of the money raised actually went to the hospitals, though his evidence for this is not clear.[9] Another author has adopted the words of the Presbyterian-oriented *Readers' Digest* in describing the Sweep as 'the greatest bleeding heart racket in the world'.[10] In the 1930s, the typical view in Ireland was no more censorious than it is today of the Lottery; the Sweep was obviously an extraordinary phenomenon.

There was, however, obviously a moral problem. From the beginning it was quite clear to the organisers and the government that Ireland alone would not be sufficient—tickets would have to be sold extensively in Britain and America, where such activities were illegal. This was at least an unfriendly international act. One can imagine the outrage if, for instance, Britain had decided to sponsor the export of condoms to Ireland. Going along with this, and the contortions relating to international postal regulations, the government soon compounded their morally dubious position by imposing a 25 per cent stamp duty on all monies paid to the hospitals. This more than doubled the stamp duty receipts. Even at home there were those with grave doubts, as there might be for instance if the government established a chain of brothels and then taxed the women at double rates.

In a rare (if not unique) burst of unanimity the *Catholic Bulletin* agreed with the Church of Ireland Archbishop Gregg in deploring the operation. The Archbishop thought that 'it would be hard to find anything more cynically callous than this trading upon greed and profiting by the losses of others. The most repellent part is that the sweepstakes are for our hospitals.'[11] For the *Bulletin* the Sweep was 'a great international scandal, a malignant menace, a putrid pool, a giant evil'.[12] (The origin of this overheated rhetoric is directly D. P. Moran's *The Leader*, which itself was perhaps influenced by the nineteenth-century papal invective against Italian liberals who were variously described as 'dropsical, impious children of Satan' and 'stinking corpses'.) Similar attacks, without the *Bulletin*'s characteristic language, came from the Dublin Presbyterians and Methodists. Some hospitals, notable the Adelaide and the Rotunda, refused to participate. Bethel Solomons later said that his greatest contribution as Master of the Rotunda was to persuade the hospital to participate in the Hospital Commission payout. Some people particularly disliked the humiliating sense of Ireland with an international begging bowl to finance the hospital system. In a meeting in Trinity the Rev. P. Hartford branded the sweepstakes as a 'form of national degradation', declaring that Ireland had become 'the thief of the world'.[13]

Others found the vision of a new type of Irishman, more like Shaw's Larry Doyle than Gaelic League, disturbing. Joe McGrath and his colleagues were hardworking, efficient, stylish and none too scrupulous. They created an enormous enterprise which was the wonder of the world in the 1930s, financed over two hundred hospitals, provided considerable if ungenerous employment in Ballsbridge, and all with money from abroad. They had also, and this was difficult to forgive, become very rich. Their like was not to be seen again until a new brand of Irish businessman appeared in the 1960s.

Whatever the terms used, the Sweep was undoubtedly (like the Eucharistic Congress) a superb feat of organisation. The tickets were priced at 10s each, and sold in books of twelve, two of which represented the agent's commission (the seller of a successful ticket was also entitled to a prize). Anyone could buy a book if they had £6 (two weeks' wages for a national schoolteacher), and enough rich friends. Notoriously, middle-class housewives regularly supplemented their dress money by judicious trips to friends in England with multiple tickets. The law insisted that every purchaser received a receipt from head office, a system which inhibited fraud and forgery by agents, and encouraged purchasers to feel a direct link with the Sweep that stimulated them to buy year after year. The enormous clerical task of supplying receipts meant that the Sweep quickly became a major employer in Dublin. With money coming into the office in more than forty currencies, 1,000 people worked in the foreign department alone. In a world where female employment was hard to come by, this alone made the Sweep a welcome addition to Dublin life, though there were frequently expressed doubts as to the low pay and onerous conditions. (The employment, of course, made it almost impossible for the Minister to refuse to authorise the three-times-a-year submission by the Hospitals Trust.)

There were jobs to be had elsewhere too. In the United States, McGrath used the arms- and cash-smuggling network of the IRA as a machine for selling lottery tickets. Their physical skills also came in handy for deterring the Mafia and others who saw the cash potential in the Sweep. However, in the early 1930s only about one in twelve of the tickets were sold in America; after the British counter-offensive in the 1935 Betting and Lotteries Act the proportion went to over 40 per cent.[14] The bulk of tickets, nearly three-quarters, went to Britain. Since the Sweep was illegal there, tickets had to be got into the country in various unofficial ways, and many people were involved in travelling to and fro with tickets. Special trains had to be laid on from Euston just before the Sweep closed to accommodate the hundreds of people coming from Britain with large sums of money to bet. The stewards on the mail boats and the Liverpool ferries were notoriously ingenious about smuggling large quantities of tickets, on one occasion inside a coffin.

Once the tickets were sold and the receipts dispatched, the six million or more counterfoils had to be taken to the place where the draw would occur. In 1932 this was the Plaza dancing and billiards hall in Middle Abbey Street. Three times a year throughout the 1930s, a flamboyant parade was organised, a touch of colour in the Dublin of the Economic War period—a period in which the most usual parade was of bedraggled herds of cattle on their way to slaughter. Hundreds of the employees dressed in fancy costumes—for the 1932 Derby Sweep 1932 8.2 million tickets were escorted through town in their boxes by 200 male and female jockeys, some on horseback. The organisers' inventive panache came up with other themes: one year it was a Haroun al Raschid theme, complete with real camels and asses; another Trojan slaves, with a wooden horse; another 'rare and strange fish'; another opera characters—two hundred Brunnhildes, Madame Butterflys, Titanias and so on.[15] These parades were not resumed after the Emergency.

The sheer physical task of ensuring that the millions of tickets were fairly mixed taxed Captain Freeman's ingenuity to the hilt. By 1932 he had devised a massive wind blowing machine, which was set up in the Plaza. After being thoroughly tumbled, the counterfoils were conducted on a miniature railway, escorted by the jockeys, Brunnhildes or Trojans, to the great 18-foot cylinder with six little doors from which they would be drawn. At the first Sweep blind orphan lads had been used to draw the tickets, but by 1932 it was felt that nurses were more in keeping with the spirit of the enterprise. The draw, like all the Sweep's operations, was conducted with maximum panache. The hall was decorated by the

Harry Clarke Studios, and elaborate precautions were set up to prevent the possibility of fraud. The operations were conducted by the publicity-loving General O'Duffy, the chief of police, in front of an audience; one year over two hundred foreign journalists attended to witness this phenomenon, including Edgar Wallace.

The unprecedented scale of the draw itself provided tremendous excitement and was a substantial tourist attraction. 'The whole town', wrote the diarist of the *Irish Independent*,

> had a holiday atmosphere this week. The number of people from every part of the country and from England and Scotland who find the draw a business which entails their presence in Dublin is extraordinary. The hotels and restaurants were working at a hectic rate. The streets were packed with motor cars and thronged with visitors. All the folk in and around Dublin who are always looking for things to fill in their leisured days were having the time of their lives sitting in the Plaza for hours on end, then meeting for luncheon and seeing everybody else they knew lunching too, then returning to the draw and sitting for more hours on end; and doing exactly the same thing for three days running.[16]

The record sale of over eight million tickets for June 1932 meant that the prize fund was divided into 28 units—28 drawers of tickets for the winning horse would each get £30,000; the second horse tickets £15,000, the third £10,000. In addition, there were the drawers of horses not scratched, and 100 cash prizes. The draw was a lengthy business, since over 3,500 tickets had to be pulled from the drum. The Sweep organisers had originally started with a single winner, but when an Italian café owner in Battersea in London claimed £354,000 with a single ticket, it was clear that individual winnings on that outrageous scale would jeopardise the future of the Sweep. Also, the publicity value of a win of £10 million is not ten times that of £1 million. So the organisers divided the receipts into units of £100,000. The more units, the more chances people felt they had.

Less than 8 per cent of prizes went to Ireland as a whole, and just over 5 per cent went to the Free State. Nonetheless, the Irish people managed to buy (for themselves or for others) over 370,000 tickets each time at 10s each. Virtually every household had an interest in the outcome; world-wide, it was estimed that over 30 million people were involved. The real value to Ireland of the Sweep, however, lay in what was not distributed as prizes. We can calculate at least the magnitude of this. Assuming that prizes were distributed in direct proportion to expenditure, the total ticket sales for the three sweeps of 1932 were £11.1 million, of which three-quarters came from Britain and Northern Ireland. Sales in the United Kingdom in 1932 amounted to £8.2 million, and £5.5 million was returned in prizes. This annual donation from Britain to Ireland of £2.7 million was enough to ensure the British government set up a Royal Commission to prevent the sales of Sweep tickets. It did not go unnoticed in Britain that this substantial 'invisible export' went a long way to recompensing Ireland for the losses caused by the Economic War.

Table 6 Distribution of 1932 Sweep receipts (£000s)*

Income

Gross Income	11,117
Less Prizes	7,436
Available for beneficiaries and expenses	3,681
Net contribution by IFS citizens	556
Purchases in Ireland	184
Prizes to Irish residents	372
Net Irish income	3,496
Less	
Expenditure	
Hospitals	2,779
Wages to employees	339
Expenses	321
Promoters' share	242

* Based on the accounts audited and presented to the Dáil by Craig Gardner and sent to every TD; does not include the controversial excluded sales expenses.

For the Sweep as a whole, the net income to Ireland in 1932, after deducting overseas prizes, was £3.5 million—the fact that this was somewhat more than the government's receipts from income tax makes the huge scale of the operation vivid. The effect of this inflow on the health system was enormous, as James Deeny, the Department of Health's Chief Medical Advisor, describes. 'Starting with forty county hospitals . . . we carried out a formidable programme. We built regional and teaching hospitals, regional sanatoria, mental hospitals, county hospitals, specialist hospitals, clinics, dispensaries and other health institutions. All in all between 1940 and 1965 more than two hundred hospitals were built, and another large number reconstructed.'[17] Deeny, however, observed that because the Sweep moneys were earmarked for hospitals, they could not be spent on, for instance, GP services, thus ensuring an uneven balance of growth in the health service as a whole.

An important further development in the health service was occasioned by the Sweep. As the money started to pour into the system, the sixty or more hospital boards started to devise ways to spend it. In the fragmented state of the medical system they did this quite on their own, with absolutely no regard to other hospital facilities in the area. Proposals were frequently presented to the Department of Health as of right, without any attempt to justify them. As a result of this lack of co-ordination the total claims quickly came to as much as eleven times the historically enormous sum of money now available. The official response was to establish the Hospitals Commission (1933) which began to co-ordinate expenditure, establish criteria for investment and generally lay the foundations for a hospital system. The medical establishment had trouble seeing the merits of this. 'It was difficult', wrote the Commission in the first report, 'to get the hospital authorities to see that the evolution of such a scheme must necessitate the subordinating of their individual interests to those of the community in general.'[18] Eventually, lured by the Sweep's funds, the proudly independent voluntary hospitals were gradually if reluctantly forced into a closer relationship with the government.

Chapter 12 Two grand narratives

The political trenches are dug

The great argument formulated in the 1880s about the development
of the nation had, it seemed, been squarely won, and not to the
advantage of the urban middle class. In Daniel Corkery's words 'the
three great forces' that made the Irish national being, viz. the Catholic
religion, nationalism and work on the land, had prevailed. With superb
timing the Fianna Fáil party, founded in 1927, expressed as its aims just
that combination of aspirations that hit the spot. As a result, for fifty
years afterwards, as the Labour activist Fergus Finlay put it, 'every Irish
election, as a broad rule of thumb, [had broken down] into Fianna Fáil
votes and anti-Fianna Fáil votes'.[1]

The objects of the radical new party were:

(a) to achieve the political independence of a united Ireland;

(b) to restore the Irish language;

(c) to create an equal opportunity social system to enable every Irish
citizen to live a noble and useful Christian life;

(d) to place as many families as possible on the land; and

(e) to establish Ireland as a self-contained and self-sufficient economic unit.[2]

These were the stirring, even radical, ideas the party started with.
They certainly upset the ruling political class who sniffed rank socialism. Once in power, however, TDs increasingly found that promoting
their constituents' local needs and maintaining a constant presence
at funerals and other gatherings took all their time, and were just as
effective in holding votes. It is a striking example of the dichotomy in
politics between what is said and what is done that the Fianna Fáil party
has been in government for 61 out of the 83 years since the party was
founded without having achieved *any* of its formal goals.

Despite this new departure, there was a frustration in the country.
The autonomy achieved by the 26 counties had proved less liberating
than hoped. The country and its open economy was still constrained
by external factors that seemed mysteriously to hold it back. Nineteen-

Two striking scenes from the Eucharistic Congress 1932.
Above: The Cardinal Legate proceeds to the altar through ranks of cassocked priests
before the culminating Mass on Sunday; the congregation stretches as far as the
camera can see.
Below: Grafton Street dressed overall in celebration. Pedestrians largely stick to
the crowded pavements, though at 4.50 pm there are only two cars in view—one
driving in the middle of the road, the other parked.

thirty-two was an election year. At the start William Cosgrave's party, Cumann na nGaedheal, was in power, as it had been since 1922. In the previous election, the second to be held in 1927, he had won 62 seats out of a total of 153; the next largest group was Fianna Fáil with 57. Six other groups held seats: Labour, Farmers, National League, Sinn Féin, Independent Republicans and independents.

Cosgrave called the election for early in the year so that the clamour of the hustings would not disturb the Eucharistic Congress in June. (A more calculating politician might have allowed the glow expected from that event to shine on him by leaving the election until the autumn.) The campaign began with the government party on the defensive. Cuts in government spending necessitated by the international situation (world trade had dropped 33 per cent in a year), had upset important groups of his voters. Even during the election campaign itself, civil servants, teachers and gardaí, natural supporters of the status quo and therefore fundamental parts of Cumann na nGaedheal's constituency, were threatened with wage cuts. Ten years in power had not improved the party's street wisdom.

Since the shooting of Kevin O'Higgins in 1927, Cosgrave had become obsessed with the idea that militant communists in the IRA presented a serious threat to the state, and had reacted with a security clampdown. The IRA was undoubtedly violent, active and dangerous. The guns and the violence of the troubled years still washed round the country. For years there had been a continuous series of shootings and attacks on police barracks. Month after month judges, jurymen and police were attacked or intimidated; '1931 was notable,' wrote one chronicler, 'for a remarkable upsurge in IRA activity, for killings, shootings and for continual seizures of arms and explosives by the police . . . the shootings of jurymen and police witnesses made it almost impossible to get a verdict in an ordinary court.'[3] When in 1932 *The Irish Times* produced its *Review* of the ten years since independence, it was not a surprise that the supplement started with a discussion of law and order.[4]

The Cumann na nGaedheal line in the election was a straightforward appeal to the conservative instinct—'keep a hold of nurse for fear of finding something worse'. 'President Cosgrave and his government have stood with you' proclaimed one advertisement. 'In the darkest hours they did not falter. They led you through the welter and chaos of civil war. They made the country safe for you. They established peace and progress. Their task is not yet done. Stand by President Cosgrave'.[5]

As the campaign wore on, Cumann na nGaedheal began to be more explicit about what exactly might be 'worse'. Previously bland and allusive statements became tinged with more vigorous scare tactics, exploiting the communistic leanings of the extreme IRA factions, and fears engendered by remarks such as Seán Lemass's comment a few years before that Fianna Fáil was a 'slightly constitutional party'. During the election Lemass developed his view that the Fianna Fáil policy was not communistic, it was the Irish equivalent of communism, a remark which did not reassure his middle-class hearers.[6]

There was undoubtedly a decisive class element in the contest, with the strong farmers and the urban middle class, strongly supported by the *Irish Independent,* frankly thinking that de Valera and his followers were, as one Cumann na nGaedheal minister saw it, 'incapable of governing—you have to have breeding to govern!'[7] Fianna Fáil proposed first of all to clear the ground by abolishing the Oath, the annuities and the governor-generalship (and those symbols of British hegemony, the frock coat and the top hat). These remnants of the ancient enemy removed, they would settle down to revitalising the economy, not by developing exports, but by stimulating home industries to meet home demand. The policy of protection, as proposed by the 1885 select committee witnesses, and taken up by Sinn Féin, was an important plank of the platform.

Although de Valera and his followers had described the Oath as an empty formality since 1927, it was a formality they found humiliating. The strength of their detestation naturally aroused a countervailing attachment to something which not even the British cared much about. ('We don't care a damn about the Oath,' said the wife of the president of the Board of Trade to Lemass at the Imperial Economic Conference in Ottawa, 'but we're not letting you away with the annuities.'[8]) The annuities were certainly another matter. They arose out of payments under various Land Acts by which British governments had financed the transfer of holdings from landlords to tenants. They and other connected payments amounted to £5 million, one-seventh of Irish merchandise exports, or one-fifth of annual tax revenue.[9] For Fianna Fáil there were economic, moral and legal reasons why they should no longer be paid. Put simply, their view was that the British had stolen the land in the first place, and now demanded to be recompensed for handing it back. For their opponents the issue was one of international credibility—a new state should not renege on its agreements. Neither side discussed what the lion might do if its tail was tweaked in this way.

In a speech on 3 February de Valera quoted at great length a legal opinion provided by various eminent lawyers to the effect that in strict legal terms the annuities could be withheld. (This opinion was echoed by one given to the British government later in the year, which partly explained their reluctance to go to independent international arbitration on the issue when de Valera suggested it.) Having proved to his satisfaction that the annuities shouldn't be paid to the British, de Valera did not explain why the farmers should go on paying them to the legal successors of the British in power. Indeed, some of the wilder Fianna Fáil orators let the farmers believe that they would not have to pay them at all.

By the end of January the election campaign began to hot up. Fianna Fáil took a large advertisement in the *Irish Independent* on 30 January describing 'The disastrous record of Cumann na nGaedheal, the greatest failure in Irish history!'. One of de Valera's favourite lines was to attack the waste of tax revenues in the payment of high salaries to public servants. Cosgrave, as President of the Executive Council (prime minister), had a salary of £2,500 at this time, and the ministers £1,700 each. These salaries, declared de Valera, would have to come down. A salary of £1,000 should be sufficient for any minister to meet his expenses and rear his family, and the same limit should apply to civil service salaries. One of the first acts of the new government was to reduce all ministerial salaries to £1,000; only de Valera's was fixed higher, at £1,500. It is not clear how this large difference between the leader's salary and that of an ordinary minister was justified, though the relationship was still maintained sixty years later. [10]

As the election wore on, Fianna Fáil were clearly making in-roads, despite the best efforts of the *Irish Independent* and *The Irish Times*, which always presented Cosgrave in the most flattering light, and as far as possible de Valera in the opposite. On 9 February, for instance, the *Independent* took great pleasure in reporting that Mr de Valera's speech in Feakle, Co. Clare had been loudly and frequently interrupted by the braying of an ass tethered to some railings.

In the country de Valera strongly appealed to the thousands of small farmers who participated very little in the exchange economy. For many of them the years of waiting to inherit the farm, and the closeness of the rural community, had implanted above all a vigorous understanding of the evils of dependence. An economic programme based on self-sufficiency was therefore extremely attractive, and if it implied that the country would have to make do with the 'plain furniture of the cottage' as de Valera put it, in order to live within its means, so be it. For them, after all, there was little to lose. The idea was, of course, less attractive to the middle-class.

In the cities it was clear that Protestant interests still held substantial ownership in the large companies and the banks and other financial institutions, and many Protestants made no secret of their continuing loyalty to Britain. The cultural freedom that nationalists had hoped for was also proving elusive (there was no sign, for instance, that book buying had increased). On the hustings and in the Dáil Fianna Fáil deputies declared they knew why this was so: Freemasons, allied with the British empire, were conspiring to prevent Ireland becoming truly free. The reason for Cosgrave's failure to govern the Irish people, said Seán Brady in Dún Laoghaire, lay in the shadow of Freemasonry. Lodge membership, he said, had grown from 21,000 in 1921 to 28,000 in 1928.[11] Two days before polling, one of the party's most senior men, Seán MacEntee, also attacked the Masons. The *Catholic Bulletin* developed the point in its usual vigorous style: 'The Mason stalks the land on imperial stilts. Tomorrow he will descend from those stilts to lay a grip on it that you will never release. Every diocese reeks with Masonic effluvia.'[12] The idea we have seen expressed by prominent churchmen that behind the Freemasons were the Jews, and behind the Jews, Satan, added unknowable power to this rhetoric.

It was clear that Fianna Fáil was offering something new, especially to the wider electorate in the country, while Cumann na nGaedheal was relying on the mixture as before, an uninspiring policy of 'proven leadership, sound policies', combined with scare tactics. The difference in message was repeated in the physical appearance of the two leaders. Cosgrave was small and conventionally dapper, with a wing collar and a trim moustache—the epitome of bourgeois elegance. De Valera appeared at election meetings in the country illuminated by rows of blazing tar-barrels in a great black cloak, riding a white horse—Emmet, Parnell and Pearse combined in one.[13]

It was not, however, merely a matter of style; organisation was a key part. The Fianna Fáil campaign book went into elaborate detail—candidates were told, for instance, always to site the speaking platform for a meeting in the corner of a square, not in the middle, so as to maximise the effect on the audience. Cumann na nGaedheal, on the other hand, had very little organisation, and what they had was pulled together more or less unenthusiastically for the occasion. Desmond FitzGerald, Minister for Defence, complained to his civil servants what a bore it was to have to go to Sunday morning chapel meetings and stand on a ditch making speeches.[14] Unfortunately for Cumann na nGaedheal, politics was rapidly becoming more professional. In UCD's L&H debating society, the political cradle of the next generation, a new worldliness had crept in. The winning candidate in the election for auditor was later unseated for having paid his supporters' membership fees. He had certainly overcooked the pudding, polling three or four times the normally successful number of votes.[15]

For his supporters, de Valera embodied Irish national aspirations, and was the recipient of intense personal devotion. In his autobiography, Robert Briscoe, who became a TD and was later Lord Mayor of Dublin, described his first meeting with de Valera: 'He took my hand in a firm grip, and shook it silently. I was too awed to speak at all. Nor did I have to. Our eyes meeting for those few seconds said all that was needed; his the warm friendly look of a leader toward a trusted subordinate, mine a pledge of utter devotion to him and to the cause he served.'[16] No one felt that way about Cosgrave.

As the first election results came in, it was clear that Fianna Fáil had done well, though there was from the first doubt as to whether they had done well enough to form a government by themselves. Both de Valera and Lemass had lost share of first preferences. In the event, Fianna Fáil won 72 seats, five short of an overall majority, but with the support of the seven Labour TDs they were able to form a government for the first time. Seán MacEntee calculated that at least 640,000 Catholics had voted for a change of government as against only 480,000 in favour of the government party: 'by a majority of one-third, the Catholics of the Twenty-Six Counties had rejected Cumann na nGaedheal.'[17] Although the source of these figures remained obscure it was certainly likely that the Protestants had followed *The Irish Times* in supporting Cosgrave. (Not all did this enthusiastically—to some he was still a 'murderous potboy'.[18])

The assumption of government by Fianna Fáil was a moment full of menace. On the right and the left (including *An Phoblacht*, the IRA newspaper) people saw de Valera as an Irish Kerensky, the bourgeois preliminary to Lenin's communist revolution, which had taken place in Russia only fifteen years before.[19] In late February, the *Irish Press* had noted rumours that a Cumann na nGaedheal clique were plotting a coup, and it is said that these rumours were sufficiently believable to encourage several deputies to enter the Dáil armed, including de Valera's son, acting as his bodyguard.[20]

The new government immediately set about doing what they had promised. The first step was to promote a bill to abolish the Oath. The next excitement came in Seán MacEntee's budget, which imposed taxes and duties on a wide range of new targets from silk underwear (90 per cent duty), and cosmetics to bachelors. Even then, income tax was not particularly oppressive. A man with two children paid only £1 2s 6d at £400 though surtax now began at £1,500, down from £2,000.

New duties were rapidly imposed on all postal packages and on soap, newspapers, wooden furniture, sports equipment, paper bags, tea, bicycles, matches and many other products. Ireland was on its way from being one of the least protected economies in the world to one of the most, a situation which held good until 1958. The range and speed of introduction of the new duties seems to have taken the business community completely by surprise, and the *Irish Independent* took a gloomy delight in reporting for weeks afterwards how the customs posts at the border were in disarray because of the duties, and on the docks the package tax meant that every parcel had to be opened.

Interest groups of all sorts made their case to be exempt from the new duties. Thus, at first all imported books and periodicals were to be taxed, later this was modified to a tax only on leather-bound books and entertainment magazines (which meant in effect largely those popular with women); at first all sporting occasions were to pay entertainment tax—then GAA games were exempted. Some of the taxes had not been well thought out. Mrs Collins-O'Driscoll (Cumann na nGaedheal) pointed out in the Dáil that vital components of women's corsets came under the newly taxable heading of Manufactured Articles of Brass and Steel, a point that had evidently not occurred to the somewhat embarrassed minister, who promised to change the regulation.[21]

Ireland calls her sons to her

In 1932 religion was important politically and personally to a degree difficult for us now to recapture. As Daniel Corkery put it: Irish 'religious consciousness is so vast, so deep, so dramatic, even so terrible a thing, occasionally creating wreckage in its path, tumbling the weak things over, that one wonders if it is possible for a writer to deal with any phase whatever of Irish life without trenching upon it.'[22] For the 96 per cent of the population whoe were Catholics, religion was simply *the* fact on the ground. Virtually all the population believed in the immediacy of the spiritual sphere, many to a starkly dramatic extent. Austin Clarke recalls that he was taught to regard a tiny ringing in the ear as the howls of a soul in Purgatory, the sound of whose terrifying agony was muffled only by the vast distance.[23]

No decision—medical, political, educational, social—could be taken outside the framework provided by the Catholic religion. De Valera himself said at the 1931 Fianna Fáil Ard Fheis, 'if all comes to all, I am a Catholic first', a remark echoed later by John A. Costello.[24] His main opponent, Cosgrave, was also a devout man, who expected guests to join in the family rosary if they arrived while it was in progress.[25] Alternative ideas could gain no foothold, for the consensus was so enveloping as to be virtually unavoidable. From childhood to deathbed, religion was dissolved throughout.

The material sphere—the normal subject of politics—was envisaged as merely part, and not the most important part, of the full world. The world was, so Cardinal D'Alton of Armagh put it at this time, 'a rugged and difficult path towards our true home in Heaven'. Life is but shadow and image in the face of this, and we are but strangers and exiles on earth.[26] This was not an attitude that stimulated a serious interest in the 'condition of the people' question.

For Irish Catholics there was added to this mighty scenario a special pride-making national role. Just as in the Dark Ages Irish missionaries had come from their remote Catholic fastnesses in the West to bring Europe back to the Church, so now, with the new barbarians (that is, communists, liberals and Jews) pressing hard once again at the citadel, the uniquely Catholic Irish could once again spread into the world and ultimately perhaps restore the glories of the thirteenth century. For some commentators even the spread of English through Ireland and the continuing emigration could be seen as part of this divine contingency plan. For the Irish nation included also those living beyond the seas: 'When Ireland calls her sons to her,' wrote the *Irish Press*, 'there is a stirring in every part of the Universe.'

A very high level of personal piety was common: serious-minded people were very often religious. Regular, often daily, attendance at Mass and the sacraments was common. Many senior civil servants were daily Mass-goers, and some, such as the new Secretary of the Government, Seán Moynihan, devoted Legionaries. At a more junior level, Frank

Duff, the founder of the Legion of Mary, was a civil servant, as was his biographer and future departmental head León Ó Broin. Mass-going was not the only arena for pious energy. Meetings, sodalities and prayer-groups were wide-spread. The 1932 Jesuit *Directory* lists as many as twenty-three separate and well-attended groups based on St Francis Xavier's in Upper Gardiner Street. These included the Confraternity of the Sacred Heart (separate branches for men and women), the Sodality of the Immaculate Conception (for young men), the Sodality of Our Lady Help of Christians (for commercial men), the Night Workers' Sodality, the Conference of St Mobhi (for Irish speakers), and the Sodality of the Assumption of Our Lady and St Martin (for civic guards).[27]

Nineteen-thirty-two was the fifteen-hundredth anniversary of St Patrick's coming to Ireland, and the Catholic Church was determined to celebrate in style, and did so with the Eucharistic Congress. Barely a century after emancipation, the present position of the Church in Ireland seemed to many commentators nothing short of a miracle. Time after time during the Eucharistic Congress foreign journalists marvelled at the sight of a nation, as it seemed, united in prayer. The celebrations were also an opportunity to copperfasten the group iden-tification of 'Irish' and 'Catholic' in a flood of boosterish rhetoric. The *Father Mathew Record* expressed the point thus:

> Because of his sins the Jew is left outcast, a wanderer, nationless; for the virtues of his ancestors the Irishman has a country, not only fair and green but one of saints and scholars . . . Irish nationality is so bound up with the foundation of all true nobleness, the Catholic Church, that the words 'Irish' and 'Catholic' are linked constantly. Our national standard is one erected by centuries of Catholic living, Catholic thinking, Catholic dying.

Throughout the year, writer after writer repeated the point. To be Irish meant to be Catholic; it was also to participate in some vague way in the ancient traditions of the Celtic way of life. (The fact that in the course of imposing a centralised church-based discipline since the 1850s, many traditionally Irish styles of devotion were prohibited in favour of Continental styles was ignored. For instance, holy wells were frowned on, and the ancient traditions of holding baptisms, weddings and funer-als from home were all abolished.)

The Irish nation had left the British empire, the greatest the world had ever seen, and joined a still greater. The *Catholic Bulletin* declared that, 'it is the pardonable pride of our Irish exiles that they founded a spiritual Empire . . . more extensive than that of Rome, more inspiring than that of Greece, more durable than that of England.' The ancient pomp and dignity of the Church was at least as spectacular as anything the British could supply, and had the inestimable advantage of being on the right side in the fight for the soul of the world. With this naturally came a certain self-conscious arrogance: thus when a British film-maker complained that the Irish censorship had no written rules or standards, an official no doubt took pleasure in replying: 'Our rules are now the oldest and shortest in the world; you will find them in any catechism. They are called the Ten Commandments.'[28]

From the beginning of the year preparations of all sorts for the congress were in hand. In January the city engineer worried in public about the water supply; daily usage had gone from 13 million gallons in 1907 to 17 million in 1932. It was not excessive bathing that roused his anxiety: for as Risteárd Mulcahy wrote of family life in Rathmines in the 1930s, a 'regular daily bath or shower . . . would have been considered a gross extravagance.'[29] The cause, he complained, was that people insisted on letting the hot water tap run to warm up before washing their hands, thereby wasting water. He feared, especially if the weather was fine, that water for the visitors to the congress would have to be rationed. The commercial opportunities of the occasion were not neglected. In the newspapers small ads began to offer items such as the 'beautifully painted' Eucharistic lamp bulbs, complete with pious slogans and papal insignia, (suitable for Shannon current, 40–60 watts, 2s each). The managing director of Clery's told his staff that 'clergy and nuns are objecting to Eucharistic emblems being put on drapery goods, carpets, linens etc.' so they were not to buy any more such items without consultation. Householders on the route of the procession were warned by the organisers to resist allowing advertising signs to be put up in their gardens. A few weeks later it was reported that Jury's had bought 190 cattle and 500 sheep in preparation for congress week. The *Irish Independent* urged householders to make sure that everything was spick and span in good time for the expected visitors.

The congress organisers defended themselves against the charge that not enough of its literature was available in Irish. They had printed 200,000 copies of one leaflet in Irish, they said, but only 15,000 had been sold, as opposed to 880,000 in English, 50,000 in French and even 10,000 in Maltese. By May the preparations were in full swing. Nearly every day the *Irish Independent*, in an increasing fever of excitement, reported some further titbit. On 3 May, for instance, readers were told of the advanced state of preparations of the floodlighting for Dublin's public buildings; that 70,000 children were expected at the children's Mass in the Park; that the government had sent out thousands of invitations for the official state reception in Dublin Castle; that as many as eleven cardinals were expected in Dublin during the congress. The following day, readers learnt that Dublin Corporation had arranged a special double shift of street cleaners for the week of the congress, and that sixty wooden huts to serve as temporary public conveniences were to be erected in O'Connell Street and other places. On 5 May, the main news page carried a story warning householders that the supply of suitable lamps and other decorations was running short. The abundance of these stories was not just a silly-season phenomenon in lieu of other news. The new Fianna Fáil government was also providing a steady stream of exciting events: on 5 May, for instance, the bill to abolish the oath was passed, a levy and bounty on butter was imposed. On the same day the Spring Show at the Royal Dublin Society opened.

In the middle of May an encyclical from Pius XI reminded everyone what was at stake. 'Subversive factions,' he told the faithful, 'taking advantage of the world-wide misery more and more brazenly unfurl their banners of wickedness and hatred of religion . . . formerly atheists were lost in the multitude, now they form a huge army that with the help of secret societies grows bolder every day.' His Holiness declared that never before in the history of the world had there been a crisis of such gigantic proportions as the present one, and he compared the danger of the situation to that of the time of Noah before the flood.[30]

As the time grew nearer, it was clear that the extent of participation was going to make this the biggest popular event ever held in Ireland, dwarfing O'Connell's 'monster meetings' or any such gathering. At every level, from decorating homes and streets to personal participation in retreats and prayer groups, people across the country wanted to take part. A *Eucharistic Congress Souvenir Number* published by the *Irish Independent* in early June ran to 96 big pages, being so successful that the journalists struggled to fill the space between the ads. It was not quite clear, for instance, how a page on the Maynooth Mission to China or a full page picture of Cobh cathedral were quite relevant, though perhaps it was no harm to be reminded that Archbishop Byrne had acquired Merrion Square for the erection of a cathedral 'worthy of the Catholicism of the Irish nation'. God willing, construction would begin soon after 1938.[31] The *Souvenir Number* did its best to make the papal representative, seventy-eight-year old Cardinal Lauri attractive, but the most interesting thing they could offer about this Curia apparatchik was the fact that when he was a professor in the Pontifical University 'punctuality was his long suit'.

TDs discussed the new duties on trousers and tennis rackets in the Dáil, and Miss Amelia Earhart set out on her bid to become the first woman to fly solo across the Atlantic (irritating some by insisting on using her maiden name). Clery's announced that they still had some pre-budget stocks in, including corsets for stout figures, usually 10s now 5s 9d, ladies' walking shoes 8s 11d, tweed skirts 4s 11d, linen table cloths 2s 11d. Special fast cheap excursion trains had been organised from Clonmel, Kilkenny and Enniskillen to enable shoppers to take advantage of the prices. The short-lived Irish magazine *Woman's Mirror* told its readers what to wear for the dances during congress week. 'On the whole, skirts are shorter, especially street frocks and suits. Garden party skirts sway just above the ankles and in the evening they clear the ground all the way round.'

Although the Papal Legate was not due to arrive until 20 June, the activities of the congress began on 5 June, with a week-long retreat for women. 'The city's womenfolk', reported the *Independent*, 'crowded the churches for the opening of the special retreat in preparation for the Congress.' A week later the men's retreat started. As the excitement mounted, rehearsals were held in the Park, and pilgrims streamed into the city. Some lived in special camps such as that erected at Marino, or the Knights of Columbanus's 1,000 tent encampment in Artane; others stayed on the numerous boats moored in Dublin Bay. The Girl Guides offered to put up Guide visitors to the Eucharistic Congress, and exposed themselves to the customary tirades of the *Catholic Bulletin*: these 'unsuspicious Catholic Girl Guides', wrote the editor, were being inveigled into camps so that they might be 'got at by Cromwellian Protestant women, whose very names drip with bitter hatred of all that the Eucharistic Sacrifice stands for.'[32] The organisers arranged for 275 interpreters to be assigned to various churches, and a special bill was rushed through the Dáil to allow vessels moored in the bay to serve drinks in their ballrooms.

Houses and streets were smothered in bunting: G. K. Chesterton described the formal decorations erected by the city, the 'great festoons of green garlands going from lamp to lamp with blazoned shields and emblems . . . there were the Lamb and the Dove and various animals fabulous or real who were symbols of medieval mysteries', and in the off streets, furnaces of colour erected by pious local groups. 'These mean streets glowed and glared like Oriental bazaars.'[33] (A similar profusion was visible, in a lower key, for Pope John Paul's visit in 1979.) Dubliners hastened to put into practice the detailed instructions in the official *Handbook of the Congress*. 'All householders are requested', wrote the organisers, 'to put a lighted candle in at least one window. Not more than a single candle should be put in any window, but all windows may have a candle, at householder's choice. Due precautions should be taken to prevent fire by tying back curtains and rolling blinds. The candle, which need not be of wax, should, it is recommended, be of Irish manufacture . . . it is hoped that business premises will be illuminated by gas or electricity.'

In an era when all businesses were clearly either Catholic or Protestant, there was much curiosity about how the Protestant firms would react. 'Several Protestant firms,' it was afterwards noted ominously, 'in response to the request of the Organising Committee, decorated their premises, but some firms, among them prominent concerns largely supported by Catholics and Catholic organisations and industries, absolutely refused to do so.'[34] The bullying note was unmistakeable. The debate in the United Arts Club was no doubt typical: the chairman, a Scots Presbyterian called Hill Tulloch (who was also senior partner of the accountancy firm Craig Gardner) resisted, on grounds of expense, the flying of flags, while Catholic members of the committee urged that not only should the national and congress flags be flown, but also the front should be painted, and flower-filled window boxes be added to the facade.[35]

The Papal Legate finally arrived at Dún Laoghaire at about 3 o'clock on 20 June, to be greeted by an enormous crowd of more than 50,000 people headed by President de Valera and his government (in suits, not frock coats). The correspondent of the *Revue des Deux Mondes* noted that 'from Dún Laoghaire Harbour to the Pro-Cathedral, a distance of ten kilometres, there was an unbroken mass of people, compact, deep, on both sides of the route. In the city the pavements and the squares were completely covered by the multitude.'[36] The *Irish Independent*'s *Eucharistic Congress Record* published at the end of June (only 64 pages this time) described the gun salutes, the aircraft squadron flying over in the shape of a cross, the speeches in Latin, Irish and English, the sixty-strong cavalry escort in a specially designed new uniform and the kneeling schoolboys outside Blackrock College as the cavalcade progressed into Dublin. The next event was a state reception in Dublin Castle, with speeches by de Valera in Irish and Latin. It was notable also for its array of ecclesiastical uniforms—'the Cardinals in their scarlet robes, the varying purples of the Archbishops, Bishops and Monsignori; the prelates of the various religious orders in grey, cream, black, white, brown; and the gorgeous robes of the high dignitaries of the East.' Over 2,500 special invitations had been issued. The guests filed past a dais on which sat the Papal Legate, the Archbishop and de Valera, before retreating to the refreshment tent. Conspicuous by his absence was the Governor General, James MacNeill, who had deliberately not been invited.

The big event of the following day was a garden party in Blackrock College given by the hierarchy and organised by the president of Blackrock, the Rev. John Charles McQuaid. It was claimed that over 20,000 people attended in the brilliant sunshine. The grounds were open to anyone who cared to go, and everyone who was anyone did; fashionables and politicals rubbed shoulders with archbishops and cardinals among the marquees and white-clothed tables. For women generally the colours of choice were blue and white, the colours of the Immaculate Conception.

Clerical uniform for this occasion and all others was elaborate and carefully laid down by the organisers. There was nothing Irish about it. Bishops were to wear house soutane, cincture (body belt) with fringe, violet ferraiola (full length cape), pectoral cross with gold chain, zucchetta (skull-cap), biretta (three-peaked clerical hat). On ecclesiastical occasions such as the opening ceremonies, bishops were to wear choir soutane (violet), cincture with tassels, rochet (knee-length white tunic often with deep lace fringe), pectoral cross, mantelata (knee length outer garment in red), zucchetta, biretta. Those celebrating pontifical High Mass would require in addition mitre, dalmatic and tunicle (white), buskins (embroidered silk socks), sandals and gloves.[37]

Irish Independent readers were told that over 250 gallons of cream were consumed at the garden party, as well as 400 lbs of slab cakes and 12,000 French fancies. A group of Dutch Catholic girl guides sang hymns (rounding off their performance with a fascist salute to the Papal Legate). There was Benediction, and then the proceedings were ended by full-throated renderings of 'Faith of Our Fathers' and the Lourdes hymn 'Ave Maria'. It was, wrote one commentator, 'the most emotional moment of an emotional day.'[38]

The formal proceedings of the congress began on Wednesday 22 June, with a ceremony in the Pro-Cathedral. Later that night all the city churches held midnight Mass; extraordinary numbers attended. At St Andrew's, Westland Row, for instance, the correspondent of the *Revue des Deux Mondes* noticed a large crowd in the street outside the church, all ten thousand of whom wanted to receive holy communion. A priest told him that it was three o'clock before the last left the altar rails; Mass ended as dawn broke.

For the next four days Dublin was in a happy, busy daze of religion and also something more—a celebration of independence. Years later Máire MacEntee, daughter of the then Minister for Finance, remembered in her autobiography the 'big element of secular triumphalism' that went along with all the devotion, and the 'splendid thread of worldly satisfaction' that ran through the proceedings of the Congress. 'There was', wrote Dr James Deeny, down for the occasion from Lurgan, 'a spontaneous excitement of religion, carnival, achievement, fun and a wonderful feeling of being all Irish together.'[39] May Green was thrilled when Count John McCormack, a native of her town of Athlone, sang at the final Mass in the Phoenix Park. 'I felt a great sense of pride to be part of this ceremony, pride in my faith and in my country.'[40] Perhaps only the executions after the Rising soldered the Irish people so effectively; it laid the basis, for instance, for the general support for the policies of the Emergency period.

The crush of people, the parties, the intense religious feeling made these memorable times. The whole city was turned into one great church by 400 loudspeakers, by constant ceremonies, and by the multitudes of foreign priests. 'Dublin the kneeling city, the city of the millions of candles, the worshipping town, Dublin the heart of the Catholic world' enthused the commentator of the Dutch paper *De Tijd*. After the ceremonies, May Green and her friends made a tour of the inner city 'to admire the many beautiful shrines erected in honour of the Congress. They made a most impressive religious spectacle.' All of the commentators, Catholic and Protestant, were struck by 'the spectacle of an entire nation, from its President to the poorest of the poor in adoration before the Blessed Sacrament (*La Croix*, France). 'One felt', wrote *Figaro* 'that one heart was beating in a whole nation.'

Behind it all was the meticulous, even nannyish, organisation. In the Phoenix Park there were plenty of latrines (men's on this side, women's on that), and 500 boy scouts with pails of water and 700 St John's ambulance staff (to look after the several people who were overcome with the emotion of it all), not to mention 1,500 gardaí and interpreters to help the foreign pilgrims. At the men's Mass on Thursday the men were told that they should hold 'in their right hands and slightly over shoulder height a lighted candle. Care should be taken to see that candle grease is not sprinkled on clothes.'[41] (It was not thought necessary to repeat this instruction for the women.)

The Protestants, whose hearts were presumably beating to a different rhythm, mostly looked on with a kind of baffled admiration. The Methodist *Irish Christian Advocate* wrote in wonder at the feat of bringing a million people together 'solely in the cause of religion'. Some of them, who still represented one in fourteen of the Free State's population, not to mention those in the North, had already attempted to rain on the parade by claiming that not only was their's the true church, but that St Patrick had had no papal mandate for converting the Irish, and was actually an early Protestant in spirit. This argument was somewhat weakened when someone pointed out that in practice Protestants very rarely called their sons Patrick. Others took a less high-minded attitude, such as the three young Protestant clerks from Bray who were fined a stiffish £5 each for uprooting several papal flags after returning late and the worse for drink from a dance.[42] In the North, pilgrims coming down to Dublin were stoned and attacked in Larne, Ballymena, Belfast and Coleraine; in Larne, a large mob attacked an old people's bus, terrifying the passengers by hurling stones, lumps of coal and bottles through the windows.

The climax of the congress was the huge Mass in the Phoenix Park on Sunday. The organisers had divided the rising space in front of the altar into eighty units, each of which was divided into eight subunits. Every Dublin parish and the rest of the country by diocese was carefully allocated a place, with the women, generally on the left, well separated from the men. Thus the women of Rathgar were in 64F, and the men in 21, the women of Donnybrook were in 76 and the men in 30. Some nice calculations were obviously to be made: the men pilgrims of France were only expected to fill half a sub-unit, while the women were allocated a whole one. The pilgrims from Scotland, on the other hand, were expected to be 3 to 1 male.

On Sunday participants began arriving before dawn. The *Irish Press* described the event thus: 'At nine o'clock there were thirty thousand people gathered in the park. At ten o'clock one hundred thousand; at eleven, two hours before the Mass was to begin, there were gathered together more than on either of the two previous nights, and it was only now that the torrent reached its height, and breaking its banks flowed by every path and pass and road and by-way into the Fifteen Acre.' When all were gathered, there were, it was estimated, perhaps a million people in the Park that morning, each in carefully pre-ordained spaces. What struck observers so forcibly during the service was the silence—the chatter that might have been expected in so large a crowd was quite absent.

At the consecration, wrote the *Press* reporter, 'through that silence, so deep and perfect that if you closed your eyes you were alone, through that silence rang St Patrick's Bell . . . down to the ground those million people bowed, down in an ecstasy of adoration that the one voice of the bell called out into silence. From all that multitude as the Host was lifted up went an unspoken intensity of devotion that gave to the air itself a sweet happiness.'

Immediately after the Mass a procession was formed, which carried the blessed sacrament down to the final benediction at a specially constructed altar on O'Connell Bridge. The order of this great procession, which took four hours to wind its way to O'Connell Street, was, like so much else of this great gathering, meticulously planned. To accommodate the multitude who wished to take part, various routes had been allocated to different sections, and the exact order of march, a demonstration of protocol that could hardly have been matched by the British empire itself, was well publicised.

> First came a detachment of cavalry, followed by the banner of the blessed sacrament; then men, (four files of eight by parish); cross bearers and acolytes; 35 different religious orders, torch bearers;
> Blessed Sacrament;
> Cardinals, Archbishops, Bishops;
> Members of the Permanent Committee for Eucharistic Congresses;
> Other Prelates;
> Ministers of State, Judges, Foreign Ministers, Members of the Dáil and Seanad;
> Bearers of Papal Titles;
> Dublin Corporation, Representative Persons from the Six Counties, Corporations, County Councillors, Harbour Boards, Vocational Councils, Urban District Councils, Boards of Public Assistance, National University representatives, others;
> Distinguished and representative women;
> Female singers;
> Women.

After the final benediction at the specially prepared altar on O'Connell Bridge, the congress was at an end. The following days were somewhat anti-climactic as the pilgrims prepared to leave (there were more stonings in Belfast) and the decorations began to be taken down. Life slowly returned to normal. General O'Duffy congratulated the guards on their handling of the occasion and gave them a day off. A correspondent to the *Irish Independent* claimed that the mayfly season had been the best for twenty years; another noted that women had a weakness for beige, despite its being a difficult colour to carry off. Guinness put its famous dray horses on the market; holidays in the Isle of Man for 8s 6d a week full board were advertised in the small ads. The Senate passed a much amended version of the Oath Bill, and the Tailteann Games opened.

The Economic War begins

The next political excitement came in July, when, true to its electoral pledge, the government refused to pay to Britain the due instalment of the annuities. Britain, rejecting arbitration, responded vigorously to this challenge and imposed a series of duties on Irish agricultural exports. As a result, by August cattle prices were at 1914 levels. Many farmers, remembering over-exuberant speeches by Fianna Fáil electoral candidates, refused to pay their share of the annuities. Faced with this grim reality, Frank Aiken announced that 'the Irish people have been producing food for John Bull to grow fat, but now the result will be that the Irish will grow fat on their own food . . . if they went down to the slums of Dublin they would find that the unemployed were damned glad of the situation brought about.'[43] The cynical manipulation of this was a bit much for the normally bland *Dublin Opinion* which responded with perhaps its most bitter cartoon ever, showing a starving tenement family with one saying, 'I see in the papers we will never be able to consume all the food we produce.'

Fianna Fáil had been taken by surprise by the speed and aggression of the British government's reaction to the refusal of the annuities. Few had supposed that so drastic a response was likely. Consciousness of this mistake and what it would mean for their hopes of a revived Ireland added sharpness to politics. In the Dáil, exchanges became more aggressive. The government took the line that its policies were a continuation of the struggle against the old enemy; so opposition was no less than treachery. Fianna Fáil deputies accused the opposition of 'playing the British game', and even of advising the British what to do.[44] De Valera himself began to get rattled, uncharacteristically accusing the ex-Minister for Agriculture, Patrick Hogan, of having been 'bought' by the British government. In August he appealed for cooperation from the Cumann na nGaedheal party in the national crisis; he appealed to the opposition to 'give them a chance'.

The language used in the Dáil darkened. The word 'traitor', for instance, was used only sixteen times in the five years from Fianna Fáil's entrance in 1927 to July 1932. But in the following five years it was used as many as sixty times. Other accusatory words such as 'anti-Irish' and 'Freemason' were used much more often in the hectic years of the Economic War than before or since.[45] This supports the idea expressed by the Ceann Comhairle, Michael Hayes, who argued that 'the bitterness generated [by the Civil War as such] had been exaggerated both in depth and duration.'[46] Something subtler was happening than the traditional story. Intense frustration, as the Economic War foreclosed so many political aims, aspirations and promises, was being expressed through a pre-existent but dormant emotional channel.

In September Seán MacEntee, Minister for Finance, joined the booster chorus, declaring that 'retention of the annuities would secure a prosperity and a standard of living here unparalleled in Europe, and far above that enjoyed in the Six Counties'.[47] Insiders saw matters less rosily. On his return from the Imperial Economic Conference in Ottawa, Joseph Brennan, head of the Currency Commission, was confronted with an alarming radio message. 'Dublin situation so threatening British business men are preparing to evacuate with wives and children. Grave fear of clash between three bodies of definitely military cast: Irish Republican Army, Free State Army Comrades Association, and a Communist organisation. Meanwhile managers of British establishments find shop windows placarded "Ban British goods".'[48]

An emergency vote of £2 million (just the sum by which, before the election, Fianna Fáil had promised to reduce taxation) was passed. The inexperience of the new government showed in the handling of this. They announced that the assistance would be distributed to the country in proportion to the number out of work. Responding to this open invitation, in Ballina, and no doubt other places, there were suddenly more registered unemployed than inhabitants. Dark suggestions were expressed that in some areas relief work was only available to those who joined the Fianna Fáil party.[49]

Frank Ryan of the IRA announced in November that 'while we have fists, hands and boots to use, and guns if necessary, we will not allow free speech to traitors', a position eerily similar to the Church's insistence that heretics should not be allowed a voice.[50] Cosgrave's meetings were broken up in May and September (on the latter occasion with 'considerable pummelling' on both sides).[51] Membership of the Army Comrades Association (later called the Blueshirts) rocketed: numbers had reached

30,000 by September, and were expected to go to 100,000 by the following March.[52]

The association had been formally inaugurated in January 1932. Its
initial purpose, as its founder Commandant E. J. Cronin explained,
was to protect the privileged access of former Free State soldiers to
local authority work.[53] This access had been attacked by Frank Aiken
and others in the Dáil in the previous April. At first membership was
non-political (although members were urged to vote against Fianna Fáil
and Labour candidates) and confined to ex-members of the national
army. However, it quickly took on a role as the protector of Cumann na
nGaedheal meetings against attacks. At the same time its aims widened.
To 'uphold the State' in the face of opposition from organisations such
as the IRA (of which Fianna Fáil was regarded as a mere front) became
an important objective.

By the end of the year, both import and export figures showed alarming declines, particularly in cattle; terms of trade were worsening, and
the Economic War was joined in earnest. However, while the agricultural economy struggled, the urban middle class were much less hit.
On the stock exchange the tone was described at the end of the year as
'optimistic and supporting, despite the budget imposts, politics and tariff
tangles'. Investment money was amply available for first class propositions. At the end of the year a Dublin Corporation loan for £650,000
was five times oversubscribed within twenty-four hours.[54] This experience was repeated later in the decade: P. J. Carroll's flotation in 1935 was
oversubscribed as much as ten times, largely by Irish investors who sold
British shares for the purpose.[55]

Politically, the government's position was precarious. In November,
de Valera survived a vote of censure by five votes. The seven-member
Labour party, who were essential to Fianna Fáil's majority, were however
becoming restless, particularly in face of the rapidly increasing unemployment. There were also by-elections outstanding in Donegal, East
Cork and Waterford, two of which were likely wins by Cumann na
nGaedheal. Rumours of an imminent general election were in the air.
In December, a new national party was mooted, combining Cumann na
nGaedheal, Farmers, Independents and even possibly Labour interests.
In the new year this group became the basis of a new party, the United
Irish Party, later more commonly called Fine Gael, the first and longest
lasting of many attempts to combine against Fianna Fáil.

—1963—

HENRI STREET . . . APRES LE COMMON MARKET

In 1963 it was assumed that Ireland would soon enter the Common Market, and most middle-class people looked forward to this future, as this cheerfully optimistic cartoon from Dublin Opinion *suggests.*

Chapter 13 A confident optimism

The Irish economy was thriving at the beginning of 1963. The *Annual Review* covering the year (published by *The Irish Times* in January 1964) was duly optimistic. The stock exchange was up 60 per cent since 1960—'buoyant investment thoughout the year gave Dublin stockbrokers their busiest dealings ever . . . Irish shares went out in a blaze of glory.' This reflected a general industrial boom. Manufacturing output was up 30 per cent or more on the levels of 1958, and 'the prospects for a major expansion of manufacturing exports are good', wrote Garret FitzGerald. New motor car sales in 1962, at 31,700, were up 11 per cent on the previous year. (In 1932 the total number of cars on the road had been only 32,000—by 1963 this had risen to 230,000.) The ESB pumped out 50 per cent more electricity in 1963 than had been used in 1958. The building industry was doing well too: 'The year 1963 has been one of the most remarkable in the history of the modern building industry in Ireland,' wrote a correspondent, and 'the industry faces 1964 in a mood of confident optimism'. The tourist trade was looking for good things too, expecting to double its income in the next few years. The government's Second Programme for Economic Expansion, undeterred by the setback in negotiations for entry, assumed Ireland would join the EEC by 1970, and that national income would be up 50 per cent by that year.

For most people these changes had an impact, not least in animal spirits, but life was, as usual, a matter of contriving to meet the gap between getting and spending. In Dublin that meant finding and keeping a job. The first problem, for half of the population at least, was that they were female. The Commission on Emigration reported that 'in this country married women do not usually take up regular gainful employment outside the home'.[1] This was a disingenuous way of conveying the fact that most large employers would not employ married women. The civil service, the local authorities and many large companies operated a formal marriage bar, which meant that on getting married, women simply left the workforce. In practice, the marriage bar simply obliged women to chose between a career and a family, a choice that men did not have to make. The looming fact of this choice deeply influenced the attitudes to the education of women, and the likelihood of their getting any serious job. This extraordinary custom was justified as reinforcing the family, according to Article 41:2 of the Constitution. Those mothers who might be tempted to work were discouraged by moral persuasion. Considering how few middle-class married women worked, the columnist Angela MacNamara was safe enough to announce that 'the grown man or woman who speaks with love, gratitude and reverence of his mother is rarely found to be the child of a "working mother"', but it was mere propaganda to continue 'much of the disappointment, failure and heartbreak in the world today is the direct result of the mother's neglect of her vocation.'[2]

The typical social pattern was therefore the Breadwinner Father model, with a dependant wife at home and several children. Few wives were able to add to the family income except perhaps by taking in lodgers. This usually involved offering bed, breakfast and frequently an evening meal for rural migrants (in the civil service and the banks), students and foreigners.[3]

For men the impetus given to manufacturing in the 1960s opened out a new range of possibilities. Of those born between 1936 and 1941, 40 per cent of those who did not emigrate worked in some form of family employment.[4] However, in the space of a few years after 1958 the Ireland of the family farm, the family firm and the family shop was to be replaced. Real wages (that is, adjusted for inflation) were up 28 per cent since 1953, though it was notable that productivity per worker (up 32 per cent since 1953) was increasing considerably faster than employment (up 17 per cent since 1953). The boom in manufacturing had as a result produced only 8,000 new jobs.[5] The significant point, for the urban middle class at least, was that the jobs were to be allocated on the basis of education and skill.

All sorts of new opportunities were being explored. When C. S. Andrews' son Christopher married in October he and his new wife honeymooned in Palm Beach, Florida—the man of no property himself had had to be content with France. An Aer Lingus ad offered seven days in Paris, Amsterdam or Brussels for 29 guineas, bed and breakfast. (The snobby price designation says much. As a coin the guinea was last minted in 1816. It represented 21s, so the actual price of the holiday was £30 9s. Until decimalisation pricing in guineas was used to add cachet to high-priced goods such as horses, prize bulls, barristers' and medical consultants' fees, fur coats and upmarket antiques.) The more adventurous could go to San Sebastian for eight days on the same basis for £51, but were warned that Spanish cooking used olive oil 'so always say *preparado en mantequilla* (prepared in butter) when ordering'.[6] Journalist Patricia Boylan had some fun in *Hibernia* at the launch of a new biscuit. This was organised by the 'dynamic' Frankie Byrne, 'one of the first and best-known PR people in Ireland', who had opened her own agency in February. Described as 'the most new important biscuit since the birth of the cream cracker in 1885', the Gye biscuit was made by Jacobs and Guinness. At the launch party,

> fine big fellows with moustaches and buttonholes and glasses in big hairy fists miminied to each other over the subtlety of the flavour, the appeal of its suntanned colour, its texture and tactile strength and its resistance to damp, not to mention its viability. Some of them congratulated others who looked so sweet and so modest as they tried to minimise their parts in the hard protracted negotiations that had gone on for months.[7]

Daily life was dominated, as ever, by one's position in the social pecking order. Nearly everything done throughout the day was a function of this: especially where one worked, how much one earned, where one lived and what one ate. It was bad form to say so; indeed there was judicial authority for the view that class distinctions were almost entirely absent in Ireland. Judge Barra O'Briain made this announcement in Limerick, while refusing to accept counsel's argument that there was a class difference between farmers and farm labourers.[8] In his survey of Ireland published in 1966, Tony Gray confirmed (as a matter needing no evidence) 'the almost total lack of a class structure in Ireland'.[9] The author Ulick O'Connor (a barrister, educated at St Mary's College, Rathmines, and UCD) agreed: in Ireland, he said, 'we have an aristocracy of personality. There is a kind of classlessness in Irish society because we are more interested in a man's mind and personality than his title or income.'[10] As so often, the implicit comparison was with England, which was racked, as everyone knew, with comic worry over the smallest of class markers. Ireland's class system was more subtle. In practice, as O'Connor would perhaps have agreed in another mood, one's inherited position dictated access to medical care, education, employment and law. Even the tax system benefitted the better-off, by assigning over half the tax take to non-progressive taxes such as excise duties.

The only place in Ireland where this legendary classlessness nearly did operate was in the pub. In this men-only haven from the rigours of life, where neither women nor priests would penetrate to bring reminders of diurnal or eternal reality, all sorts of comfortable myths could flourish. In Dublin there were some 640 pubs, each comfortably supported by an average of less than four hundred male drinkers. 'Not a place for a woman all the same,' thought Mr Sugrue, in Jack White 1962 novel *The Devil You Know*, 'they shouldn't serve one on her own, who knows what kind she might be?'[11] In fact young women were beginning to be seen more and more in pubs, but they were still not a common sight. Men would only very reluctantly allow a woman to buy a drink.[12] Here the aristocrats of personality shone; though it was quickly discovered that as soon as they were taken out of the uncritical gloom of the pub and put in front of the Telefís Éireann cameras, they hemmed and hawed like anyone else.[13] Another popular myth exploded by Telefís at this time was that the country was brimming with undiscovered talent: a national talent contest suggested merely, as one commentator put it, that 'mediocrity was here to stay'.[14]

Over the last few generations most of the old Protestant Ascendancy class had been bought out, had died out or had simply left. The newly dominant Catholic middle class blandly disclaimed any intention of replacing them. A bank director and owner of a large business got himself into a revealing muddle when he was described as upper class: 'I'm amazed,' he said, 'at your use of upper, middle and lower class. We are quite ordinary people. We do not consider ourselves in any way an upper class. We think of ourselves as ordinary middle-class people and we don't have any activities that are associated with upper-class people. There are really only two classes here—a working class and a middle class, although you might say there is an upper and a lower level in that middle class.'[15] Jesuit sociologist Alexander Humphries quoted a more nuanced response from a medical interviewee: 'between a specialist like myself and a practitioner there is a definite gulf so far as social matters are concerned and this is kept on all sides. If I were suddenly to begin inviting a general practitioner whom I know fairly well for dinner, not only other people, but he himself would start to think: "I wonder what Jim wants".'[16]

Among the middle class there were rigid standards identifying the marriagable. Jane Beaumont, writing in the *Sunday Review*, described the rampant snobbery in south Dublin. 'Girls are sent to college not to broaden their education but to meet the right people and to mix with their own class.' (As a contemporary clerical author wrote, 'women . . . are actually capable of being educated, but the kind of education suited to their nature is of a different order; they are not inferior to men in their capacities, but these are suited to other fields of life.'[17]) Daughters' boyfriends were another source of snobbery.

Mothers like to be able to announce that they're at university, or failing this, well up the ladder of success in the business world. For daughters, jobs where beauty and appearance are important count the most . . . At social functions, tuppence ha'penny must never be asked to rub shoulders with tuppence. In two suburban areas in County Dublin where residents' associations have held dances, I have been told that it was found necessary to hold two separate functions, one for the teens from the better-class houses and one for the more democratic youngsters from the cheaper housing estates.[18]

In the towns of Ireland, the same snobbery applied. Monica Barnes recalled Kingscourt, Co. Cavan in the 1950s. 'The small-town snob system was remarkably complex, very subtle. It rarely came out into the open, but everyone knew their place.' It was most visible at the reading out in church of the annual collection. Each year the ledger of contributions was read sonorously from the altar, confirming the relative social standing of each Kingscourt citizen. The names were read according to the amount each gave. Prosperous shopkeepers and professionals first; they gave a pound. Less prosperous shopkeepers and business people gave fifteen shillings; then the ten shillings, the fives and then all the plebs who gave half-a-crown. 'And if you paid beyond your amount, people talked about you getting beyond your station.'[19]

The status of most families was dependent on the status of the head of the family, a man, and his status was largely dependent on that of his father. One might move up or down one class between generations, but the high mobility implied by classlessness was non-existent. Humphries was told that 'the partitions that separate the lower middle and the upper classes are still strong . . .[and] they are getting thicker.' 'The son of an unskilled manual worker had a negligible chance of reaching managerial grade,' according to the statistician Roy Geary. Even his grandsons had only one-fifth the chance of reaching professional status (the highest class) that they might have had in a perfectly mobile society. Not only was class strong in Ireland, it was stronger than that of the much-jeered-at neighbours across the water. The mobility for Dubliners was found to be 'markedly less than in England and Wales'.[20] These conclusions were based on a study of the actual life experiences of a large sample of men born and bred in Dublin. For those coming into Dublin from the country entry to the better jobs was relatively easy, and a high proportion of the new professional and administrative jobs were filled by non-Dubliners. It was actually harder for locally born skilled and semi-skilled workers to break in.

The key was no longer inherited wealth, but secondary and third-level education. This was a speciality of the middle classes, who were therefore poised to take advantage of the new opportunities. Secondary education was not free at this time, and so only some 130,000 pupils took advantage of it; about one-third of those who might have done. For the children of professional and managerial parents, however, participation was high. The real crunch came in third level education, where one in three of student age men and women from the higher professional group attended, while the children of semi-skilled, unskilled workers and agricultural labourers achieved less than one in two hundred attendance. One in four children of the lower professional, managerial and executive class attended. Although these figures refer to both sexes, in practice a woman's chance of going to university was even more biased by social origin than a man's. In the light of the marriage bar, it is not surprising that less well-off families decided not to encourage their daughters to go. Fees in UCD, for instance, went up in May to £65 a year for arts courses and £100 a year for medical students; Trinity arts degrees cost £70 a year. This was one-eighth of the average industrial annual wage.

Many employers had ceased to enquire about an applicant's religion— the question was, could he or she do the job? in March, Senator John Ross (a leading solicitor) told the pupils of Christ Church Cathedral School that there was no need to emigrate: 'There was a time,' he said, 'when many Protestants felt that unless they could get work in a Protestant firm, they might not get work easily. But people no longer worried about whether one was a Protestant or not. If a job was well done, one would not be prejudiced against by being a Protestant.'[21] Not everyone thought that way. Another American Jesuit sociologist, Father Biever, was told: 'Religion and business might not mix in some areas, but here in Dublin they are one and the same thing. I'd starve if I had to rely on the Protestant customer, so how can being a good Catholic hurt me?'[22] For some (about half of his sample) religion was still a significant factor in making ordinary commercial purchasing decisions: 'I think we ought to keep our money among our own. God knows that they [the Protestants] tried to keep it away from us long enough.'[23]

Some professional firms were quickly sensitive to a newly business-like mood. In the leading accountancy firm Craig Gardner, which employed about two hundred staff, a committee of partners was established with a view to assessing the suitability of applicants. The old paternalist style of partners introducing whoever they liked was abandoned. The premium had been abolished in 1957. The firm cut back on its employment of the older type of unqualified clerks, and took a vigorous interest in the exam progress of young articled clerks. Articled clerks were expected to pass at least one exam every year; increments were not paid to those who did not. Graduates made up a quarter of the articled clerks.[24]

As in the other years described, there was a wide range of earnings. Top of the heap were the few businessmen making large sums from property—it is of course impossible to guess at their takings. As a group, the professionals continued to do well, with lawyers just topping doctors. The 1956 *Irish Independent Guide to Careers* noted that 'the maximum income any barrister can hope to earn in this country is about £6,000 a year.' The same publication commented that 'it is doubtful if the incomes of those few at the very top of the [medical] profession exceed £5,000 a year.' At this time the secretary of a government department earned about £3,000. The *Irish Independent Guide*, however, remarked that, although Saturday mornings were still worked, 'it may be safely assumed that work in the Civil Service is not unduly arduous'.

In 1963, when the average industrial wage was £541,[25] the twelve partners of Craig Gardner averaged £6,000 each ; eight of the firm's staff earned more than £1,500, fifty-four between £900 and £1,500 and the rest (mostly clerks, trainees and typists) less than £900.[26] These were good salaries, as might be expected in such a firm. Other positions were less handsomely rewarded. Seán Lemass, as Taoiseach, for instance got £4,000; the Secretary of the Department of Finance, including children's allowance, much the same. The newly appointed Director General of Telefís Éireann, Kevin McCourt, got £5,000, and General Costello, head of the Sugar Company, got £4,500;[27] an advertisement in *The Irish Times* (7 March) sought a new director-general of the Irish Management Institute and offered £3,000. In February Dublin Corporation advertised for a senior consultant engineer at £1000–£1300; a junior would get £800–£1000.[28] The standard tax rate was 6s 4d (32 p) in the £; surtax began with a taxable income of £2,500. In 1962/3 there were 7,520 payers, with an average taxable income of £3,500 each.[29] One of these was Gay Byrne, as he proudly admitted.

Down the scale, the two editions of the *Irish Independent Guide to Careers*, published in 1956 and 1967 give an idea of the range of salaries paid by various posts, and the rapid and general increase in real earnings between the two years.

Table 7 Getting rich—salaries for various jobs, 1956 and 1967*

Position	1956	1967	% increase
Retail Price Index (1953=100)	*107*	*153*	*42*
Average industrial wage	364	744	104
Creamery manager	526	1,275	142
National school teacher	800	1,490	86
Architect (Dublin Grade 1)	950	2,350	147
Bank manager	1,050	2,225	119
ESB engineer (basic grade)	1,070	1,900	78
Company secretary	1,200	2,200	83
Public relations officer	1,500	3,000	100
Assistant principal, civil service	1,612	2,435	51
Senior pilot captain	1,950	6,253	220
Successful junior counsel	2,500	5,000	100

*These salaries are the levels for a married man at the top of scale but do not include allowances such as rent, children, overtime etc.

In the nine years covered all of these middle-class salaries, with the notable exception of the civil service assistant principal, comfortably out-performed inflation. The cost of living in 1963 was approximately three times what it had been thirty years before. The average industrial wage went from £126 a year to £541, a rise of more than four times. The top civil servants, on the other hand, earned (excluding children's allowances) £1,500 in 1932 and £3,375 in 1963, a rise of 2.25 times. The range between the highest and lowest earnings had levelled considerably, and at the relative expense of the higher earners. In 1907 the top civil service salaries were £1,800, and a skilled labourer might expect £80 a year, a ratio of 23:1. In 1932 a senior civil servant had earned twelve times the average industrial wage. By 1963 the top civil servants earned in practice six and half times the equivalent wage. From one point of view this was admirably equalising; from another, the disinterested behaviour of civil servants had caused them to fall behind their contemporaries.

To see how people lived on a more ordinary level of earnings, we can quote the case of 'Liam Sheehan' as he was called in the Time-Life book, *Ireland* (published in 1964). Liam earned £1,375 in his job as a personnel supervisor in a Dublin factory. He was forty-two, and he and his wife Maureen had six children. Although 'Irish Government economists' pointed out that best sirloin steak was only 4s 6d a pound in Dublin, and salmon 12s a pound, that the best seats in the Abbey or the Gate were only 10s 6d and that membership of the best golf club cost £20 a year, Liam Sheehan was not impressed. 'I assure you,' he told the interviewer, 'that when you're supporting a wife and six children on a salary like mine, you eat precious little sirloin steak'.[30] The Sheehans had a small car (a four cylinder Fiat), a television, but no telephone. At this time the telephone directory for the entire country was still in one volume—there were only 66 telephones per 1,000 inhabitants across the country.

The car and the television were very likely being bought on hire purchase. Between 1958 and 1963 the amount of hire purchase and credit purchases shot up threefold. Much of this expenditure was on cars—up four times—and radios and televisions—up five times. Domestic electrical appliances were another great source of credit purchases.[31] In the fifties hire purchase had been used for cars and for machinery. In the self-confident sixties consumers felt happy to increase their indebtedness well beyond the rate of their earnings increase to buy more frivolous items.

Liam Sheehan came home every lunchtime to his meat-and-potatoes meal of the day at home. Not only was this cheaper, but the commercial provision of ordinary meals during the day was not extensive. In February the barmen of Dublin protested against a plan to serve cooked meals in pubs. 'We have no objection to cold foods, snacks, sandwiches, Bovril and soup, but the serving of heavy four or five course meals is out!' announced their leaders, which if not mere rhetoric was an interesting insight into the union's view of the average businessman's diet.[32] Maureen Sheehan spent around £10 a week on food and milk, leaving £15 a week for all other expenses. These included rates at £50 a year, two packets of cigarettes a day (the average adult smoked seven a day), and the secondary education of two of the girls at £15 each. The girls' school clothes would have cost as much. One mother complained bitterly in *Hibernia* about the costs of kitting out her daughter, which included a winter coat for £5, a beret, 15s 11d, three blouses, £3 10s 6d, an English tweed pinafore dress, £4, and a blazer at £4 2s; total cost £17 8s 5d (just over £80 in 1990 terms). Health could be dear. People earning more than £800 a year had to pay for everything themselves, except school health, tuberculosis and infectious disease services. The average fee for a surgery call was 10s, or 15s if the doctor called to the home; drugs, moreover, were getting expensive, so people were tending to go straight to hospital to get them free.[33]

Liam and Maureen lived in a six-roomed house near the Phoenix Park, for which, like most Dubliners they paid rent, at £73 a year. A slightly grander house, say with three bedrooms and two reception in Stillorgan could be bought for £4,100; one in Rathgar, five bedrooms, three reception, for £6,000, and a five-bedroom house on one-third of an acre in Foxrock for £8,500.[34] This was about two and a half times the taxable income of the average surtax payer. In all, Dubliners spent only 10 per cent of their income on housing, less than they spent on drink and tobacco. It has been speculated that Irish people, as a result of a distressful history of evictions, have an atavistic urge to own their own property. The truth is less picturesque. The *Report of the Commission on Emigration*, published in 1955, noted the small number of houses available for middle-class renting, especially in the country, and derived from this circumstance the 'relatively modern custom of house purchasing' (which, as the Commissioners noted, put a great initial financial burden on a marriage).[35] In 1961 owner-occupied houses represented one-third of Dublin dwellings, and as late as the 1981 Census, only half of the houses in Dublin were owner-occupied. Favourable tax treatment and the burgeoning of suburban estates had encouraged a surge in the previous twenty years, so that by 1991 70 per cent of private dwellings in the greater Dublin area were owner-occupied.

The average household size was still much as it had been in the 1920s. Three-quarters of people lived in households of four persons or more. Such relatively large households were to sink to just half, with striking implications for personal privacy. To live by oneself was very uncommon: no more than 3 per cent of people lived in single person households in the 1960s. This was another figure that would show a dramatic increase, especially in Dublin.

The daily patterns of another household, this time in the upmarket suburb of Rathgar, has been preserved in a series of household expenditure notebooks.[36] (Rathgar, like Foxrock, was famous for its upper-class pretensions and special accent. Girls from Rathgar, as the current joke had it, thought sex was what the coals came in.) The family is unusual in having only one child, a daughter, but in other respects was no doubt typical. The wife kept meticulous records of her expenditure of £7 or £8 a week (including on one occasion 1d for toilet when in town). During the week there would be daily purchases. On Sundays it might be: church 7d, V de P (St Vincent de Paul Society) 4d, *Irish Catholic* 4d, papers 11d. Food was bought virtually every day; in January 1963 for instance there were only three days in the entire month with no food purchase. Typical items include: chops, chicken, 'meat', ham, corned beef, potatoes, peas, onions, cabbage, bananas, spaghetti, Nescafé, sugar, butter—with the exception of the spaghetti, the staples of the not very adventurous Irish diet of the day.

Journalist Tony Gray reported that 'in the average middle-class Irish home menus trended to follow the English pattern: bacon and eggs for breakfast; a joint of beef with two veg for Sunday lunch; rissoles or other made-up dishes from the left-overs, stews or fries for lunch during the rest of the week and fried fish on Friday. The evening meal almost always consists of tea, bread and butter, and sometimes includes cold meat and salad, or baked beans on toast, or a savoury dish of that sort.' However, this staid pattern was slowly changing. With some hyperbole Gray noted, 'ten years ago there was only one delicatessen in Dublin. Now there are dozens . . . ten years ago the Irish drank tea, water or milk with their meals. The bottle of Paddy's Gold Label on the sideboard was only there in case some visitor called unexpectedly; all the serious drinking was done in the pub. Now you are quite liable to find a bottle of wine on the table.'[37] This was a bit of a stretch, since import figures recorded fewer than 300,000 bottles imported in a year. They would not have gone far among the 700,000 or so households.

Cooking in Ireland, as an American commentator put it, was 'a necessary chore rather than an artistic ceremony, and the Irishman will usually eat anything out in front of him without bothering overmuch about its flavour or seasoning.'[38] It was a vicious circle: dully cooked food reinforced the idea that to like food was somehow perverse. Monica Sheridan, who had a popular Telefís Éireann cookery programme *Monica's Kitchen,* told the story of her young sister, fresh from honeymoon, who made an omelette for her new husband. He looked at her coldly across the table, turning the omelette over with searching fork. 'If I must have eggs,' he said with finality, 'I'd rather have them boiled.'[39] In restaurants, nine out of ten men ordered 'steak, every time, and seven men out of ten will order chips with it!'[40] There was in fact very good food to be had in the old French tradition, in restaurants such as Jammet's and hotels such as the Russell, the Gresham and the Shelbourne. The Russell was one of only eight in the British Isles to be awarded three stars by the *Egon Ronay Guide* of 1963. Five other Dublin restaurants won stars. Of Jammet's Egon Ronay wrote: 'Space, grace, the charm of small red leather armchais, fin-de-siècle murals and marble oyster counters exude a bygone age. Ritz and Escoffier would feel at home here.' However, the growing trend towards suburban living (with its concomitant need for car parking) killed off Jammet's and a number of the grander inner-city restaurants over the next decade.[41]

There were, of course, less sophisticated restaurants, some daringly offering foreign dishes. In February *The Irish Times* showed there was some way to go: 'To judge by the crowded tables at the foreign restaurants in town, more and more Irish people are discovering the delights of new dishes ... from the piquant flavour of prawns in tomato sauce, to the spicy sting of a good curry, the juicy succulence of chow mein, the exotic extravagance of paella, to the solid worth of Boeuf au Bourgogne.' (The creaky descriptions hint that perhaps the leader-writer was not quite as knowledgeable as he pretended.) There was still a self-consciousness about some places. A lawyer told Father Biever that he had never been to Ireland's top French restaurant, Jammet's: 'It was a place for the Protestant country club set and American tourists. An Irishman wouldn't know what to do in a place like that!'[42]

If you were invited to a small dinner party (for six to eight people) at the home of Charles Haughey, the thrusting new Minister for Justice, his wife Maureen (so the up-market women's magazine *Creation* told its readers in April), would very likely offer you their 'special favourite, Steak Fondue. Small cubes of very tender raw steak, well seasoned, are placed on a platter. Then each guest, using a special two pronged fork selects his piece of steak and cooks them at the table exactly to his taste, in hot melted butter [sic] in the chafing dish. A variety of sauces and a tossed salad complement the dish.' 'Their guests,' commented *Creation*, 'find Steak Fondue a very amusing novelty.'

Novelty it certainly was, though later it became so popular that hardly a wedding present list was complete without its fondue set. *Creation* made a brave attempt to stimulate its readers: 'You might think,' it wrote in February, 'that Chinese food is too exotic to be attempted in the kitchen, but this is not so'. (Thirty years before, *Model Housekeeping* had made a very similar remark about omelettes and soufflés.) Breda Ryan, the wife of the businessman mayor of Galway, preferred a chicken dish with a very rich sauce, *Creation* readers were told in March, with fresh salmon or oysters for the fish course, and always a soufflé or fresh fruit to follow.

Typically, Irish men gave their wives a household allowance (in cash) plus an allowance for presents, clothes and anything personal. If more was needed, it was negotiated—'a frilly nightdress', suggested 'An Irish Housewife', who was evidently a realist, 'will get better results than browbeating ... Show me a man who will refuse anything when approached in the right manner by one lightly perfumed and lightly clad.'[43] If the husband got a rise, a percentage of that was supposed to go to the household expenditure. With little chance to earn money themselves, women were dependent but they were never helpless. Austin Clarke told the story of one of his mother's friends, a seamstress who had toiled night and day at her sewing to help keep her husband and family. The husband was given a rise, but he didn't tell her, keeping the money for his weekend drinking. When she found out a year later, she was appalled by his meanness. She looked after him for the rest of her life, but neither spoke to him nor slept with him again, despite all the admonitions of the clergy.[44]

The pattern of food-buying was changing. Although the country was dotted with shops of all kinds (actually one for every sixty-five adults or so), most of these were very small. Of the 26,000 retail establishments, 6,500 were pubs or groceries with pubs attached. The biggest category was the simple grocery, in which 8,400 establishments employed 20,000 people, with an average turnover of less than £10,000. Many of these small local shops offered bad value, bad presentation, and a narrow range of goods: 'a pack of robbers they are,' thought the 'Irish Housewife'. Supermarkets, which had an average turnover of £300,000, were springing up in city and country, being blamed indeed for the rise in shoplifting. By 1966 half the retail sales in the Leinster area were through self-service outlets.

'Today's housewife no longer buys just for one day,' said *Creation*, 'but can buy her goods in bulk, to plan ahead for a week or more. Much of this food is of a comparatively perishable nature and consequently the need for proper storage is underlined. This is where refrigeration comes in. Refrigerators are now within the reach of most families, and this is a good thing, because they are essential for keeping food fresh tasty and healthy . . . what few people seem to realise is that a fridge is not just a seasonal necessity . . . the spread of central heating in many homes in the country is another reason—yet only slightly over 30,000 homes have fridges, while one without a television set is exceptional!' (The author describes her own milieu: nationwide, only one in three households had television in 1963.) The cost for an AEl fridge giving 5 cubic feet storage space was 60 guineas.

Bread and milk were delivered daily to the Rathgar family, and paid for once a week. The general category 'groceries' appeared on fifteen days in the month, meat on ten, fish on six—the family was especially fond of kippers. Other frequent purchases include pork chops and eggs (frequently duck eggs). Cheese was not noted in January, but it was in February, so perhaps it was not bought often. Items such as stamps, newspapers, clothes from Switzers and Colette Modes, and charities appear regularly.

For ordinary transport the housewife had her Humber bicycle, which had to be repaired during the year (17s 6d); otherwise she took the bus. The family went to Mass regularly, and attended sodality meetings as well as making charitable payments to the Vincent de Paul and the Little Sisters of Charity. Other religious expenditure included the Easter dues (£1), and regular purchase of the *Irish Catholic*. Expenditure on books is recorded once a month, and the cinema about six times during the year. The theatre is more of an occasion. Only one visit is recorded, and is preceded by a special visit to the hairdresser. Other items included the monthly rent, wages to the maid—Bridie left during the year and this resulted in a lot of expensive newspaper advertisement before her replacement, May, arrived some time later. (In *The Irish Times* around this time 'A capable general' was sought for a modern house in the Ranelagh district, and was offered £4–£5 a week all found.[45]) The daughter was allowed 1s a week pocket money, and money for the Girl Guides and dancing classes. In May the purchase of a hat for 18s 9d is recorded, perhaps in preparation for President Kennedy's visit, for which the civil servant husband might have been able to get a ticket to the garden party.

The Household Budget Enquiry of 1965/6 reveals that the expenditure proportions had changed somewhat since the civil service enquiry of 1932. Thus the top earning group in 1965/6 spent 24 per cent of its disposable income of food whereas in 1932 the top group spent 29 per cent. Housing in 1965/5 took 9 per cent of income; in 1932, 15 per cent. In the 1960s much more was spent on transport and somewhat less on clothing.

The most revealing conclusion to be drawn from the 1965/6 survey is how for urban dwellers expenditure on food, like access to education, medicine and employment, was absolutely correlated with social status. On white bread, for instance, social group 5 (unskilled workers) spent nearly twice as much as social group 1 (higher professionals). The classes between spent progressively less as they got higher. In milk, the progression went in the opposite direction: social group 1 spent most, social group 5 least; the other groups broadly according to their rank in between—for some reason the families of skilled workers spent nearly as much as the higher professionals. This scaling of expenditure by class applies to most food products: on eggs, cheese, steak, lamb, chicken, tomatoes, fruit and spirits, social group 1 spent most, and the others ranked below in order. For butter (to go with all that white bread), bacon, potatoes, cabbage, tea and cigarettes, social group 5 spent the most and the rest progressively less as they rose up the scale.[46]

The Irish were generally well nourished—indeed the government boasted that according to United Nations figures, consumption of calories per head was the highest in the world.[47] Quantity was not, however, the same as quality. In theory, of course, Jammet's, like the Ritz, was open to all. In practice, what one ate depended on what one earned, which in turn depended very simply on what one's father had earned in his time.

Chapter 14 The overwhelming presence

Religion was still an overwhelming presence in the 1960s. Conformity to religious practice was universally visible, from Sunday Mass attendance and people crossing themselves as their bus passed a church, to the dab of ash on the forehead on Ash Wednesday. A French observer, Jean Blanchard, noted that in Ireland the working class, which had long since deserted the Church elsewhere, 'is probably unique in the world for its devotion to religion and its deep faith. The family life of Irish Catholic workers and employees with few exceptions is steeped in Catholicism.'[1]

Some have argued that this was in fact little more than external adherence for prudential reasons. John McGahern quotes a Leitrim neighbour as saying 'sure none of us believe . . .we had the auld Druids once and now we have this crowd on our backs.' So why go to Mass? 'We go for the old performance, to see the girls, to see the whole show.'[2] A businessman quoted by the Jesuit researcher B. F. Biever echoed this view: 'If you aren't a good Catholic here,' said one, 'you'd be blackballed by the hierarchy and you'd lose your shirt. There is nothing like attending Mass with your wife and kids, making sure to be seen of course, to help the business.'[3] Though Seán Lemass was a sceptic, writes Tom Garvin, all his life he 'attended Sunday Mass and conformed to the rituals of the tribe. Not to do so would have been politically unwise and, perhaps, bad manners.'[4] There was undoubtedly strong social pressure to conform. Jean Blanchard reported that in the rich diocese of Donnybrook '80 per cent or 90 per cent of parishioners receive Communion on Easter Sunday . . . people even wonder why all the parishioners do not receive it.'[5]

No doubt the intensity of religious devotion ranged from the fervent to the full atheist. McGahern himself recorded in the article quoted above that he 'never found the church ceremonies tedious. They always gave me pleasure, and I miss them still. The movement of focus from the home and the school brought a certain lightness, a lifting of oppression, a going outwards, even a joy.'[6] Pauline Bracken, brought up in a reasonably pious middle-class home in Blackrock in Dublin, wrote 'we loved our religion. It was our mainstay and our peace and it was always

Newly ordained priests giving their coveted first blessings to their parents in Maynooth 1963. The world of their ministry turned out very differently to what they and their families had been taught to expect. (Brian Seed)

comfortingly there ... slipping into church for a prayer was routine for most people and women always ended their shopping by popping in.'[7] If we could measure the relative intensity of devotion across a spectrum, perhaps the proportions would fall out as in the table below. Such a model would account for the diversity of memories, and the certainty with which witnesses would say 'everyone' was warm or cool, from those like McGahern's Leitrim neighbour to those who got great consolation from their religion. For most people, perhaps, religious belief and practice was simply a presence, taken for granted—like wind or snow, sometimes irksome, often exhilarating or beautiful.

Table 8 Model of grades of belief	*Proportion of population* %
Fervent/devout	2
Pious/committed	14
Accepting both belief and practice as part of life	34
Broadly believing, unenthusiastically practising	34
Practising with little or no belief	14
Not believing, not practising	2

* Theoretical proportions, taken from the normal curve that accurately models other human variables.[8]

Whatever was happening in the secret places of people's minds, there were undoubtedly extraordinary levels of practical adherence. In parishes all over the country, attendance at Sunday Mass was over 90 per cent, week in week out, a figure that might be compared with the 70 per cent audience, the highest TAM rating that the *Late Late Show* (a programme that 'everyone watched') ever achieved.[9] Father Roland Burke Savage testified that three or four hundred UCD students would attend the evening Mass in Newman's church during term.[10]

People went to Mass and Communion frequently, though for some 'getting' Mass, as the expression was, could be perfunctory. In the country churches the hardy men lurked at the back, half in and half out; in towns priests muttered through the liturgy in 30 minutes, while their parishioners said the rosary. At home, however, people hung pictures of the Sacred Heart on their walls and read missionary magazines. They joined sodalities in hundreds, said the rosary at home, and were buried in the robes of a tertiary order.

Officially the Church's special position was endorsed by the Supreme

Court (as early as 1925) and the 1937 Constitution. But, as Jean Blanchard wrote in 1963, 'the two systems, religious and political, are so closely intermingled in the mind of the Irish people' that 'there are no official relations between Church and State'.[11] Politicians from Noel Browne to de Valera declared their allegiance to the Church, and at least some believed what they said. In public, the clergy were treated with immense respect, much more than, for instance, politicians. They 'represented an older, better established order, steeped in the nation's history,' wrote Jean Blanchard. It was not always thus. In George Birmingham's *Hyacinth*, set in the early 20th century, the elderly priest reminisced: 'I can remember when a priest was no more thought of than a bare-footed gossure out of a bog, but now there isn't a spalpeen of a Government inspector but lifts his hat to me in the street.'[12]

For those inclined to go beyond the 'child-like faith' so often praised by the hierarchy, the elaborate construct of theories and principles built up over hundreds of years was a source of intellectual satisfaction and security. For them religion was, as Newman put it, a threefold package: supplying at the same time metaphysical truth about the world, a source of spiritual growth or consolation and a fountain of moral guidance.[13] As the Lithuanian writer Czeslaw Milosz has written about the attractions of Communism, the Faith

> spoke to the modern person's yearning for order, unity, harmony and a superintending design. It offered the lonely a sense of meaning in life. It appealed to the spirit of noble self-sacrifice and obedience to a higher authority. It did so by affirming that, for all its restrictions, its privations, its arbitrary rules and rites, it offered a life superior to the life lived in modern capitalist society, which was vulgar, escapist, foolishly full of optimism.[14]

Just as this mighty edifice was about to change as a result of the deliberations of the Vatican Council, a substantial book described the way the Church's views penetrated every space in Irish society. Lyrically its author decribed Christianity (by which he meant scholastic Catholicism), as 'a complete philosophy of life', which gave 'a meaning and a value to human life and its activities at every level and in every sphere ... the tremendous jig-saw puzzle of human life with all its inequalities, apparent shapelessness and jaggedness finds its pattern'.[15] Between 1940 and 1955 the author, Canon John McCarthy, Professor of Moral Theology in Maynooth, had contributed a regular article to the *Irish Ecclesiastical Record* in which he answered moral questions put to him by readers, very often as a result of dilemmas arising in the confessional. These were later collected in two volumes as *Problems in Theology* (1955 and 1960) published by Browne and Nolan.[16]

The questions are grouped by commandments and by sacraments, following the style of moral theology texts. The biggest category is, not surprisingly, sexual matters (the sixth and ninth commandments), though it is perhaps not as large as might have been imagined, taking only some 160 pages out of the 1,000—20 per cent of the commandments and only 16 per cent of text. Economic and financial issues (seventh and tenth) including the morality of going on strike, manipulating income tax returns, dealing in black market tea, and questions of commercial morality such as overcharging shop customers, make a respectable second category with 117 pages. Other commandments generate fewer problems: the first and second (prohibiting strange gods, etc.) touch on superstition; honouring the Sabbath (third) takes up a mere twenty pages. 'Thou shalt not murder' (fifth) takes 65 pages, largely on medical matters such as amputation, vivisection and organ transplants. The questions in respect of the third commandment, 'Remember the Sabbath and keep it holy', reveal the tight control exerted by parish priests. For instance, in a period of bad weather saving the hay on a rare fine Sunday could be of great economic importance. But whether or not a particular farmer did so was not to be left to his individual circumstances and individual conscience. The priest would announce from the pulpit a general permission to farmers to save the hay on Sunday—or not.

Canon McCarthy and his questioners lived in a world buttressed by certainties. Discussing the vexed question of attendance at Protestant weddings and funerals, he writes: 'We Catholics cannot forget, and cannot be allowed to forget, that truth is one and that we have the truth . . . we cannot tolerate doctrine other than our own, for such doctrine is false.'[17] ('No free speech for traitors', as the IRA put it in the 1930s.) For the Canon, God is in his heaven and his Irish people are fundamentally sound, though sorely harassed by Satan and his helpers on earth. Catholic moral law, based on the supernatural order established by God, was by definition universal; it covered every case.[18] However, within boundaries there was nearly always room for stimulating discussion and interpretation.

Characteristically of his caste and time, Canon McCarthy pays little or no attention either to what individuals owe to society for the common good (contributive justice) or to the allocation of societal resources (distributive justice). The obligation to pay tax, for instance, especially indirect tax, is discussed in a purely personal light. Thus it is argued that if a man believes his neighbours are underpaying tax, so unfairly putting more of the national burden on him, he is morally entitled to underdeclare his own income in self-defence. He is also entitled to charge any expenses that he did not in fact incur but that a person in his position might typically do (for instance by charging against tax subscriptions to trade journals actually read in a library).[19] There is no hint that the state is worth supporting for patriotic reasons, or for the common good, or perhaps because of the national struggle.

Behind many of his discussions is the very old idea of a God-created hierarchy. At the head of the great chain of being was Aristotle's unmoved mover, God himself. Beneath him were angels (nine different grades, from archangels, seraphim and cherubim to plain angels). Below the angels came man, then animals, insects, rocks. Crucially, each had a rightful position with responsibilities that could not be usurped without severe damage to the whole. As Shakespeare put it, 'when degree is shak'd, which is the ladder to all high designs, the enterprise is sick.'[20] This hierarchy is replicated in the class structure, which the Church explicitly supported.[21]

This all may seem far from ordinary Irish life, but in one well-documented episode the application of this concept had dramatic consequences. When Noel Browne introduced the famous Mother and Child scheme he included clauses to the effect that all mothers and infants would be entitled to free healthcare. To the doctors this seemed simply an invasion of their market by the state (especially deplorable since it was long known that careful attention to sick infants had a way of expanding the practice to the rest of the household). As the son of a doctor himself, John Charles McQuaid, Archbishop of Dublin, no doubt sympathised with their view, but he also saw the situation in scholastic terms. Most families could afford to pay for their own medical care. Allowing a higher organisation (the state) to usurp the duties of a lower (the family) was against natural law and fraught with danger. Some years before Pius XI had stigmatised such usurpation as 'an injustice, a grave evil and a disturbance of right order'.

In sexual matters the basic rule was simple: sex is for procreation, and only for procreation inside marriage. Any kind of sexual pleasure not *directly* so connected is an 'abuse of the order of nature and intrinsically wrong'.[22] Following the Roman originals, from St Jerome onwards, there is a marked lack of nuance; any sexual pleasure apart from procreation is presented as 'a violation of the primary precept of natural law'—every molehill, in this world, is a mountain. Anything that might lead to what they called '*luxuria*' ('the abuse of sex pleasure') was frowned on. This 'somewhat inhumane treatment of the doctrine of marriage', as a contributor to the Commission on Emigration and Population Problems put it, was thought by some to be a contributory factor to the low marriage rate.[23]

'I have heard it stated,' says one of McCarthy's questioners, 'that the vast majority of modern dances are seriously immoral and suggestive, and therefore are to be regarded as a dangerous occasion of grave sin.' Contemporary clergy often talked of 'grave' matter, the essential component of mortal sin, i.e. such as would by itself condemn an otherwise innocent sinner to eternal damnation—though so freely did they use the term that one might wonder how far they actually believed this. The Canon agreed that some modern dances, though not all, were indeed seriously suggestive of sexual intercourse. On another occasion he was asked about the morality of kissing. He answered that 'indulgence in these acts will often be fraught with some danger, and they will therefore often be at least venially sinful.' Inside marriage pleasure in sexual activity was unavoidable, but it was not to be indulged in.[24] To that end, knowledge of the lawful 'safe period' was to be given only to the married, on a one-to-one basis—and they in turn told not to tell others.[25]

Of course, few of the men laying down the law knew *anything* of the ordinary tender practicalities of sexual behaviour. Most went into junior seminaries at the age of twelve or fourteen, and apart from works of moral theology, their source of information about ordinary sexuality was the confessional, not a place where joy or simple affection was likely to be expressed. Most priests and nuns cultivated a fastidious distaste for such things, which slipped easily into wholesale condemnation. F. X. Carty, who had entered the Holy Ghost seminary after Blackrock College in the late 1950s, remembered how 'it was only when I already had taken a vow of chastity for three years and was preparing to take it for life that it dawned on me that there was such a thing as sexual intercourse . . . I had always imagined that men and women went to bed together and fell asleep and that eventually God, if he so willed it, sent them a child.' He was twenty-one at the time. With some embarrassment he consulted an older priest, who assured him that 'in humans it normally took place as in monkeys.'[26]

The laws, rules and regulations governing behaviour came from many sources. From the 'top' there was eternal (God's) law, natural law, divine law (deduced from Revelation), the law of the universal Church (canon law), state or local positive law, local custom and practice, and finally, parental or family rules. Like a nest of Russian dolls, the higher group framed the conditions and sphere of activity of the lower. Ordinary civil law was very low down in the priority order, and the clergy tended to speak slightingly of it. Except in so far as it gave expression to natural law, it imposed no obligation in conscience, any more than there was a moral content to traffic regulations.

Given the propensity of states to pass obviously bad laws, there clearly could not be a moral obligation to obey their law as such, and certainly not if the priorities established by higher laws (as, for instance, those of the Church) would thus be infringed. To an organisation with a corporate memory of the French revolution, the German Kulturkampf, the Russian revolution and National Socialism, not to mention the martyrs of the Roman Empire and the Irish penal laws, the state was by no means necessarily a benign entity. Indeed, history seemed to show that the greater the degree of sovereignity asserted by the state (as in the French and Russian Revolutions and Nazi Germany) the greater the tendency to injustice, violence and cruelty. The way in which bishops across the world have behaved in the child abuse cases of recent decades suggests that this dismissive view of the local law by no means died during the Vatican Council.

Canon McCarthy followed papal encyclicals in rejecting market-based economics in favour of the so-called 'social economics'. For instance, he believed that an employer had a moral duty to pay at least a 'family wage' to his workers, regardless of the employment market. This wage should be sufficient to maintain a worker and a normal family in, as the Canon put it, 'frugal but decent comfort'. (This high-minded attitude is in marked contrast to the attitude to the state's taxation.) Occasionally, of course, employers failed in this. If so an employee 'is entitled to compensate himself occultly to the extent that his wage falls below the standard' i.e. take the money out of the till on the quiet.[27] Canon McCarthy notes, however, that the local police tend to take a dim view of this kind of activity, and so, on prudential grounds, advises against. What, asked a correspondent, was the chaplain of a convent to do who had discovered that the mother superior was paying appallingly low wages to the nuns' servants? Answer: he was bound 'to bring her violation of the moral law to the notice of the Superioress'. He should do so privately. Even apart from his duty as a chaplain our correspondent might be bound in charity as a priest to administer a *correptio fraterna* to the Superioress.[28] (And, he might have added, good luck to you.)

As well as sex and money, Canon McCarthy touches on a fascinatingly wide range of topics. One correspondent quotes an article in the political periodical *Hibernia,* then published under the auspices of the Knights of Columbanus, to the effect that it would be sinful to vote for a Jew. 'Unduly harsh,' says the Canon. It is morally acceptable, if not ideal, to vote for any non-Christian who accepts the Constitution. In a tight job market it was well known that both Protestant and Catholic firms discriminated in favour of co-religionists. In that context was it permissable for a candidate to lie in the interview about his school (which would of course immediately reveal his religion)? No, says the Canon, for although the question is out of order, to deny the school is tantamount to denying the faith, and gravely sinful.

Long before the 1957 Fethard-on-Sea boycott, Canon McCarthy was asked to consider the morality of the boycott system. Father Peter, says the questioner, has urged his parishioners not to frequent shops run by Protestants, on the grounds that supporting heretics (the not very polite term used to refer to Protestants) is tantamount to encouraging heresy. Was this morally justified? Answer: There is no obligation in justice or charity to deal in any particular shop, and Catholics are perfectly entitled alone or together to abstain from entering any shop. On the other hand, purchasing sweets in the shop of a non-bigot is certainly not encouraging heresy, and it is socially valuable to maintain peace and harmony in the community. Boycotts also have a way of turning nasty, leading to undoubted violations of justice and charity.

In 1955, Canon McCarthy moved to the parish of St Peter's in Athlone where he became parish priest. The *Irish Ecclesiastical Record,* established as a specifically ultramontane publication, did not survive very long after the Vatican Council, folding in 1968. By the time the Canon died in 1983 the Catholic Ireland whose problems he had discussed at such length had long gone. In a short generation the elaborate moral construct he depended upon, and which traced its roots back to the Middle Ages if not further, had melted from people's minds.

And in practice

The Irish were known, at least to themselves, as a remarkably moral people. This had been a source of frequent self-congratulation since the days of the Gaelic League. By comparison with European countries, writers often pointed out, the morals of the country were almost irreproachable. This was usually ascribed to the intense loyalty of lay people to the Church. 'Look at our morality in Ireland,' said one of Father Biever's interviewees, 'we are better off than most if not all countries in the world. How can you say the Church is behind the times?'[29]

The European country everyone had particularly in mind was, of course, pagan England. Worryingly, the increasingly outspoken British media, so eagerly consumed at least in the populous eastern fringe, was beginning a new assault. 'The strong moral tradition of the country . . . can no longer be counted on, as so many corrupting forces are in direct competition with it,' wrote *Hibernia* in March 1963. The Archbishop of Tuam agreed: writing in his Lenten pastoral of advancing secularism and attacks on chastity, he feared that 'even in this country there had crept in a certain looseness, a spirit of laxity.'[30] It was, wrote the Archbishop, 'the purity of the men and the chastity and modesty of the women' that gave Ireland a special place in God's providence. Conscious of the blandishments of the 'swinging sixties' from across the water, the Irish bishops hammered home the message of chastity.

However, crime rates were still low, and the police solved a very high proportion—of the 885 crimes against the person reported in 1962, 830 were detected; 14,000 offences against property were reported of which two-thirds were detected (twenty years later, 86,000 such crimes were reported, with just over one-third detected). The pattern is characteristic: the crime of sacrilege (robbery from a church) was regularly observed, as was the offence of attempted suicide, of which in 1965 there were 11 cases recorded, as compared to 7 murders. Only two of the attempted suicide cases were prosecuted. One hopes that Mrs Mary Roberts of Fairview was lucky. She was robbed of her handbag containing her life savings (£120) while she stopped in O'Connell Street to buy her two-year-old grandson an ice cream. She carried the money around with her, she said, because there 'had been so many cases of housebreaking recently that [she] thought the money would be safer in her bag than in the house.'[31] To some extent the low rate of crime was because, as a contemporary report put it, 'Irishmen of criminal tendencies invariably went to England and improved their criminal skills there, encouraged in this by the Irish police'.[32] As a result, crime rates were one-third those of Britain. In a special article on Lemass's Ireland, *Time* magazine noted facetiously that 'the authorities admit that [the] nation's commonest transgression, larceny of pedal cycles, bears watching.'[33] By the end of the decade there were 2,469 such cases, of which only 300 were cleared up.

The most spectacular evidence of high morality was the famous Irish chastity. The Irish were so chaste indeed that demographers have speculated on some kind of racial loss of libido as a result of the Famine. Nearly one man in three never married, and very likely had no sexual experience beyond the bleak masturbations described by Patrick Kavanagh. Father Biever noted how even men-only dirty jokes were 'not really connected with sex at all; rather [they were] scatalogical bathroom humour.'[34] Those who did marry did so late—the national average age at marriage was thirty for men and twenty-six for women, and in the country four years older still. Officially, illegitimate births were less than 4 per cent of the total, though this figure was widely believed, like the equally low suicide rate, to conceal more than it showed. Pregnant but unmarried women were frequently exported, like the criminals, to England.

One hundred years of repression by lay enthusiasts and clergy had their effects on everyday life. In September, a group of young Italian tourists complained bitterly to the *Sunday Press* about this: 'If we hold hands in the street, people look askance at us; if we kiss in a public place such as a café, we are immediately put out.'[35] Though perhaps the fact that this was a news story suggests something of a thaw. In 1935 a young man had actually been fined for putting his arm around a young woman's waist in public; the prosecuting inspector claimed that the act had caused scandal, contrary to section 18 of the Criminal Law Amendment Act, and the justice felt obliged to agree.[36] Even in the family, *noli me tangere* predominated: generally a boy would not kiss his sisters or his father, ever, and his mother only on uncommon occasions. In the street a slap was more common than a kiss. 'The only human being in our old, repressed, modest and fanatically chaste society,' wrote Polly Devlin of her 1950s childhood in Ardboe, Co. Tyrone, 'that adults can unrestrainedly and unashamedly caress without inhibition' was the baby.[37]

Marital sex was often not much more enthusiastically approached. 'I'm lucky, I don't mind it', or 'he's very good, he doesn't want it very often,' were remarks that Dorine Rohan heard from her women friends in the 1960s. One man said to her, 'we're all animals after all, aren't we? I don't believe in all this spirituality lark about sex.'[38] A husband told Alexander Humphries: 'Back of everybody's mind is the notion that there is something wrong with it, something bad. It is deeply engrained in us. I know that is true of myself and of most of the people I know.'[39] Father Humphries was told that there was 'very little infidelity here in

Dublin, at least in comparison with London and Paris where I have worked. Men do not fool around with other women very much.'[40]

'What are the chief dangers to chastity?' ran the *New Catechism*. 'The chief dangers to chastity are: idleness, intemperance, bad companions, improper dances, immodest dress, company keeping and indecent conversation, books, plays and pictures [cinema].'[41] Company keeping (by which was meant ordinary courting activities between man and woman) was apparently unqualifiedly bad, and the natural companion of indecent conversation. Books, plays and pictures, as such, were equally risky.

By the 1960s a more tolerant atmosphere had grown up: the younger clergy had ceased to think of marriage as 'the shame-faced sacrament'. Dancehalls sprang up all over the country. In many a country place the gaunt barn of the ballroom, which could often fit two or three thousand people, was the biggest building and the most profitable enterprise in the area. The dancehalls were dominated by the new-style showbands, eight or ten musicians with set routines and neat suits who mostly played versions of the latest British and American pop songs. There were as many as six hundred showbands, some, such as Dickie Rock and the Miami Showband and the Capitol Showband, making considerable sums plying the roads of Ireland—except during Lent, when the dancehalls were closed, and the bands tried their luck in Britain. Huge crowds flocked to them night after night to hear songs written to appeal to Liverpool or small-town America.

It was in 1963 that Michael O'Beirne bravely set up his matrimonial introduction agency in Ely Place. His first discovery was that none of the national newspapers would take his very discreet advertisements. To overcome this problem he visited the Catholic Welfare Bureau, and was gently but firmly discouraged. 'Life provides its own introductions,' said the Monsignor, 'buying a packet of cigarettes is an introduction to the girl behind the counter.' This was not much consolation to the million or so unmarried people in the country at the time.

The most striking difficulty, O'Beirne believed, was the different expectations and aspirations between the sexes. The men were stuck in the country because of their farms, but the women wanted nothing of the drudgery their mothers had known. They were looking for something different from the regal position enjoyed by Canon Sheehan's Mary. 'The average Irish woman,' wrote O'Beirne, 'sees the average Irish man as under-educated, lacking in financial stability, deficient in ambition and initiative, careless and slovenly in dress and grooming. Their manners are boorish, and, to sum it all up the men are lacking in maturity . . . [As a result] the women have left the country in their thousands, hurrying to the towns where they imagine all the super-men were to be found.'[42] In public, of course, these things were not said. When an article appeared in the *Manchester Guardian* criticising Irish men, the normally cool and critical journalist, Bríd Mahon leapt to their defence in the *Sunday Press*: 'We Irishwomen are quite pleased with our menfolk . . . they may not be madly demonstrative in public, but oddly enough we prefer privacy and loyalty . . . We do not consider ourselves downtrodden. The Church upholds the worth and dignity of a woman, and we don't lose out as a result, but then maybe we're old-fashioned enough to appreciate respect.'[43] A Church of Ireland Synod speaker agreed. 'If premarital sex relations were to be treated as a source of pleasure . . . the stability of married life would be undermined. Men looking for wives', he warned, 'are not looking for soiled goods, a fact that young girls should keep in mind.'[44]

The students at UCD lived in a different world to these ardent lovers. They went on dates, did lines with particular friends, discussed love, marriage and kissing quite freely, both with boys and girls. 'Met John and Noel on the way to College,' wrote a UCD student in her diary for 25 November 1963. She was then in her second year of an arts degree.

> We were discussing boys and girls, etc. They asked me did I ever turn down invitations. Said yes. They were horrified. 'Some poor guy after weeks of effort finally works up enough courage to ask you out and then you turn him down!' I was saying how different it was for girls. You have a good run maybe going out with 3 or 4 different boys at the same time (they thought this was fantastic) and then there might be a month where you'd be going out with nobody. N said there was always someone keen on you and all you had to do was to be extra nice to him—give him a big smile etc.

More intimate details were for girl-talk only: 'Coffee in the DBC with S, who was looking for advice on what to do when boys make advances. Personally I think it is quite all right to kiss a boy when you're keen on him. S was being very vague . . . she gave me the impression that I was awful even to contemplate kissing someone before I was engaged to him.' The next day she meets another friend for lunch in the Annexe in UCD. 'J said she had done it [that is, kissing] with V . . . was amazed, but realise we can talk really frankly, which is great.'[45]

In the Gaeltacht to learn Irish, Patricia Craig and her friends enjoyed long kissing sessions with the local boys. But as she wrote in her mem-oirs, there were strict limits:

Looking back I am sometimes amazed that my actions or non-actions never provoked more unpleasantness; that my obstinate withdrawal of my person at one crucial moment or another didn't cause my co-experimenter, whoever he was, to cut up rough. Still it's true that I could call on widely held notions of goodness to back me up—that the whole weight of religion, social usage, even intrinsic Irishness was on the side of abstinence. Who, without renouncing their birthright, could argue all that out of existence? 'But it's nice' didn't amount to much of a countervailing assertion against the brick-wall pronouncement 'it's a sin'.[46]

This was not a climate in which people knew or talked much of sex—Angela MacNamara, who was just starting her long career as an advisor in these matters, believed that 80 per cent of the young girls who wrote to her would not even mention the word to their mothers. Many a middle-class girl was shocked and terrified by her first period. As Marie Stopes had found some years before in England, children grew to maturity with only the vaguest ideas of their own physiology, let alone that of the opposite sex. Angela MacNamara noted that when she offered to write a series of articles for a popular newspaper the editor told her that 'Ireland is not yet ready for the frank, open approach . . . the word "womb" is considered objectionable by some.'[47] Doctors treated with gentle advice childless couples who had been concentrating on the navel or other areas for insemination. Finding a little booklet in her daughter's room called *The Glass Woman—Facts of Life Explained*, Pauline Bracken's mother reported that 'she found it very enlightening, having borne six children without a word in print on the subject.'[48]

In the urban Ireland of the 1960s sexual matters were beginning to be aired, slowly. The *Irish Times* search engine reveals that the word 'sexual' was used in various contexts only 24 times in 1958, but 64 times in 1963 and 215 times in 1968—and 561 times in 1988. 'Erotic' was used 5 times in 1963 and 50 times in 1988. However, the Church's view of sex was not unpopular. Four-fifths of Father Biever's sample rejected the idea that the Church's views on sex were out of date.[49] The young Bunny Carr, despite great theoretical interest in women, was not untypical: 'It never occurred to us actually, really, to sleep with a girl . . . Hell was real and sex was its close bedfellow.'[50] Not everyone was quite so innocent. Lee Dunne's racy 1965 novel *Goodbye to the Hill* described the sexual exploits of a young lad from the poor flats in Ranelagh, near Mountpleasant Square. Even at the time it was felt to contain a good deal of wishful thinking (notably our hero's relationship with the big-breasted widow who pays him for sex)—today, perhaps the most jolting revelation is that he was sixteen before he owned a pair of underpants.

Flashes of anecdotal evidence, like lightning in a night sky, suggest the existence of an unofficial sexual world. What people say, what they believe, and what they do, are rarely the same, especially in a society that puts such a high value on observance of demanding moral laws. The historian's difficulty is to assess the weights to be given to the three.

There were, of course, ribaldries, usually gentle: 'If I said you had a beautiful body, would you hold it against me?' asked a student paper Patricia Craig worked on. Or from an older generation:

> God bless the breezes
> That rustles the treeses
> And lifts the chemises
> From the lovely girls' kneeses
> O Jeeeesus.

No doubt many little girls and boys had 'greatest secrets' like Edna O'Brien's Cait and Baba when they 'took off our knickers and tickled one another'.[51] In the 1940s, Stanley Lyon revealed that 14 per cent of first babies in Dublin were to women married less than eight months. There was in addition an official illegitimacy rate of 4 per cent.[52] In March 1963 it was reported that six dead babies had been abandoned in various parts of Dublin in recent months.[53]

Other types of sexual experience are even less well-documented. Most women certainly encountered sexual harassment, if only a fumbling self-exposure on the banks of the Dodder. In her autobiography *Stealing Sunlight* Angeline Blain records being groped by her boss in the Regent Cinema, and Angela MacNamara the dreadful day when a family friend exposed himself, and 'showed me what happens to men when aroused'—she was ten.[54] As Diarmaid Ferriter has reported, these incidents and court cases frequently unveiled a sexual life that 'contrast[ed] strongly with the picture Irish society wanted to paint of itself and to present to others.'[55] There were also unknown quantities of incest and child abuse: June Levine describes an encounter in her childhood with a white-headed old neighbour, who had a grand, Protestant, accent. One day he put his hands into the pockets of her dress and rubbed her budding breasts: 'Nice little pocket', he said, and I felt very strange'.[56] Joyce, Kavanagh, O'Faolain and McGahern all describe boyhood sexual encounters with men. The brutal encounters forced on boys and girls in industrial schools are now well documented.

Homosexuality was rarely mentioned and then not sympathetically.

The word is recorded first in *The Irish Times* in 1936 in an almost technical Freudian context; then it occurs very occasionally in the context of
Roger Casement's 'degrading and unnatural practices'; Oscar Wilde and
others crop up, but it is not until the British Profumo scandal hit the
headlines that the term occurs regularly. Typically, it was from the BBC
that David Norris (born in 1944) discovered the existence of other gays.
Then he became aware of 'hints of a dark subterranean world popu-
lated by balding old men, who were probably alcoholics, lived in greasy
raincoats, hung around public lavatories, or the Phoenix Park, and tried
to lure small boys into bushes with Smarties.'[57] But, in common with
other sex words, 'homosexual' occurs with increasing frequency in *The
Irish Times* in the 1960s and beyond: four times in 1958, three of which
condemned the British Wolfenden Report's recommendation that
homosexual behaviour between consenting adults be outside the law, 17
times in 1963, 77 times in 1973, and 160 times in 1988, by which time 'gay'
was becoming the term of choice.

Transport early 1960s style at O'Connell Bridge: the uncomfortable-looking process on the right was called 'getting a bar'. The scooter, the pipe, the sharp trousers and the short mac of the man on the left are of a style. Both the young women (they would have said 'girls', and perhaps still do) wear decorous on-the-knee skirts with scarves and gloves—minis arrived later in the 1960s. (Brian Seed)

Chapter 15 Codes and aspirations

The 1960s was a pleasantly affluent time, as everyone agreed. It was also an age when the Irish seemed to be taking control of their own destinies, even in the previously disappointing economic field. For the first time for generations the adventurous young did not feel they had to go overseas to invent a future for themselves. It was, or at least it might be, possible to do it in Ireland. Not that the old tunes were totally silenced. The ultra-Catholic publication *The Word* still hammered on about Freemasonry, international Jewry, Marxism and Communist dupes; the Department of Foreign Affairs (under Frank Aiken) produced *Facts about Ireland* which described the foundation of the state and coming to power of Fianna Fáil, but in a feeble attempt to rewrite history, barely mentioned Michael Collins or Fine Gael.[1] In December ex-boxing champion Garda 'Lugs' Branigan became a sergeant. His technique of quieting trouble makers by what he called 'a few taps' from his formidable fists had made him a local character.

People got married and had babies in the old way too. And in 1963, for the second year running, the population actually went up. Because of the late marriage age, half the births in Dublin in 1963 were to women over thirty. (In England and Wales 70 per cent of births were to women under thirty.) Despite the current belief that there was an abnormal birth rate nine months after St Patrick's Day, in fact the peak month was May, with nearly two hundred births per day. These babies could look forward to between 62 and 67 years of life, depending on sex and whether they lived in town or country. Country people lived longer than townees, and women were expected to live two or three years longer than men. In 1932 the expectation for both sexes had been about 57 years, with women living a mere six months longer.

Antibiotics had dramatically shifted the horizon of death. In particular, the proportion of deaths of children under ten had collapsed from nearly 16 per cent of all deaths in the 1930s to just over 3 per cent, a proportion that was to drop to less than 2 per cent of all deaths by 1989. For the first time in human history, the death of a child was ceasing to be a common family event. The old scourge, tuberculosis, was down to 1 per cent of deaths. Pneumonia ('the old man's friend' as it was called) and bronchitis made 8 per cent; the big killers were heart attacks, strokes and cancer, which together accounted for over 40 per cent of deaths.

During their upbringing the children would have noticed a sharp difference between the way boys and girls were treated. Boys were nearly always exempted from household chores, while girls were expected to help with everything. 'My brothers do nothing to help at home. Is this usual? How can I change that?' a schoolgirl asked Angela MacNamara. In extreme cases they cleaned the boys' shoes and vacated favourite chairs when the the young master came into the room.[2] The marriage bar and other prevailing attitudes reinforced the sense of separate castes. While boys were to be toughened into breadwinners, girls were already undergoing an apprenticeship before becoming house-makers. The intense relationship that resulted between mother and son was proverbial. 'Only a mother knows the taste of salty tears,' one woman was told as she wept after her son's curly locks had been cut for the first time. 'The first haircut, the first day at school, they go to work, maybe across the sea and get married. You keep breaking your heart from the minute they are born—you never lose them though, you will always be their mother.'[3] Daughters had to learn to put up with this favoritism with wry resignation. Only when a mother-in-law attempted to continue the relationship with her son after his marriage was there likely to be serious tension. A middle-class male interviewee told Alexander Humphries 'my mother was very reluctant indeed about my marriage . . . she did not think any girl was good enough for me, or could take care of me.'

Two books of etiquette published in the 1960s were aimed at the future (male) breadwinner. Martin Molloy justifies his *Book of Irish Courtesy*,[4] on the grounds that 'social assets have a very solid market value, and the young man who possesses them is usually assured of a buyer . . . in the next few years this market value is certain to rise at a very rapid rate as Ireland draws nearer to entering the Common Market.' In their little etiquette book published in 1962, the successor to *Christian Politeness*, the Christian Brothers aspire to rather higher motives. For them Christian Courtesy 'is the fulfilling of the Divine precept . . . as you would that men should do to you, do you also to them in like manner.'[5]

There was some unease about the genre—if Ireland is as classless as we have been told, what place should there be for all this? Was there not what Martin Molloy called 'the aristocratic temper of the Irish mind'? 'This is,' he wrote, 'very much in evidence. Despite their long years of hardship, the Irish never became bourgeois: their minds were too fine, too sensitive. They have an inordinate respect for good breeding, not in any class-conscious sense but in their regard for the integrity and other personal qualities which they rightly associate with members of the Old Stock. This aristocratic stamp is very clearly exemplified in the average Irish countryman, than whom there is no finer gentleman to be found anywhere; and no shrewder judge of what constitutes a true gentleman.' In so far as books of etiquette are now needed, it is because 'centuries of serfdom, poverty and misery' have engendered 'plebeian attitudes and outlooks'.

Having thus elaborately side-stepped the question, the books concentrate on laying down a set of rather basic rules. If you want to get on, the simple message is, you must have, or pretend to have, middle-class manners. As Molloy explained: 'There are few social activities more revealing of the individual than his table manners. In normal society they are always interpreted as a pointer to one's upbringing and education ...no one with ambition to succeed in life can afford to risk having them called into question.' Judging by the prohibitions, both books assume a distinctly rougher starting-point than the 'Member of the Aristocracy' in the 1880s. For the table, we are told: don't play with your knife and fork, don't dip bread into the soup, don't put your knife in your mouth; don't stuff your mouth with food, or pile your plate mountain high; don't reach over others to get the salt, don't speak with your mouth full, shut your mouth while chewing. The two books handle differently the vexed question of how to hold the knife. Molloy says categorically to hold the handle in the palm, and only use the 'fountain-pen' grip for implements when taking soup or sweet; the Christian Brothers duck the question, leaving it to parents or teachers.

All this was taken quite seriously. The schoolboys at Catholic University School had regular elocution lessons, and F. X. Carty remembers his etiquette lessons in the Holy Ghost Seminary around this time. The lessons were given every Monday by the Sub-Master, who solemnly took his place at the speaker's rostrum complete with napkin, knife, fork, spoon and perhaps boiled egg, as he prepared to teach these future African missionaries the niceties of table manners. For instance, 'bread was to be cut into eight pieces and each piece buttered separately. Butter was to be placed on the side of the plate . . . under no circumstances was butter to be spread over the whole slice together . . . twenty-eight chews per moderate mouthful was the ideal. This would make us more like Christ, showing that we had control over the things of the flesh.'[6] One absolute rule was never to talk about food; to enjoy eating as such was unbecoming to a serious person. Lonely in the mission-field, many a Holy Ghost father felt that instruction on how to run a bank account, how to mend a car or how to build a school would have been rather more use.

In St Patrick's teacher training college in Dublin, John McGahern had experienced a different regime in the 1950s:

> Things were pretty savage really. One fellow got badly beaten [by the authorities] over an egg. There was a crew of students from the Gaeltacht who had come through special preparatory schools and really they were still savage. Rations were very small, so if you had any table manners at all you starved. This fellow anyway, complained that he hadn't got his boiled egg, so he was called up and given a battering in front of the whole refectory. Likewise, if you didn't go to daily Mass, you could be expelled.[7]

Authoritarian outrage was usually expressed physically. Beatings, slappings, hair-pulling, ear tweaking, bashing with books, canings, whippings, 'batterings' for all sorts of infringements and none were normal in homes, in élite schools, in Christian Brother establishments, in national schools, in the Irish language school in Ring, and in industrial schools. (The hidden reign of terror in the latter put them in a special category.) James Joyce described it in Clongowes: as the ferocious Father Dolan and his pandybat (whose 'loud crashing noise and fierce maddening tingling burning pain made his hand shrink together with the palms and fingers in a livid quivering mass'); and the boys were told: 'Father Dolan will be in every day to see if any boy, any lazy idle little loafer wants flogging'.[8] Discipline had to be maintained, and the obvious way was to instil physical fear. Smacking of children was common in the home, in the shops and in the streets, though in the 1960s decreasingly so among the middle class. Corporal punishment was finally banned in Irish schools in 1982 and became a criminal offence in 1996.

As with table manners, a chap's dress could unwitting reveal his origins, and more. 'Dress is often a reliable pointer,' wrote Martin Molloy, 'not alone to personality but also to character. It is the mark of a mature and balanced person that he does not follow every fad.' In practice Molloy recommended that his readers concentrate on the all-purpose lounge suit. 'This is the correct dress in Ireland for: informal dinners, cocktail parties, funerals, receptions, christenings, opera, ballet, race meetings, openings of Churches and Schools. On all of these occasions it is bad taste to appear in sports clothes.' Wearing of hats was no longer *de rigueur*, but if they were worn, correct hatmanship must be shown. 'Greeting a lady in the street, a gentleman who is wearing headdress raises it with the hand farther away from the lady.' The Christian

Brothers expected boys wearing caps to be particularly alert. Their cap should be raised:

— whenever they pass a church or cemetery;

—when they meet a Priest, Brother, Nun or a lady they know; (the naive clericalism that capitalises Priest, Brother and Nun but not church or lady is striking, and, in a book about courtesy, the significant order in which the groups appear.)

—when they are walking with a lady and someone salutes her;

— when they meet a friend with a lady (for example a class mate walking with his mother);

— when they are spoken to by a lady or by any person of high rank. They should also raise their caps when they finish speaking to such people. (We will no doubt easily recognise such a 'person of high rank'.)

—when they have done a lady some little service, such as picking up her handkerchief;

—when the National Anthem is being played (in this case the cap should be held in the right hand over the heart).

The courtly deference offered on all occasions to senior churchmen, from verbal buttering to ring-kissing, was, like their honorific titles and their vestments, from another era. A striking instance (being unforced and private) occurs in a secret report prepared in 1962 for Archbishop McQuaid about the conditions in Artane School, where 400 boys were sent for mitching from school, as orphans or petty criminals or as transferees from other institutions. The author, an experienced prison chaplain, condemns the poorly planned diet ('the boys are undernourished and lacking calcium and other components'); the clothing ('the boys' clothing is uncomfortable, unhygienic, and of a displeasing sameness. They are constantly dirty, both themselves and their clothes.'); the poor healthcare (the Brother in charge had no medical training, having recently been transferred from the poultry farm); the beatings ('constant recourse to physical punishment breeds undue fear and anxiety. The personality of the boy is inevitably repressed, maladjusted, and in some cases, abnormal.'); and even religious observance was criticised ('religion seems to make little impression on the majority of the boys. With many ex-pupils the practice of their Faith is a burden to be shunned'). At the end of this damning indictment the author of the report declares, in no ironic spirit: 'This Report would be incomplete without a special mention of the personal interest which Your Grace has taken in the welfare of these boys.'[9]

When this report was circulated secretly to the Department of

Education and the Christian Brothers, they of course resented it strongly. They explained the squalors by the fact that the Brothers were all men (and, they might have added, generally from not particularly well-off households) who could not be expected to know better. Their proposed solution was to introduce a more womanly touch to the arrangements, by asking some nuns to participate.

In general, dress at all levels was sober and dull. 'The variety and eccentricity of modern fashion' so much deplored by Martin Molloy was hardly in evidence. One returning emigrant, going for a stroll in a short-sleeved shirt and sunglasses on a fine Sunday morning in Dublin was embarrassed to find himself the only one so casually attired. Everyone else conformed to a formal dress code: 'The men in dark going-to-Mass suits and the women looking most refined in their carefully ironed dresses, veiled hats and white gloves'.[10]

Even for students suits, grey flannels and sombre sports jackets were the style. When a London photographer came to UCD in October 1963 to take photographs for a book on Ireland, he put on what he supposed would be suitably studentish suede jacket and red tie. He was therefore quite taken aback when he saw the anonymous grey mass of male UCD students. The weight of convention was felt quite heavily: when one student went for a day in Malahide with a male friend she noted: 'G. very scruffy, long hair, suit, no tie.' A few days later the boy had had his hair cut, and apologised for not having worn a tie.[11]

Women of course were driven by a much more exacting code. They were, for instance, forbidden to wear trousers inside UCD, and they covered their heads in church. They were expected to conform as far as possible by wearing clothes that recognised such norms. 'Keep away from pants and jeans' advised the author of *Dating Without Tears* (a book in which there is a sympathetic postscript for the over twenty-fives) 'unless you have slim hips and a very flat tummy *and* long legs . . . whatever you've chosen, you must be wearing the right size and shape of girdle and brassiere underneath.' For a Christmas party the thirteen-year-old Caroline Walsh wore 'the woollen red skirt I wasn't so sure about but which the lady in the shop had deemed ideal, the little blouse, the inevitable black patent shoes, and—oh thrilling moment—my brand new, first-time-ever suspender belt and nylons.'[12] These were very soon to follow the corset and the crinoline into history: in September Ida Grehan noted in *The Irish Times* the arrival of tights—'a one-piece 15-denier arrangement not at all unlike a leotard—dressing would certainly be considerably faster'.

To help women undergraduates to conform, a modelling and beauty class was organised for Trinity students. Run by Mrs Zoe Weinman, who owned a modelling agency in Dublin, it included daily classes in deportment, clothes coordination, colour sense, make-up and hair. In her preliminary talk on The Secret of Attraction, Mrs Weinman revealingly 'stressed the need to shock girls into realising that people were commenting on their general sloppiness.'[13] In the authoritarian style of the day the young women were to be 'shocked' into abandoning casual student habits for some ideal of clothes-coordinated rectitude—and the weapon of choice was 'people are talking', the great sanction of a small, conformist society.

There were eight modelling agencies in the city, some offering 'improvement courses'. A young woman who had taken such a course told the *Sunday Press*: 'I had worn no make-up except lipstick until then, and the beauty woman told me I would have to take care of my skin— that meant the purchase not only of cold cream and face powder but of skin tonic, nourishing cream, tinted foundation, eye make-up and face packs. After the course I felt very glam., all those deportment exercises made me feel two inches taller. I knew how to pluck my eyebrows the right way.' Her boyfriend was less enthusiastic—with the ungracious directness many men prided themselves on, he 'said the course made me look less like a model than ever.'[14] No doubt the same woman read with interest beauty consultant Bronwyn Conroy's interviews with TV personalities Gay Byrne and Terry Wogan. They were asked what they were looking for in a 'living doll' as the 1959 Cliff Richard hit put it: Gay Byrne thought he liked femininity, intelligence, a nice voice and figure, good legs in dark stockings, blonde hair, brown eyes and sensible clothes. Wogan was more interested in a sense of humour, good dress sense and grooming, and his pet hate was bad make-up.[15]

Boots and trousers for women were the new thing. 'Boots, boots, boots and more boots' commanded *Vogue*; in Paris Saint Laurent concentrated on 'showing women how to dress for their boots.' One of his models was shown with alligator boots shockingly high up her thigh. The rule for 1963 was: legs first. If they weren't in boots, they were in knitted stockings, in paisley, cable knits, rugger socks, diamonds, tartans.[16] Women's trousers, depressingly called 'slacks', were another source of scorn to the old-fashioned, for whom the so-called 'Gigi look' (derived from a Leslie Caron film about a French courtesan) was much more the thing. During the great freeze in the early months of 1963, when there was skating on the pond in Dublin Zoo for the first time since 1947, 'Cherchez la femme' wrote to the *Sunday Press* complaining that 'it is rare these cold days to see a woman under forty wearing a skirt while out shopping. The streets are full of muffled, duffled and betrousered travesties of womanhood . . . come on girls, let's have some glamour to brighten up the streets!' 'My father doesn't approve of slacks', Angela MacNamara was asked. 'What do you think?' And S. Ó Cuanac agreed with him: 'The masculine clad female', he considered, 'is one of the most revolting sights for mankind to behold.' The readers of the *Sunday Press* would not have won prizes for feminist thinking—in March another complained about having to pay when he took a girl out: 'It takes a brave man,' he wrote, 'to take out one of these painted, trousered, fashion ladies of today. These painted ladies are not worth a smoke to any man.'[17] In Jack White's 1962 novel *The Devil You Know*, in Italy Eileen Sugrue found being pinched was about as erotic as a mosquito bite, but at least 'it aroused in her an awareness that she was a Woman and they Men, a fact of which she had rarely been made conscious on top of the 11 bus to Ranelagh.'[18]

Although they might have been more graceful, the *Sunday Press* readers could be excused for not being feminists; Betty Friedan's path-finding book *The Feminine Mystique* was only just published, and Val Mulkerns, reviewing it in *The Irish Times*, wasn't much impressed: 'She forgets that the full life of the mind only works if there is a mind there in the first place. . . . It is my belief that if the cage doors were suddenly opened, the prisoners would scuttle back to the kitchen at the earliest possible chance.'[19] Others, such as June Levine, also had trouble with *The Feminine Mystique* when it first came out: 'How could she really know what life was like for a girl like me? I was twenty-nine years old and had three children, and still did not call myself a woman.'[20] Women were discouraged in various ways from thinking of themselves—in some households even saying 'I' was frowned on. A middle-class woman told Alexander Humphries: 'In our family if you started to express any ideas of your own, or to take on any projects, my father would put a stop to it. He would tell you not to be ridiculous, and he would put you in your place.' Later in May 1963 the Chief Justice Cearbhall Ó Dálaigh told the Irish Housewives Association that 'the women of this country had equal rights with men six years before the women of Britain.'[21] (He meant of course voting rights, and did not refer to the Constitution-led closing-in we have seen occurring from the 1930s.)

In the month that Mulkerns' review was published, Dublin was reading less challenging matter: top of the fiction best-sellers was Ian Fleming's *On Her Majesty's Secret Service*, then Daphne du Maurier's *The Glassblowers* and Monica Dickens' *Cobbler's Dream*. Top of the non-fiction list was Cecil Woodham-Smith's *The Great Hunger*, then Mícheál Mac Liammóir's *The Importance of being Oscar*, Cardinal Suenens' *The Nun in the World*, and Kevin Danaher's *Ireland Long Ago*.[22]

A more realistic estimate of relative positions of the sexes even in middle-class Dublin was revealed by a Ballsbridge housewife who wrote to *The Irish Times* in January complaining bitterly about an architect's proposed scheme of three-storey houses. 'No woman,' she declared, 'will single-handedly take on a three storey house. . . .'

> This is not prejudice or obstinacy, but working knowledge gained seven days a week winter and summer, most days doing at least fourteen hours. Can I really manage to carry my sick husband's breakfast tray, the week's washing, the parcel from the cleaners, and the toddler's damp mattress down the stairs all at once, and without letting the baby slip out from under my arm? . . . Naturally while she nurses four consecutive cases of measles on the third floor, the good housewife finds time to organise neat piles at the front door for the milkman and the breadman, the notes and the key for the ESB or the gasman, the key at the back door for the coalman, not to mention the procession of beggars, sales folk, children next door and, dear oh dear, not another beastly friend calling in? Of course reliable, consistent help from a loving husband would be fairly useful, but so many men seem to have an 'anti-attitude' to running up and down stairs on messages for their wives.[23]

Since the husband would very probably have been exempted by his mother from any contribution to housework since he was a boy, this was not a surprise.

One great solvent to so many of these attitudes was to be television. Telefís Éireann (TE) had been launched with great fanfares at the end of 1961. It was given the typically contradictory task of making money, while at the same time 'bearing constantly in mind the national aims of restoring the Irish language and preserving and developing the national culture'.[24] Despite constant carping from critics, the first aim tended to predominate: Irish language programmes, for instance, took up only half of broadcast time. Television had become a fact of Irish life by 1963, broadcasting five or six hours a day, of which 55 per cent were programmes bought in from abroad, mainly America. The average set was switched on for nearly three hours every day of the week. When the Charles Haugheys advertised for a nanny (£5 a week) they were careful to stress that both central heating and television were available.[25]

Pundits began to worry about the effects on family life: 'Only at meal-times does a family meet with a common object in view ... those homes where meals are eaten on a tip and run basis, with one eye on the clock or the TV are missing something irreplaceable.'[26]

Evidence of the 'loneliness, dullness and generally unattractive nature of life in many parts of rural Ireland, compared with the pattern of life in urban centres' had greatly impressed the 1955 Commission on Emigration,[27] so the impact of television was marked. Advertising man Peter Owen told Tony Gray:

> I know a farming family who live in a cottage which used to have a plain concrete floor. A few weeks ago I called on them and the boys were busy putting down plastic tiles. They had seen how to do it on TV. No sooner had they got the tiles down than they decided that the old turf grate didn't look right with their lovely new floor. So they put in a Kosangas cooker. The walls then began to look out of place so they redecorated the whole room. And because people kept carting mud into their beautiful new kitchen they put an apron of cement around the house. That's the impact of televison.[28]

Television was by no means universal however, perhaps because it was seen primarily as entertainment. People as news conscious as journalists did not necessarily possess a set. F. X. Carty recalls that his father, then editor of the best selling newspaper in the country, the *Sunday*

Dublin Opinion

"Dí fear ann fadó agus fadó a bí——*will ye listen to me?*"

Press, only bought one in the middle of 1963.[29] As Frank Duff resignedly admitted, 'we had better face up to the fact that amusement is one of the special purposes to be served by TE'. 'What,' he asked, giving an interesting list of desiderata, 'is TE doing about the following—Emigration, Unemployment, Clean Sport, Excessive Drinking, the Slaughter on the Roads, the Building of Industry (including the buying of Irish products, Honest Work, Giving Value) Duty and Discipline, modest Living, Public Order, Proper Administration of the Law, Untidy Towns, Public Spirit and Christian standards generally?'[30]

Favourite programmes included (from America) *Sergeant Bilko, Bat Masterson, Have Gun will Travel, Dr Kildare* and *The Jack Benny Show*; locally made programmes with high TAM ratings included *The Showband Show*, the *News, Country Style, Jackpot* and *O'Dea's Your Man*. Popular English TV, for those who could get it on the East coast, included *Sunday Night at the London Palladium, 6.5 Special, Emergency Ward 10*. The bright young names were Terry Wogan, Bunny Carr, then a continuity announcer but later to compère a long-running quiz show, and Gay Byrne. Byrne had just completed his first season of the *Late, Late Show* to some acclaim, but he was taking no chances. He was at this time also working four days a week in England for Granada and BBC Manchester.[31]

Just as the Eucharistic Congress had stimulated radio purchase, the great events of 1963, in particular Kennedy's visit and the election of Pope Paul VI, stimulated TV sales. At the beginnng of the decade one house in three had a TV set. There was active and persistent licence evasion: in 1962 11,000 people were prosecuted for not having radio or TV licences.[32] The relatively slow acceptance of TV in rural areas surprised local pundits, but by the end of the sixties three quarters of homes had TV.[33] In 1980 more households nationwide had TV sets than had indoor lavatories, running hot water or baths.[34]

It took a little time to get used to the reality presented by television. Although the *News* as such was always high in the ratings, audiences for home-produced public affairs programmes, which tended to be straightforward studio discussions, were not large. But it was noticed, that as Maxwell Sweeney observed, 'there has been less inhibition in discussions on television than on the radio'. This phenomenon was to become more marked as the *Late Late Show* got into its stride in the next few years. The broadcasting of religious services, such as Benediction, caused problems. They were often at awkward hours, for example just when the children were being put to bed, or the family tea was in progress. The viewer was puzzled how to react with proper reverence—should domestic chores be stopped, should one kneel, or put out cigarettes? In June a Dublin woman sued TE for libel on the grounds that her husband, an actor, had been portrayed in an advertisement apparently married to another woman. She claimed that this was taken by several people (including her sister, who gave evidence) to mean that she was not her husband's lawful wife, and that she was living in sin with him. The case got to the High Court, but was dismissed before going to the jury.[35]

Television was the flashy medium of the sixties: advertisers echoed its jargon: 'I guess I'm tuned in to the wrong channel—I'm right out of the picture' ran one Colgate ad. In her list of 'What's In' journalist Bríd Mahon included: two-button suits (for men); doing the Bossa Nova; going to an island for your holiday; calling your son Seán and your daughter something old-fashioned like Sarah, Miriam or Deborah; serving Irish stew or pigs feet, bacon and cabbage for your party; and watching *TW3*. This last was the BBC satire programme *That Was The Week That Was* which infuriated the staid with skits such as the Consumer Guide to Religions. 'Cheap smart alec superficiality' declared *The Irish Times* TV critic John McDonnell. 'Satire sounds smart, but it covers prejudice, cruelty and sheer bad taste.'[36] 'Bad taste', like the previous generation's 'vulgarity', was a marker of the respectful attitude to hierarchy and authority which was very much still part of Irish social life.

One way or another daily life in urban Ireland was becoming more and more open to the world—not only to the 'great moral laxness of Britain', as Angela MacNamara put it, on the television screens, but also to the exciting possibilities for a country that could produce such men as the President of the United States. Kennedy was, for many in Ireland, the symbol of the potential of a new successful dynamic Ireland. No wonder so many took him to their hearts during his extraordinarily successful visit in June 1963.

The Nice Man Cometh

After the drama of the Cuba crisis, Ireland was hardly braced for the dramas of 1963. As *The Irish Times* political correspondent wrote: 'There has not been its like both in the extraordinary significance of the foreign events and in the manner of their effects on the country.'[37] The year began with a disappointment. Throughout 1962 people had been getting used to becoming European—to joining the EEC. The British reference book the *Annual Register* covering 1962 was full of articles analysing the likely impacts of EEC membership on Britain and Ireland.

One of these was a reduction in tariffs, the first since 1932, put in place in January 1963. And then General de Gaulle, rightly suspecting the wholeheartedness of Britain's conversion to Europe, vetoed the British application and the Irish fell with it. Such was the mood in the country that this set-back hardly dented confidence at all. Economic planning (the Second Programme for Economic Expansion) went ahead on the assumption of EEC membership by 1970. The tariff reduction was left. And there were other matters to distract attention. In June the saintly Pope John XXIII died, leaving his work on the Vatican Council to be completed by others.

Very soon after this President Kennedy, the hero of the Cuba crisis, the symbol of youth and widening possibilities to all young Irishmen and women, arrived in Dublin airport. During his three-day stay, Kennedy visited Dublin, Wexford, Cork, Limerick and Galway. At every stage there was a curious compound of large measures of rhetoric with equally large measures of affection on both sides. His visit was a great excuse for a party: 'Off to Clonliffe Road to see Kennedy,' wrote a student diarist. 'Scrumptious tea laid out and almost entire family there ... Flags waving, music over loudspeakers, we all got up on the wall ... the President arrived at last, looking young and fit and bronzed, smiling. Buses and cars full of security and press men all American looking.'[38] This was Kennedy's fourth visit to Ireland. (On his previous visit in 1957, just three years before he became President, Jacqueline Kennedy rang the *Irish Independent* from the Shelbourne to offer an interview, but the journalist decided to take the details over the telephone. It was Sunday, as he said, and 'three fellows are waiting for me on the golf course.'[39])

Kennedy himself seemed genuinely to enjoy the visit, perhaps because in Ireland he could get away for a time from the enormous problems he was facing. He had left an America that was on the brink of racial explosion. Led by Martin Luther King, blacks had begun to assert their right to eat at downtown lunch counters, to ride on buses, to go to university, to vote. As King fought his battle of wits and courage against the dogs and fire hoses of police chief Eugene 'Bull' Connor (another Irishman), in Birmingham, Alabama, many were waiting for New York, Chicago, Philadelphia and other cities to explode with riots. Just before his arrival in Dublin Kennedy had been in Berlin, the most sensitive theatre of the Cold War. Artfully mixing German phrases among the English rhetoric, he restated his commitment to keeping West Berlin non-communist—*Ich bin ein Berliner*, he declared. To those who believed that communism was the way of the future: '*Lass die nach Berlin kommen*' (let them come to Berlin), and the hairs stood up on the heads of men and women across the developed world.

On his arrival at Dublin, he was greeted with no such tensions. De Valera addressed him in Irish, 'our native language, the language of your ancestors, the language that was spoken by the great Kennedy clan of the Dal gChais who, under the mighty King Brian Boru smashed the invader and broke the Norse power forever.' Kennedy himself played vigorously to this audience, reaching back to a rhetoric that had in many Irish ears begun to sound a little hollow. In his speech to the Oireachtas, he spoke glowingly of Irish progress and rising living standards. 'Other nations in the world in whom Ireland has long invested her people and her children are now investing their capital as well as their vacations in Ireland . . . this revolution is not over yet.'[40] The description of a hundred and fifty years of enforced emigration as the nation 'investing her people' was certainly tactful.

The Irish view of Kennedy was wholly approving, though not always very knowledgable. In a comment after his visit to Ireland in June 1963 *Hibernia* wrote in its July issue: 'Whatever hostile historians may do to the political record of John Kennedy, his status as the model head of a perfectly natural family is above assault. Kennedy's impregnable personal position, buttressed by private wealth and a truly Christian family life is of prime value to the nation he leads.' His visit gave a tremendous boost to national self-confidence. Here was 'one of our own', who had 'fled from the famine ravaged potato fields' to achieve the most powerful office on earth. He gave a kind of presidential seal of approval to the nation's new look, and as a plus put the old enemy in its place. Reviewing the just-published *The Great Hunger*, John Connell hit a similar note: 'From the embattled Kennedys and Fitzgeralds and Curleys would one day spring a President of the United States who would be the leader of the Western world and who would spell out in a friendly way the end of Britain as a great Power. It would be a foolish Irishman who will rejoice at the eclipse of Britain in this age; our economies are too closely linked. But he would be a poor Irishman also who did not recognise that we have in us the power to be a greater people.'[41]

In Wexford the President was shown 'documentary proof of the rebel blood of his ancestors.' These were the prison records of a distant cousin who once spent two months in hard labour in Wexford Jail in 1888 for resisting arrest and obstructing the sheriff. As the *Sunday Press* put it, 'the hatred of oppression, the belief in the God-given freedom of man that are so much a characteristic of President Kennedy may have come down from the rebel blood which coursed through the veins of his ancestor James Kennedy who preferred jail to submission to an injustice.' At Galway the mayor spoke his words of welcome entirely in Irish and Kennedy matched the moment. He 'rounded off his address by telling the crowd that if they ever went to Washington and told the man at the gate that they were from Galway, there would be a Céad Míle Fáilte for them.'

On his return from New Ross, where his distant cousins had given him tea and cake in a smiling and informal atmosphere, there was a garden party in Áras an Uachtaráin. Two thousand had been invited, and for weeks beforehand fashion writers had been worrying about What To Wear. Simple, well-tailored clothes, recommended one, no chiffon or silks. Hats were essential—by 26 June a leading milliner reported that she hadn't a hat left in the shop, everything from thirty shillings to thirty guineas had walked out of the door. On the big day, ministers' wives favoured chic blue and white, and wild silk two piece suits were also popular. Since it rained, the most useful accessory spotted by fashion writer Ida Grehan was a plastic parasol decorated with bright red flowers.

When the President came out of the Áras, the guests surged forward. An obviously distraught de Valera tried to motion the pressing crowd back with his hands, but to little avail. 'Especially the elegantly dressed women wanted to shake hands with the smiling young president,' wrote *The Irish Times* reporter.

> Toes were trampled on, high heels sank into the lawn, shoes were lost, beautiful hats were crumpled, guests fell over chairs ... all the while Kennedy shook as many of the grasping hands as possible, including the white gloved hand of a woman who shouted and waved frantically over the heaving shoulders of the security men. 'Jack, Jack, my hand, shake my hand!' When he did she turned away and adjusted her hat, expressing utter satisfaction to her friends and the others on whom she had trampled.

Politely ignoring this display by the great and the good of the nation, the *Sunday Press* summed up the visit emotionally.

> In three short days this young man of destiny, great grandson of an Irish emigrant and leader of a mighty nation had written his own footnote in our history. He has given us a new pride in our heritage, won his way into our hearts and touched the very core of our being by honouring our patriot dead. They were three days of crowded incident, of welcome, of civic function and national honour for this boyish-looking statesman. But for the Irish people

who gave their hearts it was a mighty period of burning pride, affection and esteem ... For many the most lasting memory of President Kennedy will be his moments with the little schoolgirls outside the Ryan homestead. Watching their shyness melt away away and seeing them whisper excitedly into his ear was a heartstopping business.

The new note of the sixties was youth. The children of the post-war baby boom in the western world came bumptiously into their own, demanding appropriate services and products. Entrepreneurs, from record companies to clothes manufacturers, tumbled over themselves to supply this market. For the first time to be young was not a sign of unstable immaturity, but a positive value. Advertisers used 'young' as vigorously and with as much justification as they used 'green' in 1990. Fashions became informal; young designers fresh from art college, such as Mary Quant, made clothes they themselves liked to wear. The fiercely expensive fashions of Paris took a back seat. Even in Ireland this was felt. At Lady's Day at Punchestown *The Irish Times* noticed that 'informality rather than high fashion was the keynote ... one of the most interesting evolutions over the last two or three years is the equalising of fashion.'

In general, politics was still in the hands of the old men whose original claims had been staked between 1916 and 1922. Lemass' government did contain the 'men in mohair suits', O'Malley, Lenihan and Haughey, who were in their thirties, but their attitudes were not exactly youthful. 'I am not one of those,' remarked Mr Haughey (aged thirty-eight) 'who think that the young of today are to be despaired of.'[42] By contrast, a large part of President Kennedy's attraction for so many people was that he was young: a mere forty-five. 'To the rest of us who still have old men at the top,' wrote Mary Holland in *Vogue*, Kennedy's 'youth, vitality and firecracker energy made them seem like tired Victorians.'[43] The Beatles came to the Adelphi in Dublin in November and teenagers rampaged in O'Connell Street. Seán Moore, the Lord Mayor, a Fianna Fáil TD, couldn't understand what he sniffily described as 'a display of moronic barbarity after a performance by a cross-channel theatrical group.' Perhaps he would have preferred the Waterford showband star Brendan Bowyer and the Royals who were packing thousands every night into dance halls across the country. Bowyer had Irish No 1 hits in 1963 with 'Kiss me quick' and 'No more'.

New American-style high office buildings began to rise above Dublin's natural four-storey skyline, to the disgust of the refined. Liberty Hall, O'Connell Bridge House and Hawkins House were the most conspicuous of these. A new concern with appearance was burgeoning: 'One can see it in simple things like the replacement of the traditional green paint on doors by more subtle colours; in the brighter interiors of homes and offices; the government has had its Scandinavian report and the *Irish Press* its facelift. Dublin city has a mushroom growth of modern architecture.'⁴⁴ The controversy over the ESB's houses in Fitzwilliam Street was just getting under way. For many, there was satisfaction in the idea that at last the Ascendancy's Georgian buildings, attractive as they were, could be replaced with something truly Irish.

Kennedy left, promising to come back as soon as possible. Five months later he was dead. On Friday 22 November in Dallas, Texas he was assassinated. The shock was felt across the world, but especially deeply in Ireland. 'Nowhere in the free world,' wrote James Meenan in the *Annual Register,* 'did the assassination at Dallas bring a sharper sense of personal loss'. One diarist records fulfilling a theatre engagement (*A Man for All Seasons*), but leaving at the interval: 'I was shocked all through.' And on Saturday only the one line entry: 'still dreadfully upset by Kennedy'; on Sunday 'watched news on TV all day. Dead hopeless feeling. B rang, but I didn't go out.'⁴⁵ Many sports fixtures were cancelled on the Saturday, and normal Saturday night activities came to a standstill. In a letter to an American diplomat friend, Garret FitzGerald summed up his feelings and those of most Irish people.

> What I wanted to say was simply how shattered we are at Kennedy's death. No one here realised how much he meant to us until he died. All have felt a sense of loss that normally arises only on the death of some near relative. For once Irish cynicism was silent, and even the most hard-bitten Dubliners have been moved. Had you been here I think you would have been moved yourself at the reaction of the whole Irish people to this tragedy. Even now, a week later, we have not recovered.

Over the next decades, driven by the great equaliser television, the aspirations of the Dublin middle classes were to become (with some lags) the aspirations of the country as a whole. In the past, urban children had learnt Irish through tales of reaping and sowing, harrowing and winnowing. Now country children were to learn the language through images of pop stars, boxing matches and housing estates. Ireland was undoubtedly becoming richer, but very little thought was given to how the newly enlarged cake might be divided. Most subscribed to Lemass' comfortable dictum that a rising tide lifts all boats. Lemass himself, however, did not believe that this was the whole story. In a speech in May he said there was growing evidence that 'all have benefited in some degree [from economic success] . . . but that inequalities and distortions have emerged or widened is also true. It should be possible for a Christian nation ... to develop methods of sharing the benefits of better living which economic progress makes realisable.'[46]

The advancing Catholic urban middle class saw such remarks as addressed not to them, but to the trade unions, which no doubt they were. However, the audience to whom this speech was given (the National Convention of Junior Chambers of Commerce) suggests that Lemass may have had a wider target in mind. The middle class ignored this possibility, and quietly got on with the business of consolidating their social position, control and ultimately wealth.

It was not only the economic and social fabric that needed to be renewed. The structure of these tenement houses in Fenian Street, Dublin, was so rotten that on 12 June 1963 they simply collapsed into the street, killing two children. (Illustrated London News)

Chapter 16 Cracks begin to show

The 1960s came late to Ireland. The intention and effect of de Valera's policies since 1932 had been to insulate the country from rough winds overseas. 'It would be a fine thing for us in this country,' he once said, 'if we could shut ourselves off from the rest of the world and get back to the simple life I knew as a boy in Bruree.' (De Valera and his family actually lived in the comfortable suburb of Blackrock in Co. Dublin.) From inside, the country had been seen increasingly as the last bastion of real Catholicism and of the ancient traditions of the Celtic race. From outside, as one journalist put it, the country summoned up images of 'pints of Guinness, Brendan Behan, wet macintoshes, Sweep tickets, rosary beads, Irish coffee, turf bogs, round towers, Donegal tweed, bacon and cabbage, banned books, racehorses, fist fights, ballad singing, rain.'[1]

The Economic War, emigration, neutrality, protectionism, the 'sore-thumb' policy in relation to the North, and a complacent authoritarianism from the professional class had each added to the effect. Isolation, and the willingness of other countries to accept Irish emigrants, reinforced the conditions that created it, as Father Biever discovered. 'Mister,' a middle-aged man told him, 'the Irish have the answer to any social problem that might come up. It might not be the best answer, but it is the one we have come to use—out! Thousands do it every year. I like it here, but the youngsters don't seem to, so they move. Why get all involved for someone who is going to leave the country just as soon as they can anyway?'[2]

For thirty years the country had been conservative and protectionist in cultural, economic and religious terms. Its citizens had left in thousands whenever they could; for those at the top it was too easy to excuse this depressing fact by blaming the unreasonable aspirations of those who had gone.[3] From the time of Burke, the acid test of governance had been the increase of population. In Ireland, uniquely in Europe, this was not happening. But why? If only, said the politicians, our people would be satisfied with a frugal rural life, all would be well. Leading solicitor and Fine Gael *eminence grise* Alexis FitzGerald no doubt expressed a common view of the well-got middle-class when he declared that in the order of values it seems more important to preserve and improve the quality of Irish life than it is to reduce the numbers of Irish emigrants . . . high emigration, granted a population excess, releases social tensions which would otherwise explode and makes possible a stability of manners and customs which would otherwise be the subject of radical change.[4]

De Valera had begun his long period of dominance of Irish parliamentary politics as a radical, with a ringing statement of intent. He declared that 'if we fail to make the radical changes obviously necessary to provide for all our citizens so that everyone may be at least reasonably housed, clothed and fed, we shall be failing in our duty, and failing cruelly and disastrously.' Years in office took the edge off this ambition, though his personal charisma ensured that he remained by far the most popular politician in the state. The 1961 Census revealed that at least half of all houses outside the urban areas simply had no lavatory facilities whatsoever, indoors or out. In Longford, for instance, there were only 1,600 indoor lavatories in the whole county of 30,000 people. To be fair, this was some improvement on the 1946 Census which revealed that a mere 4 per cent of all dwellings had a fixed bath, and 82 per cent of farm dwellings across the country had no fixed sanitary arrangements. Not that this was as exceptional as it might seem; the 1954 Census in France revealed that only a quarter of homes had indoor toilets and a mere 10 per cent had a bathtub or shower.[5]

Commentators spoke of 'threadbare villages, half ruins and half tacky shops, almost as dreary as ghost towns . . . rank country towns spreading out and out like spilt drink.'[6] The rural-idyll writer Alice Taylor described removing the acumulated squalor before the Stations in one country farmhouse. 'Dunghills disappeared from the yard . . . loose sheets of galvanised iron were nailed down and missing slates replaced. . . . Mice and spiders who had nested comfortably in the house for months [were swept away]. . . . Broken window panes patched with bits of old timber were replaced.' In a neighbour's house the milk sat on the table in a bucket, hens nested under the table, and mice infested the linen box.[7] Edna O'Brien's description of the grim country towns in Clare (in her 1960 novel *The Country Girls*) echoed this.

In the 1950s four hundred thousand Irish out of just under three million decided that de Valera's idea of reasonable comfort was not theirs. De Valera was however more concerned with the other objectives of his party, notably the reinvigorating of the Irish language and the reunification of the national territory. To the end of his life he was said to regard the preservation of the Irish language as more important

than combating unemployment or emigration. Few in the 1960s, even in
Fianna Fáil, agreed with him. In the lower ranks, as in the property and
business community, men waited. 'It can't stay like this,' said a character
in Brian Cleeve's novel of the times *Cry of Morning*. Things have got to
start moving sooner or later . . . all it needs is a few things to happen—
like the Long Fellow shifting up to the Park and letting Seán Lemass
take over. And some smart money coming in. This Common Market
everybody's talking about.'[8] The objective of putting more people to
work on the land had also failed: the very opposite had occurred. In
fact by the 1960s the national project seemed to be stalling—the old
consensus was slipping away. The new men, in mohair suits, with quite
different ideas about service, personal wealth and power, awaited their
opportunity.

Dev's magic lay in his great personal charm, and in allowing the people to feel good about themselves, without their actually having to do
very much. In Ireland, he was reported to have said, 'you can do what you
like, as long as you say the right thing'.[9] In a rough post-colonial world
it was undoubtedly comfortable to be regularly reminded, as one writer
put it, of 'the aristocratic stamp of the Irish, their innate refinement,
delicacy of feeling, artistic sense, their interest in culture and learning,
their strong spirituality . . . and side by side with these their manliness,
physical vigour and courage.'[10] If things went wrong there was always
the English to blame. If the Irish were occasionally worse than 'the true
greatness of their aristocratic past' would lead one to expect, the same
writer continued, this is simply because of 'centuries of serfdom, poverty
and misery'.[11]

In a speech in the 1860s, John Stuart Mill had pointed out that 'Ireland
is not an exceptional country but England is. Irish circumstances and
Irish ideas as to social and agricultural economy are the general ideas
of the human race; it is English circumstances and English ideas that
are peculiar. Ireland is in the mainstream of human existence and
human feelings and experience; it is England that is in one of the lateral
channels.'[12] It was Ireland's bad luck to be so exposed to this abnormal
force. We have seen in previous chapters how the gravitational force
of England drove tastes, social customs and economic arrangements, a
factor in the Irish circumstance that was still strong in 1963 and is hardly
gone yet, despite the collapse, to continue the metaphor, from a Red
Giant to a White Dwarf.

The excuse had begun to wear a bit thin. *Hibernia* quoted an old man's
story about how he and a friend had left Clare as young men to make

their fortunes in Liverpool. Amid the customary lamentations they set out, and after great travelling they arrived at the great city, where to their disgust, though not to their surprise, very few people seemed able to speak Irish. Exhausted by the trip they lodged for the night in a cheap hotel. When they awoke they found that all their possessions—packed into suitcases—had been stolen. It was just the kind of thing to be expected when one ventured into ruthless pagan England. The writer said that he could well understand that such a traumatic experience could cause a profound and life-long hatred for the English, particularly since it had been English economic policy that had driven him out of the West in the first place. 'And there was worse to it than that,' continued the old man. 'Later in the day we found that after all that travelling we hadn't got to Liverpool at all, and the place we were in was Dublin!'

By 1963, after a miraculously successful switch in economic policy the Irish economy was growing faster than any in Europe, and the heat of economic success was warming stiff bones. After so long a hibernation, the warmth of an economic spring-time was very pleasant on the skin. For the young the isle was full of noises, sounds and airs that gave delight and hurt not.

For most of the old men in power, however, this new warmth was a mixed blessing. Prominent among the old men in power was the sixty-eight-year-old Archbishop John Charles McQuaid, who had been Archbishop of Dublin since 1940. McQuaid, like so many of his priests, was a countryman—he had been born in Cootehill, Co. Cavan. Educated as a Holy Ghost father in the traditions of Fathers Cahill and Fahey, his flinty public image concealed acts of private generosity and public social concern. But like de Valera, he longed for a mythical past. For him, the scholastic philosophers of the 12th and 13th centuries had moulded Europe into a civilised unit of social, juridical and religious culture. In this imaginary world kings and emperors bowed to the Church; there were no Protestants, Freemasons, Liberals or Communists; Jews were kept in ghettos; heretics were firmly dealt with. This was, as Edward Cahill SJ put it, 'the Golden Age of Christianity', the time when 'the Christian State then approached most nearly its full development.'[13]

The problem was how to recover that glory in modern conditions. It was certainly not likely that mere economic success would do it, and neither would ecumenism. McQuaid had after all been instrumental in closing down perhaps naive Legion of Mary attempts to draw Jews and Protestants into the Church by debate and discussion.[14] The Church's discipline, which included its control of education, offered the best opportunity. McQuaid's two preparatory suggestions to the great Vatican Council which started in October 1962 were typical of his approach. Firstly, he asked that religious orders be no longer exempted from the power of the local bishop, an obvious strengthening of episcopal power. Then he called for the the much loved doctrine of Mary as the mediatrix of grace to be elevated from its current lowly status as no more than a 'pious opinion', a move which would of course deeply alienate the Pope's 'separated brethren', the Protestants.[15]

In common with many Irish bishops McQuaid quite mistook the importance of the Second Vatican Council, which in the event completely changed the face of Catholicism. They regarded it as merely finishing off the abruptly terminated business of the Council of 1870, whose most celebrated act had been to copperfasten the doctrine of Papal infallibility. At least one member from a southern diocese attempted to stay at home rather than attend, and there was a general expectation that, as McQuaid famously announced, 'no change will worry the tranquillity of your Christian lives.' Dr Lucey, Bishop of Cork, assured his people in his Lenten message in 1963 that 'nothing sensational will emerge from the Council.' Throughout the debates McQuaid held grimly to his conservative position against a rising tide of reform. Xavier Rynne, the contemporary chronicler of the Council, reported that in the discussion on the development of the Mass, 'Archbishop McQuaid came out once more against any thought of change.' He was at least listened to. Cardinal Browne, the Irish Dominican, suffered the indignity of the fathers retreating to the nearby coffee shop as he 'droned on' about St Thomas Aquinas.[16]

This clerical complacency stemmed from a deep assurance of being right, reinforced by the position the Church held in the esteem of the Irish people. The American Jesuit B. F. Biever found that nearly 90 per cent of his sample agreed with the proposition that 'the Church is the greatest force for good in Ireland today.'[17] Clergymen benefited largely from the still-strong culture of deference to politicians, professionals and priests. Biever describes being startled by so many 'ostensible signs of respect, men tipping their hats to clergymen on the street, women bowing or crossing themselves, policemen stopping the traffic at a busy crossing so that the good father may cross without delay'.[18] In the libraries of University College Dublin the students stood for the Angelus at twelve o'clock and six o'clock. Church-derived images saturated conversation: even in the pubs the barman was known as the curate and the snug was called the confessional; a certain type of active, competent, bossy woman was called a Reverend Mother, and a different type of unctuous authoritative man was referred to as a lay bishop. The American Jesuit describes how he joined a queue to make a telephone call, 'when to his chagrin the person in the booth, who was already in the middle of her call, hung up, came out and surrendered the booth to him. He protested, but the reply was simple: "no priest should be standing in line waiting for the likes of me"'.[19] English Catholic visitors were astounded by the matter-of-fact way Irish priests accepted these obeisances.

There was no great popular pressure for change: 88 per cent of the sample refused to declare the Church 'out of date'—Father Biever's respondents declared complacently: 'when you've got the truth, lad, you don't worry about keeping up with the times', and 'I wouldn't change a thing the Church is doing; it keeps the society here in Ireland a God-fearing one, and in the end there is nothing else worth doing. The Church may not be getting us jobs, but it is keeping our people happy and with their feet on the ground.'[20] A mere 0.2 per cent of the population refused to declare a religion in the 1961 Census.

But here and there cracks were appearing in this long-established 'grand narrative' of the Irish people. Among those with more than twelve years of education four out of five disagreed strongly with the Church's dominance, feeling that (as one of Biever's respondents put it) 'the world is too complex today for a clerical state, and that is what we have in Ireland. What do priests know about politics, except that it leads to socialism?' These thoughts had been tentatively voiced by both priests and lay people in print, particularly in the late 1950s, in journals such as *The Furrow* and *Doctrine and Life*.

The clergy themselves on the whole agreed with the majority in thinking of themselves as natural leaders. In terms that remind one of Cumann na nGaedheal comments about the Fianna Fáil party lacking the class to govern, one priest told Father Biever 'no one questions our authority. How can they? We have more education, thank God, and with that education comes responsibility to lead.' Another commented 'I look at Ireland and I say to myself—who else could lead? The politicians are new at the game, we have few economists, our professional people leave. Who stays? We do.'[21] They were conscious of some criticism, but called on two hundred years of history to provide their justification (always a sign of weakness): 'Some of your smart intellectuals have forgotten that it was the Church that never deserted the people when they needed help and guidance the most. We deserve the place we have in the nation, and we do not intend to give it up. What has made Ireland unique is the Catholic Church, and nothing else.' There spoke the typical parish priest as described by Bishop Newman, 'a manly friend and fellow-citizen rather than a scholar'—terms that were highly old-fashioned even then.[22] Newman's study of Maynooth students (published in 1962) revealed, to no one's surprise, that three quarters of them had rural backgrounds, half being farmers' sons; half had a priest in the family; they also had an average of six children in the family—the national average was just under five.

Whatever its claims to leadership, the Church could do little to stop the changes brought in on the tail of economic growth. In the five years since the publication in 1958 of *Economic Development* wage rates had gone up 32 per cent in Dublin (and slightly less in the country). People began to feel rich; for the first time since the early 1930s it was reasonable to feel cheerful about Ireland's future. In Shannon Michael Viney noted 'the sweet tang of optimism . . . like an aura of aftershave applied freshly every morning.'[23] Visitors noted the reduction in public drunkenness. 'There was,' wrote one returned emigrant, 'an unaccustomed briskness about the way Dubliners moved, and a freshness of complexion I had not noticed before. . . . Even the grumbles were indicative. There were complaints about all the money being spent on jet airlines and luxury hotels, and it was annoying that the upsurge in car ownership meant that the Irish would now have to take examinations for driving licences.'[24]

In January Lemass proposed a break with republican tradition: that there should be an Irish honours list. *Hibernia*'s readers were asked by the editor (then Basil Clancy) to nominate suitable recipients. The list provides an insight into the great and the good of the day, at least as perceived by that magazine's thoughtful but largely conservative readership. Seventy per cent voted for de Valera; the next most popular name was Mac Liammóir with 43 per cent. After him came William T. Cosgrave and Seán Lemass; then Seán T. O'Kelly, General M. J. Costello of the Sugar Company, Cardinal Browne and F. H. Boland, the diplomat. Then, with 27 per cent voting for him, came Frank Duff, the founder of the Legion of Mary, and Seán McEoin, the fighting blacksmith of Ballinalee. Other names mentioned were Siobhán MacKenna, Ronnie Delany, Christy Ring, Rev. Dr Lucey, Rev. Dr Philbin, Mother Mary Martin, J. A. Costello, Seán O'Casey and Brendan Behan. In summary, politicians comfortably led the field, with six names out of nineteen. Next came religion with five names (John Charles McQuaid very obviously not featuring); two each for sports, acting and writing; one businessman (state-sponsored—no McGraths) and one civil servant. The range of possible stars was not wide, but it is notable that men with primarily fighting reputations (as for instance Dan Breen) did not feature.

Despite the rapid changes, an older, simpler, rougher Ireland was not quite dead. In February *The Irish Times* reported that a heifer being walked to the slaughterhouse had escaped and jumped through some-one's front window in Dún Laoghaire. The beast was recaptured, but only after causing considerable damage. Two women were admitted to hospital with shock and head injuries. On the Feast of St Blaise twenty-two priests blessed the throats of the thousands of people who attended the Franciscan church in Merchants' Quay for the purpose. The mini-mum marriage age for girls was still only twelve: in May the Church of Ireland Synod heard that between 1957 and 1959 four girls aged fourteen had married and 60 girls and one boy had married aged fifteen.[25] In June two elderly people died when their house in Bolton Street, Dublin, collapsed; three weeks later the Corporation, in a panic, had evacuated 520 families from 156 dangerous houses. One of these families reported that they had been buying a tin of rat poison every day. Also in June small retailers began to pressurise the Dáil members to vote against the turnover tax (an early form of VAT). One TD found a .303 bullet in his post and the anonymous message: 'this is for you if you vote in favour' … another was threatened with kidnapping—the bullying spirit learned during Land League days lived on.[26]

During the Dáil debate on the turnover tax, Oliver J. Flanagan, the Fine Gael TD from Leix-Offaly, compared Taoiseach Seán Lemass to an Irish Krushchev or Castro. He also accused two independent TDs of having sold their votes to Fianna Fáil for £3,500 each. In the melée, dur-ing this speech Flanagan was called a perjurer and the dirtiest mouth in Irish politics. Old scandals were revived. References were made to the Locke's Distillery case of 1948, to the Civil War, to the 77 executions and of course to the Blueshirts. Much of this came from Brian Lenihan, one of Fianna Fáil's promising young men, then Parliamentary Secretary for Lands: 'Is this tout to be allowed to make such statements?' he demanded 'the gas chamber is the place for you … you are good manure that is all you are.'[27] This violence of language from a new generation harked back to the rough days of the 1930s, and did not suggest that the new generation was going to take political ideas any more seriously than the old.

Intellectual life flickered but scarcely flared in the pubs around *The Irish Times*, in small theatres and publishing companies. The quality of public debate on social and political issues was not high. Those from the non-possessing classes who might in another country have challenged the system either emigrated or were sucked into the civil service or the Church. From there, like Brian O'Nolan, they conducted private sniping campaigns against their paymasters. Even in the universities 'the market for ideas' was not lively. In general a university degree was looked on as a qualification leading to a career, rather than a search for enlightenment. The choice of a course of study was governed by the student's vocational aspirations, or those of the parents. Not surprisingly, half of Irish students reported feeling little or no enthusiasm for their studies.[28] For their seniors, the 'ennervating minutiae' of university politics were more eagerly addressed than the national condition.[29]

On the other hand, the censorship laws, which had been since 1929 the favourite battle ground of philistine and anti-philistine, were slowly beginning to lose their grip. In the peak year of the 1950s over a thousand books had been banned—in 1963 the number was 454. These however included important titles such as Sylvia Plath's *The Bell Jar*, James Baldwin's *Another Country*, Jack Kerouac's *Dharma Bums*, and a paperback edition of Simone de Beauvoir's *The Second Sex*. There was also Barbara Cartland's *Husbands and Wives*, and a good sprinkling of books about orgies, eager mistresses, nymphs, forbidden ecstasy and the like. The previous year had seen Joseph Heller's *Catch-22*, Iris Murdoch's *A Severed Head* and Edna O'Brien's *Girl with Green Eyes* and *The Lonely Girl* banned. In practice, much *bien pensant* powder had been spent on an imposition that was more symbolic than serious. As Tony Gray pointed out, 'books are rarely banned until they have been on sale for a month or two, by which time anyone who is likely to buy the book will have already done so . . . in any case the number of people who buy books in Ireland is so small that the Irish royalties would hardly keep an Irish author in toothpaste.'[30] At St Patrick's teacher training college in Dublin in the 1950s John McGahern recalls that 'even though we were 18 to 20 year olds, there was still supervised study every evening, and we were only to read what was prescribed. If you were caught reading T. S. Eliot, for instance, you were biffed across the back of the head.'[31] When Brendan Behan wanted a copy of the Penguin edition of Plato's *Symposium*, a bookseller told him 'we saw a slight run on it, and the same sort of people looking for it, so we just took it out of circulation ourselves. After all we don't have to be made decent minded by Act of Dáil. We have our own way of detecting smut, however ancient.'[32]

It was notably a paperback that stimulated this remark. The huge increase in paperback publishing in the late 1950s and early 1960s, as *The Irish Times* commented at the time, 'made the task of the Censorship of Publications Board almost impossible. Not only has the number of publications increased, but the paperback industry has made available to the many books which hitherto had been within the grasp of the few.'[33]

Paradoxically, the country's isolation from the world for a generation or more had produced an almost neurotic obsession with what the world thought about Ireland. This was the international version of 'what will the neighbours say?', the social and moral sanction of daily life that stifled so much spontaneity. Visitors' opinions were eagerly sought. In May, *The Irish Times* devoted half a column to the thoughts of Miss Norma Lynn Knobel, a High School teacher of American and world history at Richardson, Texas. 'The Irish', she told the reporter, 'are a fun-loving but deeply religious people.'

International successes for anyone remotely Irish (especially if Catholic as well) was very important to national self-esteem. They were widely discussed, perhaps as an antidote to self-doubt, in public and in private. Kennedy, as President of the United States, was of course in a class of his own, but when the British Variety Club marked Peter O'Toole as Best Actor for his role in *Lawrence of Arabia*, the Irishman's Diary called it 'a bit of a score for Irish performers'—that O'Toole had been rejected by the Abbey some years before on the grounds that he spoke no Irish was not commented on.[34] When Seán MacBride became Secretary General of the International Commission of Jurists in November, *Hibernia* became lyrical. 'The appointment . . . is a compliment not alone to a distinguished Irishman, but to Ireland as a nation. It marks our position in the family of nations in a special way. It recognises that this ancient people has a special role to play in the community of peoples. It says in effect that we are called upon to serve the cause of freedom everywhere.' There is an almost pathetic yearning and boastfulness in this, since few of the readers would have more than the vaguest idea what the Commission was. In the review of *The Great Hunger* quoted previously, John Connell concluded: 'Truly the Irish are a great people. We are a great people, for within one hundred years of this appalling Famine we came back strong enough to challenge a great empire and win.'[35]

Serving the cause of freedom was as usual easier said than done, as the Irish Army had already found in the Congo, where an inexperienced patrol had been massacred by Baluba tribesmen a few years before. The international stage was dominated by two large and aggressive coalitions. They were if anything even more self-righteous than their predecessors of the early part of the century, and, with the help of technology, more vicious. On one side of the Cold War lay the Western alliance dominated by the United States—the Free World, as it was called. Against them were the Russians and their allies. There was no question as to which side Ireland was on.

At the time the contest seemed by no means one-sided. The USSR had launched Sputnik in 1957, well ahead of anything the Americans had done in space and in 1961 they had repeated the triumph with the first manned space flight. This was the Soviet moment. The USSR was genuinely growing economically, and its citizens were able to buy new clothes, new apartments, even new cars. By planning, by application of cybernetics and by a science-led command economy the country seemed to be surging ahead. Worried White House advisors took seriously the possibility that Russia and its planned economy really was going to outpace the West economically and militarily.

The most dramatic point of confrontation was Berlin, where the famous Wall was now two years old. Marxist/Leninist ideology told the Soviets that in due course history would bury the West, as the Russian leader Mr Krushchev regularly pointed out to Western leaders. The Reds, as the press called them (thus in one *Sunday Press* headline: 'Red kids eat more cabbage') were not going to be content simply to let history take its course. In May *Hibernia*'s special correspondent noted the dangers of Russian paratroopers. 'The Russians are adept at falling free for 100 seconds. The reason that they jump from this great height—20,000 feet—is that the sound of their planes will not be detected. This tactic is obviously planned only against countries which have no radar defences, like Ireland. There would be definite advantages for Russia (no need to set them down) in occupying Ireland. If that should happen here, we should wake up one morning to find the country in Russian hands.' Why the USSR should want to invade Ireland, or what they would do once here, was not explained. As the IRA found during the Second World War, the view of Ireland's importance taken from inside the country was sometimes rather different to that from outside. In April the editor of *The Distributive Worker* warned his fellow trade unionists of the growth of communism in Ireland. 'The number of card-carrying members is less than one hundred, but its influence is immense . . .

obviously there is no time for smug complacency. If these facts awaken Irishmen to the true nature and extent of the danger of Russian influence in our country, they will have served their purpose'.[36]

If history was to bury the West (and the East too very likely), it was more generally expected that it would come through what was called 'the unthinkable'—global thermo-nuclear war. Far from it being unthinkable, in practice millions of roubles, dollars, pounds and every other currency were spent brooding on its consequences. By accident or design, it was thought, a nuclear exchange might occur any day. Although it was the subject of jokes, 'living under the shadow of the bomb' was an indigestible and nightmarish reality, particularly for sensitive young people.

Books and newspaper articles told readers in detail what might happen. The blast from a 20-megaton bomb exploded over the GPO in O'Connell Street would leave a 600-foot deep crater stretching from the North Circular Road to Trinity College and the Four Courts. This would instantly fill with scalding water from the Liffey. Children playing in schools in Crumlin, Ranelagh and Glasnevin would be incinerated; people seeking refuge from the overpowering heat in the Dodder or the Tolka would be boiled alive; seminarians walking to Mass in Maynooth would find their soutanes bursting into flames; a massive firestorm would sweep the city, worse by far than Dresden or Hamburg; virtually all buildings between Kippure and Donabate would collapse. After this would come radiation sickness, and then panic and disease. 'Such a device', it was estimated, 'exploded in mid-town Manhattan, for example, would probably kill six million out of the New York City's eight million inhabitants, and produce an additional million or more deaths beyond the city limits.'[37]

The Irish Times, in common with most Irish people, chose not to think about it: 'Our civil service,' wrote a journalist casually, 'is probably right in assuming that it wouldn't have to deal with more than one or two misguided missiles in the 10 or 20 megaton range.'[38] The prevailing winds, it was felt, would blow any fall-out from Britain away to the northeast. Nonetheless it was with some relief that the country greeted the first Nuclear Test Ban Treaty signed in November—the fruit of the telephone hot line established between the heads of the Soviet Union and the United States after the Cuba crisis. Many believed that the rich from Europe and beyond were buying up property in the West at an alarming rate. Oliver J. Flanagan raised the matter in the Dáil—'if we go on as we are' he said, 'rural Ireland will be stripped of its population.'

This was, 'he claimed, 'a new invasion by a new type of landlord. The land buying was often caused by Germans and others looking for a bolthole in the event of nuclear war'—what was the Minister going to do about it?[39] This was in fact xenophobic nonsense, as Tony Gray pointed out: 'There is no breakdown into nationalities of the foreigners who bought land, but even if they were all German, which they certainly were not, only one Irish acre in every four hundred was in German hands.'[40]

One entrepreneur tried to cash in on fears of nuclear war by launching an anti-fallout sweet. This product, which came in three flavours— barley-sugar, butter mint and fruit drop—filled 'the body's reservoir with minerals such as potassium or carbohydrate complexes; radioactive materials are absorbed in these and are passed straight out . . .' The spokesman of the Irish Association of Sweet Manufacturers was not amused, and called the product 'a clever gimmick'.[41]

There was plenty of international news to distract one. In the 1960s Swinging London became the centre of world attention. Macmillan was still Prime Minister, and Harold Wilson had just come to the leadership of the Labour party, and promised to replace the tired, corrupt Tory regime with the white heat of technological revolution (a distinct but discreet nod in the direction of Soviet success, complete with a new civil service department of economic planning). 'England swings like a pendulum do' went the song. Across the water, glimpsed in magazines and on the television, there was *Private Eye* and *That Was The Week That Was*, Wimpy bars, Vespa scooters, Jean Shrimpton and Julie Christie, John le Carré, the Liverpool sound, bright plastic whatnots in primary colours, pop art, the Twist, Sunday colour sections, Minis (the car, not quite yet the skirt). Even Hollywood stars such as Elizabeth Taylor and Richard Burton turned out to be British.

In the spring an extraordinary crop of rumours spread from London: one of them told how a member of the Cabinet had served dinner at a private party stark naked except for a mask and a small lace apron. Quite soon it became clear that behind these rumours there was at least one substantial scandal. The Secretary of State for War, John Profumo, had been sharing a mistress with a naval attaché of the Russian embassy. Profumo initially denied any impropriety with Christine Keeler. However as stories of naked romps round the pool at Cliveden, obscure intermediaries connected with MI5, slum landlords and other seedy characters became public, he could not sustain this line. Irish readers snapped up the *Daily Telegraph* to relish the sight of the British establishment, from Macmillan to Lords Hailsham and Denning, making fools of themselves. Macmillan was forced out of office, and, as the *Annual Register* put it, with a valedictory speech 'polished, philosophical, and delivered with something of his old flare', the Macmillan era in British politics finally closed.

In August another extraordinary insight into the British character was revealed. The Great Train Robbery was a brilliantly organised theft of some two and half million pounds of used notes from a mail train. Although the engine driver was clubbed on the head with an iron bar and permanently disabled, it was quickly clear that the British public regarded the train robbers not as violent thugs, but as folk heroes. Students of Southampton University elected the crime's organiser an honorary member of the Union.

The best-known Irish criminal of 1963, Shan Mohangi, was not so lucky. Mohangi was a South African Indian medical student, who became engaged to sixteen-year-old Hazel Mullen. On 17 August she called at the Green Tureen restaurant in Harcourt Street where he worked as a part-time chef and told him that she was seeing someone else. In a fit of jealous rage he strangled her. In between 'helping' the distraught Mullen family to find Hazel, he dismembered the body in the restaurant's basement; he later attempted to burn the remains, but the smell he created attracted the attention of the fire brigade. Eventually he confessed to the murder, and was convicted first of murder (and sentenced to death) then, after a retrial, of manslaughter (for which he got a seven years). He was eventually released and now lives in South Africa.

In the early 1960s, Ireland was like an icebound lake to which spring had come later than to countries south and east. The country resounded with the sound of long set structures—economic, social, political, religious—creaking and cracking as the ice melted. The pressures released caused friction as old attitudes were confronted. Garret FitzGerald wrote at the time (in words that he might have recycled for the Celtic Tiger years), 'the outlook of the people has changed gradually, but radically, from one of cynicism and near despair to one of confidence and self-assurance. This psychological break-through is of far greater importance than any purely economic achievements.'[42] In the February issue of the women's magazine *Creation*, under the heading 'Super living in the super sixties' journalist Caroline Mitchell enthused: 'This country is on the way up. We are going up financially, industrially and artistically; . . . the first whiffs of outside air have been stimulating, enabling us to see ourselves more clearly as other see us, and in many cases for the first time.'

—1989—

Partners in Progress: Bertie Ahern (Minister for Labour) and Charlie Haughey (Taoiseach) at a Fianna Fáil general election press conference in the Shelbourne Hotel 2 June 1989. (Derek Spiers)

Chapter 17 Look, we have come through

A lot of history happened in 1989.

In Ireland there was a general election, and the Fianna Fáil party again failed to secure a majority. To retain power, Charles Haughey made a deal with the break-away Progressive Democrats (PDs), and even gave them seats in the cabinet. The political mould, it was believed, was broken. As Haughey, Taoiseach again, said 'this was a new departure in our political life.'

But events in the rest of the world were even more memorable. For anyone aged forty-five or under (which included 70 per cent of the Irish population) the key world fact for their whole life had been the Cold War. On the one side there had been the Soviet Union and its allies and on the other the West (the Americans and their allies). The great and bloody symbol of this conflict was the wall dividing East and West Berlin. This was officially dubbed the Antifascist Protection Barrier, and erected, so the GDR explained, to stop West Berliners from taking advantage of the subsidised prices in East German shops. Like the code of so much Irish public life, this rhetoric was not expected to be taken literally.

Ireland's stance in the Cold War had long been ambiguous (neutrality) and unambiguous (fear and hatred of godless Communism)—but in global terms irrelevant. The island's strategic position, which had indeed been critical from the days of the Armada and the Napoleonic wars to the world wars, had in the era of inter-continental ballistic missiles become a sideshow.

The great pro-democracy movement that flared through the world barely flickered in Ireland; the most passionate public demonstration of the year was a peaceful march of 10,000 people to mark the twentieth anniversary of the deployment of British soldiers in the North. The North was a constant backdrop of violence and hatred—in February the solicitor Pat Finucane was murdered by loyalists after provocative statements in the House of Commons by Douglas Hogg—later famous for charging expenses for cleaning his moat—following a slanted RUC briefing. On the march, a Union Jack was burned, and Gerry Adams told the crowd that the solution to the Northern problem was freedom from Britain, from British partition and British military occupation. Neil Blaney, the TD from Donegal, told the gathering: 'I object to the Border totally completely and absolutely and until the British get out of our country there is no hope for this country'. This was felt sufficiently remarkable to appear in the 'They said this week' column in *The Irish Times*. A headline noted 'DUBLIN-CORK GAME HIGHLIGHT OF THE WEEKEND'.

At the beginning of the year it seemed that all was running normally. In January an era ended as President Reagan handed over the Oval Office to his successor George Bush; in London Mrs Thatcher continued her preparations for the hated poll tax that was to prove her downfall. Elsewhere old men ruled. In China, eighty-five-year-old Deng Xiaoping and his associates were firmly in power. In East Germany, seventy-seven-year-old Erich Honecker presided, helped by nearly one in seven adult East Germans who worked as *Mitarbeiter* of the Stasi. In Rumania, Nicolae Ceaucescu, and in Bulgaria Todo Zhikov were in their seventies. In February, the eighty-seven-year old Ayatollah Khomeini declared a murderous fatwa on Salman Rushdie for his book *The Satanic Verses*; the author immediately went into hiding.

By the middle of the year there were one or two signs of change. In Moscow, Mikhail Gorbachev (only fifty-eight) had preached for four years now *glasnost* (openness) and *perestroika* (restructuring)—an easing that the gerontocrats in the Soviet satellite countries watched uneasily. In his first speech as President of Czechoslovakia in 1990 Vaclav Havel (speaking in terms that had application also in Ireland) strongly criticised the moral atmosphere these men had thrived in: 'We have fallen morally ill, because we became used to saying one thing and thinking another'. In Poland, the Solidarity movement was officially recognised and in Hungary the anniversary of the 1848 revolution was marked with nationwide demonstrations. In South Africa, after twenty-six years in prison, Nelson Mandela was released in July. Later in the year the Apartheid Act was scrapped, and *Slegs Blankes* (Whites only) signs were pulled down. On a visit to the US in September, Boris Yeltsin was stunned by the casual profligacy on display in the supermarkets— clear evidence, he was dismayed to realise, that the Soviet system did not work. The Soviet moment, whose zenith had been between 1957 and 1964, was well and truly over. Only in China, now officially with a population of 1.1 billion people, did the hardliners hold against the pro-democracy wave. In June, they sent in the tanks to crush a long-lasting protest in Tiananmen Square: 'Tanks and armoured personnel carriers cap seven hours of bloody attack, killing scores of unarmed civilians and mowing down student demonstrators', as *The Irish Times* reported.[1]

The event that made 1989 especially memorable was the collapse of the Berlin Wall, the central point of the whole division between Warsaw Pact and NATO countries. Cracks in the Iron Curtain began to show early in the year. Judy Dempsey, who reported on the year's events in *The Irish Times* from Vienna, identified the key change that had made all this possible.

> It was the erosion of fear [following *glasnost*]. Fear of repression, of losing one's job, of having a passport confiscated, of children banned from university, of speaking the truth, of imprisonment, of sacking for not voting, of not waving the flags, of not displaying the correct party slogan on May Day, of not joining the party. It was fear of the Power.

When Gorbachev signalled that Russia would no longer morally or physically support the old regimes, the people slowly realised that the forty-year-old repression was at an end. In May, the Hungary-Austria border was opened, and Rumania had to put up a makeshift wire fence to stop its citizens fleeing. But the hole in the Curtain meant that East Germans, who had long been allowed to go to Hungary without trouble, could now abandon their Trabants there and creep into capitalist Austria. Although this was still illegal, the border guards did little, and the hundreds of escapees quickly turned into thousands. Eventually pressure inside East Germany mounted. As Judy Dempsey wrote, 'the spark ignited by Hungary in May ignited a massive unquenchable flame throughout East Germany . . . on the night of November 9th, a Friday, bricks once set deep in cement and mortar fell one by one from the Berlin Wall'.[2]

Ireland in 1989

While all this was going on, the Irish people were beginning to see the end of a depressing period of high taxes and special levies, inflation, seemingly endless cuts in public expenditure, and emigration of the brightest students. Every year in the 1980s tens of thousands had left to find work, primarily in England. This time, however, it was not the unskilled rural masses of the past, but educated urban professionals, perhaps with second degrees, looking for work, ideally to match their qualifications. They were accountants, architects, computer analysts, doctors, engineers. But once again beloved children, many of them perhaps the proud first graduates in the family, had to leave home to find work. On the plus side, air transport and good communications and the fact that most of the emigration was to the next-door island gave emigration less of a desperate air than in the past. Ryanair, founded in 1985, established a service from Luton to the new airport at Knock in 1986, making it practical to return home to the West several times a year.

For some too, the opportunity to recreate oneself away from the dense culture of home had its positive sides. The British writer John Ardagh quoted a Monaghan woman working in a bank in London: 'I hate that old-fashioned sentimental nationalism, that SPUC morality, that prying gossip. Yet I'm glad to be Irish, and I miss Ireland. So what do I do?'[3]

Economic muddle and mismanagement had resulted in a waning of the national self-confidence that had flowered in the 1960s. The 1980s recovery (the essential precursor of the Celtic Tiger) had begun with Charles Haughey's third government, which took office in 1987. Having campaigned on a platform of total rejection of public expenditure cuts, when in office he completely switched to a new regime of austerity. He and his Minister for Finance Ray MacSharry (succeeded by Albert Reynolds in 1988) had been able to take advantage of various factors. In the first place, the experience since the late 1970s had made the public mood chastened and malleable, and so willing to put up with severe government action. Unemployment had increased from 126,000 or 10 per cent of the labour force in 1981 to 232,000 or 18 per cent of the labour force by 1987. Secondly, the inflation rate declined from 20.4 per cent in 1981 to just 2.1 per cent by 1988. Thirdly and crucially, they inherited from the FitzGerald government a broad stabilisation of the public finances—public sector borrowing as a percentage of GNP was reduced from 20.1 per cent in 1981 to 14.4 per cent by 1987, providing the incoming government with a degree of flexibility that had not been enjoyed by its predecessor.

There was even a stroke of luck. A tax amnesty declared in 1988 provided a much larger than expected windfall to the revenues, though as a tax official commented dryly: 'If you throw a party for every crook who ever robbed you and a lot more people turn up than expected, that is a success—of sorts.' The amnesty was good news for accountants, and not such good news for banks. Anglo-Irish Bank, for instance, reported a withdrawal of £10 million by customers to meet amnesty payments.[4] 'Parasites from the so-called entrepreneurial class,' growled Proinsias de Rossa, the newly elected President of the Workers Party.

Nonetheless there were nettles to be grasped. As the economic commentator Paul Tansey put it:

> The three principal planks of the Haughey strategy, in chronological order, were severe cutbacks in public spending; the re-establishment of national pay agreements, though with a novel twist; and the phased introduction of reductions in personal income taxes. Public spending cuts were introduced almost immediately, with no changes in tax rates, allowances or bands.
>
> Then, the minority Fianna Fáil government received a political bonus from an unexpected quarter. In October 1987, the new Fine Gael leader, Alan Dukes, announced his Tallaght Strategy. Dukes said that Fine Gael would not oppose the government where it was seeking to bring the public finances under control, thereby clearing the way for future reductions in personal taxes.
>
> This provided the opportunity for the government to introduce further deep cuts in public spending in 1988 and in 1989. The pruning of public spending was both quick and deep. Current government spending was actually lower in cash terms in 1989 than it had been in 1986.
>
> The second strand of the strategy was the revival of national agreements. The trade unions had been excluded from corridors of power since the collapse of the national understandings of the early 1980s. Their bargaining power was severely diluted by the very high levels of unemployment then prevailing.
>
> The Programme for National Recovery provided for basic pay increases of 2.5 per cent annually in each of the three years 1988 through 1990 in return for a promise of £225 million in tax cuts over three years. Whatever about the long-run impact of national agreements on rates of pay increase, the PNR delivered two crucial results. First, it provided employers and foreign investors with a degree of certainty about the evolution of Irish wages in the medium-term. Second, it safeguarded a recovery strategy from being undermined by a proliferation of industrial disputes.
>
> And for the trade unions? Well, the boys were back in town. Personal tax reductions provided the final leg of the recovery strategy. The initial easing of the personal income tax burden was provided from 1988/89 through a widening of tax bands. Reductions in tax rates only became a feature from 1989 onwards.[5]

In June, Charles Haughey went to the country, claiming that minor Dáil spats made government impossible. He was confident that the discipline imposed since 1987—when, as *The Irish Times* declared, Fianna Fáil 'forsook its spendthrift ways'[6]—was bearing fruit, and that it was now in a position to reap the rewards with a comfortable majority. However, without ignoring the successes, *The Irish Times* could not see why further improvements required a majority Fianna Fáil government, as opposed to the cooperative arrangements currently in place. The days of trusting Fianna Fáil to govern alone, said the paper, were over, especially with Charles Haughey in the driving seat. The outcome of the election suggested that the people in general agreed. Fianna Fáil lost four seats and was faced with the choice of going back to the country or some form of coalition.

This was deeply traumatic for the rank and file Fianna Fáil members, for as Pádraig Flynn put it, 'all the members of the cabinet are unanimous for no coalition. The national executive, the parliamentary party and the grassroots have indicated this is a core value which we must preserve.'[7] Flynn spoke too soon, for Bertie Ahern and Albert Reynolds were negotiating with the PDs, driven by Haughey's determination to hold on to power. After a wearisome series of negotiations (made particularly so by the PDs' insistence on writing everything down, a discipline both unfamiliar and uncongenial to the Fianna Fáil negotiators[8]) a coalition was patched up, giving the PDs two seats in the cabinet and a junior ministry. It was hardly a coincidence that while the negotiations were progressing, the ailing Irish Press group, brought into existence specifically to support the Fianna Fáil party, also lost its independence, in this case by a take-over by the American Ingersoll Publications group.

Although Charles Haughey was flexible enough to accept the idea of coalition, he and his party were at the same time deeply set in an older mode of politics. As he told the columnist Nuala O'Faolain in an interview after the election, 'he saw the politician as protecting the individual against the indifference of the state.' Bizarrely, despite his own life-long ambition to be its chief officer and the party's years in power, he and his colleagues honestly saw the state as something alien, outside, to be exploited or protected against. Haughey vigorously supported the simple structure of personal clan-like relations, a kind of political *meitheal*. The voter was to rely not on his or her legal rights but on the TD to gain benefits. 'Why should they hear from some faceless bureaucrat that they've got a pension? Why shouldn't they ask someone they know to get it for them? Why shouldn't someone they know personally tell them they've got it?'[9] Simpler voters vaguely thought that, as John Waters recalled his Roscommon friends arguing, 'sure, if [Charles Haughey] made himself rich, mightn't he make us rich as well?';[10] this sentiment was common in Dublin, too.

In this simple, direct world there was no social contract, no rule of law, just 'them' and 'us'. It is almost as if the British (or at least Cumann na nGaedheal) were still in power. The phrase 'vote early and vote often' was of course an old joke, but activists did if they could, as May Green admits in her memoir of life in Athlone,[11] and no one was very shocked when in 1992 solicitor Pat O'Connor was accused (and acquitted) of attempting to vote twice in Haughey's constituency. From this point of view the TD's primary job, and even more so the minister's, was not so much to govern the country as to ensure that this voter or that electoral district 'did well out of the system'—which ultimately meant receiving state resources that were not available to others. On achieving office, ministers picked civil servants whose sole task it was to continue this service to the constituents. Politicians who did not follow this path were generally punished at the polls. At the very least this was an obstacle to good governance, necessitating cabinet-making by province. It quite likely also amounted to a sin against distributive justice, since funds thus arbitarily allocated were denied to more needy causes. The Catholic Church generally failed to pursue this analysis. Indeed, they would have been paid scant attention if they had.

Since the TD's intervention seemed to work (the pension came through, the bridge was built, the parking fines disappeared), the system's apparent effectiveness copper-fastened an ultimately mendacious view of how the state worked. In some cases, of course, the TD's intervention was necessary and valuable—to make the best of a bad case or steer a voter through bureaucratic complexity. Frequently, however, TDs were no more than free-riders, writing letters that they knew would change nothing, or claiming to have engineered a pension that was automatic. A much-repeated story of the time told how one TD (usually Oliver J. Flanagan) used his privileged access as a county councillor to find out where road works were due. A day or two later he would ostentatiously pull up by the site of the proposed works, and ask locals 'what was being done?' They would relate how many complaints had been made to the council to no effect, etc. The TD would promise immediate action, and in accordance with the work roster, action would of course occur. Later, in the pub the voter would have the satisfaction of telling his friends: 'I said to him [the TD] that it just wasn't good enough, something would have to be done.' And it was. Everyone was happily confirmed in a simple and delusive view of how government worked. In 1988 on the *Late Late Show*, Brian Lenihan, lining himself up for the presidency, showed his practical contempt for the rule of law in an anecdote he told of how Donogh O'Malley was caught drinking in a pub after hours. As the guard became officious, O'Malley coldly asked: 'Will you have a pint, or a transfer?' Even as a joke the remark had a sting. In 1987 Seán Doherty reportedly threatened to sack a Dáil barman who refused to serve him an after-hours drink, saying 'Fianna Fáil is back'—but that was just another joke.

Despite apprehensions aroused by the forthcoming shakeup of the EC (eventually enshrined in the Maastricht Treaty), the Economic and Social Research Institute (ESRI) was cautiously optimistic about the Irish economy in its September forecast. Industrial growth had stabilised in 1988 and was forecast to grow in 1989. Actually, canny readers had expected this, having been told of the dramatic rise in executive advertisements in the early part of the year,[12] and an equally cheering lift-off in general advertising in the early weeks of 1989. In November, the Confederation of Irish Industry analysed 40,000 job advertisements placed between August and October in Irish newspapers, and found a rising demand for computer people, marketing and sales staff and machine operators. A steadily growing demand for accountancy and finance staff was also notable.[13]

House price boom

A property boom was under way as well, with house prices in Dublin and Galway doing especially well. The rise was fuelled by the banks' newly aggressive lending policies. For generations, banks had always refused to make long-term loans—the safe old policy of 'borrow long, lend short' was their maxim. As George McDonnell put it in *Buying a House* (1972), 'you will not find your bank manager very interested in giving you any long term financial facilities. He is not in this business.'[14] But there was a mortgage famine, and in 1975 Ritchie Ryan as Minister for Finance persuaded the banks to allocate £40 million for two years to be used for house loans. By 1980 banks were providing 5 per cent of house purchase loans (the building societies provided most of the rest), scantily doling them out only to higher income people with a good savings record at the branch. By the mid 1980s, however, the 'buy or rent?' debate seemed to have been definitely decided on the buy side, and the banks began to see that mortgage business could be profitable. By the end of the 1980s they had 40 per cent of the market. A Building Societies Act was passed in 1989 to level the playing field for building societies, putting them under the Central Bank rather than the old-fashioned and under-staffed Registrar of Building Societies; they were freed up in other ways too.

In this newly competitive situation, traditional standards were quickly abandoned. In *The Irish Times* John Stanley wrote of how the maximum 80 per cent of purchase price rule was the first to go, with some institutions 'lending up to 95 per cent of the purchase price, while traditional salary multiples have been extended. Instead of a maximum loan of two-and-a-half times salary, some lenders have been advancing in excess of three times.'[15] The fact that the same lending house might be supporting two or three bidders in an auction was noted as a new factor stimulating prices.

But behind the boom was the fact that the improvement in the Irish economy gave, as John Stanley put it, 'a renewed confidence, particularly in the middle class'. *The Irish Times* had launched its property supplement in September 1988 (the sports supplement had been launched in 1986).

The years of job uncertainty and economic gloom that now seemed to be coming to and end had prompted people to sit tight rather than trade up, with the result that the average length of a mortgage increased from seven years in the 1970s to ten years at the end of the 1980s. It takes an effort of the imagination to realise the amount of 'putting-up-with' that this 40 per cent increase implies, in terms of the cramping of growing families—lack of privacy with teenage children sharing rooms, inadequate study space, perhaps long school journeys and commutes, and daily toleration of less than satisfactory living conditions. This phenomenon represented pent-up demand. At the same time, the relative cost of housing was coming down. A National Economic and Social Council report showed that a house that would have taken 5.8 years of average industrial earnings to buy in 1981 now took only 4.3 years' worth. In addition, those who remembered the house price rises of the 1970s realised that since it was not subject to capital gains tax the housing market was one of the few ways open to ordinary individuals to make windfall money.

The tinder that set the market alight, so it was believed at the time, was young Irish professionals who had done well in Mrs Thatcher's City of London and who came to Dublin with enough money to buy at the top of the market a much more impressive house than they would have been able to afford in London. Once this new money started to appear, a cascade began. Pent-up demand, reduced housing costs, increased money flow and low interest rates were kindled by this input. Confidence grew by what it fed on—when the house down the road sold for much more than seemed probable, everyone exclaimed, told their friends, and felt richer. This so-called 'wealth effect' encouraged general expenditure.

The result was clear. The Department of the Environment's report on the housing market produced in April 1990 showed that the average price of a second-hand home in Dublin at the end of 1989 was £54,700, up 27 per cent on the previous year.[16] Prime areas such as Ballsbridge, Blackrock, Rathgar, Foxrock and Killiney had done even better. Even previously seedy flatland Ranelagh was attracting buyers, as young professionals began to build up its reputation as a trendy place to live. In May, the property pages reported that a house in Albany Road which had sold for £57,000 in 1985 now fetched £141,000. This result was described as 'a neat illustration of Ranelagh's transformation in recent years from "flatland" to an expensive residential area.'[17] In An Irishman's Diary Kevin Myers snorted at the 'sudden desire for the Dublin middle class to pay insane prices for the privilege of moving into Ranelagh, and once there to simper with revolting twittering self-congratulation'.[18] The average second-hand house in Dublin now cost 80 per cent more than it would have done at the beginning of the decade.

People to watch

On 1 January 1990, Kathy Sheridan introduced to *Irish Times* readers a list of 'the people most likely to make an impact in the 1990s'. The choices reflect the world as they saw it at the end of 1989. Dividing some of this list of potential movers and shakers into sectors, results as follows:

Category	Number	Examples
Academia	5	John Coolahan, Frank Convery, Peter Humphries
Arts	23	Orla Brady, Mary Clarke, Hugo Hamilton, Alan Gilsenan, Brid Harper, Elisabeth Magill, Jimmy Vaughan, Joe O'Connor
Business	5	David Dilger, Frank Fitzgibbon, John Teeling
Civil society	5	Ivana Bacik, Karin Dubsky, Joan McGinley
Fashion	4	Lisa Cummins, Kip Carroll
Hospitality	4	Patrick Guilbaud
Media	4	Joe Duffy, Anne-Marie Hourihane
Medicine	1	Michael Kearney

Politics	10	Albert Reynolds, Ivan Yates, John Bruton, Gay Mitchell
Professions	9	Adrian Hardiman, Anne Rowland, Tony Reddy
Public service	4	Brendan O'Donoghue, Michael Dowling
Religion	5	Robin Eames, Diarmuid Martin
Sport	7	Ken Doherty, Angela Farrell, Stephen Staunton, Ronan Rafferty
Trade unions	3	Des Geraghty, Joe O'Toole

In hindsight, it is notable that there are hardly any money-men: no bankers, no economists and no property developers. Only two of the ten politicians are Fianna Fáil (Albert Reynolds and Minister for Agriculture Joe Walsh). Given the provenance, it is not surprising that arts feature so largely, but perhaps more so that there are four bishops and a Vatican official (Diarmuid Martin) in the pick. Despite the publication of Paddy Doyle's *God Squad* in 1988, the dark shadows of the child abuse scandal were in the future, and *The Irish Times* confidently expected Bishop Magee to rise in the Hierarchy, perhaps as high as the Archbishopric of Armagh. The civil society campaigners are mostly concerned with environmental matters; they include John Gormley and 'the extraordinary Ms Dubsky' whose campaign against the raw sewage deposited in Dublin Bay made a good deal of effective noise in 1988 and 1989. The sports people include a couple of soccer players, a sailor and a snooker player, but no-one from the GAA or, perhaps more surprisingly, from the rugby world. Since Ireland only won its first entry into the World Cup in 1990, there are no football managers.

As well as professional rugby players, economic commentators and property developers, other character types not yet in the public view include celebrity chefs, Riverdancers, boy bands, female Presidents (Brian Lenihan was still regarded as a shoo-in to the Park) and paedophile priests. It was going to take a bit of time also before we were regularly shown B-list and C-list celebrities sipping their lattes and macchiatos (all terms that first appear in English usage in 1989 according to the *Oxford English Dictionary*). In fact, the new celebrity cult was barely under way: *Hello!* was only launched in 1988, and *OK!* followed in 1993.

Musically, U2 were top of the heap, with two Irish hits ('When love comes to town' and 'All I want is you') not to mention an album *At the eleventh hour;* their manager Paul McGuinness was felt to have achieved something by being invited to join the board of the Arts Council in January. International musical hits came from Michael Jackson ('Leave me alone'), Madonna ('Like a prayer') and Celine Dion, who had won the Eurovision Song Contest in 1988 and impressed Irish buyers in 1989 with 'My heart will go on'. Jason Donovan and Kylie Minogue, from the Australian soap opera *Neighbours,* had seven No 1 hits between them. *Neighbours* had been broadcast at teatime on BBC 1 since 1986 and had a big teen following. Apart from U2, the leading Irish artists were The Pogues (just about hanging together), Sinead O'Connor and Something Happens.

A new breed of middle-class achiever was coming to prominence, a generation that built on the opportunities and expectancy created by the Fianna Fáil men in their mohair suits in the sixties, but were significantly different. 'The world they inherited,' wrote Paddy Woodworth in an *Irish Times* profile of U2 manager Paul McGuinness, 'holds a lot less hope and innocence than the world which formed them, but it can take for granted a certain degree of personal freedom and conspicuous consumption which most of the Taca men could only have imagined.'[19] Paul McGuinness, wrote Woodworth, 'loves fine wines and good food', and 'epitomises the heady mixture of hedonism, hard work, expertise and style which distinguishes his generation from its predecessors.' The slightly scratchy profile makes no mention of McGuinness' religious views or indeed any other opinion, other than a belief that Arts Council subsidies should be 'market-oriented'.

First of all, of course, McGuinness was extremely successful, and as a consequence rich—'estimates of his personal wealth have run as high as £30 million, though £20 million is probably closer to the mark.' The thirty-eight-year-old 'shares a beautifully decorated house in Dún Laoghaire with his wife Kathy', and has 'recently bought another house in the Holland Park area of London'. There are hints of the so-called new man—'he has taken an active interest in the redecoration' of the new house, apparently, and 'in a world where such devotion is hardly usual, he is deeply attached to his family.' But the core is his 'appetite for playing hard which seems at least as well developed as his remarkable capacity for sheer hard work.'

This generation, thought Woodworth, 'which grew up in the turbulent 1960s is coming into its own in the late 1980s. A network of individuals whose interests span the arts, the entertainment industry and the world of business and investment has slipped almost imperceptibly into a dominant position in Irish life.' Among those identified as part of this group were Michael Colgan, the financial journalist Paul Tansey, Senator Shane Ross, and McGuinness associates Chris de Burgh and James Morris. History was to show that their position was important, but scarcely dominant, and that a fortune of £20 million, or even £30 million, was nothing like enough to satisfy a real player.

Money

There was a creeping feeling that existing attitudes to wealth were old-fashioned, even holding the nation back. Nobody went so far as the egregious Gordon Gekko in the film *Wall Street* or his real-life counterpart Ivan Boesky, to say that 'greed is good, greed works', but the saying was in the air (the film was shown in Dublin from May 1988). People began to think that they wanted what John Healy had dismissively called America's 'ice-boxed riches', and if the 'materialism and competiveness' had to come with it, so be it.[20] Something like this attitude was now represented in government by the PDs, and in public discourse by such as Dr Edward Walsh from the new University of Limerick who used to lament that if only those who worked hard could become wealthy, all Ireland's problems would be solved.

In the February issue of *Irish Business*, the caterer Pat Campbell, who had taken over Bewleys in 1986, deplored the 'stigma attached to making money in this country, as if every businessman was by definition greedy. "This", he declared, "is a bad attitude."' *Irish Times* columnist Mary-Ellen Synon brought the new flavour of neo-con thinkers such as Ayn Rand and Robert Nozick from the US, to the fury of *bien pensant* readers. In her very first article in September she declared 'making money for oneself is the only ethical way of life. The alternative is to be a thief or a beggar.' She scorned as slavery the idea that one person's need is another's obligation. International data proved, she argued, that Ireland would only have an economy which was both rich and just if producers and workers were allowed to keep what they have, as of right. Everyone else—unmarried mothers, bureaucrats and others such as artists and presumably clergy—should be told to stop looting someone else's pay packet.

Others clung to the idea of Ireland as a caring society. Nuala O'Faolain described how once every ordinary Irish person had some intimate sense of poverty, even if it was only a beggar on the steps of the club, a class-mate or a family member who had not quite made it. There was as a result a widespread participation in charitable activity, occasionally by quite surprising people. But now she feared a new kind of Irish person was emerging, who had never known anything but comfort, and lacked that sympathy born of personal experience of poverty—'maybe they will eventually form a stable, demanding, middle class which insists on tax cuts for itself and public service cuts for everyone else.'[21] At the end of 1989 the Labour leader Dick Spring put the dilemma in slightly different terms: by creating, he said, 'a more efficient and less equal society' there was an increasing polarisation of society.[22]

To the impoverishment of the Letters column, Mary-Ellen Synon left *The Irish Times* at the end of the year to join the newly launched *Sunday Business Post*. The new paper's publicity made clear that it was aimed at the 'yuppie' market, 20–45-year-olds 'who earn a lot of money and tend to spend it by credit or charge card'. (Yuppie—standing for young urban professionals—was a classic marketing catch term of the mid-1980s.) This was the first new publication in the Irish Sunday market since the *Sunday Tribune* was launched in 1980. It was of its time, concentrating on business, politics and economics; there was to be a Lifestyle section with property, personal investments and a wine column by John Bowman of RTÉ; there would be gossip but no book or arts reviews. In this hard-nosed world, the opinions of long-dead economists, as portrayed by Mary-Ellen Synon, were sufficient.

Stimulated by American theory and practice, Irish boardroom salaries were to escalate remarkably in the next twenty years. With them went the salaries of top officials, a rising tide that certainly did not lift all boats equally. By 2008, a departmental secretary-general was paid four times what his predecessor had in 1989. The salary of the Chief Justice went from £65,000 to €302,000 in that time, and the salary of the Garda Commissioner rose from £46,948 to €240,453. The average industrial wage over the same period increased from £12,500 to just under €40,000.[23]

Straws in the wind

The video rental shop Xtravision, founded in Ranelagh in 1982, now had seventy stores across the country; allowing a much wider and raunchier range of viewing in private than was possible on television or in the local cinema. In September the ban on *The Joy of Sex* was lifted. The nation's drinks bill was steadily increasing—the unlicensed ballrooms had gone, and drink and entertainment were becoming locked together.

The first legal radio station outside RTÉ was opened, with the special help of the Minister, Ray Burke. Struggling to survive, Century Radio was rumoured to have offered £1 million to Gay Byrne, whose autobiography was a Christmas bestseller. Still selling well was the phenomenal 1988 nostalgia-fest *To School Through the Fields,* which quickly joined Noel Browne's *Against the Tide* (a book with an equally post-modern view of truth) as the two best-sellers of the decade. On the highbrow side, John Banville's *Book of Evidence,* based on the MacArthur murders, was the flavour of the season and was nominated for the Booker Prize.

The Taoiseach Charles Haughey announced in June his support for the idea of regenerating the Temple Bar area of Dublin as a centre for cultural activity. He was also influential in the decision to make use of the restored but now empty Royal Hospital in Kilmainham as the base for a museum of modern art.

The diseases of old age, cancer and heart failure, were now responsible for two out of three deaths; maternal mortality was at an all-time low, pushing Ireland to the top of the industrialised countries' league for safety in childbirth.[24] With some 500 deaths of children under five, there was some way to go to achieve the same for infant mortality. The structure of the health service was, as usual, a matter for debate. A Commission on Health Funding, chaired by Miriam Hederman O'Brien, proposed abolishing the health boards in favour of a single unified body, providing free hospital service for all. The scheme also proposed that consultants 'would virtually become employees of the hospitals to which they were appointed.'[25] The report was shelved. The consultants later proposed a 50 per cent pay rise for themselves, though commentators felt this was mere sabre-rattling. Another idea vigorously opposed was the amalgamation of the Adelaide, Meath and National Children's hospitals, which the *Church of Ireland Gazette* condemned as 'monumental insensitivity to the feelings and rights of the whole Protestant community'. The Irish Society for Prevention of Cruelty to Children reported that its newly-introduced helpline had received 26,000 calls in its first year of operation. A quarter of these related to sexual abuse.

Among other straws in the wind was the increasing tendency of business people not to drink during the working day—'lunch is for wimps' as Gordon Gekko declared in *Wall Street.* This change, which followed the removal of tax reliefs for entertaining in the early 1980s, signalled a new 'work-hard, play-hard, winner takes all' ethic in the business and professional community. The solicitor's profession had followed the accountants to an obsession with billings and time sheets (recorded in some cases in six-minute intervals throughout the day), and losing much of the old civility in the process. The loss of the lunch business seriously affected the restaurant trade. Another new mood (later identified as the *Bowling Alone* phenomenon) switched ordinary sports activity from the convivial team games (followed by a few pints, which the drink-driving laws had made problematic) to the solitary intensity of the workout and the gym session.[26]

Fax, photocopy and filofax were still the smart technologies. In May it was reported that mobile phones, which had surfaced in Sweden in 1981, were growing in business use. But they were dear, at £2,000 each, and looked like small bricks. It was reckoned there were some 9,000 customers in Ireland. In *Irish Business* in May, Jonathan Philbin Bowman told its readers about the exciting new possibilities of electronic mail, and reported that there were now as many as 600 users in Ireland. Unbeknownst to all but specialists, in March Tim Berners-Lee circulated his proposal for a combination of hypertext, browser and hyperlinks that within a few years became the internet.

There was a sense that significant change was in the air, that established ways were unravelling. In the summer, Professor Francis Fukuyama published his essay 'The end of history?'—though the dramatic title in fact referred to a restricted form of history, the apparent triumph across the world of the ideas and practice of liberal democracy. There was a reasonable apprehension that Ireland was too weak to meet the great changes in the EC expected in 1992. A survey reported that half the population had only the vaguest idea about the expected cultural and commercial onslaught as the barriers to free movement of people, capital and goods were to be pulled down. 'We have now the sense,' wrote Fintan O'Toole at the end of the year, 'that something—the post-war order of the world—is ending but something else—whatever is to follow—has not yet begun.'[27]

Chapter 18 Getting and spending

Getting

Money was a private subject, still carrying a lingering but deep feeling that there was something unseemly about excessive concern with it, and that it was definitely rude to probe into another's financial affairs. D. P. Moran's identification of Irish and anti-materialist was still (just) alive, and it was possible for a secretary of the Department of Finance lyrically to describe how his officers were not motivated by self-interest, but 'by other interests such as religion, patriotism and professional ethics. Practical patriotism was not yet a dead formula in a country such as Ireland where national independence was achieved within living memory.'[1] But this was even then perhaps an old-fashioned attitude, which had arguably cost the service dearly. In the years of the national project, up to the 1960s, the purchasing power of senior civil servants such as assistant secretaries had fallen by over half.[2]

Intrusion into other people's money affairs was as sensitive as prying into their sex lives. Charles Haughey was able to fob off journalistic enquiries on the source of his wealth for years by exploiting this fact (aided by fears of the stringent laws against libel). The idea that tax records should be as openly available to ordinary public scrutiny as they have been for decades in Sweden and Norway would simply have been regarded as rank socialism. In newspapers there was still a curious reluctance to express incomes in plain figures: the re-appointed Ombudsman, Michael Mills, we were told, for instance, had a salary 'on a par with that of a High Court judge'.[3] How much exactly people were paid, or how much they spent on this evening out or that bauble, was generally not in the public domain.

As a result of this secrecy little was really known (even by the tax authorities) about who had what. When the manager of the Bank of Ireland's newly launched private banking venture—itself a sign of things moving—was asked how many millionaires there were in Ireland, he was obliged to admit that even after confidential enquiries among lawyers, accountants and bankers, no one knew: 'Some say 1,000, some say 2,000 and others put the figure even higher. I'd put it higher rather than lower.'

New Men
Above: Managing Director Seán Fitzpatrick in his office at Anglo Irish Bank, November 1989—the power-dresser's double breasted suit, and a desk full of paper, with a coffee-cup, matches and an ashtray, but no computer or document shredder. (Derek Spiers)
Below: A different style of New Man, shopping with the family in Blackrock—shell suit trousers, white socks, deck shoes. (Derek Spiers)

In January 1989, the magazine *Irish Business* broke a taboo and produced a Rich List for Ireland, a notion that would have been condemned as hopelessly 'vulgar' a generation before. At the top of the list was Larry Goodman, the beef baron backed by Haughey, with assets of more than £200 million, though during the year increasing questions were asked about exactly how this had been amassed. The magazine next identified three men (there were no women in the list) with more than £100 million: Martin Naughton of the electrical concern Glen Dimplex, Tony O'Reilly of Heinz, Fitzwilton and the Independent Group, and Tony Ryan of GPA and Ryanair. In the next tranche, with £50 million or more, were Ben Dunne, the Earl of Iveagh, Chairman of Guinness (the only one remotely representing old money), Charles Gallagher of Abbey builders, and Michael Smurfit, whose print and packaging group had an Irish market capitalisation greater than AIB or the Bank of Ireland.

Others, identified with lesser assets, were the Doyle hotel family, the McGraths of Sweepstake fame, Feargal Quinn the supermarket owner, Dermot Desmond the stockbroker, Vincent O'Brien the horse trainer, the mysterious Pino Harris (trucks and property) and Austin Darragh with his pharmaceutical interests. Motor interests were prominent in the rich list, with Toyota (Tim and Denis Mahony), Renault (Bill Cullen) and Volkswagen (O'Flaherty) all creating multi-millionaires. Property interests were, of course, featured, including the Sisks and McInerneys; and, as a straw in the wind, there was John Byrne, described as 'a friend of Charles Haughey and the Fianna Fáil party, [his] empire is controlled through the Guinness and Mahon Cayman Trust in the Cayman Islands.' The only representatives from the worlds of arts and media were the rock group, U2 and their manager Paul McGuinness. There were no bankers, sportsmen, millionaire novelists or software creators.

Although they were not at all ashamed of their riches, the magazine was clear that the members of the Rich List 'tended to be less flashy and more discreet in their spending' than foreign millionaires. They had big houses in the country, but behind walls; they invested in stocks and shares, but only anonymously, through bank nominee accounts. They bought art, but as often as not 'discreetly imported' it from abroad. 'For the most part,' the magazine commented, 'the Irish rich eschew private planes and helicopters—they are too much trouble and are too high profile.' They certainly did not take high-profile jaunts to Morocco for the weekend on the private jet. When Charlie Haughey was photographed for *In Dublin* magazine he refused to be taken outside Kinsealy, saying it represented 'too much Georgian splendour'.[4] Otherwise, the magazine reported, the rich's activities were 'similar to international millionaires, except with consideration to the tax man and the terrorist' (in that order) with both of whom, the magazine implied, they had as little to do as possible. The possibility of IRA kidnap, as had happened in 1983 to Don Tidey and the racehorse Shergar, was a daily concern for the rich.

The one thing they did have in common was hard work, a value that was frequently expressed with a self-congratulatory smirk at being 'self-confessed workaholics'. This term, which had started out in the early 1970s as identifying an obsessive, pathological inability to cut loose from the job, had become the modern way of identifying a new work ethic. Larry Goodman was clearly a workaholic, and the fact that Martin Naughton 'had few leisure pursuits' gave the game away. In fact it became hardly possible to be taken as a serious person unless you were 'a bit of a workaholic'—just as in the 2000s if you were not 'tremendously busy and stressed' you were scarcely participating in society. In January, for instance, *The Irish Times* told its readers that Seán Cromien, the Secretary of the Department of Finance, was a workaholic, and then described his hobby of bird watching, broad reading of literature and presidency of the Half Moon swimming club. Later in the year a hotel advertised bargain accommodation 'for all you fun-loving workaholics'.

Very large salaries, reported the Irish Management Institute, were unusual in Ireland. Few earned six figures, unless they were in large companies with multi-national ramifications.[5] There was a row when Alex Spain, appointed Chairman of B+I ferries, insisted on nearly twice the pay of a normal state-sponsored body chief executive (especially since he was also chairman of the extremely successful video rental chain Xtravision). Data from a survey of 30,000 European managers published in a German magazine showed that Irish managers were the worst paid in Europe, averaging £41,600 for the managing director of a company with sales of £80 million. The UK managing director of an equivalent company could expect £61,500 and a Swiss as much as £98,750.[6] The recently retired European Commissioner, Peter Sutherland, had been on £100,000. An IMI survey published in October showed that the chief executive of a large company operating in Dublin earned £51,000, £4,000 more than his counterpart outside the capital. Over 90 per cent of chief executives had a company car, and only 18 per cent received a bonus, typically based on profit performance.

As in the previous periods studied, there was a spectrum of earnings (see Table opposite). At the lowest was the minimum wage level

Table 9 Who earned what in 1989

Over £60,000	President (£72,000), Taoiseach (£65,796 plus allowances), Chief Justice (£65,798), CEO of £60m+ company (av £76,624), medical consultants (£36,000 basic, up to £100,000 with private fees), senior counsel.
£50,000– £60,000	High Court judge (£50,061), President of SIPTU (£51,000), Secretary, Department of Finance (£54,882), Supreme Court judge (£55,032)
£40,000– £50,000	Dublin City Manager (£45,634), CEO state-sponsored body e.g. IDA, ESB, Aer Lingus (£42,800), Attorney-General (£47,581), CEO of £10m company (£47,824), government minister (£47,991), Secretary of government department (£49,227),
£30,000– £40,000	District Justice (£33,897), CEO health board (£36,587), assistant secretary in government department at top of scale (£37,623), head of finance in company employing 250-500 (£38,000)
£20,000– £30,000	Economics correspondent RTE (£20,000), engineer for Louth Council, seven years experience required, (£22,233), newly qualified chartered accountant (£23,000), TD (£24,777),
£10,000– £20,000	Programmer in UCD computer department (£10,000), average male industrial wage (£12,500), staff nurse at top of scale (£12,532), garda top of scale (£13,328), execuive officer Department of Education £14,053), senator (£14,061), pensions for former Taoisigh Jack Lynch and Garret FitzGerald (£16,180), personal secretary to CEO (£18,000), teacher (married male) at top of scale £19,047
Up to £10,000	Old age pension (£2,600), £60 pw minimum wage proposed by Labour Party (£3,120), long-term unemployed married man with two children (£5,044), three-quarters of all farmers (<£7,500), average female industrial wage (£7,800), AIB starters (£8,250), Garda new recruit (£8,553), pastry chef in Galway (£8,800), book-keeper in small office (£9,000), clerical assistant Department of Education (£9,607)

Source: Irish Times advertisements and articles throughout 1989 especially 'Examples of Revised Pay Scales' 29 July 1989

proposed by the Labour Party of £60 a week, or £3,120 a year, rising to the Taoiseach at £65,796 plus allowances, or the President (Dr Hillery) at £72,000 plus a free house in the Park. The Minister for Labour, Bertie Ahern, vigorously opposed the idea of a minimum wage on the grounds that it would push costs up and 'probably lead to the loss of jobs'.[7] His own salary, in common with all his colleagues, had gone up by just short of £3,000 a year in July.

The seven grades given in the table show the nice calculations of how the society valued contributions. At the bottom, earning less than £10,000, were the farmers (no longer the fêted darlings of the economy), clerical staff in a small office, and a pastry chef in Galway. The next level, from £10,000 to £20,000, contained the average (male) industrial wage at £12,000, clerical assistants, office workers, recruits to the guards or newly-qualified nurses; then senators, staff nurses and married male teachers, who at the top of the scale were paid 50 per cent more than top nurses. This was the level at which most Irish citizens found themselves. The Revenue Commissioners reported that only 2 per cent of PRSI payers reported incomes of more than £20,000.

Above these, in the £20,000 to £30,000 range, a newly qualified chartered accountant was worth more or less the same as a TD, and a bit more than the economics correspondent of RTÉ. The reputation of the chartered accountancy exams was high, and the accountancy profession had considerably enhanced its standing over the previous twenty years, overtaking the solicitors in the range of services provided, and, some said, in the professionalism with which these services were provided. Notably, they had completely captured the lucrative tax consultancy and advice business, unlike their cousins in the United States where that business had remained with law practices. Newly qualified chartered accountants, unlike lawyers, had a very mobile qualification, and could easily move to the 'glittering salaries' often advertised by British firms looking for 'really young Europeans'.

A qualified accountant acting as head of the accounts function in a sizeable business could look for £40,000, while his staff might expect £23,000. Perks at the top levels included company cars, VHI subscriptions, non-contributory pensions and share participation schemes.[8] In the £40,000–£50,000 bracket distinctions were nicely calibrated. The chief executives of state-sponsored bodies earned just a little less than secretaries of government departments, who in turn earned a little less than ministers; always excepting the Secretary of the Department of

Finance who, as the titular head of the civil service, had traditionally been paid a little more.

Spending

Since 1951 the Central Statistics Office had at irregular intervals identified the details of household expenditure. The information was based on two-week diaries kept by the chosen households. As always, such self-reporting introduces bias; people significantly understate the amount they spend on certain sensitive items such as alcohol (and overstate what they spend on others, such as toothbrushes). That said, the surveys done in 1980 and 1987 do reveal a reduction in consumption during those economically stressed years. Taking inflation into account, we can see for instance that expenditure on food fell in real terms by some 17 per cent, as families cut back. Expenditure on clothing fell by as much as 30 per cent. Fuel, household disposables and transport expenditures were also reduced. Reported expenditure on alcohol and tobacco more or less kept up with inflation.[9] Overall, Irish households spent one-twelfth less on themselves in 1987 than they did in 1980.

At the same time, there was a long-term trend to adjust the *pattern* of expenditure. As incomes grow over time, it seems that the pattern of expenditure chanages and, with variants, gradually approximates to the pattern adopted by social group 1 (urban professional class). The very earliest household survey (covering urban households only) showed that in 1951 households spent 38 per cent of their income on food; by 1987 the figure was down to 25 per cent. This is very near the proportion for food consumption recorded by social group 1 households in 1965.

The very clear differences in expenditure between the social groups, almost a ladder of preferences, that we saw in the 1960s had become blurred by the late 1980s. Nonetheless, there is sufficient of a pattern to distinguish the lifestyle of the urban professional class (social group 1) from, say, the urban manual workers (social group 5). The survey records that the professionals' weekly expenditure was almost exactly twice that of the manual workers—probably an underestimate of the real differenc. But the interest lies in how this two-fold expenditure was deployed. For the most basic items such as food, household consumables, fuel and lighting actual cash expenditure was similar, manual workers' families spending about 20 per cent less than the professionals, although the items bought in each category were differently balanced. For instance, families in the two groups spent almost the same (in cash) on meat and vegetables, but the manual workers spent absolutely more on white bread, milk and butter, the professionals buying considerably more fresh fruit. The reported alcohol and tobacco expenditure was the same for both groups.

Not surprisingly it was on more discretionary items that the professionals recorded greater expenditure. They spent twice as much on clothing and twice as much on 'miscellaneous goods' such as reading materials, music recordings, jewellery and sports goods. Unsurprisingly, the professionals were also able to spend more money on restaurant meals (five times the manual workers), new cars (eleven times) and holidays abroad (four times). In social terms, however, the most significant differences were in the amount spent on medical expenses—the professionals reported expenditure of five times that of the manual workers—and on education—the professionals spent twelve times as much as the manual workers.

The perhaps mythical concern of ordinary Irish people with education (hedge schools, etc.) seems to have waned. But it was this continuous investment in education that ensured the class inheritance. As two ESRI scholars commented ten years later, the 'accumulating evidence provides no support for any trend towards equality of educational opportunity'. There was no concerted plan or coordinated activity to that end; to maintain their privileged position all the middle class needed to do was to 'set their superior resources strategically against whatever changes—in institutional arrangements, public policy etc.—may appear threatening to them. The middle classes of the Republic of Ireland have succeeded admirably in this while continuing to espouse the rhetoric of equality of opportunity and denying the reality of class.'[10]

In the home

Whatever the class or social group, the first requirement was housing. On average, professional families spent three times as much as manual workers' families on housing. Most of this went on mortgages. The buying of houses, rather than renting, was now a firmly established phenomenon, with the 1981 Census reporting that for the first time more than half of the houses in Dublin were owner occupied. The Household Budget Survey revealed that the middle class was spending over 10 per cent of its income on housing, the bulk of this being mortgage repayments. The practice was spreading quite slowly, so far only 35 per cent of all households were actually making mortgage repayments.

The practical implications of this increase in home ownership were becoming clear, as the rate of house moving, especially in the early years of marriage (which in earlier, renting, generations had been frequent), slowed down considerably. On the other hand, as the property market warmed up, people began increasingly to see a house as not just a home, but also as an investment. For those prepared to be light-footed, this presented a pleasant chance to make money.

Another implication, pointed out by *The Irish Times* columnist Maev-Anne Wren, was 'unprecedented transfers of wealth from one generation to the next as elderly parents leave their middle-aged, already well housed offspring with inherited property'.[11] She did not mention another equally significant inter-generational transfer as young first-time purchasers were able to borrow from aggressive lending banks (who only ten years previously had to be cajoled into entering the market at all) to pay inflated prices to those a little older who were 'trading up'.

Having established a home, the next thing to do was to fill it. Virtually everyone had a television now, and 87 per cent of urban households either owned or rented a colour set—double the figures of the beginning of the decade. Home computers were not unknown, but were typically hobbyist machines such as Atari, Commodore 64 and Sinclair. In the office the IBM PC (launched in 1981) dominated, though the cool types in design and related spheres preferred the Apple series. As we have seen, mobile phones were brick-like objects typically sported by salesmen; in fact so little did people feel the need to be connected that fewer than 60 per cent of urban houses in the state had a telephone. This was however a considerable advance, since at the beginning of the decade only just over one-third had a phone. Just over half of urban households had a car.

Urban houses now generally boasted a vacuum cleaner (85 per cent), a washing machine (79 per cent) and a fridge (98 per cent). However, fewer than 10 per cent of urban households had a dishwasher. For each of these goods ownership had significantly increased over the decade, representing a progressive investment during the decade in household equipment. For instance, the proportion of urban households with washing machines had gone from 66 per cent to 79 per cent; the proportion with vacuum cleaners had moved up from 73 to 85 per cent.

Another area of marked investment in the 1980s was in central heating. At the beginning of the decade only 18 per cent of urban houses had central heating, and the largest group of these used oil. In the early

1980s the government tried to reduce its oil import bill by encouraging those using oil to switch to solid fuel. In an unintended consequence, considerable numbers of those who previously had had no central heating took advantage of the grants to install back-boilers. By the end of the decade solid fuel or mixed systems were installed in a third of all urban households. In its advertisements the coal lobby encouraged the feeling that a house without a coal fire was not a home. Unfortunately the government had paid no attention to environmental warnings, and by the mid-1980s Dublin was suffering severe atmospheric pollution in winter, such as had been eradicated in London in the 1950s.

Although the introduction of natural gas had some small effect, after an experience of freezing smog in November 1988 more and more voices began to be heard decrying the incidence and dangers of solid fuel systems. In January 1989 Environment Minister P. Flynn declared that 'Dublin's smog was Ireland's most serious air-pollution problem'; but then, reluctant to upset voters, and unwilling to face the various interests, notably the coal lobby, he merely initiated a publicity campaign urging households to burn smokeless fuel. 'The solution to the problem' he feebly urged, 'lies in our own hands. People have an opportunity to make an investment in their own good health.'[12] The smog stayed as bad as ever until Mary Harney became Minister of State for the Environment later in the year and enforced the use of smokeless fuel.

Shopping

Buying a house, a central heating system or, more mundanely, the groceries, was not usually thought of as 'fun'. According to market research, many women working at home ('housewives') actually enjoyed their weekly foray into the bright modern spacious arenas of the supermarkets.[13] The 'big shop' was typically done at the end of the week, in preparation for the minor festival of the weekend. This shopping expedition was a serious business, typically done by the woman alone, except in middle-class Dublin where the men occasionally lent a hand. Here the housewife juggled her budget, her consciousness of the need to provide healthy foods, her suspicions of the value of the growing range of convenience foods, and the culinary conservatism of her husband and children. To add to the complexity, 'the whole repertoire of the diet (white bread, eggs, potatoes, sugar, butter, salt, cakes) that in her mother's day included the very symbols of goodness, she is now told is questionable.'[14]

At the weekend the daily routine was broken, leisure was enjoyed and special foods were eaten, for instance a fry for breakfast (no longer usual during the week) and notably the Sunday roast (ideally beef). Many women still felt that the occasion deserved the ceremony of purchase of the roast at a butcher's, rather than buying pre-packed joints from the supermarket. During the weekend there was a vague atmosphere of leisure and 'plenty' in the household, as befitted a festival, shown perhaps in the increased consumption of cakes, minerals and other drinks. Most families would mark Sunday by attendance at Mass.

During the week there would typically also be 'small shops' most days, for things that had run out, such as bread, milk, sugar, fruit, cigarettes and perhaps a magazine (newspapers were typically bought by the husbands). These expeditions were as much a jaunt, a walk, a social occasion as a commercial one.

Especially in Dublin, other kinds of shopping, particularly for clothes, had become much more than a utilitarian activity. Indeed Fintan O'Toole proposed that shopping was to the 1980s what cinema was to the 1930s, a consolation and an escape. Inside the new Stephen's Green Centre (opened November 1988), with its outside decorations like filigree sugar, was a little community of its own, complete with its restaurants and buskers and police and of course more and more things to buy.[15] In the nineteenth century promoters of the department store concept had advertised their shops as the ideal place for otherwise stay-at-home housewives to spend the afternoon, buying whatever they fancied to decorate the nest (anything from a ribbon to a piano from under the same roof), and then taking afternoon tea. Now the increasing numbers of shopping centres combining a wide variety of different shops required a different message. Already there was the ILAC Centre and the Stephen's Green Centre in central Dublin and others in the suburbs; the vast Square in Tallaght was to open in 1990; a new complex was being planned to extend from Jervis Street almost to O'Connell Bridge and another huge one in Blanchardstown (finally opened in 1996). Across the country smaller centres also sprouted, selling the same message. To sustain these centres, as Nuala O'Faolain noted, shopping was promoted as a newly meaningful, family activity: 'Dad will buy something Dad-ish, like a power drill, and Mum will buy food and Sharon will buy a Bros video and Kevin will buy a denim jacket. Then they will all go home in a haze of happiness.'[16]

It was in this context that the word 'shopaholic' appeared. First appearing in America in the mid-1980s, it was most used in Ireland to describe Princess Diana (still married, just). In 1989 the term still retained its obsessive-compulsive tinge, but before too long it became normalised, and in a few years rich women (particularly women) would be saying with a smirk, just like their high-achieving husbands, 'I'm a bit of a shopaholic' as they flew off to New York to buy their Christmas presents.

Buying clothes had become both easier and harder, for in common with other areas of life, authority was draining out of fashion. As fashion writer Arminta Wallace noted, 'style, not fashion, had become the watchword'. The rigidity of the old days when everyone hung on the words of the great Paris couturiers to find out what colours, what skirt lengths, what accessories were in, had gone. In this as in other things, a looser, less regulated, even post-modern variety was now adopted. In 1967, fully 92 per cent of skirts illustrated in *Vogue* had been of a single length, at or just above the knee; by 1987 no such rule applied—some skirts (11 per cent) were at thigh length, some on the knee (22 per cent) some at mid-calf (14 per cent).[17] Now, one author claimed, we were hurtling towards 'stylistic tribalism' in which multiple style groups co-existed, each with their shops to cater for them.[18]

At the same time the idea that there was an appropriate style for particular occasions had withered. At the RDS Horse Show in August, for instance, fashion writer Gabrielle Williams noticed without enthusiasm 'one girl in a bustier bodice and little else', another apparently dressed as a New Orleans tart, and there were several 'flowery, flouncy dresses more suitable for a Godfather wedding breakfast'.[19]

Trust me, I'm an alternative practitioner

In another area of expenditure, too, the norms of the past were cracking. For generations doctors had been among the most respected members of the society, revered for their compassion and their secret knowledge of the human condition. Paradoxically, just as the antibiotics and other drugs had enabled the profession to be really effective, to the point of seriously improving both survival rates and quality of life, patients began to look for more. 'People are no longer prepared to sit down under a system which says doctor knows best, when he patently hasn't got the answers to many of their problems' the organiser of a Natural Health and Complementary Medicine Conference told *The Irish Times* in March.

The number of alternative and complementary practitioners advertising in the *Golden Pages* shot up from 26 in 1985 to 241 in 1995, only some of which increase could be accounted for by the increase in telephone availability and use. There were acupuncturists, aromatherapists, chiropractors, homeopathists, hypnotists, osteopaths and reflexologists all jostling for business, to the general exasperation of the medical establishment. In the same period the number of counselling services advertising equally soared, from 27 in 1985 to 265 ten years later.[20]

As official medicine became increasingly sophisticated and arcane, people looked for a simpler picture. One such was provided by dietary therapist Bernadette Connolly-Martin. Her speciality was dietary therapy, which identified four key areas of the body (skin, kidney, bowel or liver) where all the bad toxins you have ever consumed manifest themselves. The key to her treatment was a full hour and a half initial session in which the patient's personal medical history, intimate details of eating habits and current life-style were explored. (This was a long way from the ordinary GP's brisk prescription after a ten minute consultation and perhaps a test or two.) Then you were given a cleansing regime which eradicated the bad effects of past self-indulgence—no wonder the attendance at Confession was down. Bernadette was particularly successful, she claimed, with sinus and migraine, and had soothed her husband's sore knees by taking him off pork and tomatoes.[21]

At the Mansion House conference, members of the public paid £3 a head for access to a 'remarkable range of professed cures for physical, emotional and spiritual problems as well as promises of opportunities for creative growth and improving relationships.' If there was nothing physically wrong with you, you could try 'loving relationship training' which apparently promised to bring users to the point 'where there is no conflict between pleasing yourself and pleasing others'.[22] By all accounts, brisk business was done at all the stalls.

This trend is clearly part of the growing resistance to authority, and the groping for alternatives. Many of the alternative practitioners were in fact competing not with conventional medicine but offering spiritual benefits—in fact invading the increasingly weakly-held territory of the clergy. This is clear from the fact that the use of the standard medical services, whether of GPs or hospitals was equally increasing.

Frolicking in the sun

The two great and expensive family festivals of the year were Christmas and the annual holiday. The annual summer holiday figured high on the family budget, being a one-off drain of perhaps several hundred pounds. As the *Independent* put it, you 'saved all year for a week or two basking and frolicking in the sun'. A huge weight of expectation rode on this one crucial fortnight: 'For most of us the annual holiday abroad is what makes life living. We look on it as an escape from routine and chance to let our hair down and an opportunity to recharge our batteries ready for winter'.[23] The holiday was 'the thing that makes working for the rest of the year bearable'.

Just as in the 1989 film *Shirley Valentine*, the sun, sea and freedom might just possibly change everything. "Holidays can do wonders for your sex life", says therapist Eddie McHale' reported the *Independent*. Or, conversely, we were told that couples who were having problems with their marriage might find them magnified in the isolation of the holiday. The weight of expectation gave a poignancy to articles about 'holiday nightmares' including airport delays with the chartered flights, appalling plumbing, unfinished hotels, oily and monotonous food, lager louts (usually British), accidents and the inevitable results of tender white Irish skins being exposed to scorching sun. Food was always a problem, given the notorious conservatism of the male Irish palate. By way of softening up the resistance to anything but steak and chips, *The Irish Times* in May introduced its readers to some French specialities. 'Do French people really eat frogs and snails?' asked the headline, as the article introduced foie gras, caviar, snails, frogs' legs and truffles, describing what they were, what they cost, how to eat them and what they tasted like.[24]

The marvellously sunny season of 1989 even encouraged a few of those white skins to reveal themsleves in Ireland. In July 'Dollymount strand became the Costa del Dublin' wrote Kathryn Holmquist. 'Thousands of people bared their bodies to the sun. In the privacy of the dunes women sunbathed topless to salsa music.' Others were more sensible, and 'shaded themselves under sombre rain umbrellas and sunhats that had not seen the light of day since the 1960s'. In Stephen's Green, to the sound of the Army No. 1 band playing Strauss, people of all ages lounged on the ground and enjoyed the gardens, baring as much of themselves as they thought decent.[25] Although people had experience of topless sunbathing from their continental holidays, and in the heat of this summer, 'naked bosoms had begun to appear in Brittas beach',[26] many were still very uncomfortable with such nudity. In the *Irish Independent* in July Mary Kenny voiced a residual feeling that such nudity was not suitable where there were children, and perhaps not in Ireland at all.

The all-in flight and accommodation booked through the tourist agent was only part of what the saving was for. In the special sunlit place 'abroad' clearly a quite different type of clothes was necessary. Luckily, Sasha of the Stephen's Green Centre and all over the country could kit you out in vests, print blouses, Bermudas, T-shirts, culottes, a print dress and all accessories including wedge shoes and sunglasses for less than £150. What's more the whole lot will only take up half a carry-on bag (no cumbersome case, please), leaving plenty of room for souvenirs, presents and the all-important duty-free on the return journey.[27]

According to a survey by Bord Fáilte, in 1988 some 844,000 Irish people had holidayed in Ireland, many in the traditional way on the farms of relations. That tradition was waning, however, and the majority of home-holidaymakers now stayed in hotels, guest houses and rented accommodation. Cork or Kerry (with one-third of visitors between them) were the most popular destinations, with Galway next. Three-quarters of a million people went abroad, with Britain by far the most popular destination, taking 38 per cent. The next most popular destinations were European, headed by Spain (18 per cent), France (8 per cent), Greece (4 per cent) and Italy (2 per cent).

For a variety of reasons, including the fine weather at home, 1989 was a near disastrous season for the travel agencies. They had expected that the confidence in the economy would push the previous year's numbers up by 10 per cent or more, so they pre-booked for 250,000 travellers. By mid-season it was clear that they were not going to achieve this so they cut to 200,000. By the end of the season it was 'now estimated that only 160,000 Irish people have taken sunshine holidays'.[28]

Speculation suggested that people were put off air travel by the Lockerbie bombing of December 1988, or the previous summer's airport strike hassles, or mounting publicity about skin cancer. Others thought that the high emigration figures of previous years limited the number of young holiday-makers, while their parents saved the holiday fund for family reunions with emigrants in Britain and America. Confirming this speculation, Bord Fáilte had reported that in 1988 over a third of holidaymakers went to Britain, and as many Irish people went to America as to France.

The simple attractions of the crowded sandy beaches were beginning to lose their allure, with holiday-makers looking for something a bit different. The market for holiday cottages in the Irish country was picking up. In May Nuala O'Faolain told her *Irish Times* readers about an idyllic walking holiday in the Alps near Grenoble, and her colleague Mary Dowey recommended the newly formed 'Hidden Ireland' group of Irish country houses. Here, Dublin's middle-class could live the Anglo style for a while. '*Real* country houses,' urged the group's promoter John Colclough (pictured complete with a monocle), 'as opposed to ghastly modern houses that happen to be in the country.' The atmosphere, readers were told, 'is of a home rather than a hotel. The owners greet you, pour drinks, serve you dinner.' Family heirlooms, Victorian plumbing, tattered curtains and hosts who never stopped talking were all part of the charm. This was as Mary Dowey reported, a notch up on 'that same old stretch of Spanish costa (but of course the children love it)'.[29]

'Tis the season to be jolly

The other annual highlight of most people's years, with an equal weight of expectation and apprehension, was Christmas.

Christmas Day in 1989 was a Monday, so many factories and offices were shut for a full ten days to Monday 1 January. In this blank time was fitted a cascade of rituals: the office party, the candle in the window, the Christmas tree complete with lights, Midnight Mass, Santa, relatives to stay/visit and the apparently compulsory family rows, turkey, pudding, crackers, presents, too much rich food and drink, carols, endless television repeats, all the pubs closed, the sales, ringing-in the New Year. Religion was certainly present, but as an additional extra for those who cared for that kind of thing.

If there was a problem with Christmas, it was that, as Maureen Gaffney put it, 'Christmas was not big enough for the feelings we put into it'. Over 100,000 people travelled specially to Ireland from Britain to be with their families, and nearly half a million crammed the intercity rail services (45 extra trains laid on) and the provincial bus services. For the adults it was an aspiration, an occasion for a party and a revisiting of memories of the best bits of their childhood. For children it was simpler. Alice Taylor, in her best-selling 1988 book *To School Through the Fields.* captured some of the sentimental yearning: 'Christmas in our house was always magical and for weeks beforehand my toes would tingle at the thought of it.' Gene Kerrigan, remembering his Christmases in Cabra in the 1950s recalled ' the noise and the smiles and hugs and the taste and the smell and the sheer joy of it.'[30]

Anxious to recreate those feelings for their children, parents spent a fortune on presents to provide competitive kids with the requisite delight, tramping round town to find the must-have toy of the season. For the adults increasingly elaborate meals were prepared for the 'Christmas dinner'. It was not enough just to do what your mother had done, though paradoxically little bits of family ritual could not be omitted--it wouldn't feel quite right. On special television programmes, in Darina Allen's 1989 *Simply Delicious Christmas* recipe book published just in time (and containing a disastrous misprint in the recipe for Christmas pudding[31]) and in the newspapers, eager cooks urged you to add 'that perfect finishing touch'. Decorations, special crackers, personalised gifts were proposed, all in anxious-making pursuit of the elusive perfection. Rose Doyle suggested that the already over-worked cook provide porridge, oysters, kidneys and cranberry for breakfast; and restaurant critic Sandy O'Byrne proposed 'anything but turkey'—actually goose, pheasant, guinea fowl or just a brace of quail for 'the luxury of a Christmas table *à deux*' (with wild mushrooms and wine butter, of course).

Christmas was supposed to be the time of celebrating family, of the clan coming together, of identifying who was looking after whom in the world. But the fact was that over half of Dubliners lived either by themselves or with one companion/spouse/child. These were not the jolly family groups that the memoirists lovingly recalled. Olivia O'Leary recounted an experience that must have been common: 'I came from a family of eight children and I thought for years that that was how families had to be: large, rumbustious, noisy. So at Christmas time I'd fuss about setting a long table, preparing an epic meal and then wonder why my own small household with our only child didn't quite fit the space. Then, one Christmas, because I was ill, dinner was served in front of the fire at a table just big enough for us: intimate, simple and lovely—the right-sized Christmas for our family.'[32]

For many singletons, as everyone knew, Christmas could be a bit of an ordeal. No doubt invitations could be forthcoming, but as Nuala O'Faolain pointed out, perhaps there was nothing worse 'than clinging to the edges of someone else's household, wondering where they keep the kettle and whether it would be rude to open a window or why that child isn't given a good slap.'[33]

For traders, and here was a major source of tension, Christmas was a profit centre. Many shopkeepers, such as the booksellers, toy shops and jewellers would do 40 per cent or more of their annual business in November and December. It was not a coincidence that the current image of Santa was based on an advertisement. They needed people to buy things, and the dearer the better. Nobody said it out loud, but the idea in the air was that the more one spent, the more one loved. Wine sellers, record shops (just stocking the new CDs at £10 to £15 each), chemists, even hardware shops did their best to join in the bonanza. Anything, it seemed from the ads, could be the 'perfect gift'; and Maeve Binchy had some fun with this idea as she recalled the baffled or insulted recipients of a draught excluder, some telephone cleaning fluid, Bridge lessons, half an ox for the freezer and, of course, the special lingerie.[34]

By 1 January it was all over. Shops, offices and factories went back to work, and the people who had travelled to all parts of Ireland for the holiday returned home. 'How was your Christmas?' one asked another across the country, 'Quiet'.[35]

Ladies at leisure
Above: opportunities for outdoor eating, with or without the BMW, (here, at Woods of Baggot Street) were not anything like as common as they became after the smoking ban. (Derek Spiers)
Below: pondering form at the Phoenix Park races. (Derek Spiers)

Chapter 19 Shifting sands

For generations the Irish people had nourished various images of who they were and what sustained them. There was the Land, for the real Irish were country folk. There was the Catholic religion, for Ireland was the jewel in the Vatican's crown, the most devout nation on earth. And there was the Family, enshrined in the Constitution as the source of identity and comfort—as the ISPCC had declared in a 1932 appeal, 'no country in the world counts its children more precious'.

A host of lesser myths supported these—among them that the Irish were continually 'agin the government' (as the joke went, if the Irish language was forbidden everyone would want to learn it); that the Irish were too fine and too sensitive to fall into the crass love of money or goods; that the Irish were much given to fighting; that the Irish were an aristocratic people who had no class system; that the Irish had a deep interest in culture and learning, combined with an instinctive spirituality; that it was simply unnatural that the whole island was not under Irish rule; that the Irish language was the unique key to the Irish soul; that the Irish really had more in common with the people of the European continent than with the British; that in the country everyone knew everything about their neighbours; that the Irish were prodigious book-readers; that the inherited fear of eviction had made the Irish obsessive about owning property; that the Irish had been more cruelly oppressed by the brutal English than any other nation in the world.

Unnervingly, in the late 1980s doubt shone on each of these props of the Irish identity. People felt acutely this ebbing of the old certainties. Some resisted vehemently, the majority embraced the changes with more or less enthusiasm.

The crumbling monolith

Despite a momentary revival caused by Pope John Paul's visit in 1979, a series of self-inflicted wounds since the 1960s had gradually added to the pressures of the outside world in weakening the Church's position. The process began with the changes consequent on the Vatican Council of 1962–5.[1] For generations, Catholics had been told categorically that the use of Latin was a unique identifier of Catholic worship, and a sign of the universality of the Church. In 1963, worshippers were suddenly told that the traditional order of Mass which had been declared perpetual and universal in 1570 (with Latin and an elaborate web of gestures and prayers which many had grown to love since childhood) was now positively forbidden. Henceforth, all worship was to be in the vernacular and the prayers and ceremonies revised.

More fundamental, perhaps, was the view Catholics were now to take of their position in the world. In the past, as we have seen, Catholic churchmen had insisted that their faith was the only truth. No other had any rights. Protestants, Freemasons and Communists were a contaminant and a danger to the soul to the extent that it was inadvisable to play football with them, to be a member of the same Boy Scout troop or to attend lectures on public administration in their colleges. In a majority Catholic country such as Ireland the state had a duty to profess, promote and defend the faith—ideally this meant suppressing all other religions, though this requirement might be temporarily waived. Now the Council proposed that since the act of faith must be unforced, religious liberty was essential, and governments should be forbidden to impose penalties on citizens worshipping one way or another. The long-serving Archbishop of Dublin, John Charles McQuaid, made no contribution to this debate, which contradicted his most fundamental beliefs.[2]

A few years after the Council the Church delivered a second, more personal, shock. There had been rising expectations that the Church would respond to the development of the contraceptive pill and loosen the existing rigorous prohibitions. Dublin's Holles Street Hospital (whose ex-officio Chairman was the Archbishop of Dublin) established a pioneer 'Marriage Guidance Clinic' providing the pill to those who could in conscience accept it.[3] So, when in July 1968 Pope Paul issued his long-awaited encyclical *Humanae Vitae* absolutely forbidding any form of artificial contraception, it was intensely controversial. Limitation of birth as such was not forbidden, but only by the precarious 'rhythm method'. Holles Street immediately closed the clinic. In his encyclical, the Pope drew a firm line between his God-sourced rulings and those of secular public authorities, who, he writes, might be tempted 'to intervene in the most personal and intimate responsibility of husband and wife.'[4] The sanctity of this area no doubt came as a surprise to an older generation of Irish women, for, as one put it to a market researcher, 'years ago when we got married if you didn't start a family straight away the parish priest was down your neck'.[5]

The statistics of birth rates, however, soon made it clear that more and more people, initially only the better off and then everyone, were using some form of contraception. The number of births to women over forty had halved since 1969. Market research published in 1986 made it clear that 'there is a general feeling amongst housewives that contraception within marriage is now an acceptable and desirable thing. Older house-wives, especially in rural areas, are likely to reject artificial contracep-tion.'[6] In 1989 the newly appointed Archbishop Connell of Dublin told *The Irish Times* that he recognised that the decree was widely ignored by the otherwise faithful. But, he asked sadly, 'how many people were happy in their hearts about the way they were behaving?'

Actually, married women approved of contraception because they had abandoned the 'tumble-up' theory of child-rearing—'with seven children in the family, we were as free as birds,' as Alice Taylor put it. Despite nostalgic glances backward, they knew that the extra sup-port and education that they now wanted to give their children was not possible either physically or financially for a large family. What's more, they were not prepared to put up with the isolation, long hours, and the drudgery their mothers had. So everyone was having smaller families, and this was regarded as a good thing.

A host of smaller changes slowly accumulated in the years after the Council closed in 1965. Catholics were told they no longer need fast on Fridays, nor was it now a sin to attend a Protestant funeral. The popular name-saints Christopher and Philomena, among others, were demoted from the Roman calendar. In March, Aer Lingus announced that it would no longer fly Irish pilgrims to Lourdes. The Pilgrimage to Lourdes Association described the move as 'a bombshell', and remarked sourly that Aer Lingus had been glad enough of the business when they had no other customers. Attendance at Sunday Mass slipped to 85 per cent. On the other hand, research in 1984 had shown that as many as 29.6 per cent of parishioners went to Mass more than once a week (suspiciously precise numbers, perhaps, that would nonetheless have made the hierarchy of any other Catholic country burst their cinctures with pride).[7]

There was, moreover, a long and active tradition related to the Chris-tian year: Christmas, St Patrick's Day and Easter had taken on secular meanings, of course, with Santa, the parade and Easter bunnies. Lent, however, was very commonly observed, and politicians appeared on Ash Wednesday with foreheads decorously smudged with ash. On Good Friday 1988 Nuala O'Faolain went to the Pro-Cathedral, while her friends (so she declared) took the day off to swig vodka and watch videos. In the cathedral she found 'bus conductors, girls in skintight jeans and high heels, neat couples with neat children in matching coats, ancient men, women who carried carrier-bags full of shopping they took with them when they went up to the altar to kiss the cross and again when they went up to receive communion.'[8]

During the 1980s a series of pitched battles were fought between the proponents of the so-called liberal agenda and the opponents of the permissive society. In 1989 it seemed to observers that the latter were winning, and that the liberal gains of the 1960s and 1970s were about to be rolled back. As *The Irish Times* religion correspondent John Cooney put it, 'the 1980s were marked by Church-State conflicts in which the score was 2–1 in favour of the former: a referendum in 1983 amended the Constitution to impose a total prohibition on abortion and another referendum in 1986 rejected a proposed amendment to introduce a limited form of divorce.'[9] In between, in 1985, the Dáil liberalised the sale of contraceptives, by a small margin. From the point of view of the future Supreme Court judge Catherine McGuinness (a Protestant from Northern Ireland), 'the same forces [that had fought against abortion and contraception earlier in the decade] regrouped under a number of banners for a bitter, determined and successful fight against the introduction of civil divorce in the 1986 divorce referendum.' Pessimistically, she perceived a 'regression towards an authoritative specifically Roman Catholic state.' 'Ireland,' she declared, 'is not prepared to grant minority rights to either Catholics or Protestants where these clash with a traditional view of Roman Catholic morality.'[10] As a lawyer, Catherine McGuinness would have been very conscious of the notably less liberal line that the Supreme Court had travelled in the 1980s, notably in Norris *v* Attorney General and the abortion information cases, in which the implications of the anti-abortion amendment were pushed to the point of interfering with free speech.[11]

Faced with the moral dilemmas of abortion, divorce and contraception, many country people optimistically clung to the ideas expressed by 'Pádraig from Bruree' to Fintan O'Toole: 'Moral standards are the same as they have always been. We'd be leading a different kind of life from the cities and towns. In a rural area everyone knows everything about everyone else. You can't be a Jekyll and Hyde character. No matter what you do it's common knowledge. That helps keep people on the straight and narrow.'[12] This was, sadly, a myth, as the Kilkenny incest case, and the fates of Anne Lovett (the Granard teenage mother) and Joanne Hayes (the Kerry babies mother) underlined.

For the liberal wing it was dismaying to see the Hierarchy going back on their brave statements in the New Ireland Forum about cherishing cultural diversity. To some extent the bishops had been, perhaps not reluctantly, pushed by the outspoken vehemence of the traditionalists, aided by inputs of American energy. Although they had recognised in theory the right of each person to vote according to conscience, in practice no one who attended Mass on Sunday was allowed to be unaware which way their conscience should go. One priest noted in *The Furrow* that there were 'sermons for five or six Sundays consecutively on the topic alone; use of church buildings and grounds for pro-amendment canvassing and collections; sermons on Sunday by members of SPUC [the militant Society for Protection of Unborn Children]; sermons which ran counter to the conscience clause in the bishops' letter.'[13]

The family

Everyone—pro or con—was conscious that notable changes were in train to the Irish way of life. As the market research company, Irish Consumer Research, found, 'the dominant fact—when considering social and moral attitudes is the fact of change . . . change in moral and social attitudes is perhaps the most acutely felt and most painfully experienced of all the change reported here. Just as we see how the staple, traditional foodstuffs are now being questioned and partly abandoned so we see at a more fundamental level that social values and traditional beliefs and practices are also being questioned and to a degree abandoned.'[14]

The progress of these changes could be seen all over: here we have a journalist complaining that there are no places in most shops (not even in the pristine Stephen's Green centre) where a 'new man' could change his child's nappy—except in Mothercare, where there was a magnificently appointed space 'by the prams and buggy section. Its name: "The Mother's Room".'[15] More darkly, Fintan O'Toole lamented (after free samples of heroin, with syringes, had been offered to ten- and eleven-year-old pupils leaving his old primary school) that the once familiar was becoming unknown, unrecognisable. 'Ireland has become so multi-layered, unrecognisable, so much a matter of one set of images superimposed on another that it's hard to tell what's in the picture in front of us.'[16] A simple image of the changing world of the family could be seen every day in *The Irish Times*' wedding announcements. In a random choice from August 1989, there was the family-free model— 'Ken and Sheila are happy to announce their engagement'—the slightly more inclusive 'Catherine and Declan together with their families are delighted'—the more formal 'Joe and Noreen are happy to announce the engagement of their daughter'—and the grand and traditional 'The engagement is announced, between . . .' (this last model covered about one-fifth of the insertions).

As we have seen, the real battlegrounds where these issues crystallised were the controversies about abortion, divorce and contraception. Voices proposing the freeing of the ancient anti-abortion law alarmed right-wing Catholics, and stirred vehement opinions on both sides. Perhaps the real majority view was a great distaste for abortion, mitigated by a new consciousness of possible hard cases. This was expressed by respondents to the housewives survey: 'I don't believe in abortion, but then again suppose you'd been raped and your life was in danger', and 'a mother who is seriously ill—wouldn't it be terrible to let her die rather than have an abortion. But where is the line to be drawn? Definitely I'm against abortion, but we have to think of all the consequences.'[17] These women, the survey reports, did not see themselves as feminists, indeed distanced themselves from the only (unnamed) feminists they were aware of, on the media, whom they regarded as too radical, even men-hating, and certainly remote from their own lives.

Divorce had been made impossible soon after the state had been founded, and in 1986 a divisive referendum had resulted in its being rejected by 63.5 per cent of the voters. But most people, it seemed from market research, believed that divorce would eventually come to Ireland, for good or evil. The new closeness of husband and wife had led to higher expectations from marriage, and 'most housewives knew at least one marriage which was in difficulty. It was widely held that divorce might be a good thing in the case of marriages that were extremely painful or unhappy for those concerned.'[18] On the other hand, if divorce were too available, perhaps people would not make the effort to make their marriages work. Many feared for the future of the children of such marriages. This was argued as an experiential question, with pros and cons. Few now believed, as W. T. Cosgrave had when divorce was first made impossible in Ireland, that 'the whole fabric of our social organisation is based upon the sanctity of the marriage bond and that anything that tends to weaken the binding efficacy of that bond to that extent strikes at the root of our social life.'[19] Once again, long discussion of the issue changed the ideas of people who in the normal course of events would have happily accepted the received opinion. They were stimulated to think for themselves, and evolve nuanced views of difficult issues. Television greatly helped this process, by allowing different opinions to be heard without condemnation, and by showing strong women getting their way, and enjoying it.

The traditional values of the authoritarian institution, whether family, school, church or business were steadily giving way to the interests of the individual. In *The Irish Times* in September Mary-Ellen Synon proclaimed: 'The family exists to support the individual', not the other way round. This was, of course, in direct contradiction of the traditional Catholic and Irish view. For Mary-Ellen Synon, the Constitution was simply wrong. The state should support the individual and leave him or her to support the family if they chose to have one.

Few would have wished so wholeheartedly to throw the baby out with the bath-water, but many men and women had less than idyllic memories of childhood. A heartbreaking survey conducted by the Irish Society for Prevention of Cruelty to Children in 1989, as part of its campaign to abolish all physical punishment of children, revealed that despite the warm images, the Irish family had at times been a chilly and a violent place. Nearly one in six adults remembered no close relationship with their mothers, and one in four 'had not been close to their fathers'.[20] As many as 20 per cent of respondents reported that they had received no demonstrative affection from their mothers. (Once they ceased to be babies, as Polly Devlin had pointed out, all sorts of inhibitions kicked in.)

Although the harsh disciplinarian father of older times was less in evidence, with only 6 per cent of adults remembering such, 86 per cent of respondents had been physically chastised, and three-quarters felt that at least ocasionally this had been unfair. (The considerable reduction in the number of stammerers in schools has been associated with the effective disappearance of the authoritarian father and his repressive punishments.) For most children, however, physical punishment in the family was unusual, as opposed to verbal threats, shouting and extra chores. Nonetheless, physical punishment, the ISPCC believed, was deeply embedded in the Irish childhood experience at home and in school. One-third of adults had no problem in endorsing the practice—from which, given people's tendency to tell researchers what it's thought they want to hear, we can take to mean that at least half of parents actually did deliver the occasional slap.

One of the striking elements of change that the Irish Consumer Research report on women working in the home outlined was the way the marriages of all classes worked in practice. In the previous generation, as for instance Angela MacNamara saw, 'in most homes there was firm discipline and little space was given for argument or discussion.' In her own family, 'Daddy ruled the roost with kind but no-nonsense strictness and discipline. My quiet and gentle mother bowed to his authority. She had her role as mistress of the house and mother, but was without power in the wider decision-making.'[21] Risteárd Mulcahy's 'remote and impersonal' relationship with his famous father was typical.

'Husbands,' said current market research, 'are said to be markedly different nowadays than were those of previous generations. In the past the husband might come in from work and be waited on by his wife and have a very limited span of interest and involvement in the home and the family. Now that is changing. Especially it is felt that younger husbands take a more interested and active role as husbands and fathers than used to be the case. They are now more by way of being partners.'[22] Modern husbands, it was said, take their wives out socially more than before, they communicate more freely; they even do the chores around the house, at least sometimes.

There was a downside to the new woman-oriented men. 'There was considered to be more marital infidelity among husbands today than in the past.' It was just too easy for husbands in work, in clubs or out and about to form relationships with young girls. 'My daughter,' reported a Dublin woman from the AB social group, 'has had so many propositions from married men, I think she's scared to get married.'

Behind this change between husband and wife was another that affected more than just the family. The culture of deference was very slowly being replaced by a more individualistic one. In the past everyone had a known place, and the world was supposed to be better if that place was kept to. The 'narrative of the group' dominated daily life and its typical expression, the sanction 'people will talk', was deeply felt. John Healy lovingly described how, in his small country town, there was 'a hierarchy in which every family, every individual had a fixed place. Everybody knows practically everybody else, and the collective memory in most cases will stretch back over several generations'.[23] Nuala O'Faolain confirmed how 'from de Valera down to the parish priest, from the home to the guards barracks, to the doctor's surgery, the two poles of that world were authority and obedience.'[24] This was an ancient ideal, which C. S. Lewis described as how 'the goodness, happiness and dignity of every being consisted in obeying its natural superiors and ruling its natural inferiors.'[25] The Catholic Church actively supported the idea. Indeed, it was in church that the full local hierarchy was most on display, in the clothes worn, in where one sat, in the size of donation to the priest. The practice of reading out donations from the altar reinforced everyone's sense of who was who in the community, and at the same time the Church's approval of the status quo. Pope Leo XIII had written that 'no society can hold together unless there be some one over all, impelling individuals efficaciously and harmoniously to one common purpose'.[26] But now people began to wonder—who was 'one over all' in a market? who in a democracy 'impelled individuals'? who in a free society decided the 'one common purpose'? Healy's vision of a small town society, where everyone had a place and the collective memory over generations conspired to keep you in it, began to seem oppressive, perhaps even a good reason for emigration.

Furthermore the old national projects that had underpinned these hierarchies began to lose their appeal. An increasing number of floating voters began to assess the offerings of politicians as they did the blandishments of the shopping centre. As one commentator said, 'politicians no longer stood for things, they were merely on the same side as people who had once stood for things.'[27]

The 1991 Census showed that the traditional household of husband, wife and more or fewer children was in a minority, though with 40 per cent of households in Dublin it remained the most common ménage. However, there were substantial numbers in other configurations, and the number of marriages celebrated every year was declining. For instance, 66,000 people (21 per cent of households) lived on their own, and there were 30,000 lone parents with children, mostly mothers. These different arrangements were becoming normalised. It was increasingly practical, if not unstressed, for unmarried or abandoned mothers to bring up their children on their own, as, of course, widows had always done; in June *The Irish Times* showed readers how a group of middle-class women had done just that. Among those pictured were the cartoonist Wendy Shea and Eileen O'Mara Walsh, managing director of O'Mara Travel, both coping with residual prejudice, anxious to present their normal, stable children doing ordinary things. The number of births recorded as occurring outside marriage had gone up by 50 per cent in five years and now stood at 12.6 per cent of all births.

Another ménage that was very slowly becoming accepted, not without difficulty, was the gay couple. In 1983, the Supreme Court rowed back on the idea (which had formed the basis of the 1973 McGee case) that the state had no role in enforcing codes of private morality. In the resounding words of Chief Justice Finlay, it declared that 'on the ground of the Christian nature of our State and on the grounds that the deliberate practice of homosexuality is morally wrong, that it is damaging to the health of individuals and finally that it is potentially harmful to the institution of marriage', homosexual acts between consenting adults would remain forbidden.[28] But since then David Norris had appealed the case to Europe, and Ireland's prohibition was found to infringe Article 8 of the European Convention on Human Rights, on the individual's right to privacy. In 1985, Dublin's famous gay bar the George had opened, and in 1989 the wittily named 'Out and About' gay hiking group was started. To general applause, Minister for Justice Ray Burke added sexual orientation to the prohibitions in the 1988 Incitement to Hatred Act. But there was a long way to go. Fintan O'Toole recounted the story of a gay couple: 'Alone and discreet they could get by and be tolerated. Living together they would be a challenge to the Family, and an affront to normality. They would cease to be two ordinary people and become a symbol. This was too much to carry. As one of them said, "I would rather do a menial job in a foreign city and be normal than have a good job in Dublin and be regarded as a freak."'[29] Incidents of 'gay bashing' on a Saturday night were still regularly reported.

Among the 60,000 people living alone in Dublin were many elderly citizens, some of whom at least were threatened with the new scourge of the 1980s, Alzheimer's disease. This had been introduced to the public notice at the beginning of the decade at a meeting in the St John of God hospital in Stillorgan. The now-familiar symptoms of memory loss, confusion, irritability, restlessness were recounted in an article by Kathryn Holmquist in which the estimate of 20,000 Irish sufferers was proposed, with very little help from state services.[30] The strain on the new smaller families of having, for instance, to care for an elderly father who could not be left alone as well as growing children was obvious.

Nice people and rednecks

The proposed amendment of 1986 permitting divorce was rejected in the country and passed in middle-class Dublin areas. This exemplified what journalist Desmond Fennell called the contest between 'Nice People and Rednecks' that ran throughout the 1980s. 'Nice People' in his eyes were anything but. Rednecks (a term from the lexicon of US political abuse) were everyone else; anyone in fact who supported 'Ireland's right to unity, rebel songs, Charlie Haughey or the IRA, or Catholic bishops preaching Catholic sexual morality, the legal prohibition of divorce, the limited availability of contraceptives, the Constitution's claim to Northern Ireland, public criticisms of sexual libertinism or harsh words about abortion'[31]—a list carefully compiled to tease right-on liberals.

After so long a time in which the archetypal Irish person was seen as a Catholic male living in the country, the emergence of a loud and effective urban voice had come as a shock. The opponents of this new Irish voice responded with a violent rhetoric which precluded any reasoned response. For Desmond Fennell, the cosmopolitan proponents of the liberal agenda with their 'barren, shoneen atavism' were surreptitiously trying to refit Ireland back into the British sphere. They were a paralysing incubus preventing national development. They were snobbish, anti-democratic, anti-Irish and impertinently frivolous. They would turn bitter anger on anyone who proposed an idea at variance with those current in New York or London.[32] Another of this school, John Healy, wrote that Dublin was 'a monstrous swollen head on a shrunken rural body, a gross cancer which feeds and devours its body'.[33] Echoing the nineteenth-century Russian Slavophiles, Healy believed profoundly in the culture of mutual help exemplified by the *meitheal* and represented by Fianna Fáil, as a model for a larger social regeneration. (The fact that, as Arensberg and Kimball had pointed out, only insiders participated in the *meitheal*, just as barely half the population voted Fianna Fáil, was always skated over.) Like the Russians, Healy believed that 'the cosmopolitan is a nullity, worse than a nullity. Without national sense there is no art, no truth, no life, nothing.'[34] His successor at *The Irish Times*, John Waters, wrote that the people of the legendary 'Dublin 4' were Pharisees, were fundamentally unjust and dishonest, were hectoring, dismissive hypocrites, and filled with self-loathing. With their blinkered refusal to face reality all they wanted was for the rest of the country to lie down and die.[35] The baleful name-calling of D. P. Moran's *Leader* and the *Catholic Bulletin* echoes in the ear.

Part of the problem for those wishing to cling to an older image of Ireland was the advertising on television and other media. As one commentator saw it, to judge by the advertisements, 'we lived secure, comfortable lives in a prosperous, single-class economy which is urbanised but does contain a minority who farm intensively. That there can be a poorer class is never alluded to, and when the occasional worker or "man in the street" is required then he is depicted literally in the street or at his work-place, often a building site or factory. We are never shown a happy relaxed family in the corporation flat, council house or rural cottage, only in a beautiful open-plan house with gardens.' In this ad-Ireland men are the providers, women the carers. Conservative tastes encourage new products to be launched with the patina of age already in place. ('Old Mr Brennan').[36]

Programmes seen across the country reinforced the middle-class aspirations. Half of viewers in multi-channel land regularly switched to British channels between seven and nine in the evening. Soap operas were strong favourites. Well-watched programmes included *Brookside* (TAM rating 48 per cent of sets), the Australian *Neighbours* (44 per cent) and *Coronation Street* (40 per cent). *Brookside*'s popularity in Ireland was no doubt aided by the fact that Sheila Grant, one of the central characters, was a staunch Catholic, moving up the social ladder from a council house to a four-bedroom house in a secluded close. US fantasy soaps such as *Dallas*, *Dynasty* and *Falcon Crest* were also popular as were Irish-based soaps such as *Glenroe* and the new *Fair City*. In its first transmissions in the autumn of 1989, *Fair City* attracted 1.3 million viewers. The producers of *Nighthawks*, an innovative mix of soap, chat and music, popular in Dublin 4, were delighted with their *succés d'estime*—and a TAM rating of 15.[37] In March RTÉ announced with pride that nine out of ten of the top programmes watched on RTÉ, headed by the *Late, Late Show*, were locally-produced.

Despite the myth of Irish love of culture and things of the mind, in practice there was a strong anti-intellectualism in the air. Men and women of the world—making money, organising things, living lives—thought theories effete, academic, irrelevant. The only ideas that anyone had taken seriously were theological, and they were exploded. The civil service could see no reason to employ graduate specialists, and an old joke was fostered on to Garret FitzGerald, a central proponent of the liberal agenda: 'That's all very well in practice,' he was supposed to have said, 'but how does it work in theory?'

John Healy idealised the anti-intellectualism of the small town. In the 1950s the Jesuit researcher Alexander Humphries had politely described the Irish countryman as 'suspicious of the pride of mind, and so wary of ultimate rationalisms that he shies away from reasoned discussions of high truths', a feature he also found, to a lesser degree, in Dublin. John Healy loathed 'Dublin 4' for what he thought of as 'its attempts to deny the reality of Irish life, its failure to understand that politics was first of all about people. You could not impose systems or ideologies on people who had no use for them . . . left and right was the way you learned to goose-step, but it had nothing to do with Irish politics.' Like a true provincial, he believed that his own place was the *beau idéal* of all. His intense belief in 'the reality of Irish life' prompted him to assume that all other places were much the same: Dublin, he claimed, 'was only a string of villages' and moreover he could enter any village 'from Achill to the steppes of Russia' and know its hierarchical structure.[38] The Dublin 4 brigade, so John Waters claimed, was 'impatient with reality', they 'had been to university and studied concepts like dialectical materialism, positivism, gradualism and democratic centralism. They had long been appalled at the fact that their own country refused to reveal itself in terms of the learning they had accumulated. They wanted to squeeze the nation's politics into the neat packets of their own understanding.'[39]

The identity question

One regular source of irritation was revisionist history, whose locus classicus, Roy Foster's *Modern Ireland,* was published at the end of 1988, with the explicit intent of identifying the realities behind the 'desires and regrets' of romantic observers of Irish history. Colm Tóibín's emotional reponse to this revisionist stance was an indication of the enormous psychological value put on the conventional narrative. 'Imagine,' he wrote, 'if Irish history were pure fiction, how free and happy we could be! It seemed at the time a most subversive idea, a new way of killing your father, starting from scratch, creating a new self.'[40]

The 'Irish identity' question was worried away at by groups of intellectuals centred round the *The Crane Bag* journal, and the Field Day pamphlet series. In *The Crane Bag* the national identity had been elaborately pursued for issue after issue. It ceased to be published in 1985 and was briefly followed by other journals, the *Irish Literary Supplement* (1986–8), and *The Irish Review* (1988–91). These took a philosophical, poetic and literary-critical view of Ireland. The writers were well versed in the latest

Continental theories and were also much influenced by Edward Said
and his theories of post-colonialism, as expressed for instance in his
1988 pamphlet *Yeats and decolonisation*. *The Crane Bag* group made no
attempt to be social scientists or social researchers. Empirical questions
about the condition of Irish society, what Richard Kearney called 'the
paralysing immediacy of facts', generally took a back seat. None of these
publications of course had large circulations, so it is difficult to assess
their general impact. Nonetheless 'Dublin 4', to use John Healy's term,
certainly took them seriously enough.

Since the lines were drawn in the 1880s, there had been a struggle
between those who believed that getting the economy right was the
essential first step in creating a New Ireland, and others, notably de Valera, who believed that there was no point in 'getting the economy right'
if in the process the Irish lost their soul. By losing the Irish language
the people would lose the only way of allowing that soul fully to express
itself. This would inflict a great injustice on future Irish people.

In 1987 and 1988 Richard Kearney's somewhat different ideas about
Irish identity were given a full airing in long articles in *The Irish Times*.
'What does it mean to be Irish?' was the question he posed, and it was
clear that the old triumvirate—Land, Religion and Nationalism—were
not to be part of the answer. Rather we were, a little vaguely, to find our
'affirmation of dynamic cultural identity in an exploratory dialogue with
other cultures.'[41] There was an appetite for this level of discourse: in 1989
The Irish Times published another six long articles by Kearney exploring
the nature of modern republicanism. On a smaller scale, in the course
of a short review of some novels by Cormac McCarthy, John Banville
threw out references to Hegel, Joyce, Proust, Gadamer, Celan, Beckett,
Valéry, Boehme and Nietzsche.[42] At the end of 1988, diarist Kevin Myers
devoted a column to reviewing Richard Kearney's new publication *The
Irish Review*, describing it as 'extremely stimulating—so stimulating in
fact that my copy was stolen within an hour of my getting it'.

Narratives

In the late 1980s nearly all the myths, narratives and identities that the
Irish people had been comfortable with for generations were under
challenge. It was becoming clear that at least some Irish were not very
religious, the countryside was thought fine for a holiday home but fewer
and fewer people wanted to live there, the Irish were not always very
kind to their children, and did not care much about the North. They

were not anti-materialist, nor classless, nor belligerent (being devoted in fact to neutrality), nor much interested in ideas; their most extreme expression of being 'agin the government' was pretending to live abroad for the purposes of avoiding DIRT tax, or perhaps failing to pay for a rod licence.

Fianna Fáil had perceived itself as the sacred embodiment of the nation, to the extent that an attempt to unseat its leader had quite seriously been talked of as treason. But in 1989, to retain power, it had been forced to step down from this elevated position and cooperate in coalitions, just like everyone else. In his book *All Things New* the experienced political commentator James Downey wrote that the result of the June election 'gave a shock to the political system from which in all probability it will never recover.' 'It will take a least one more general election', he thought, 'before we can see with any clarity the future shape of Irish politics. But it is at least certain that the future shape will be different from that of the past.' 'The task now,' he continued optimistically, 'is to build a better political system, as well as a better society.'[43]

The problem was, with the decline of the grand nationalist project and other narratives and myths, how to identify the elements of that better society? Automatic deference was decreasingly offered to anyone in a suit—politicians, clergy, professionals and pundits. Like Fintan O'Toole, people began to find many aspects of modern Ireland unrecognisable. Or worse, not at all how they had seemed, like Nuala O'Faolain, who 'used to see the farmhand and her little niece going off hand in hand and I used to think it was sweet'—only to discover later that the farmworker (a daily mass-goer) had been sexually abusing the child since she was very small.[44] No wonder that *To School Through the Fields* had such enormous appeal, with its re-creation of a 'close-knit rural community', in a time when 'life moved at a different pace', when children were 'as free as birds', when 'the old were never alone as neighbours joined hands around them and the young too were included in the circle' and when 'sharing was taken for granted'.

Despite the best efforts of the traditionalists, the most cherished identities were now found to be, as the historian argued, 'neither natural, unchangeable nor true'. They passed, they were reinterpreted, they were (like the Irish language) abandoned. If it was true that 'identities are fictions which are formulated and adapted through narratives and performances . . . as a way of interacting with prevailing historical circumstances,'[45] the how and the why were still open. The citizens were on their own, without any of the traditional guides. In these circumstances, Noel Browne's 1986 self-serving memoir *Against the Tide*, with its almost prophetic image of a visionary, driven leader, was extremely popular. Dr Jim Deeny's attempt in his 1989 memoir *To Cure and to Care* to put the record straight was resented with a vehemence that showed the emotional hunger for such a leader.

Where all this would lead was more than usually unclear. 'It seemed to me,' wrote John Waters at the time, 'that we were at a turning point of our history, but that there was a distinct possibility that we were being diverted down an avenue of expediency no better than that from which we were now voluntarily emerging.'[46]

Chapter 1

1 D. Cannadine *The Decline & Fall of the British Aristocracy* (London 1990) pb revised 1992 p 27

2 For instance, S. Buxton *Handbook to Political Questions of the Day* (London 1880) p 124

3 G. Fottrell *How to Become the Owner of your Farm* (Dublin 1882) p 8

4 W. Bence Jones 'Landowning as a business' *Nineteenth Century* (London 1882) p 346

5 *Report from the Select Committee on Industries (Ireland)* (1884–5 288) p 193

6 It was common for landlords and their agents to escort, or drive, their tenants to the polling booth and listen intently to how they cast their votes.

7 E. Œ. Somerville and M. Ross *Irish Memories* (London 1918) p 27

8 8 January 1882, quoted by Gifford Lewis in *Somerville and Ross—The World of the Irish RM* (London 1985) p 13

9 Somerville & Ross *An Irish Cousin* (London 1889) chap xii. 'Uncle Dominick' is admittedly not intended to be an attractive character, but he is not a caricature.

10 G. Moore *A Drama in Muslin* (London 1886) reprinted Belfast 1992 book 1 chap 6

11 One of these was the great-grandfather of the developer Paddy Kelly. Patrick Kelly, from Abbeyleix, was prosecuted in 1882 for surreptiously posting notices at night 'calling on the people to boycott several respectable farmers for paying their rent and land-grabbing'. (*The Irish Times* 28 January 1882)

12 G. Moore *A Drama in Muslin* (London 1886) pp 74–5

13 'The Irish Landlords' *Contemporary Review* (London 1882) p 160

14 Somerville & Ross *Mount Music* (London 1919) chap 7. This was the first novel written after Martin Ross's death, and its defects (notably an excess of adjectives and a tendency not to leave well alone) show what she had contributed to the literary partnership.

15 *Nation* 21 Jan 1882 p 3

16 Somerville & Ross *Irish Memories* (London 1918) p 35

17 Lady Fingall *Seventy Years Young* (London 1937) p 45

18 The fact that these salaries are all recoverable in such detail from the Official Estimates is a tribute to the late-Victorian worship of Facts.

19 L. Cullen *Eason and Son—A History* (Dublin 1989) pp 110, 124

20 T. Farmar *Heitons—A Managed Transition* (Dublin 1996) chap 2

21 M. Hearn *Thomas Edmonson* (Dublin 2004) p 19

22 M. Hearn 'How Victorian families lived' in Daly, Hearn & Pearson *Dublin's Victorian Houses* (Dublin 1998) pp 66–70

23 T. Farmar 'Setting up home in Dublin in the 1850s' *Dublin Historical Record* vol liv no 1 (Spring 2001) pp 16–27

24 L. Cullen *Eason and Son—A History* p 156

25 *Thom's Directory* 1864 and 1868. Nowadays Sherry FitzGerald expect about 2½ per cent of houses to change hands every year.

26 Geraldine Plunkett Dillon (ed. Honor O Brolchain) *All in the Blood* (Dublin 2007) p 24

27 M. Hayden *The Diaries of Mary Hayden* (Killala, Mayo 2005) 13 April 1882

28 As late as 1946 the Census revealed that over 40 per cent of households in Dublin had neither bath nor indoor WC. Even in the relatively well-off district of Rathmines one in five houses had outdoor toilets in 1946.

29 M. Hayden *Diaries* Oct 1883

30 *Thom's Directory* 1882

31 *The Irish Times* 26 Dec 1883

32 Retail prices listed in *Nation* 13 May 1882 p 16

33 'Short' *Dinners at Home* (London 1878) preface

34 Ibid. p 10

35 Ibid. pp 115–124

36 Ibid. pp 18–19

37 M. Hayden *Diaries* 12 Mar 1881

38 Ibid. 3 Apr 1881

Chapter 2

1 M. Hayden *The Diaries of Mary Hayden* (Killala, Mayo 2005) 19 Sept 1881

2 George Bernard Shaw reproduces these arguments in the preface to *The Doctor's Dilemma* (London 1911).

3 M. Hayden *Diaries* 14 Mar 1880

4 Ibid. 31 Dec 1900

5 F. Pim *The Health of Dublin* (Dublin 1891) p 30, (Dublin 1892) p 5

6 *Weekly Irish Times* 25 Mar 1882

7 *The Irish Times* 17 Mar 1888

8 Ibid. 27 October, 2 Nov 1888

9 *Irish Ecclesiastical Review* Jul 1883

10 M. Holroyd *Bernard Shaw Vol 1—The search for love* (London 1988) pb 1990 p 100

11 E. Œ. Somerville and M. Ross *The Real Charlotte* (London 1896) pb Dublin 1999 p 296

12 'A Member of the Aristocracy' *Manners and Tone of Good Society or Solecisms to be Avoided* (London 1879) p 166

13 *The Irish Times* 6 Jun 1882

14 *Manners and Tone of Good Society* chap 6

15 M. Hayden *Diaries* 16 Nov 1882

16 Ibid. 14 Mar 1880

17 Ibid. 30 Oct 1881

18 L. Atthill *Recollections of an Irish Doctor* (London 1911) p 233

Chapter 3

1 T. Grimshawe 'A statistical survey of Ireland from 1840 to 1888' *Journal of the Statistical and Social Inquiry Society of Ireland* part lxviii (Dublin 1888) pp 331–61

2 Ibid.

3 *Report from the Select Committee on Industries (Ireland)* (1884–5 288) q 10122

4 E. R. R. Green 'Industrial decline in the nineteenth century' in L. Cullen (ed) *The Foundation of the Irish Economy* (Cork 1969) p 97

5 W. C. Sullivan *Royal Commission on Technical Instruction* C-3981-III Appendix x p 492

6 *Select Committee on Industries* p 821

7 Ibid. p 359

8 B. Irish *Shipbuilding in Waterford 1820–1882* (Bray 2001)

9 During the campaign to establish creameries, a story was told of a meeting in Limerick in the 1890s when one of the organisers was proposing the establishment of a creamery. 'A local solicitor (probably Patrick Liston) sprang to his feet and declared: "Rathkeale is a Nationalist town—Nationalist to the backbone—and any pound of butter made in Rathkeale will be made in accordance with Irish Nationalist principles, or it will not be made at all."' (P. Bolger *The Irish Cooperative Movement* (Dublin 1977) p 67).

10 *Select Committee on Industries* q 3978

11 Ibid. q 3223

12 Ibid. q 10272

13 Ibid. q 43

14 Ibid. q 10258

15 Ibid. q 3004

16 Ibid. q 6723

17 G. Moore *Hail and Farewell—Vale* (London 1914) pp 113–5

18 *Select Committee on Industries (Ireland)* q 616

19 T. Garvin *Judging Lemass* (Dublin 2010) p 173

20 *Select Committee on Industries* q 2906

21 Ibid. q 1101

22 First edition 1848, seventh 1871

23 J. S. Mill *Principles of Political Economy* 1871 ed book v chap x

24 *Select Committee on Industries* q 10126

25 Ibid. q 2918

26 Ibid. qs 4128, 4129

27 Ibid. qs 2974, 911

19 M. Hayden *The Diaries of Mary Hayden* (Killala, Mayo 2005) 31 Oct–3 Nov 1881

20 *Weekly Irish Times* 2 Sep 1882

21 *The Irish Times* 25 March 1882

22 Ibid. 12 May 1882

23 'A Member of the Aristocracy' *Manners and Tone of Good Society or Solecisms to be Avoided* (London 1879) chap xii

Chapter 4

1 Quoted in R. Fulford *Votes for Women* (London 1956) p 65

2 S. Buxton *Handbook to Political Questions* (London 1880) pp 41–2

3 *Popular Science Quarterly* 1879 p 208

4 3 *Hansard* ccxxxiv at 1413

5 O. Schreiner *The Story of an African Farm* (London 1883) p 187

6 M. Hayden *The Diaries of Mary Hayden* (Killala, Mayo 2005) 18 Jul 1884

7 Ibid. 20 Feb 1881

8 Royal Commission on Technical Instruction 1884 2nd *Report: Evidence relating to Ireland* C-3981-iii p 118

9 C. Dickens *Great Expectations* chap xxv

10 *Weekly Irish Times* 26 May 1894

11 W. Blackstone *Commentaries* 1765 vol 1 p 430. The first pirated edition published in Dublin appeared in 1766.

12 M. Hayden *Diaries* 16 Oct 1883

13 Ibid. 21 Jan 1879

14 Ibid. 13 Aug 1880

15 Ibid. 5 Aug 1880

16 Ibid. 26 Apr 1882

17 Ibid. 16 May 1882

18 Ibid. 20 Mar 1883

19 *The Irish Times* 15 Apr 1882

20 G. Moore *Drama in Muslin* (London 1886) book 1 chap 8

21 Ibid. p 76

22 Ibid. p 98

23 Ibid. p 89

24 B. Becker *Disturbed Ireland* (London 1881) p 270

25 *Journal of the Statistical and Social Inquiry Society of Ireland* 1882 p 315

26 *Weekly Irish Times* 20 Jan 1883

27 *The Irish Times* May 1880

28 *Weekly Irish Times* 26 June 1884

29 M. Hayden *Diaries* 26 Apr 1884

Chapter 5

1 W. P. Ryan *The Pope's Green Island* (London 1912) p 1

2 *Weekly Irish Times* 16 Mar

3 Ibid. 23 Mar

4 *The Irish Times* 9 Aug 1907

5 Seanad Éireann 11 Apr 1929

6 *Freeman's Journal* Jun 1907

7 Canon Sheehan *My New Curate* (New York 1899) reprinted Dublin 1928 p 276

8 Rev. B. O'Reilly *The Mirror of True Womanhood* (New York 1877) reprinted from the 13th American edition (Dublin 1927) pp 55, 113. This book was published in Ireland by M. H. Gill in 1882 and reprinted six times between then and 1895.

9 *Freeman's Journal* 22 Apr 1907

10 J. Meenan (ed) *Centenary History of the Literary and Historical Society* reprint (Dublin 2005) p 89

11 M. Bradshaw (ed) *Open Doors for Irishwomen* (Dublin 1907) p 37

12 *The Leader* 2 Mar 1907

13 *Studies* (Dublin 1915) p 433

14 *The Leader* Mar 2 1907

15 M. B. Pearse (ed) *The Home Life of Pádraig Pearse* 2nd ed (Cork 1979) p 106

16 P. L. Dickinson *The Dublin of Yesterday* (London 1929) p 1

17 C. S. Andrews *Dublin Made Me* (Cork 1979) pp 10–12

18 *Studies* (Dublin 1915) p 434

19 *The Irish Times* 30 May 1907

20 E. Hales *The Catholic Church and the Modern World* (London 1958) pp 199–200. John Charles McQuaid has been harshly criticised for establishing just such a vigilante group in Dublin.

21 *Irish Ecclesiastical Record* (Maynooth 1907) pp 1, 587. In the Catholic and Lutheran listing of the Ten Commandments (learnedly called the Decalogue) 'Thou shalt not commit adultery' comes as number six.

22 S. Browne *The Press in Ireland* (Dublin 1937) pp 242–259

23 M. Carbery *The Farm by Lough Gur* (London 1937) p 90. The narrator was born in 1858, which suggests that her grandmother would have been born perhaps in the 1790s. By this time Dublin street directories and maps (eg Rocque 1756) had long clearly indicated where Catholic chapels and convents were.

24 John Fiske, quoted in B. Werth *Banquet at Delmonicos* (New York 2009) p 210

25 *The Irish Times* 11 Dec 1907

26 H. Robinson *Memories: Wise and Otherwise* (London 1924) p 224

27 Ibid. pp 148–9

28 P. L. Dickinson *The Dublin of Yesterday* (London 1929) p 14

29 'The Irish Council Bill in brief' *The Irish Times* 8 May 1907

30 *Freeman's Journal* May 8 1907. This remoteness, incidentally, was not merely part of the British-Irish relationship; the English educated classes had the same problem with their own people. A generation before, Matthew Arnold had noted, 'how often it happens in England that a cultivated person . . . talking to one of the lower classes . . . feels, and cannot but feel, that there is a wall of partition between himself and the other; that they seem to belong to different worlds. Thoughts, feelings, perceptions, susceptibilities, language, manners—everything is different.' M. Arnold 'Equality' in Noel Annan (ed.) *Selected Essays* (Oxford 1964) pp 198, 203

31 N. Robertson *Crowned Harp* (Dublin 1960) p 24

32 A. Jackson *Ireland 1798–1998* (Oxford 1999) p 145

33 H. Sutherland *Ireland Yesterday and Today* (Philadelphia 1909) p 108

Chapter 6

1 M. Daly *Dublin—The Deposed Capital 1860–1914* (Cork 1984) pb 1985 chaps 1 and 2

2 R. Barry O'Brien *Dublin Castle and the Irish People* (London 1909) pp 385–401

3 Royal Commission on Trinity College Dublin *Appendix to First Report* (Dublin 1906) pp 10–18

4 M. McCarthy *Five Years in Ireland* (London and Dublin 1901) p 336— UCD Fellows p 282

5 *A Century of Service—A Record of One Hundred Years, published for the centenary of St Vincent's Hospital* (Dublin 1934) p 84

6 G. Birmingham *The Search Party* (London 1909) 16th printing 1918 p 15

7 R. Barry O'Brien *Dublin Castle and the Irish People* (London 1909) p 387

8 L. Cullen *Eason & Son—A History* (Dublin 1989) pp 286–93

9 P. L. Dickinson *The Dublin of Yesterday* (London 1929) p 76

10 Ibid. p 76

11 T. Farmar *The Legendary, Lofty, Clattery Café* (Dublin 1988) pp 29–30; *Irish Independent* 2 Dec 1932

12 Letter from 'An Intolerant Protestant' in the *Freeman's Journal* 15 Nov 1907

13 L. Ó Broin *No Man's Man* (Dublin 1982) pp 7, 12

14 T. Farmar *Patients, Potions and Physicians* (Dublin 2004) pp 114–5

15 C. S Andrews *Dublin Made Me* (Cork 1979) p 35

16 G. Birmingham *The Search Party* p 15

17 C. S. Andrews *Dublin Made Me* p 24

18 P. Costello *Dublin Churches* (Dublin 1989) p 124

19 T. Farmar 'The Building Society that refused Patrick Pearse' *Dublin Historical Record* vol lv no 1 Spring 2002

20 *Consumption and Cost of Food for Workingmen's Families in UK Urban Districts* (1905) Cd 2337 lxxxiv p 25

21 *Economic Cookery Book* (Dublin 1905). This little book was reprinted in 1906, 1908, 1910 and 1913.

22 Mrs C. S. Peel *How to Keep House* (London 1902) 57. Dorothy Peel (1868–1934), was a prolific journalist and writer of numerous books on household management and domestic history including *Ten Shillings a Head per Week for the House Books* (1899) and *Entrées Made Easy* (1905).

23 A. Findlater *Findlaters—The Story of a Dublin Merchant Family 1774–2001* (Dublin 2001) pp 129–130

24 Ibid. pp 541–7

25 See p 86

26 J. V. O'Brien *Dear, Dirty Dublin* (California 1982) pp 122–4

27 A. Clarke *Twice Round the Black Church* (London 1962) p 35

28 C. S. Andrews *Dublin Made Me* p 42

29 E. Bowen *Seven Winters* (London 1943) p 21

30 C. S. Andrews *Dublin Made Me* pp 30–33

31 Beatrice Elvery's grandmother did hers, at least while she was a girl. (Beatrice Lady Glenavy *Today We will only Gossip* (London 1964) p 20)

32 W. Bulfin *Rambles in Eirinn* (Dublin 1907) p 63

33 A. Clarke *Twice Round the Black Church* (London 1962) p 114

34 *Freeman's Journal* 14 Dec 1907

35 M. Halliday *Marriage on £200 a Year* (London 1903) pp 79–80

36 *Freeman's Journal* 5 Jan 1907

37 H. Robinson *Memories, Wise and Otherwise* (London 1924) p 175

Chapter 7

1 C. S. Andrews *Dublin Made Me* (Cork 1979) p 34
2 Unless otherwise mentioned the statements on the Exhibition are based on W. Dennehy *Record: Irish International Exhibition 1907* (Dublin 1909).
3 *Freeman's Journal* 10 Aug 1907
4 Lord and Lady Aberdeen *More Cracks with 'We Twa'* (London 1929) pp 140–1
5 *Freeman's Journal* 11 Nov 1907
6 J. V. O'Brien *Dear Dirty Dublin* (California 1982) p 188
7 *Freeman's Journal* 29 Aug 1907
8 W. Dennehy *Record: Irish International Exhibition 1907* (Dublin 1909) ccvi
9 The remark is not original, having been originally a *Punch* cartoon in the 1880s.
10 Dr Langford Symes 'Report of a Country Dispensary' in *Dublin Journal of Medical Science* vol ci Jan–Jun 1896 pp 259—267, 350–357
11 'Sick' (defined as bedridden, unable to perform normal duties) was obviously a highly imprecise category, and it is possible that the apparent trend is merely a result of more accurate scrutineering. Nonetheless the decade on decade drops reported by the Censuses do echo both the improvement in other indicators such as life expectancy, mortality rates etc, and the general European experience (see R. Schofield et al *The Decline of Mortality in Europe* Oxford 1991).
12 J. Moore 'Clinical Case-taking' in *Dublin Journal of Medical Science* vol cxx (Jul–Dec 1895) p 392. Moore was quoting, with approval, an article in the British publication *The Pracititioner*.
13 *Ireland's Crusade against Tuberculosis* vol 3 p 40
14 Lord and Lady Aberdeen *More Cracks with 'We Twa'* (London 1929) p 162
15 See for instance F. Meenan *St Vincent's Hospital 1834–1994* (Dublin 1995) p 75
16 *Ireland's Crusade against Tuberculosis* vol 3 p 41. The success of the campaign was such that a generation later an etiquette manual declared: 'It is excessively rude and offensive to spit on the floor, or into the fire, or even on the footways in the street. To spit on the floor in church is irreverent as well as rude.' Christian Brothers *Christian Politeness and Counsels for Youth* (Dublin 1934) p 89. The health imperative had been quite lost.
17 *Woman in the Home* (Dublin CTS pamphlet) p 20
18 Lord and Lady Aberdeen *More Cracks with 'We Twa'* (London 1929) p 160. Her figures are not quite accurate: Deeny *Tuberculosis in Ireland* (Dublin 1954) gives 2.55 as the rate for all forms in 1907, 2.10 in 1913 and 1.53 in 1924.

Chapter 8

1 E. Œ. Somerville and Martin Ross *Mount Music* (London 1919) chap 22.
2 See O. Figes *Natasha's Dance* (London 2002) pb 2003 pp xxx, 60, 100, 155 etc.

3 M. Molloy *The Book of Irish Courtesy* (Cork 1968) p 17

4 G. A. Birmingham *Hyacinth* (London 1906) p 100

5 E. O'Duffy *The Wasted Island* (Dublin 1919) 2nd ed 1929 p 256

6 K. A. Kennedy (ed) *The Economic Development of Ireland in the Twentieth Century* (London 1988) p 12

7 L. Paul-Dubois *Contemporary Ireland* (Dublin 1908) pp 361–6

8 G. A. Birmingham *Hyacinth* (London 1906) p 195

9 'My Dublin year' *Studies* (Dublin 1912) p 706

10 E. J. Riordan *Modern Irish Trade and Industry* (London 1920) p 77

11 G. A. Birmingham *Hyacinth* p 170

12 J. Kelly and E. Domville (eds) *The Collected Letters of W. B. Yeats Vol 1 1865–1895* (Oxford 1986) pp 296–7

13 'My Dublin year' *Studies* (Dublin 1912) p 705

14 G. A. Birmingham *The Search Party* (London 1909) chap 2

15 T. Farmar *A History of Craig Gardner* Dublin 1988 pp 98–99

16 15 February 1902, quoted in R. Kee *The Bold Fenian Men* (London 1972) pb 1989 p 152

17 Quoted in G. Owens 'The Carrickshock incident 1831: Social memory and an Irish cause célèbre' in *Cultural and Social History* (London 2004) 1: pp 36–64

18 *Freeman's Journal* 2 Jan 1907

19 W. Bulfin *Rambles in Eirinn* 2nd ed (Dublin 1912) p 98

20 E. McCabe *Arthur Cox* (Dublin 1994) p 18

21 G. A. Birmingham *The Seething Pot* (London 1905) p 64

22 *The Irish Times* 28 Nov 1890. A porch to contain the draughts was subsequently built inside the door of the Reading Room.

23 See A. Wierzbicka *English Meaning and Culture* (Oxford 2006) pp 25–34

24 T. Jones *The Dark Heart of Italy* (London 2003) pb 2007 p 282

25 P. W. Joyce *English as We Speak it in Ireland* (Dublin 1910) p 130

26 A. Zamoyski *Holy Madness* London 1999 pp 46–7; E. Hobsbawm *Nations and Nationalism since 1780* (Cambridge 1992) p 51–63

27 E. O'Duffy *The Wasted Island* (Dublin 1919) 2nd ed 1929 p 299

28 M. Moynihan (ed) *Speeches and Writings by Eamon de Valera 1917–73* (Dublin 1980) p 468

29 L. Paul-Dubois *Contemporary Ireland* (Dublin 1908) p 412

30 G. Robb *The Discovery of France* (London 2007) p 53

31 Cited by L. Paul-Dubois *Contemporary Ireland* (Dublin 1908) p 399

32 The reference was to an appalling case which had been widely reported in the 1890s, where a group of villagers in County Tipperary, attempted to burn the evil spirits out of a woman, who subsequently died; see Angela Bourke *The Burning of Bridget Cleary* (London 1999).

33 W. Starkie *Scholars and Gypsies* (London 1963) p 37

34 G. A. Birmingham *Hyacinth* (London 1906) p 27

35 *The Leader* 2 Feb 1907

36 *Freeman's Journal* 5 Feb 1907

37 R. Kee *The Bold Fenian Men* (London 1972) pb 1989 p 208

38 J. Meenan (ed) *Centenary History of the Literary and Historical Society* reprint (Dublin 2005) p 74

39 J. V. O'Brien *Dear Dirty Dublin* (California 1982) p 62

Chapter 9

1 *The Irish Times* 8 Aug 1924

2 Address to An Ríoghact reported *Irish Independent* 27 Oct 1932

3 *Irish Independent* 25 Jun 1932

4 J. Cooney *John Charles McQuaid: Ruler of Catholic Ireland* (Dublin 1999) pp 69–70

5 In his *Shape of Things to Come* (London 1933)

6 M. Ward *Chesterton* (London 1944) p 435

7 *Irish Independent* 9 May 1932

8 P. Kennedy *The Rise and Fall of Great Powers* (New York 1987) pb p 283

9 H. Williamson *The Story of a Norfolk Farm* (London 1941) p 29

10 *Catholic Bulletin* Jun 1932 p 446

11 From the late 1920s small numbers of promising young people, identified by the Party, had received training in the Lenin School in Moscow; see E. O'Halpin *Spying on Ireland* (Dublin 2004) p 16

12 The *Independent* agreed with the British Ambassador in Berlin, who told Harold Nicholson in late January 'The Hitlerites have missed the boat and are losing ground every day'. This was eight days before he became Chancellor. (H. Nicholson *Diaries* 22 Jan 1933)

13 D. Binchy 'Adolf Hitler' *Studies* (Mar 1933) pp 29–47

14 *Irish Independent* 24 Oct 1932

15 *The Irish Times* 18 Dec 1936

16 J. McGahern *Love of the World* (London 2009) p 162

17 M. Brennan *The Springs of Affection* (London 1999) pp 58, 60, 48

18 I am grateful to my friend Frank Litton for this memory from his past.

19 D. Ferriter *Occasions of Sin* (London 2009) p 141

20 *The Irish Times* 31 Mar 1938

21 L. Doyle *The Spirit of Ireland* (London 1935) p 18

22 E. Boyd Barret *The Magnificent Illusion* (New York 1930) p 237

23 L. Doyle *The Spirit of Ireland* (London 1935) pp 19–20

24 Daniels *v* Heskin [1954] IR 73

25 The Hospitals Commission *First General Report* (Dublin 1936) p 80

26 R. Mulcahy *Richard Mulcahy 1886–1971: A Family Memoir* (Dublin 1999) p 334

27 *Irish Independent* 23 May 1932

28 E. Boyd Barret *The Magnificent Illusion* p 237

29 A. Burke *Maeve Brennan—Homesick at the* New Yorker (London 2004) p 127–8

30 *Irish Builder* Feb 1932

31 R. Mulcahy *Richard Mulcahy* p 337

32 E. MacCarthy 'Public health problems created by louse infestation' *Irish Journal of Medical Science* 1948 p 67; D. Coakley *Baggot Street* (Dublin 1995)

P 79
33 *Bunreacht na hÉireann* (Dublin 1937) article 41
34 Quoted in J. Lee *Ireland 1912–1985* (Cambridge 1989) p 283
35 D. Murphy *Wheels within Wheels* (London 1979) pb 1981, p 4
36 *Irish Independent* 29 Jan
37 Jefferson Smurfit snr, unpublished memoir
38 D. Murphy *Wheels within Wheels* (London 1979) pb 1981, p 56
39 (W. Hale) *Mark Rutherford's Autobiography* (London 1881) chap 3
40 P. Craig *Asking for Trouble* (Belfast 2007) p 40
41 C. Buckley and C. Ward *Strong Farmer* (Dublin 2007) p 114
42 O. Robertson *Dublin Phoenix* (London 1957) p 91
43 B. Inglis *West Briton* (London 1962) p 15
44 G. Seaver *John Allen Fitzgerald Gregg, Archbishop* (London and Dublin 1963) p 126
45 B. Inglis *West Briton* (London 1962) p 19
46 C. S. Andrews *Man of No Property* (Cork 1982) p 13
47 E. McCabe *Arthur Cox* (Dublin 1994) p 43
48 T. Farmar *A History of Craig Gardner* (Dublin 1988) p 172
49 C.S. Andrews *Man of No Property* (Cork 1982) p 30
50 *The Outlook* Jan 1932
51 *Irish Independent* 14 Jan 1932
52 From Brendan Kennelly's poem 'De Valera at 92'

Chapter 10

1 C. Arensberg *The Irish Countryman* (London 1937) pp 57–8
2 J. Lee *Ireland: 1912–1985* (Cambridge 1989) p 197
3 *Statistical Abstract* 1931 P. no 516 (Dublin 1931) pp 111, 112
4 D. McCartney *UCD—A National Idea* (Dublin 1999) p 60
5 See T. Farmar *Heitons—A Managed Transition* (Dublin 1996) pp 78–81 for William Hewat's Dáil career
6 *Census* 1926
7 T. Farmar *A History of Craig Gardner* (Dublin 1988) p 171
8 C. S. Andrews *Man of No Property* (Cork 1982) p 67
9 R. Briscoe *For the Life of Me* (London 1958) p 212
10 *Irish Independent* 20 Dec 1932
11 C. S. Andrews *Man of No Property* (Cork 1982) p 66
12 T. Garvin *Judging Lemass* (Dublin 2101) p 137
13 *Irish Builder* Jan 1932; Westmeath labourers were paid 10s–15s (*Irish Independent* 12 Dec 1932)
14 *Irish Independent Careers Book* (Dublin 1936) passim
15 *Irish Independent* 12 May 1932
16 *Committee on the Cost of Living Figure*, P. no 992 (Dublin 1932). This Committee was part of a large controversy on the size of civil service pay stimulated by the new Fianna Fáil government; see R. Fanning *The Irish Department of Finance 1922–58* (Dublin 1978) pp 223–44

17 'Other People's Incomes' *The Bell* Aug 1943–Nov 1943

18 Irish Marketing Surveys *The Irish Housewife—A Portrait* (Dublin 1986) p 26

19 T. Farmar *The Legendary Lofty Clattery Café* (Dublin 1989) pp 37–8

20 *Irish Independent* 9 Sep 1932

21 *Irish Nursing and Hospital World* Jul 1932

22 *Model Housekeeping* 1931/2 p 493

23 C. S. Andrews *Man of No Property* (Cork 1982) p 232

24 Garret FitzGerald interview by Dr Máirtín Mac Con Iomaire from his unpublished PhD thesis 'The emergence, development and influence of French cuisine on public dining in Dublin 1900–2000' (DCU 2009)

25 R. Mulcahy *Richard Mulcahy 1886–1971: A Family Memoir* (Dublin 1999) p 336

26 T. de Vere White 'Social life in Ireland 1927–1937' in F. MacManus (ed) *The Years of the Great Test 1926–39* (Cork 1967) p 25

27 K. Sarr *Somewhere to the Sea* (London 1936) p 140

28 N. Robertson *Crowned Harp* (Dublin 1960) pp 160–162

29 O. Robertson *Dublin Phoenix* (London 1957) p 27

30 Quoted in T. de Vere White 'Social life in Ireland 1927–1937' in F. MacManus (ed) *The Years of the Great Test 1926–39* (Cork 1967) p 25

31 A. Findlater *Findlater's* (Dublin 2001). Compare the little 12-page 'Shopping Guides' issued in the 1930s with the lavish 'Grocery List' published before the First World War. A similar shrinkage was experienced in Britain, (J. Burnett *Plenty and Want* (London 1966) reprint 1979 pp 296–7)

32 Christian Brothers *Christian Politeness and Counsels for Youth* (Dublin 1934) p 43. This is the twentieth edition, which, so the preface says, 'has been carefully revised to meet the requirements of the present day'.

33 K. Sarr *Somewhere to the Sea* (London 1936) p 140. It was common practice to set opened bottles of red wine near a fire to warm before drinking.

34 O. Wuest *Gastronomy* (Dublin 1930)

35 *Committee on the Cost of Living Figure*, P no 992 (Dublin 1932)

36 *Irish Independent* 1 Aug 1932

37 Advertisements in *Model Housekeeping* 1931/2 169, 275; *Irish Independent* Jul 1932

38 Christian Brothers *Christian Politeness* p 40.

39 *Irish Ecclesiastical Record* vol xxxix p 537

40 G. Seaver *John Allen Fitzgerald Gregg, Archbishop* (Dublin and London 1963) p 204

41 M. Butler *The Ethics of Dress* (Dublin 1927)

42 *Irish Independent* 19 Jan 1932

43 O. Robertson *Dublin Phoenix* (London 1957) p 71

44 *Talkie Topics* Oct 1932

45 *Irish Independent* 16 Feb 1932

46 C. Bewley *Memoirs of a Wild Goose* (Dublin 1989) pp 114–5

47 B. Inglis *West Briton* (London 1962) p 29

48 L. Ó Broin *No Man's Man* (Dublin 1982) p 145

Chapter 11

1 *Irish Independent* 20 July 1932
2 Christian Brothers *Christian Politeness* (Dublin 1934) p 78
3 *Rerum Novarum* (1891) quoted in E. Cahill *The Framework of a Christian State* (Dublin 1932) p 382
4 *A Century of Service—A Record of One Hundred Years, published for the centenary of St Vincent's Hospital* (Dublin 1934) p 118
5 Hospitals Commission *First General Report* P. no 1976 (Dublin 1936) pp 116–7
6 The basic information about the origins and progress of the Sweep are from M. Coleman *The Irish Sweep 1930–87* (Dublin 2009).
7 *The Irish Times* 3 Feb 1931
8 *The Irish Times* 23 Jun 1931
9 *Sunday Independent* 21 Jan 1973. MacAnthony claimed that less than 10 per cent of the ticket sales went to the hospitals. This would make the Sweep about the size of the Irish cattle industry before the Economic War.
10 D. Corless *The Greatest Bleeding Hearts Racket in the World* (Dublin 2010). Since the author provides no references, this work is difficult to assess, though the fact that he apparently thinks the *Catholic Bulletin* is an American publication is not encouraging.
11 Quoted in C. L'E. Ewen *Lotteries and Sweepstakes* (London 1932) p 366
12 *Catholic Bulletin* 1932 p 517
13 *The Irish Times* 23 Feb 1932
14 Marie Coleman "'A terrible danger to the morals of the country": the Irish Hospitals Sweepstake in Great Britain 1930–87' in *Proceedings of the Royal Irish Academy* vol 105c no 5 (2005)
15 Details from the published programmes of the Irish Hospitals Sweepstake
16 *Irish Independent* 3 Jun 1932
17 J. Deeny *To Cure and to Care* (Dublin 1989) p 142
18 Hospitals Commission *First General Report 1933–4* (Dublin 1936) p 4

Chapter 12

1 F. Finlay *Snakes and Ladders* (Dublin 1998) p 6
2 Summarised from a document reproduced in D. Ferriter *Judging Dev* (Dublin 2007) p 113.
3 T. P. Coogan *The IRA* (London 1970) pb 1971 pp 71–3
4 This *Review* was published in January 1932 and was the precursor of an annual *Review* that was published thereafter every year until the late 1960s.
5 9 Jan 1932
6 *Irish Independent* 3 Feb 1932
7 Quoted by David Hanley in D. Ferriter *What if?* (Dublin 2006) p 115
8 L. Ó Broin *No Man's Man* (Dublin 1982) p 146
9 K. A. Kennedy et al *The Economic Development of Ireland in the Twentieth*

Century (London 1989) pp 41–2

10 *Irish Independent* 12 Mar 1932

11 *Irish Independent* 9 Feb 1932

12 *Catholic Bulletin* 1932 p 99. The *Bulletin*, published by M. H. Gill, claimed a circulation of 25,000 copies every month, about twice what *Business and Finance* currently sells.

13 T. P. Coogan *Ireland Since the Rising* (London 1966) p 71

14 L. Ó Broin *... just like yesterday ...* (Dublin nd) p 92

15 J. Meenan *Centenary History of the Literary and Historical Society 1855–1955* reprint (Dublin 2005) pp 190–3

16 R. Briscoe *For the Life of Me* (London 1958) p 60

17 *Irish Independent* 22 Feb 1932

18 N. Robertson *Crowned Harp* (Dublin 1960) p 176

19 D. Keogh *The Vatican, the Bishops and Irish Politics 1919–1939* (Cambridge 1986) pp 182, 185

20 T. de Valera *A Memoir* (Dublin 2004) p 44. Vivion de Valera apparently made it quite clear 'to those who wished to see' that he was armed.

21 *Irish Independent* 8 Jun 1932

22 D. Corkery *Synge and Anglo-Irish Literature* (Cork 1931) pb 1960 p 20

23 A. Clarke *Twice Round the Black Church* (London 1962) p 21

24 Quoted in J. Bowman *De Valera and the Ulster Question 1917–1973* (Oxford 1982) pb 1983, p 107

25 T. P. Coogan *Ireland Since the Rising* (London 1966) p 52

26 Cardinal D'Alton Lenten Pastoral 1955

27 The Irish Jesuit *Directory and Year Book for 1932* (Dublin 1932) pp 90–94

28 J. Kenney 'The Catholic church in contemporary Ireland' *Catholic Historical Review* (Washington 1932) p 169

29 R. Mulcahy *Richard Mulcahy (1886–1971) A Family Memoir* (Dublin 1999) p 337

30 *Irish Independent* 19 May 1932

31 The delay was caused by the (Protestant) Commissioners of Merrion Square, whose statutory remit expired in May 1938. The Square was purchased from Lord Pembroke for £10,000 in July 1930; acquisition of the Commissioners' interest at the same time 'was found not to be feasible'.

32 *Catholic Bulletin* vol xxii p 162

33 G. K. Chesterton *Christendom in Dublin* (London 1932) p 15

34 *Irish Independent* 24 Jun 1932

35 P. Boylan *All Cultivated People* (Gerrard's Cross 1988) p 185

36 Unless otherwise stated, all quotations from newspapers describing the Conference are from the collection of press comments reprinted in *Eucharistic Congress 1932—Pictorial Record* (Dublin nd)

37 Organising Committee of the Eucharistic Congress *Handbook of the Eucharistic Conference* (Dublin 1932)

38 The feature writer JAP in *Irish Independent* 22 Jun 1932

39 J. Deeny *To Cure and to Care* (Dublin 1989) p 38

40 M. Green et al *Growing up in Arcadia* (Privately published 2004) p 36

41 Irish Independent *Eucharistic Congress Number* Jun 1932 p 46

42 *Irish Independent* 13 Aug 1932

43 Dáil Debates 15 Jul

44 This was no light accusation, for the IRA were believed to be importing arms in great numbers, and the assassination of Kevin O'Higgins was fresh in the memory; Dáil Debates 5 Aug

45 The Houses of the Oireachtas search engine makes these statistics readily discoverable.

46 M. Hayes 'Dail Eireann and the Civil War' *Studies* (Dublin 1969) p 22

47 *Irish Independent* 19 Sep 1932

48 L. Ó Broin *No Man's Man* (Dublin 1982) p 147

49 *Irish Independent* 1 Dec 1932

50 T. P. Coogan *Ireland since the Rising* (London 1966) p 70

51 *Irish Independent* 5 Sep 1932

52 *Irish Independent* 5 Sep 1932, 20 Sep 1932

53 The inaugural meeting of the Army Comrades Association is customarily assigned to 9 Feb, following a report of that date in the *Irish Independent*. However, it is clear from a previous report (28 Jan) that a meeting explicitly said to be of the ACA was held in Wynn's Hotel on 27 Jan, and this was confirmed by a long letter from Commandant Cronin, the initiator of the Association, giving the precise reasons for the Association's initial impetus (*Irish Independent* 3 Feb). Neither report has a byline, so it is not obvious why the Association should have been reported as twice-born.

54 *Irish Independent* 31 Dec 1932

55 T. Farmar *A History of Craig Gardner* (Dublin 1988) p 144

Chapter 13

1 Commission on Emigration and other Population Problems 1848–1954 *Reports* Pr 2541 (Dublin 1955) p 81

2 *Sunday Press* 1 Sep 1963

3 F. Kennedy *Family, Economy and Government in Ireland* (Dublin 1989) p 53

4 D. Rottman & P. O'Connell 'The Changing Social Structure' in F. Litton (ed.) *Unequal Achievement* (Dublin 1982) pp 68–74

5 Workers Union of Ireland *Report of General Executive Committee for 1963–64* (Dublin 1964)

6 *The Irish Times* 9 May 1963

7 *Hibernia* Sep 1963

8 *The Irish Times* 1 Feb 1963

9 T. Gray *The Irish Answer—an Anatomy of Modern Ireland* (London 1966) p 352

10 Quoted in D. Connery *The Irish* (London 1968) pb 1972, p 97

11 J. White *The Devil You Know* pb (Dublin 1970) p 21

12 M. Fitzgerald in *Sunday Review* 3 Mar 1963

13 The First Director of Programmes at Telefís Éireann, Gunnar Rugheimer, quoted in D. Connery *The Irish* (London 1968) pb 1972, p 109

14 M. Sweeney 'Irish Television: A compromise with commerce' in *Studies* (Dublin 1963) p 414

15 A. Humphreys *New Dubliners* (London 1966) p 196

16 Ibid. p 196

17 B. Haring *The Sociology of the Family* (Cork 1959) p 56

18 *Sunday Review* 10 Feb 1963

19 D. Purcell 'Interview with Monica Barnes' *Sunday Tribune* 3 June 1990

20 R. C. Geary and F. S. O'Muircheartaigh *Equalisation of Opportunity in Ireland: Statistical Aspects* (Dublin 1968, 1974)

21 *The Irish Times* 2 Mar 1963

22 B. F. Biever SJ *Religion, Culture and Values* (New York 1976) p 240. This thesis contrasted Catholic values in Ireland with those of Irish Americans in the United States. The Irish research was done in 1963–5 and involved 1,500 questionnaires and 55 follow-up interviews.

23 Ibid. p 385

24 T. Farmar *A History of Craig Gardner* (Dublin 1988) pp 189–90

25 The average industrial wage is calculated, as before, from *Statistical Abstract* as the cost of salaries and wages for all industries divided by the average number of persons employed. This figure includes administrative and clerical staff.

26 T. Farmar *Craig Gardner* p 191

27 *Sunday Review* 3 Feb 1963

28 *The Irish Times* 15 Feb 1963

29 *Report of Revenue Commissioners* 1962/3

30 J. McCarthy *Ireland* (New York 1964) p 132

31 *Statistical Abstract* 1958 & 1963

32 *The Irish Times* 11 Feb 1963

33 *Sunday Press* 19 May 1963

34 *The Irish Times* 28 Feb 1963

35 Commission on Emigration and other Population Problems *Reports* Pr 2541 (Dublin 1955) pp 81–2

36 Beatrice Dixon diaries, Public Record Office

37 T. Gray *The Irish Answer—An Anatomy of Modern Ireland* (London 1966) p 300

38 J. McCarthy *Ireland* p 135

39 M. Sheridan 'The Gastronomic Irishman' in O. D. Edwards (ed.) *Conor Cruise O'Brien introduces Ireland* (London 1969) p 229

40 Mab Hickman in *Creation* Mar 1963

41 M. Mac Con Iomaire 'The emergence, development and influence of French Haute Cuisine dining in Dublin restaurants 1900–2000: an oral history' Unpublished PhD thesis DIT 2009 pp 26, 271

42 B. F. Biever SJ *Religion, Culture and Values* p 241

43 An Irish Housewife *I'm not Afraid to Die* (Cork 1974) p 119

44 A. Clarke *Twice Round the Black Church* (London 1962) p 116

45 *The Irish Times* 1 May 1963

46 *Household Budget Inquiry* 1965/6 (Dublin 1969) Table 5

47 In *Facts about Ireland* (Dublin 1963) p 73

Chapter 14

1 J. Blanchard *The Church in Contemporary Ireland* (Dublin 1963) p 30. This
   author is not to be confused with the American Paul Blanshard who
   also wrote about the Irish Catholic Church, but from a very different
   standpoint.
2 J. McGahern *Love of the World* (London 2009) p 147
3 B. F. Biever SJ *Religion, Culture and Values* (New York 1976) p 239; T. Garvin
   Judging Lemass (Dublin 2010) p 45
5 J. Blanchard *The Church in Contemporary Ireland* (Dublin 1963) p 31
6 J. McGahern *Love of the World* (London 2009) p 137
7 Pauline Bracken *Light of Other Days* (Cork 1992) p 82
8 The assumption of normality is by no means automatic; it is likely that
   the distribution was in fact skewed one way or another. A similar analysis
   today would probably produce a bipolar graph. However, given the virtual
   universality of practice in the 1960s and evidence (eg from Blanchard) that
   intensity of belief was not a function of social forces but rather depended
   on random personal factors, the basic assumption of normality can probably
   be sustained.
9 Mass attendance was measurable by the use of communion wafers, the *Late
   Late* audience by TAM ratings as published in the *RTV Guide*.
10 *Studies* (Dublin 1965) Winter
11 J. Blanchard *The Church in Contemporary Ireland* (Dublin 1963) p 68
12 G. Birmingham *Hyacinth* (London 1906) p 110
13 J. Newman *Via Media* (London 1877) p xii
14 Quoted in P. Elie *The Life You Save May Be Your Own: An American
   Pilgrimage* (New York 2003) p 362
15 J. McCarthy *The Christian Doctrine of Work* (Dublin 1955) p 14
16 The *Irish Ecclesiastical Record* was a monthly publication emanating from
   Maynooth, and published 'by authority of the hierarchy'. In 1948 the
   manager of Browne and Nolan had explained to the *Bell* that the cost of
   printing made it hardly worth while to publish fewer than 2,500 copies
   of any title, so we can assume that these handsome volumes, with at least
   1,000 pages of text between them, were produced in at least that quantity.
   This was evidently a society that took its moral code seriously.
17 J. McCarthy *Problems in Theology* (Dublin 1959) vol 2 p 47
18 Ibid. vol 2 pp 1–2
19 Ibid. vol 2 p 362
20 W. Shakespeare *Troilus and Cressida* Act I scene iii line 101
21 J. McCarthy *Problems in Theology* vol 2 p 156
22 Ibid. vol 2 p 195
23 Alexis FitzGerald 'Reservations' in Commission on Emigration and Other
   Population Problems 1948–1954 *Reports* Pr 2541 (Dublin 1955) p 223. In his
   comments FitzGerald, a serious Catholic, goes as far as he legally could

to advocating a less restrictive approach to family planning; any further and the Report could have been banned by the Censorship Board as the British Royal Commission on Population had been a few years before for 'advocating contraception'.

24 This too has a long tradition, going back to the early Fathers. St Augustine deplores the fact that procreation is not possible without 'the greatest of all bodily pleasures'; how much better, he speculates, would things be if it were possible to beget children without it (*City of God* book xiv chap 16)

25 J. McCarthy *Problems in Theology* (Dublin 1955) vol 1 p 216

26 F. X. Carty *Why I said No to God* (Dublin 1986) p 94

27 J. McCarthy *Problems in Theology* (vol 2 p 376

28 Ibid. vol 2 p 348. The concept of *correptio fraterna* (fraternal correction) derives from Matthew 18: 15: 'If thy brother shall offend against thee go and rebuke between thee and him alone'.

29 B. F. Biever *Religion, Culture and Values* (New York 1976) p 163

30 *The Irish Times* 25 Feb 1963

31 *Sunday Press* 14 Jul 1963

32 *The Irish Times* 1, 25 May 1963

33 *Time* 12 Jul 1963

34 B. F. Biever *Religion, Culture and Values* (New York 1976) p 418

35 *Sunday Press* 18 Sep 1963

36 Case reported in *The Irish Times* 28 Nov 1935

37 P. Devlin *All of us There* (London 1983) pb 1984 p 24

38 D. Rohan *Marriage Irish Style* (Cork 1969) pp 69–70

39 A. Humphries *New Dubliners* (London 1966) p 139

40 Ibid. p 143

41 Quoted in B. MacMahon 'Getting on the High Road Again' in J. O'Brien (ed.) *The Vanishing Irish* (London 1954) p 211

42 M. O'Beirne *People People Marry, People People Don't* (Dublin 1976) pp 29, 66

43 *Sunday Press* 8 Sep 1963

44 *The Irish Times* 17 May 1963

45 A. Boylan diaries (unpublished) 25 Nov, 9, 10 Dec 1963

46 P. Craig *Asking for Trouble* (Belfast 2007) p 97

47 *Hibernia* Jan 1963

48 P. Bracken *Light of Other Days* (Dublin 1992) p 52

49 B. F. Biever *Religion, Culture and Values* p 241

50 B. Carr *The Instant Tree* (Cork 1975) p 7

51 E. O'Brien *The Country Girls* (London 1960) pb p 11

52 T. Farmar *Holles Street* (Dublin 1995) p 115

53 *The Irish Times* 5 Mar 1963

54 A. MacNamara *Yours Sincerely* (Dublin 2003) p 21

55 D. Ferriter *Occasions of Sin* (London 2009) p 243

56 J. Levine *Sisters* (Dublin 1982) p 30

57 R. Sweetman *On Our Backs* (London 1979) p 139

Chapter 15

1 Department of Foreign Affairs *Facts about Ireland* (Dublin 1963). Collins' photograph does appear once, and Fine Gael appears in one table. In the pictures of the Cabinet of the First Dáil, Collins, though Minister for Finance, is put right at the bottom of the page below the Ministers for Labour, Defence and Foreign Affairs.

2 A. Humphreys *New Dubliners* (London 1966) p 163

3 'An Irish Housewife' *I'm not Afraid to Die* (Cork 1974) p 73

4 M. Molloy *Book of Irish Courtesy* (Cork 1968)

5 Christian Brothers *Courtesy for Boys and Girls* (Dublin 1962) p vi

6 F. X. Carty *Why I said No to God* (Dublin 1986) pp 24–5

7 John McGahern interviewed by Fintan O'Toole, *The Irish Times* 13 Oct 1990

8 J. Joyce *Portrait of the Artist* pb (Harmonsworth 1960) pp 50–51

9 Quoted in *Village* magazine August 2007. The short report makes no mention of sexual abuse, which the Ryan Commission on Child Abuse found to be common. The school was finally closed down in 1969. The report by Fr Moore was discussed at length in the Ryan *Report* vol 1 paras 7.784–7.844, where it is noted that McQuaid's attitude to Artane was as an ineffective critic, a notably untypical stance for McQuaid in anything remotely connected with the Church.

10 D. Connery *The Irish* (London 1968) pb 1972, p 90

11 A. Boylan diaries (unpublished) 16 & 24 Jul 1963

12 *The Irish Times* 17 Mar 1990

13 Ibid. 16 Feb 1963

14 *Sunday Press* 7 Apr 1963

15 Ibid. 1 Dec 1963

16 G. Howell *In Vogue* (London 1975) p 280

17 *Sunday Press* 17 Mar 1963

18 J. White *The Devil You Know* (London 1962) pb 1970 p 146

19 *The Irish Times* 20 May 1963

20 J. Levine *Sisters* (Dublin 1982) p 48

21 *The Irish Times* 29 May 1963

22 Ibid. 20 May 1963

23 Ibid. 25 Jan 1963

24 Most of the information in the next few paragraphs comes from Maxwell Sweeney's contemporary study 'Irish Television: A compromise with commerce' in *Studies* (Dublin 1963) Winter.

25 *Sunday Review* 6 Jan 1963

26 *The Irish Times* 7 May 1963

27 Commission on Emigration *Reports* (Dublin 1955) p 175

28 Quoted in T. Gray *The Irish Answer* (London 1966) pp 164–5

29 F. X. Carty *Why I said No to God* (Dublin 1986) p 104

30 *Hibernia* Apr 1963. The answer to his question was, of course,—just as much and as little as the government.

31 *The Irish Times* 27 Jan 1963

32 Ibid. 20 Feb 1963

33 M. McLoone and J. MacMahon *Television and Irish Society* (Dublin 1984) p 150

34 The *Household Budget Survey* of 1980 reported that 91 per cent of households had TV, 81 per cent running hot water, 83 per cent internal lavatory.

35 *The Irish Times* 19 Jun 1963

36 Ibid. 20 Jan 1963.37 Irish Times *Annual Review 1963* (Dublin 1964) p 10

38 A. Boylan diaries (unpublished) 26 Jun 1963

39 M. N. Hennessy *I'll Come Back in the Springtime* (London 1967)

40 D. Connery *The Irish* (London 1968) pb 1972, pp 30–31

41 *Sunday Review* 6 Jan 1963

42 Quoted in *Sunday Press* 15 Sep 1963

43 Quoted in G. Howell *In Vogue* (Harmondsworth 1975) pb 1978, p 254

44 R. Carroll 'The religious image' *The Furrow* vol 15 no 8 p 508

45 A. Boylan diaries (unpublished) Nov 22–24

46 Speech in Tramore to National Convention of Junior Chambers of Commerce, quoted in the *Sunday Press* 19 May 1963

Chapter 16

1 T. Gray *The Irish Answer* (London 1966) p 3

2 B. F. Biever *Religion, Culture and Values* (New York 1976) p 240

3 A. Post et al *History of Private Life: Vol 5—Riddles of Identity in Modern Times* (Harvard 1991) p 56

4 D. Connery *The Irish* (London 1968) pb 1972 p 57

5 A.   Taylor *To School through the Fields* (Dingle 1988) pp 8, 17

6 B. Cleeve *Cry of Morning* (London 1971) pb 1972 p 75

7 Quoted by J. Lee in *Irish Values and Attitudes* (Dublin 1984) p 110

8 M. Molloy *The Book of Irish Courtesy* (Cork 1968) p 15

9 Ibid. p 16

10 *The Irish Times* 3 May 1963

11 Quoted in R. Rose *Governing Without Consent* (London 1971) epigraph

12 E. Cahill *The Framework of a Christian State* (Dublin 1932) p 24

13 L. Ó Broin *Frank Duff* (Dublin 1982) pp 62–7

14 J. Feeney *John Charles McQuaid—The Man and the Mask* (Cork 1974) pp 30–31, 44–7

15 X. Rynne *Letters from Vatican City* (London 1963) p 118

16 B. F. Biever *Religion, Culture and Values* (New York 1976) p 226

17 Ibid. p 264

18 Ibid. p 265

19 Ibid. p 375

20 Ibid. p 229

21 J. Newman *Irish Ecclesiastical Record* (Maynooth 1963) p 90

22 *The Irish Times* 13 Feb 1963

23 D. Connery *The Irish* (London 1968) pb 1972, p 29
24 *The Irish Times* 17 May 1963
25 *Sunday Press* 23 Jun 1963
26 Dáil Debates vol 204 no 8 pp 1311–2
27 M. Nevin 'A Study of the Social Background of Students in the Irish Universities' *Journal of the Statistical and Social Society of Ireland* 1968
28 J. J. Lee *Ireland 1912–1985* (Cambridge 1989) pb 1989 pp 562–643
29 T. Gray *The Irish Answer* (London 1966) p 231
30 John McGahern, interviewed by Fintan O'Toole in *The Irish Times* 13 Oct 1990
31 B. Behan *Brendan Behan's Ireland* (London 1962) pb 1965 p 19
32 *The Irish Times* 8 Jan 1963
33 Ibid. 19 Feb 1963
34 *Sunday Review* 6 Jan 1963
35 Quoted in *Sunday Review* 21 Apr 1963
36 T. Stonier *Nuclear Disaster* (Harmondsworth 1964) p 26
37 *The Irish Times* 23 Oct 1962
38 Dáil Debates 29 May 1963
39 T. Gray *The Irish Answer* (London 1966) p 145
40 *The Irish Times* 3 Mar 1963
41 *Studies* (Dublin 1964) Winter

Chapter 17

1 *The Irish Times* 5 Jun 1989
2 Judy Dempsey in *The Irish Times* 28 Dec 1989
3 J. Ardagh *Ireland and the Irish* (London 1994) pb 1995 p 312. SPUC stands for the anti-abortion group the Society for the Protection of the Unborn Child which came to prominence during the campaigns of the 1980s.
4 *The Irish Times* 23 Nov 1988
5 *Sunday Business Post* 18 Jun 2006
6 *The Irish Times* 7 Jun 1989
7 Quoted in J. Downey *All Things New* (Dublin 1989) p 78
8 Ibid. p 68
9 *The Irish Times* 1 Sep 1989
10 J. Waters *Jiving at the Crossroads* (Dublin 1991) p 95
11 M. Green et al *Growing up in Arcadia* (privately published 2004) p 35: 1932 'I voted several times in that election'.
12 *The Irish Times* 20 Jan 1989
13 Ibid. 24 Nov 1989
14 G. McDonnell *Buying a House* (Dublin 1972) p 24
15 *The Irish Times* 16 May 1989
16 Ibid. 19 Apr 1990
17 Ibid. 18 May 1989

18 Ibid. 7 Mar 1989
19 Ibid. 2 Jan 1989
20 J. Healy *The Death of an Irish Town* (Cork 1968) p 59
21 *The Irish Times* 9 Jun 1989
22 Ibid. 16 Dec 1989
23 Data from *The Irish Times* 29 Jul 1989, *Sunday Tribune* 22 Nov 2009;
   average industrial wage is calculated as the average payment to industrial
   workers, including managers, and so is higher than the overall average wage.
24 UNICEF *The Progress of Nations* (New York 1993) p 38
25 M-A. Wren *An Unhealthy State* (Dublin 2003) pp 83–4
26 This phenomenon can be tracked in, for instance, T. Farmar *Celebrating 25
   years—Sportsco 1979–2004* (privately published Dublin 2004) pp 18, 51
27 *The Irish Times* 30 Dec 1989

Chapter 18

1 *The Irish Times* 24 Jan 1989
2 J. Fairbanks 'The income of the higher civil servant' *Administration* vol 3 no
   2–3 p 63
3 *The Irish Times* 14 Dec 1989
4 J. Waters *Jiving at the Crossroads* (Dublin 1991) p 142
5 *The Irish Times* 24 Nov 1989
6 Ibid. 7 Jul 1989
7 Ibid. 24 Nov 1989
8 Ibid. 3 Nov 1989
9 A certain nervousness in respect of this data arises from the fact that the
   average household income reported in the Survey is very considerably
   less than in the National Accounts. Expenditure on alcohol was always
   underestimated on the self-reporting forms, perhaps, as the 1965 HBS
   discovered, by as much as 50 per cent.
10 C. Whelan and D. Hannan 'Trends in educational inequality in the
   Republic of Ireland' *ESRI Working paper no 100* (Dublin 1998) p 17
11 *The Irish Times* 17 May 1989
12 Ibid. 24 Jan 1989
13 This paragraph is based on *The Irish Housewife: A Portrait* (Dublin 1986).
   This is the report of a research project by Irish Consumer Research
   combining interviews with a sample of housewives backed with qualitative
   data. It is emphatically not an academic or politically motivated study, being
   designed simply for marketing purposes.
14 *Irish Housewife* p 23
15 *The Irish Times* 5 Jan 1989
16 Ibid. 10 Apr 1989
17 A chart in the English academic Ted Polhemus' book *Body Style*
18 T. Polhemus *Body Style* (London 1988) reviewed by Arminta Wallace in *The
   Irish Times* 21 Jan 1989
19 *The Irish Times* 11 Aug 1989

20 T. Farmar *Patients, Potions and Physicians* (Dublin 2004) pp 210–211
21 *The Irish Times* 23 May 1989
22 Ibid. 18 Mar 1989
23 *Irish Independent* 14 Jul 1989
24 *The Irish Times* 30 May 1989
25 Ibid. 17 Jul 1989
26 Ibid. 1 Sep 1989
27 *Irish Independent* 17 Jul 1989
28 Ibid. 28 Aug 1989
29 *The Irish Times* 16 May 1989. These houses were certainly not the 'Hidden Ireland' that Corkery had in mind in the famous book of that title.
30 G Kerrigan *Another Country* (Dublin 1998) p 179
31 D. Allen *Simply Delicious Christmas* (Dublin 1998); when the error was revealed, Darina heroically cooked a new pudding for every complainant.
32 M. Daly (ed) *Families and Family Life in Ireland* (Dublin 2004), Chairperson's introduction
33 *The Irish Times* 14 December 1989. Nuala O'Faolain has obviously not quite internalised the ISPCC guidelines which deplored physical punishment.
34 Ibid. 16 Dec 1989
35 G. Kerrigan *Another Country* (Dublin 1998) p 181

Chapter 19

1 A case could be made for the Mother and Child row of the early 1950s, but this was of more interest to the political classes than the plain people. It had no effect on Mass attendance.
2 Xavier Rynne *The Third Session* London 1965 pp 53–61; J. W. O'Malley *What Happened at Vatican II* (Cambridge Mass 2000) pp 211–218
3 T. Farmar *Holles Street 1894–1994* (Dublin 1995) pp 152–4
4 *Humane Vitae* chap 17
5 Irish Consumer Research *The Irish Housewife: A Portrait* (Dublin 1986) p 64
6 Ibid. p 64
7 Quoted in 'Semper fidelis—but is the hold weakening?' by John Cooney in *The Irish Times* 29 Sep 1989
8 *The Irish Times* 11 Apr 1988
9 Ibid. 29 Sep 1989
10 C. McGuinness SC address to the Merriman Summer School Aug 1989, quoted in J. Downey *All Things New* (Dublin 1989) pp 106, 108
11 Br. Murray 'The Supreme Court and the Constitution in the nineteen-eighties' *Studies* (Dublin 1990) p 160
12 F. O'Toole *A Mass for Jesse James* (Dublin 1990) p 79
13 *The Irish Times* 29 Sep 1989
14 *The Irish Housewife* p 82
15 E. Duffy *The Irish Times* 16 May 1989
16 *The Irish Times* 28 Sep 1989
17 *The Irish Housewife* p 75

18 Ibid. p 68

19 Quoted in A. Shatter *Family Law in the Republic of Ireland* 2nd ed (Dublin 1981) p 144

20 ISPCC Survey broadcast on *Today Tonight* 7 Dec and summarised in *The IrishTimes* Dec 1989

21 A. MacNamara *Yours Sincerely* (Dublin 2003) pp 62, 12–13. The family lived in Rathgar, in some style, with three servants and a weekly washer-woman. Her father, George A. Little, a GP, had been a medical officer with the Old IRA.

22 *The Irish Housewife* p 68

23 J. Waters *Jiving at the Crosroads* (Dublin 1991) p 31 quoting John Healy

24 *The Irish Times* 5 Jun 1989

25 C. S. Lewis *A Preface to Paradise Lost* (Oxford 1942) pb 1963 p 73

26 Encyclical *Immortale Dei* 1885

27 J. Waters *Jiving at the Crossroads* (Dublin 1991) p 62

28 Norris *v* Attorney-General *Irish Law Reports* 1984 p 65

29 *The Irish Times* 30 Nov 1989

30 Ibid. 2 May 1989

31 D. Fennell *Nice People and Rednecks* (Dublin 1986) p i

32 Ibid. p iv

33 J. Healy *Death of an Irish Town* (Cork 1968) p 88

34 I. Turgenev *Rudin* trans Alec Brown (London 1950) p 226

35 J. Waters *Jiving at the Crossroads* (Dublin 1991) pp 11, 14, 86

36 C. Moran 'The advertising agency view of Ireland: a conservative mono-culture' *The Crane Bag* vol 8 no 2 p 86

37 The Television Audience Measurement company calculated from a sample the percent of televisions turned on the to programme, and this was referred to as its TAM Rating.

38 J. Waters *Jiving at the Crossroads* (Dublin 1991) p 152

39 Ibid.

40 *London Review of Books* 18 Nov 1993

41 *The Irish Times* 28 Oct 1988

42 Ibid. 11 Mar 1989

43 J. Downey *All Things New* (Dublin 1989) p 102, 109

44 'How can a little girl know what to tell?' *The Irish Times* 20 Feb 1989

45 John Brannigan *New Historicism and Cultural Materialism* (London 1998) p 61

46 J. Waters *Jiving at the Crossroads* p 14

INDEX

'crim. con.', 54–5
Court of Chancery, 12
Cowen's printers, 25
Cox, Arthur, 63, 109, 136
Craig, Patricia, 134, 218–19, 220
Craig Gardner, 10, 78, 181, 196–7
    Protestant, 136, 142
    salaries, 77, 143, 197
    and Sweep, 161, 162, 166
Crane Bag, The, 306, 307
Cranny, Josephine, 11, *45*
Cravan 'A' cigarettes, 129
Creation, 202, 203, 255
cricket, 18, 19, 48, 67, 126
crime, 128
    1907, 77, 83–5, 97
    1932, 128, 132, 170
    1963, 215, 255
Crimean War, 73
criminal conversation, 54–5
Criminal Law Amendment Act, 216
Cromien, Seán, 278
Cromwell, Oliver, 96
Cronin, Commdt E. J., 188
croquet, 19, 48
Cross, The, 69
Crowley, Vincent, 136
Crown jewels, Irish, 77, 97
Crown Solicitor, 75
Crusade against Immodest Fashions, 131
Cuba crisis, 234, 235, 253
Cullen, Bill, 277
Cullen, Louis, 10
Cumann na nGaedheal, 95, 121, 122, 186,
  247, 264
    election, 1932, 170–1, 172, 173–5
    and ICA, 188
Cummins, Lisa, 268
Curran, C. P., 115
Currency Commission, 187
Cusack, Michael, 19
Customs and Excise, Board of, 80
cycling, 18
Czechoslovakia, 111, 260

Dáil Éireann, 61, 73, 141, 156, 175, 180, 188,
  297
    Economic War, 186–7
    FF-PD coalition, 263–4
    government salaries, 172, 197, 280–1
    Kennedy visit, 236

turnover tax debate, 249
Daily Telegraph, 254–5
Daimler, 21–2
dairies, 85–6, 131
Dallas, 305
D'Alton, Cardinal, Archbishop of
    Armagh, 176
Danaher, Kevin, 231
dancing, 24, 212, 217
Dargan, W., 96
Darragh, Austin, 277
Darwin, Charles, 16, 18, 20, 47, 69
Dating Without Tears, 228
Davis, Thomas, 110
Davitt, Michael, 46–7
Dawson, William, 104, 106
de Beauvoir, Simone, 250
de Burgh, Chris, 271
de Gaulle, General C., 235
de Jongh, Dr, 22
de Rossa, Proinsias, 262
De Tijd, 183
de Valera, Eamon, 115, 149, 161, 245, 248, 302
    dress, 154
    Economic War, 186
    election, 1932, 172–3, 173–4
    Eucharistic Congress, 181
    and Irish language, 110, 243–4, 307
    isolationism, 242
    and Kennedy, 236, 237
    and MacNeill, 157
    religion, 176, 209
    Taoiseach, 174–5
de Vere White, Terence, 149
debt, 67
decimalisation, 192
Deeny, James, 166, 183, 309
Delaney, Commendatore, 38
Delany, Fr, SJ, 63
Delany, Ronnie, 248
delicatessen, 201
democracy, 121, 259, 260–1, 302
Democratic Party, USA, 121
Dempsey, Judy, 261
Deng Xiaoping, 260
Denmark, 36, 37
Dennehy, William, 93
Denning, Lord, 254–5
department stores, 47, 78, 153–4
Derry, 78
Desmond, Dermot, 277